Juris Zoology

Juris Zoology

A Dissection of Animals as Legal Objects

Geordie Duckler

LEXINGTON BOOKS
Lanham • Boulder • New York • London

Published by Lexington Books
An imprint of The Rowman & Littlefield Publishing Group, Inc.
4501 Forbes Boulevard, Suite 200, Lanham, Maryland 20706
www.rowman.com

86-90 Paul Street, London EC2A 4NE, United Kingdom

British Library Cataloguing in Publication Information Available

Library of Congress Cataloging-in-Publication Data
Names: Duckler, Geordie, 1959– author.
  Title: Juris zoology : a dissection of animals as legal objects / Geordie
     Duckler.
  Description: Lanham : Lexington Books, [2022] | Includes bibliographical
     references and index. | Summary: "At the intersection of law and
     biology, Juris Zoology provides a comprehensive and realistic framework
     to objectively assess the role and significance of animals in American
     civil and criminal law"—Provided by publisher.
  Identifiers: LCCN 2021045337 (print) | LCCN 2021045338 (ebook) | ISBN
     9781793655721 (cloth) | ISBN 9781793655745 (pbk.) | ISBN 9781793655738 (epub)
  Subjects: LCSH: Animals—Law and legislation—United States. | Animal
     welfare—Law and legislation—United States.
  Classification: LCC KF390.5.A5 D83 2022 (print) | LCC KF390.5.A5 (ebook)
     | DDC 344.7304/9—dc23/eng/20211028
  LC record available at https://lccn.loc.gov/2021045337
  LC ebook record available at https://lccn.loc.gov/2021045338

Contents

Preface

"The Spangle of Existence"[1]

Law and science share a preoccupation with relationships and with their perception by others, a fixation also shared by poetry. Of the poems that inform and illuminate both disciplines, one favorite is the 1803 epic *The Temple of Nature, or The Origin of Society* by the physician, philosopher, botanist, and naturalist Erasmus Darwin. *Temple* is an ode on nature, but within its five hundred lines rests a complex joining of two relationship and perception themes, in forms both hidden and overt.

The first is on how biotic and abiotic pressures impel changes across generations of organisms, musings on changes in form arising out of a balance sheet of lives and deaths that Erasmus assembled half a century before his grandson Charles' work *On The Origin Of Species*. The second is on how particular social mores and rules governing human conduct relate to natural processes, an idea expounded in the poem through speeches by personified ideals. Together, the themes form an argument in prosody about how to perceive the complex forces at work entwining the organic and social worlds, and how our relationships with nature affect our relationships with each other.

Like law and science, *Temple* is also both academic and recursive. It is academic in that it supports its observations with citations to authority in the form of "philosophical notes" that nearly match its text in length. It is recursive in that its thrust refers to, and relies upon, lines from other poems, most notably Virgil's *Aeneid*, written centuries before. *Temple* embodies scholarship from both its present and its past, including by opening with a quatrain in the original Latin from the *Aeneid's* sixth book:

> Hence men and beasts the breath of life obtain,
> And birds of air, and monsters of the main.
> The ethereal vigor is in all the same,
> And every soul is filled with equal flame.

vii

Temple also plays extensively with the notion of descendants being intimately connected to their ancestors, in rough parallel to the *Aeneid*'s recount of its protagonist Aeneas learning of the exploits of those who came before him. As a result, *Temple*'s lines are "nested" in the same complex fashion that lawyers and scientists tend to nest their arguments in support of their conclusions: embedding appeals to reason within an applicable history, referring to past relationships and present effects of other actors, and imbuing each layer with reliance on select observations—in the form of biased and unbiased perceptions—about the world that both author and listener inhabit.

Like the characters inside its verses, *Temple* encourages attention to nature's and history's details, and both Virgil and Darwin took pains to cherish insights assembled from the close inspection of past facts. *Temple*'s nesting constructs a "wondrous maze with a thousand doors and a thousand winding ways" comparable to a legal statement or scientific study, and wandering through its "realms, yet unrevealed to human sight" to find "gliding ghosts in the mystic wonders of their silent state" evokes feelings listeners often have during involved discourse on an academic subject.

Both *Temple* and *Aeneid* encourage the art of keeping human enterprises in perspective and of discerning how nested one's own purposes and goals might be within the field of other human endeavors. Virgil's poem has lasted over two thousand years, and Darwin's poem over two hundred, with no guarantee that either will last indefinitely. For their part, lawyers and scientists, during their small fractions of those lengthy spans, while away their time gnawing over the magnitude or transience of each particular project upon which they have that day embarked.

Charles Darwin began his celebrated path with the H. M. S. *Beagle*'s voyages across the southern hemisphere from 1831–1836, a journey also nested within others' works, including inside another favorite poem by Craven Langstroth Betts from 1916, one quoted by the evolutionary biologist J. B. S. Haldane in his classic study *The Causes of Evolution*:

> They saw the day, how brief, the night how long;
> The right how faint, how stark the groping wrong;
> Man's lighted world how narrow, and how wide
> The untrodden dark where all dark things abide.
> With what grim toil the high gods keep at bay
> The desperate leaguer of the haunts of day;
> To their side the souls of men outworn
> Battle to hold off the perilous pass of morn;
> And, overborne, in agony maintain,
> The high adventure of the world, in vain.

Charles lived in a world narrowed by his peers' delusions of an all-powerful creator summoning forth life from nothing, and he broadened it with a remarkable argument of his own, a proof founded on incontestable details of organismal and geological features that revealed all life having actually developed from past life without any preternatural aid. To establish his thesis, he struggled not just with physical obstacles of earthquake and storm aboard the *Beagle*, but with conceptual tempests as well, religious and cultural rejections of science, many of which continue to this day. On the *Beagle*, Charles navigated across three difficulties: his own burgeoning skills as a naturalist and geologist, the realities of a hard daily existence aboard a working gunner brig in the 19th century, and the uncertainties and confusion presented by the vast regions to be explored at each port. Patient maneuvering in all enabled him to eventually fashion a premise that a meaningful explanation of things as structurally and behaviorally complicated as animals and plants demanded that those things must, by necessity, have complicated histories.

Attorneys and scientists have their own historical and literary predecessors, have their own traverses encircled by the thoughts and opinions of previous authors, and are equally buoyed and dogged by precedents and commands issued by earlier generations. In the specialty field of animal law that this book addresses, it is a hallmark of my thesis that those practitioners are especially circumscribed by the biological realities of animal life, a sphere of knowledge with wide but significant boundaries. For that reason, lawyers, in their role as participants in the human enterprise of animal law, seem to me to be charged with a distinct professional obligation to locate their goals soundly within the confluence of law and biology.

In reverse from how nature works, lawyering is a highly directed activity, requiring that one act purposely with a specific aim in mind. Legal questions, disputes, and answers—like animals, poems, and ideas—are never spontaneously "brought forth" from thin air as religions propose for the origin of organic life, but instead are the products of long and convoluted processes dovetailing together time, chance, thought, and error. Law specifically arises from an untidy froth of individual and social behaviors, writings, procedures, and an ever-shifting multitude of personal histories of actors and environmental pressures on those actors. A lawyer's grasp of objects as structurally and behaviorally complicated as animals thus requires acknowledgment not just of the lawyer's own predecessors, but of the complicated histories of people and of the prehistories of animals as well.

That project is not easy. Goethe, the German scientist-poet, alluded lyrically to the difficulties and frustrations that all investigators encounter in uncovering significance in natural mechanisms:

Still secretive in the light of day,

> Nature will forever remain veiled,
> And whatever she will not give away,
> Cannot be pried loose or unnailed.

While most scientists loathe the suggestion that nature cannot be ultimately understood and its secrets ultimately remain hidden, lawyers—who regularly embrace dramatic and theatrical interpretations of the world—are more apt to commiserate. Goethe's words illustrate a tension between attorneys and their goals, evoking the anxiety generated in people who might sometimes wish to pry loose and other times wish to veil knowledge of the world's social or biological complexities.

Virgil and Darwin recognized every lineage to have its ghosts, and two other ancestors also haunt these pages. The first is the physiologist Claude Bernard, the French anatomist and biochemist who wrote his famous work *An Introduction to the Study of Experimental Medicine* in 1865 when Charles Darwin was publishing the 4th edition of *Origin*. Bernard poetically imagined science as a superb lighted hall that could be reached only by passing through "a long and ghastly kitchen," his metaphor for the intellectual route along which the practicing scientist is often beset by the obstacles of poor thinking and prejudice—as he called them "bad methods and defective processes of research." Bernard was a scientist's scientist, and his thoughtful *"La vie, c'est la mort"*—"such is life, such is death"—reflected a desire to transcend the mysticism of Virgil's "ethereal vigor," Darwin's "gliding ghosts," and Betts' "desperate leaguer," seeking instead to ground all explanation for "what life is" entirely within observed processes.

Bernard was a physiologist in the way that both Darwins were naturalists and in the way that lawyers should emulate: finding the genuine meaning of actions, reactions, and phenomena revealed by careful observation of the moment regardless of what others demand shouldn't be revealed. As lawyers should strive to be, the good scientist to Bernard was one who "reasons, compares facts, puts questions to them, and by the answers which he extracts, tests one by another where control, by means of reasoning and factors constitutes experiment and is the only process that we have for teaching ourselves about the nature of things outside us." Every lawyer would recognize the importance of Bernard's postulate that testing for material differences in explanatory ideas can clarify the most difficult questions, and it sounds far more like a trial attorney speaking than a physiologist when he exhorts:

> Facts materially alike may have opposite scientific meanings, according to the
> ideas with which they are connected. A cowardly assassin, a hero and a warrior
> each plunges a dagger into the breast of his fellow. What differentiates them,
> unless it be the ideas which guide their hands? A surgeon, a physiologist and

Nero give themselves up alike to mutilation of living beings. What differentiates them also, if not ideas?[2]

The second ghost rattling the lighted hallways of this book lived a thousand years before the others, and penned his own nested verses about life, nature, and law, verses that formed the seeds from which *Aeneid* and *Temple* later germinated and flourished. The Persian poet-astronomer Omar Khayyam compiled his astonishing *Rubayait*, reflections on life and death in the form of quatrains written in the 11th century BCE, phrases of which adorn this book's chapters. Khayyam helped construct the hallway for Bernard to eventually stride in medicine and the Darwins to stride in biology, a walkway lined with queries about how things live, how things die, and what marks the boundary, the critical membrane, between those realms.

Khayyam remonstrated about the ethereal and difficult nature of deciphering problems of free will and mortality, and he considered his quatrains to be ultimately neither scientific nor metaphysical but simply "such as they are," a monkish commentary on human existence in all its messy and beautiful details. A lawyer who deals with the life and death of organisms—as lawyers in animal law do—may find great truths in Khayyam's philosophy as it nests throughout the later works of his intellectual descendants.

I cherish reading from Bernard and the *Rubayait*, and—to quell my own anxieties about the spangle of existence—have tried to attend carefully to Bernard's insistence on clear observation and to Khayyam's insistence on accepting the limitations of that observation. The path that has unfolded has wound through a variety of disciplines, including Buddhism, Freudian analysis, the minutiae of legal practice, and evolutionary biology, conjoined and interlacing curtains of knowledge where the artificial is hopefully brushed aside to view the real.

That project is its own meta-poem with nested lines of thought. In Zen, the lifting is achieved through satori, individual enlightenment by a flash of sudden awareness; in analysis, through the attainment of personal insight into private conduct; in law, through the revelation at trial of the fruits of marshalling allegations, evidence, and issues to present disputes; and in evolutionary studies, through accumulation of knowledge about organic life by the scientific method, discerning explanations for adaptations illuminating how organic bodies are constructed and operate. Freud, in his own brand of poetry, posed it as a special manner of internal speech:

The voice of the intellect is a soft one, but it does not rest till it has gained a hearing; in the long run nothing can withstand reason and experience. The scientific spirit brings about a particular attitude towards worldly matters; before religious matters it pauses for a little, hesitates, and finally there too crosses the threshold.

In this process there is no stopping; the greater the number of men to whom the treasures of knowledge become accessible, the more widespread is the falling-away from religious belief at first only from its obsolete and objectionable trappings, but later from its fundamental postulates as well.[3]

In a search for explanations, those disciplines' similarities are greater than their differences, each devoted to lifting objective group awareness above subjective self-awareness, yet all using tools of induction, deduction, introspection, and perception to scout out intimate details of how intuition and experience may unmask the why of nature, people, and organisms.

Buddhists, scientists, analysts, lawyers, and poets all observe and perceive relationships, and all manipulate aspects of their study-object by using tools to pry apart layers. As a lawyer, I like the image of a lifted veil; as a poet, of the structure of a quatrain; and as a scientist, of the anatomies and physiologies of bodies in life and death. The lure of revelation and the reality of knowledge position this book as its own ode on the intertwining of law and animals "such as they are."

For well over three decades, I have learned and practiced about law and animals, yet nevertheless find that at the sixth decade into my life far more education awaits me in that enterprise. This book is dedicated to my wife Lori, a remarkable person who has shown me glimpses of both the Veil and What Might Lie Behind the Veil, and I love her for that gentle Lifting, through the poetry she has created in my own life and through the life she has founded with me in all its poetry.

NOTES

1. *Rubáiyát* of Omar Khayyám, Quatrain XLIX.
2. Bernard, Claude. "An Introduction to the Study of Experimental Medicine. Translated into English by Copley Green, with an Introduction by Lawrence J. Henderson and a Foreword by I. Bernard Cohen." (1865).
3. Freud, Sigmund. *The Future of an Illusion*. Peterborough, ON: Broadview Press, 2012.

Introduction

"A Lamp Amid the Darkness"[1]

Because the public today tends to view science in terms of its tools, there is a subtle danger that biology students (who, after all, emerge from the public) will find it easy to confuse technology with science. Given the proper equipment and training, it is not difficult to make monoclonal antibodies. What is infinitely harder is to walk through the woods and decide, on the basis of your observations, against which antigens you should make monoclonal antibodies. Until you are able to make this decision, or perhaps more important, until you are willing to try, you will remain a technician instead of a biologist. To make the transition, however, you must acquire the mindset of a naturalist. If you are successful in doing so, your apprenticeship is likely to end, for you will begin to apply your tools to the raw material of organisms' lives to develop understanding.[2]

This book poses an intersection of two pursuits, law and biology, the *juris* of the enforcement and violation of social rules, and the *zoology* of the origination and termination of organic forms. From the vantage point of both disciplines, I have confronted the panoply of conflicts that arise from people interacting closely with animals, as well as from animals interacting closely among themselves in ways directly affecting people and their rules: As an evolutionary biologist, I have practiced law, and as a lawyer I have practiced biology—in both guises analyzing animal-related issues by whatever light might be shed across the twin perspectives. To that end, Janovy's classic reproach to biologists cited above—imploring them to sagely wield their technical tools when seeking to understand organisms at a deep level—resonates strongly for me in my twin vocations.

One entanglement of the legal and scientific worlds arises through curiosities cropping up within specific techniques lawyers use in their daily practice, techniques that have peculiar parallels with those employed via the scientific method. The odd formality of stating allegations in a pleading or motion is not that distant from the odd formulation of propositions in a hypothesis, both being awkward proposals of a thesis in its infancy that has not yet reached adulthood as a set of established facts. Similarly, the arrangement of rules of evidence and of civil and criminal procedures seems strangely close to the tricky structure and nested hierarchies of certain scientific protocols, tables, and charts.

Both rule sets swirl around the concepts of "materiality" and "relevance," and both cleave closely to what is specifically *useful* in answering a dispute as opposed to what may simply be *interesting* in doing so. The artificial restrictions of certain variables in motions to strike, *in limine*, and to suppress and exclude used to circumscribe a particular issue of fact or law in a court proceeding have frequently seemed to me close thematic companions to the limiting variables employed in data collection and biostatistical analyses. The narrowing down from the first "ask" of a plea or complaint to the final verdict of a fact finder is remarkably akin to the narrowing down from the broad proposal of a field study to the particular confidence level of a statistically significant set of data points.

Those parallels are something more than coincidence, and in recognition of those similarities in my cases and research, I have desired to invest them with meaning in my practice in both science and law. Doing so requires that I wisely use technique—Janovy's "infinitely harder" task—and in the failures and successes encountered in that thornbush I have concluded that there is every reason to apply the tools of a scientist to develop a "lawyer's mindset" about animal lives and deaths similar to Janovy's admonishment regarding the mindset of a naturalist.

One aim is for lawyers who litigate animal-related legal issues—in order to be good practitioners of such a peculiar art—to play the role of being good scientists as well, and not merely as scientific technicians. A lawyer-scientist's task is to rigorously and carefully observe, and then rigorously and objectively analyze, the picayune aspects of organic life, death, utility, and value in the natural world, a world of which people and their various worldly possessions (the true objects of study for lawyers) are a crucial component. Currently, that task seems unaccomplished.

It isn't simply the marginal element of acting "scientifically" that is required, it's also an investment into really using the substantive ingredients. An animal law attorney who actively neglects (or passively avoids) science-based reasoning about their case's furred or feathered subject imperils their clients' interests no differently than a real property attorney who maintains a blithe ignorance of plot maps, stake surveys, or drilling samples. In turn, an animal law attorney who actively neglects (or passively avoids) law-based reasoning and the specific procedural apparatus that affects the initiation, treatment, and outcome of their case disserves law's goals, and would be better off appreciating animals in some other discipline unburdened by law's rigors.

Laws about animals require curiosity about detail and technique aimed hard in both directions: at the perplexing form of a writ, warrant, or special verdict; at the necessary redundancy of certain allegations in a code-based pleading; at the archaic subsections to the exception to a century-old rule of evidence; at the artificial restriction of one category in a statute where other, alarmingly similar, categories lie unscathed—and at the same time at the peculiar suite of adaptations affecting locomotory skills in a horse; at the jumble of cultural-based terms dog breeders utilize in outlining specialty dog breed standards; at the archaic distinctions that define and delimit what counts as "socialization" in dog and cats; at the boggle of objective-yet-subjective nutritional require-ments imposed on a rancher's milk-producing cows.[3] All these coordinates and many more beside position themselves as variables in an equation far more complex than the superficial "love and respect for animals" criterion presently deemed to be sufficient.

One imposing obstacle in the path toward being good scientists is that law-yers historically have had great incentives to be *antagonistic* to the cloak of objectivity that scientists are encouraged to drape over themselves; lawyers are often encouraged to be *unscientific* to prosper. Lawyers use rhetoric and persuasion to help others obtain or recover profits and to reduce or avoid losses; scientists do no such thing. Lawyers are approvingly paid by society for the private citizen's use of their time and of their brains; scientists rarely so (and when it does occur it is considered distasteful). Lawyers tend to mea-sure success or failure in the muddied vernacular of sports events, "winning" or "losing" a case or a point in a manner hardly distinct from scoring in a tournament; scientists, for their part, don't keep tally in that fashion as to what they might consider success or failure in testing a hypothesis or conducting an experiment.

Legal procedure and precedent, moreover, don't adhere to the scientific method, and prevailing in an argument can often be far more effective by a lawyer's reliance on personality and stagecraft then on appeals to logic and rational analysis. Lawyers, in their dual role of advocates and performers, are hardly immune from subjectivity since subjectivity is a great tool in law. The history of American jurisprudence affirms it is lauded and acceptable that quite personal criteria be employed to achieve a client's goals and to deny an opponent's victory. The lawyer, not the scientist, is the one expected to effec-tively frame issues along the path to a goal through eye-catching acts of pure persona, stepping behind or in front of (depending on how advantage might be gained) ever-shifting veils of personal preference, personal ambition, and personal benefit. The respective approaches are not easily reconcilable:

[L]awyers and scientists continue to see the world through very different lenses. Because neither discipline will or should have to adopt the other's world view, they must reconcile their differences. In practice, however, scientists are very often frustrated and disgusted by their experience with the law. This is in part attributable to some lawyers' failures both to articulate clearly what their scientific needs are and to comprehend the science and respect the scientists who enter the legal process. Lawyers too are very often frustrated and disgusted by their experience with science. Many scientists fail to make science manageable rather than magical, and some are willing to stretch science to mystical heights for the right fee. . . . The law will never become a sophisticated consumer of science until the lawyers and lawmakers become conversant in the language of science and are comfortable in its culture. But science does not exist like a schoolhouse that can be entered and exited as necessity requires. To be scientifically literate does not involve memorizing the terms or supposed content of "science." Science is an approach or methodology. It is a direction, not a destination. . . . It is a rigorous and critical form of analysis, one that seeks well-supported and parsimonious explanations for empirical questions.[4]

Since emotional bonds easily form and are easily exploited between clients and the animals they own, as a consequence the practice of animal law then both heightens and degrades that distinction between the stagecraft of legal practice and the harsh light of scientific inquiry. I believe it should be otherwise. I believe that a more scientific approach, not a more lawyerly approach, to being the advocate in an animal case is beneficial. Encounters with clients, colleagues, jurists, and the public about pursuits of claims, defenses, decisions, and judgments in animal law cases have exposed invocations of all manner of political and religious agendas in order to progress or impede an inquiry as to what a particular animal is, how it should be treated or disposed of, or what laws should apply to it. My dismay that those agendas disserve the task of understanding law, understanding science, and understanding animals, stirs me to attempt something better.

A core understanding of law, science, and animals begins with understanding evolution by natural selection as the crucial and distinctive force by which animals and humans have come to be. It is a process which informs the origins and trajectories of all three areas of inquiry, and from which even non-scientific social concepts such as "law," "reason," "value" and, the subject/object distinction all ultimately are derived. A grasp of how evolution works leads to a grasp of the immense *prehistorical* foundations from which humans developed, which in turn founds appreciation for *historical* foundations on which law then developed. Evolution is a powerful tool for both lawyer and scientist to use in their joint goal of unearthing exactly where the laws affecting animals have been buried and in what form they have been exhumed. As evolution by natural selection has inexorably "engineered" people to behave in ways radically distinct from all other animals, then the reasons why law treats animals differently than people can be disinterred from a complex mixture of prehistoric and historic events.

An application of legal rules, economic principles, biological concepts, and prehistorical and historical observations on "what animals are," posited from the stance of a practicing scientist, demands the acknowledgment that animals are legally separate objects from human beings. Many contest that point, and, wishing it otherwise, large swaths of the public actively seek to recast animals into the legal equivalents of persons. They do so by rejecting and subverting aspects of animals as legal mechanisms, market goods, organisms evolved in tandem with human communities, and carefully selected personal properties owned, controlled, and utilized by people for critical social reasons. In embracing animals as objects, rules regarding property, contract, and tort can solve the unique puzzles that animals and their ownership regularly create. Across nearly three thousand animal law cases, it has become clear to me that there is a huge benefit to resisting immersion in the enticing bath of guilt, religious belief, and childhood fantasy in which we all wallow to some extent about animals—a tub of half-truths and prejudices that can distract the bather from acknowledging colder but more crucial truths.

To that end, know that there is a specter haunting the major themes of this book—the specter of animal rights activism—and that I aspire to exorcise that ghost. It posits animals as personal subjects of "self," as analogues of people, and is propounded by a bevy of highly intelligent, yet emotive, morally judgmental, and politically motivated thinkers. My purge of those propositions starts and ends with the recognition of animals as animate items fashioned by natural selection to in fact not be our equals at all, but instead to be elaborate pieces of the natural world with which humans have long engaged, and currently engage, in a plethora of intricate use-based relationships. While effective control and realistic valuation of animals likely needs to be better addressed in the law than it has been so far, their foundational status need not be transformed at all.

Animal rights advocates take serious issue with such a stance, and rail against treating animals as objects or as property.[5] That position, however, is enmeshed in a normative and moralistic view of the universe, not a descriptive and scientific one—a "how things ought to be" argument for change, as opposed to a "how things actually are" description for analysis. In certain spheres of life there is nothing wrong whatsoever with espousing change via moral judgments; religious and charitable organizations, for example, are commended, not reviled, for postulating possible worlds in which animals and humans act in idealistic tandem or as stand-ins for each other. No one blinks when businesspeople decide which relationships to foster and which to avoid based on moral judgments they may make about the use of animals:

business decisions and business morality are phenomena which, unremark-ably, are closely linked, and a corporation's proclamation that its products don't harm animals is invariably proudly broadcast, not privately suppressed.

The legal profession, on the other hand, steps poorly when it applies moral criteria to analyzing interactions with animals; the selection of a lawyer's clients or a case's subjects is presumed to at least begin by transcending decisions affected by personal mores. Lawyers are not just urged, but pro-fessionally obligated, to employ a quasi-scientific filter in that selection, the apertures for which developed from, and are subsequently regulated by, democratically derived ideals and concepts, including and especially that lawyers are supposed to work from foundational principles concerning equal access to justice for all.

Areas of legal practice in which a moral treaty would be imposed on its practitioners would be abhorrent in any other respect. Consider the alarm raised in our legal system, for instance, were it learned that lawyers in avia-tion law had bound themselves to only represent "good" pilots as opposed to "bad" ones, or that all landlord-tenant attorneys had made a group pact assur-ing that only "noble" landlords were assisted, while "evil" ones were left to their own devices without representation. At the very least, the principles of equal access to justice and of equal protection of laws would seem heavily degraded by such an arrangement.

Yet in the realm of litigating animal cases, moral judgments about who are to be helped and who are to be hindered have permeated the practice. The earnest feeling among many law school animal law programs and graduates is that attorneys should represent only those who would "protect" animals, not those who might exploit, manipulate, confine, alter, or destroy them. Animal breeders, animal hoarders, animal eaters, animal hunters, and animal wearers are frequently shunned from consideration or from obtaining legal assistance by an agenda of "promoting animal welfare." This restriction of exposure to differing viewpoints unfortunately weakens the richness of legal inquiry, drains value accumulated by embracing divergent approaches, and cuts short important questions to be resolved about human-animal relationships:

The ecocentrist helpfully asks, Is therapeutic culling of "management species" (especially ungulates such as deer or elk) ecologically obligatory, regardless of whether anyone desires to pull the trigger? The biocentrist inquires, Is nonsub-sistence hunting compatible with respecting an animal as a fellow "teleological center of life" pursuing its own evolved good? The virtue theorist wonders, What traits of character are cultivated by sport and trophy hunting, and do these contribute to the best shared life? Do humans have predatory instincts that are most healthily expressed through hunting? Is hunting essential to a healthy relationship with the land, as Aldo Leopold believed? The deontological rights theorist inquires, Do other animals have rights; that is, might their interests as we perceive them override any direct benefits they might offer humans as prey? The feminist ethicist of care asks, Does hunting affect our ability to care for animals; indeed, are we genuinely capable of caring about beings with whom we have no sustained relationship? The utilitarian questions, Should all sentient animals' preferences or interests as we perceive them, including our own, have equal weight when we evaluate consequences? Can human preferences for hunting, if nonbasic, justifiably trump basic animal interests in life, liberty, and bodily integrity?[6]

A large component of the equal access to justice for which those voices speak, the access to which animal breeders, hoarders, hunters, ranchers, and the like are entitled, is not just equal access to consideration, but equal access to reasonable *justifications*, in particular to that which can be gleaned from scientifically valid bases of information about where prehistorical and historical relationships between animals and humans have led us.[7] As those voices reveal, wide avenues of explanation are open to the tolerant as to how the breeding, hoarding, eating, and hunting of animals are in many ways actions as respectful or protective of animals as would be their buffering from interference or their "liberation" into the wild.

Much of that dialogue starts with realistically grasping the object role that animals play and have played in human societies. The enlightenment possible from that exchange flows from the revelation that the breeding, buying, selling, capturing, altering, repairing, and disposing of animals aren't automatically abusive practices. While it is easy to concur with a generic concern about protecting animals from intentional abuse, the lawyer-scientist should pause hard at accepting claims to locate support for expanding that concern into the territory of rights via the scientific evidence regarding animal behavior and life in captivity and in the wild.

Some advocates' claims that animals are "healthier" and have "richer emotional and social lives" in natural environments have been well explored and found to have some scientific basis.[8] An unblinking readiness to inextricably link animal abuse or behavioral abnormalities to animals' placement in artificial environments, however, stretches that concept far too thin intellectually. Many animal rights advocates inexcusably disregard what detailed scientific evidence on animals in the wild and in captivity actually describes; the raw emotional appeal of life "in the wild" being the preferable alternative often turns out to be in fact dismantled, not supported, by modern field studies in those areas.

Take the retention and breeding of elephants in captivity as an example. An ever-increasing set of zoological research articles in professional academic journals demonstrate well that habitat loss and habitat fragmentation have operated to expose dying, isolated populations of elephants in the African wild to vastly greater sources of pain and torment than any zookeeper could possibly inflict.[9] A significant body of literature in turn indicates that captive breeding programs for elephants are not just necessary adjuncts to, but truly the only realistic methodological option for, elephant habitat protection; and that zoos not only do *not* turn the vast majority of captive elephants into zombielike supplicants or walking pathological disasters, but actually provide them greater physiological health benefits, more enriching behavioral experiences, and longer life spans than would currently be obtainable for them in the wild.[10] Advocates cannot in good faith look to "the scientific evidence" to lambaste elephant captivity because the actual scientific evidence does not help that effort.

Restraint from unblinkingly adopting such a position allows a healthier acceptance of the role people play and have played in the natural world, a recognition that the advocate mindset should be more open to. The role is not necessarily richer in the amorphous sense of greater "respect" for animals or of finding greater moral "worth" of animals—rather, throughout the course of evolutionary time the role has been one of humans being involved participants in the biological landscape in which the evolved adaptations of complex sociality and language have propelled us on a path fundamentally distinct from animals. A richness develops from embracing our participation at all levels as self-formed subjects—sometimes wresting, and sometimes failing to wrest, control of animals as immediate and long-term environmental objects. That role doesn't propose we are "above" animals, or "not animals anymore" since both propositions are empirically untrue. It is a stance that instead accommodates where we fit evolutionarily within a tangled network of other biological organisms around us. Critiques of humans as exploiters, in discounting our integral inclusion in food webs as being the exploited as well, miss out on that richness:

> Our teeth, alimentary system, metabolism bear it out: neither carnivore, nor herbivore, nor frugivore, nor granivore, we are all these at once. To get by on a diet of any one of these is to be either painfully stressed and malnourished or preoccupied with substitutions and additives. To willfully "be" an herbivore—i.e., a vegetarian—is a special arrogance masquerading as ethics. . . . To harvest any food is to kill living beings. This realization has become painful to us because of our lack of a philosophy of death as part of life and because in industrial societies we pay someone else to do the killing. Such a philosophy would include not only the moral necessity of killing, as the source of life, but recognition that we too are food.[11]

In recognizing ourselves as the eaten as well as the eaters, the manipulated as well as the manipulators, the captives as well as those capturing, pathways to understanding open up to us, not just cultural and historical paths, but ones hewn from far more ancient trackways carved by forays into anthropology and evolutionary biology. In one light, this book is a treatise because it examines "laws" of the scientific, social, and legal varieties. In another, it is something of a construction manual dissection manual since it pries apart superficial tissues to reach underlying structures. For the biologist who seeks a better grasp on laws about animals and for the lawyer who seeks a better grasp on laws about biology, this work assembles several steps toward accomplishing both tasks.

Chapter 1 sets out the basic apparatus by which questions and answers are suitably collected, tools that scientists and lawyers both require for building strong and useful arguments. Chapter 2 digs into history and then into prehistory with those tools to carve out foundations for an origin story of animals as objects, of law as a record of social agreements, and of morals as a fruit of the conjunction of law and language. Chapter 3 constructs a framework around competing ways of defining animals, and then ponders the viable and unviable uses supported by those definitions. Chapter 4 considers those uses to craft arguments about animals as properties having owners and as owned objects requiring attempts at control in ways effective and ineffective. Chapter 5 grapples with economic principles and practices that help identify bargained and transactional realities imposed upon interactions between humans and animals, the results of which then allow us to construct useful value schemes. Chapter 6 homes in specifically on the problems and promises raised by zoos, facilities where the exotic animals within them as specially held objects amplify relationship difficulties with people. Chapter 7 disentangles concepts of animal and human intent, spots key distinctions emanating from the concepts of culpability and provocation, and promotes objectification as a valuable concept. Finally, chapter 8 confronts head on the myth of animal "rights" in light of the strengths of human rights, hard-won concepts contingent on identifying that crucial separation of humans and animals by the evolutionarily driven phenomenon of language.

NOTES

1. *Rubáiyát* of Omar Khayyám, Quatrain XXXIV.
2. Janovy, John. *On Becoming a Biologist*. Lincoln: University of Nebraska Press, 1996.
3. See, e.g., Berleant-Schiller, Riva, and Eugenia Shanklin. *The Keeping of Animals: Adaptation and Social Relations in Livestock Producing Communities*. Totowa, NJ: Allanheld, Osmun, 1983.

4. Faigman, David L. *Legal Alchemy: The Use and Misuse of Science in the Law*. Macmillan, 2000. pp. preface xiii, 203–204.

5. A professional publication on animals and the law, for instance, talks about "improving the legal status and/or treatment of animals such that their interests and inherent worth are recognized and protected," and chides those who would call them objects or property as not using "ethically sensitive language." *See* Schaffner, J. *An Introduction to Animals and the Law* at p. 5.

6. McKenna, Erin, and Andrew Light, eds. *Animal Pragmatism: Rethinking Human-Nonhuman Relationships*. Bloomington: Indiana University Press, 2004 at p. 46.

7. Clutton-Brock, J. *Domesticated Animals from Early Times*. Austin: University of Texas Press, 1981; Clutton-Brock, J. "Origins of the Dog: Domestication and Early History" at pp. 8–20 in *The Domestic Dog*. Serpell, J. (ed.). Cambridge: Cambridge University Press, 1995.

8. Bekoff, Marc. *The Emotional Lives of Animals: A Leading Scientist Explores Animal Joy, Sorrow, and Empathy—and Why They Matter*. New World Library, 2008.

9. See, e.g., Chase, M. J., and S. Schlossberg, C. R. Griffin, P. J. Bouché, S. W. Djene, P. W. Elkan, S. Ferreira, F. Grossman, E. M. Kohi, K. Landen, P. Omondi, A. Peltier, S. A. Selier, R. Sutcliffe. "Continent-wide Survey Reveals Massive Decline in African Savannah Elephants." *Peer J.* 2016 Aug. 31;4:e2354.

10. See Veasey, J. S. "Assessing the Psychological Priorities for Optimising Captive Asian Elephant (*Elephas maximus*) Welfare. *Animals* (Basel). 2019 Dec. 23;10(1):39.; Bansiddhi, P., and J. L. Brown, C. Thitaram. "Welfare Assessment and Activities of Captive Elephants in Thailand." *Animals* (Basel). 2020 May 26;10(6):919; Hildebrandt, T. B. and R. Hermes, J. Saragusty, R. Potier, H. M. Schwammer, F. Balfanz, H. Vielgrader, B. Baker, P. Bartels, F. Göritz. "Enriching the Captive Elephant Population Genetic Pool through Artificial Insemination with Frozen-Thawed Semen Collected in the Wild." *Theriogenology*. 2012 Oct. 1;78(6):1398–404.

11. Shephard, P. *The Only World We've Got*. San Francisco: Sierra Club Books, 1996.

Chapter 1

Tools for Inquiry

"A Hair Perhaps Divides the False and True"[1]

The things that lawyers know about,
Are property and land.
But why the leaves are on the trees;
And why the waves disturb the seas;
Why honey is the food of bees;
Why horses have such tender knees;
Why winters come when rivers freeze;
Why faith is more than what one sees;
And hope survives the worst disease;
And charity is more than these . . .
They do not understand.[2]

How do you answer a question? Traditionally, most investigatory systems employ three levels of analysis: the ontological, the epistemological, and the methodological. Scientists and lawyers, though often using their own jargon and equally as often finessing certain steps at one or more of the levels, are at least familiar with the schema in general.

The first level, the ontological, simply asks "Did a thing happen?" It attempts to identify what the core issue is for the question that needs an answer. Ontological queries set the stage by inquiring *outward*, contemplating the very existence of the problem itself and its workable definition, if it even has one. Ontology concedes at the start that we have to first know, usually via our direct senses, what we are even interested in exploring to begin with—including what we already know about the world as well as what we don't know about the world but would like to—in order to be able to even hope to attack a new problem at its inception.

1

The second level, the epistemological, asks the more complicated and internally directed question "How reliable is our knowledge about the thing that happened?" It attempts to discern what proof is sufficient to eventually answer the question once the first threshold is crossed. As a line of inquiry, the epistemological delves *inward*, toward ourselves as being good or poor questioners, and it seeks some assurances that we can develop criteria for, and hopefully rely upon, certain types of support regarding the job of accepting one answer as being more likely or more correct over another answer as being less likely or less correct. It is here where we try to winnow out causation from correlation as the rationale for suspected relationships between events. Epistemological inquiries come to grips with outlining the limits of explanatory power, the definable boundaries of the strengths and weaknesses of our explanations for certain phenomena being linked at all.

The third level, the methodological, raises the most practical problem of the series: "What process will best determine a good answer?" It attempts to identify the specific tools of thought required to effectively apply the proof to the question in order to ultimately get to a workable answer. To accomplish our result, we accept a need to employ discrete methods that are hopefully reliable, internally consistent, and somehow usefully repeatable in the future, and which can thus be transmitted to ourselves later on and to the next generations so that others may later not just follow our steps and repeat our inquiry for their own satisfaction, but also build on our answers using the same process, and appreciate the combined results as universally informative and locally useful conclusions. To the extent that knowledge "accumulates," it is the methodological level that enables it to do so effectively.[3]

Identifying an issue, proving an issue, and applying methods to obtain that proof, are all activities lawyers engage in every day. A lawyer asks, "Did A steal B's wallet?"—the ontological component. They then ask, "What actual evidence supports the belief that A did or didn't?"—the epistemological component. Finally, they ask, "What rules should be used to present the evidence and reach a usable and reliable answer as to whether A truly did or didn't?"—in this, the inquiry process is closed with the methodological component. Making allegations, engaging in discovery to support or refute those allegations, and then holding a hearing or a trial via a detailed set of rules to determine the validity of those allegations based on what was found are all classic lawyer activities entangled in solving a case, i.e., "answering a question."

In an odd disconnect between the real world and the perceived world of law, laypeople (whose beliefs about how cases operate and conclude often stem from dramatic portrayals in fiction and on screen) often think that the end of a case comes at the award or the verdict, whereas lawyers, versed in a pursuit conducted through assertion, collection, and presentation of evidence, generally consider the case to actually be over when the evidence has been presented—the award or verdict is more of an afterthought, the excess icing on an ontological, epistemological, and methodological cake that has already been planned, baked, and served.

Identifying an issue, proving an issue, and applying methods to obtain that proof are all activities in which scientists engage every day as well. A scientist asks, "Did A evolve from B?"—forming a hypothesis that sets forth the ontological component. They then ask, "What evidence supports the belief that A evolved from B?"—stepping up to the task of the epistemological component. Finally, they ask, "What method or mechanism should be considered sufficient to present the evidence and thus reach a usable and reliable answer as to whether A really did evolve from B?"—the methodological component imparting "scientific" value to a conclusion. Making hypotheses, engaging in research to support or refute those hypotheses, and then conducting an experiment or test to determine the validity of those hypotheses are all classic scientist activities entangled in "answering a question."

SIMILARITIES AND DIFFERENCES IN INQUIRIES BY LAWYERS AND SCIENTISTS

It is initially encouraging that lawyers and scientists broadly share those three areas of focus. Both would agree with Claude Bernard proclaiming "Observation, then, is what shows facts; experiment is what teaches about facts and gives experience in relation to anything" as both practitioners seek to show and teach about facts. A lawyer would consider and describe the ontological level to be that of "issue spotting"—what is the event in the world that even raises any legal issue to begin with? If that inquiry is "Did A take B's wallet," and if taking another's wallet implicates a legal concern, then ontologically a lawyer becomes interested—but the fact has to be brought to attention by the client and then identified by the lawyer as a legally motivating one before anything else happens.

A lawyer would consider and describe the epistemological level to involve "evidentiary proof." What, they ask, is the verification, the concrete support, for the claim that A took the wallet? At these two levels, the messiness of human language often interferes with a clear analysis, given that many terms are ill-defined enough to overlap in confusing ways. For instance, a lawyer's use of the term "fact" itself is supremely untidy. What one lawyer might claim to be a foundational fact, a statement about the world to be necessarily accepted as true without having to be proven (what the lawyer claims must be "judicially noticed"), another might well claim isn't "judicially noticeable" or axiomatic at all and must itself first be proven before it could be accepted as a threshold.

Similarly, since the law says that those matters that a jury ultimately decides are facts and cannot further be refuted as true statements about the world ("The wallet was not in the plaintiff's pocket when the defendant first touched it"), then lawyers might vehemently proclaim something to be a fact that "in fact" turns out to be "not a fact" given what six or twelve strangers have decided themselves might be otherwise. Timing is key. The rules of evidence, in combination with jury instructions, orders, and verdicts, comprise a lawyer's epistemological field guide to a host of judicially approved methods, alternately boring and exhilarating, employed to prove in a certain period of time that things, events, and conditions either must be or couldn't be so.

That linguistic messiness brings us to the final analytic level, the methodological, which a lawyer would consider to be encompassed by the nitty-gritty of "paperwork," the heavily rule-bound motions, pleadings, petitions, affidavits, applications, submissions, and exhibits that lawyers find themselves alternatively on top of or buried under throughout their practices. The pettiness and rigidity of court documents, legal forms, and transactional papers conceal huge subterranean tectonic plates of rules that—slowly shifting back and forth as they groan under the weight and force of legislative action and judicial precedent—are what finally enable the law to reach the legal conclusion that A took B's wallet.

Legal rules of procedure can be complicated, voluminous, and picky enough that they can sometimes seem like ends in themselves, and it is a danger that a clear view of the overall landscape—the crucial ontological issues—can become obscured or even forgotten by stepping around all those pesky epistemological and methodological (read, evidentiary and documentary) divots, cracks, and gopher holes. The phrase "They got off on a technicality" is code for an instance where a subsequent methodological hole has swallowed up an initial epistemological expedition.

Scientists, for their part, use all three levels in a fairly standard scientific fashion: First, for example, they pose the hypothesis "Did B evolve from A?" Second, they look to what empirical and measurable evidence might support any claim that B did so evolve. Third, they ask themselves just what specific method or mechanism should be used to describe the evidence for or against accepting an evolutionary relationship between B and A. Without delving into the complicated swamps in which scientists often mire themselves at each level, lawyers can at least start emulating scientists with some obvious similarities, and can always begin and end by saying that, like scientists, they too are trying equally hard to use proposals to determine something specifically true and useful about relationships both past and present.

The comparison begins to break down the closer the two disciplines are forced to parallel their methods of inquiry and decision. For one, a lawyer's "evidence" is certainly not a scientist's "evidence." Lawyers, judges, and jurors frequently weigh a wiggly and weird quality called "the credibility of the source of a claimed fact"—scientists don't put much sway in assessing the "credibility" of people directly since truthful statements are measured by scientists from the support of data, not from the taking of personal oaths or the staking of social status, personal reputation, or penalties for perjury on claims of "speaking the truth," an activity that law finds fascinating and useful. Lawyers, judges, and jurors will rely on the power of a sworn oath alone sometimes to establish that a fact can exist while scientists could really care less about who individually swears or doesn't about the correctness of a proposition, a piece of evidence, or a claimed hypothesis. Where lawyers comfort themselves with universally recognizing some truths via the vehicle of judicial notice as "truths that automatically cross the entire board," the vast majority of such truisms are ones scientists dispute as truths at all, or at least not axioms from which to locate other similar truths.

Similarly, a lawyer's "laws" are almost definitely not a scientist's "laws." Lawyers accept history and tradition as support for a rule to exist and be applied as consistently as possible across a wide swath of cohorts—scientists are famous for rejecting history and tradition if the previously established "law of nature" does not turn out to comport with a new observation or data set. Lawyers rely on uniform agreements among socially authorized groups of people such as legislators, judges, arbitrators, and juries to help construct laws, many of which can be nonsensical and downright antithetical to reality. The idea of a consensus reached by voting is key to a lawyer's "laws," whereas scientists care not one whit for the countable agreements of social groups; some cohort's unanimous or majority accord is no test whatsoever for the acceptance of a workable scientific law.

> [B]oth science and law are seeking truth, but scientific findings are tested continually in looking for general understanding of nature, whereas the legal system is looking for a quick determination of truth in a particular case and prefers not to revisit the issues. It is no secret, but rarely admitted, that one of the two advocacy groups in any given legal case can be wholly disinterested in the truth—to the point of seeing irrelevant technical reasons for suppressing evidence. This is counter to the best practices of science.[4]

When one actually asks a lawyer to be "scientific" or to use the scientific method, distress expands in the same manner that it does when one asks a scientist to epistemologically depend on opinion alone to resolve a question. Scientists rely on the rigorous work of other scientists, on established peer-reviewed publications, on tightly controlled experiment, and on repeated testing to verify that a fact has been (mostly) proven or a question (mostly) answered. Lawyers rely instead on "the fact finder" to do so, either a judge or arbitrator or jury, but always in the form of other people and invariably (at least with juries) people who are neither lawyers nor scientists themselves, who are untrained and often unschooled, and who have merely been randomly selected from an enormous pool of other untrained and often unschooled candidates and then formally "instructed" by lawyers (through the advocacy of lawyers and the rulings of judges) as to how to decide.

There is no "mostly answered" for the lawyer as there is for the scientist—the fact is eventually final and unavailable for challenge in its end stage (realistically after all avenues of judicial review have been completely exhausted), albeit that it might take some exasperating amount of time and possible lapses of reason to get there, particularly within the harsh parameters, economic limitations, and political realities of an often systemically broken adversarial system of justice.[5] At least, lawyers will be the first (and loudest) to tell everyone else just how valuable their services are in arriving at the truth and just how important a path it is that the law treads:

> The profession of the law possesses extraordinary powers. Lawyers can make the arrogant humble and the weak strong. In control of the course of litigation and armed with the knowledge of right and wrong, they are most able to abjure illegal or tortious conduct; it is their duty to do so. As occupants of a high public trust and officers of the court, they are expected to conform their behavior in legal affairs to a higher standard of rectitude and spirit of obedience than those who are willing to endure the dust of transgression. Guided by oath, duty and obligation, the lawyer's path avoids the vices from which the virtuous abstain.[6]

Scientists find the finality and arbitrariness of the legal system to be outright infuriating—why, they fume, would anyone accept that a thing is "true" simply because one, or six, or twelve other people personally voted and agreed that thing to be true? People in small groups are notoriously and ridiculously fallible[7]; what if further inquiry or further facts reveal that one or two or all of them were flat wrong? Moreover, what about the pursuit of different results in light of the receipt of new information regardless of whom first provided the old information? To scientists, law seems dangerously subjective and bewilderingly myopic; it artificially restricts the pursuit of knowledge by making it a function of human personalities and topical desires, and by cementing mistake and prejudice together into the unyielding concrete block of legislated compacts and majority rule.

Lawyers, correspondingly, find the inconclusiveness and wishy-washiness of doing science to be comparably irksome and unfulfilling: How can any problem ever be settled and counted upon if people keep continually reopening its examination and questioning every result? There has to be an end to a dispute, satisfying or otherwise, says the perplexed lawyer who disdains the scientist's methodologies and is baffled by the rejection of decision procedures. If twelve smart and capable scientists closely agree about something being so, muses the lawyer, how is that one scientist can then later completely override their earlier well-reasoned determination? Alternatively, they might ask, if twelve capable scientists *disagree* about something, how can the subject of the disagreement nevertheless later be deemed to have been of no consequence at all? To lawyers, much of the practice and process of science seems foolishly impractical as a real-world tool in that it repeatedly and perilously compromises the social utility of firm and final conclusion-reaching.

> The best case that could be made for the epistemological efficacy of an adversarial system, given the special circumstances under which the legal search for truth is conducted, would run somewhat as follows. Since for good reason the legal process, unlike the process of scientific inquiry, has to be concluded within a relatively short time-frame, we need a way of ensuring that the search for and scrutiny of evidence are as thorough as that time-frame allows. An adversarial system is one way to do this. If everyone involved knows that eventually, at the trial stage, the determination will be made by an impartial jury weighing the evidence developed and presented by the parties, each subject to cross-examination by the other, this should encourage precisely the kind of thoroughness we are aiming to achieve. . . . Nevertheless, a trial is very different from an open-ended scientific or scholarly investigation sifting for as long as it takes through all the evidence that can be had; legal determinations of fact are subject both to limitations of time and to constraints on how evidence may lawfully be obtained and what evidence may lawfully be presented. What the legal finder of fact is asked to do is *not*, strictly speaking, to determine whether the defendant is guilty, or is liable, but . . . to determine whether the evidence establishes the defendant's guilt or liability to the required degree.[8]

While both are inquisitors independently trying to determine something true about the world, and while both rely on inferences and presumptions as logic tools to help get there, lawyers and scientists' paths diverge sharply as to how far logic will take them to finally reach a particular answer. The lawyer's path is strewn with impediments in the form of interferences by others on the same or crossing paths, fellow travelers and competing tourists and annoying tour guides in the guise of clients, opponents, witnesses, jurors, arbitrators, judges, legislators, and politicians, and those travelers' own opinions and voices help define and lead toward an end. Euphemistically, older generations of lawyers used to call the whole navigational experience "hanging onto the sled," an image summoning forth the simultaneous sensations of exhilaration and dread while accelerating down an incline.

The scientist's path avoids those people-oriented obstacles (or at least considers them as "obstacles" as opposed to "stepping stones") and confronts instead a more removed set of voices, figures, and shadows as seen through the scrim of other independent investigators, primarily their employment of reason, their insistence on measurement, and their reliance on the most direct perceptions possible. It is a hallmark of the weirdness and wonder of science that the "end" of the scientist's path appears at its heart to be no end at all but merely "more path" with little end to note. The scientist deals with their impediments in the form of funding, available apparatus and techniques, and lab space, but their sled careens down a hill that wondrously has no bottom.

It isn't just that vastly distinct routes get lawyers and scientists to their vastly distinct answers, it is also that there is a monumental disconnect between their aspirations as well. Lawyers deal with the physical world in small part but are far more involved with the social world, an area composed of often interlocking, and just as often severed, personal and political interactions between related parties in which an end is sought within an amorphous cloud of principles confusingly termed "justice." An overarching lawyer theme for manipulating those interactions to get to whatever "justice" might be that day involves the basic childhood game of asking and answering unknown questions, and a suitable inquiry into the potential solution to any solvable puzzle uses the ontological, the epistemological, and the methodological routes.[9] Yet lawyers are also heavily invested in trying to determine "what is right and good," an aim frequently recognized as unobtainable stemming as it does from a very limiting, self-centered, and intuitive view of the universe constrained more often than not by personal preference, fueled by personal greed, and espoused through voices amplified, muffled, and distorted by personal history and prospect.

"Trying to eliminate the incorrect," on the other hand, the scientist's constantly shifting and seemingly unreachable goal, is a broadening scientific proposition, a "how things actually are" assessment, fueled by the appreciation of empirical fact, constrained by an objective sense of the history that came before the question and the context in which the question is being asked, and is espoused and proven via the use of direct observation, induction, and rational analysis—or at least the brave attempt to use those things. Intuition and anecdote, hopefully, having nothing to do with attaining the objective.

AN EPISTEMOLOGICAL DIVIDING LINE

Why the difference? Why the deep disjoint between the aspirations if both sets of practitioners truly are inquisitorial colleagues? A basic split seems to develop at the middle, at the epistemological level. To explain why, consider a metaphor.

In chemistry, several substances mixed together (where none have dissolved into each other), are called a *mixture* and the process of *filtration* is used to separate the substances out, with the substance of interest called the *filtrate*, and the leftover substances called the *particulates*. To identify the filtrate, one uses *filters*, porous devices or materials with a number of openings, *apertures*, in them. Aperture number affects how long filtration takes: the fewer the apertures, the longer, and the more apertures, the shorter. Aperture size affects effectiveness of filtration: the larger the apertures, the less discriminate the filtration, the smaller the apertures, the reverse.

Law may perhaps be described as a mixture with many substances in the form of ideas for what is, and what has historically been, deemed morally "good" for people, mixed up with what is, and what has historically been, deemed morally "bad," also for people. Society conducts filtration to separate out the former as the filtrate (laws that command or reward certain acts), and the latter as the particulates (laws that prohibit or penalize certain acts). Extraction is conducted in an atmosphere of pragmatism and political reality that pervades the laboratory in which this unusual chemistry experiment takes place, and that atmosphere infects the filtrate so that it becomes "pragmatic and politically acceptable and workable laws," and the particulate becomes "unacceptable and unworkable laws."

Two different filtration methods are employed: the codification method and the common law method. The first, codification, is intrinsically *political* and the filters comprise what we call "the legislative process," from coarse to fine being initiative and referendum in which the investigators are the public; hearings and committee review in which the investigators are the legislators; and the electoral or voting process in which the investigators are a heady mix of the public and legislators. Political analysts note that it is often so difficult to tell what the number and size of the different apertures might be at any given moment in such filters that you might as well label the whole process as a mysterious black box in which many ideas are poured in and, later, a few supposedly helpful and applicable statutes trickle out.

Odd chemical transformations take place in the codification laboratory such that the filtrate frequently looks nothing like the original substances, and there is regular disagreement by the chemists involved as to which products should even be filtrate and which particulates. The codes and statutes that result form an imposing set of volumes stacked high in every law library, the words of which fluctuate between precedence and obsolescence with each new legislative session. The value of the filtrate is unrelated to its quantity: no one cares a jot about last year's four-million-word, 14,000-page Internal Revenue Code, while lives have been lost on construction of the single adjective "unreasonable" in the search-and-seizure language of the Fourth Amendment.

The second method, the common law, is intrinsically *judicial*. The filters comprise what we call "the legal process," from coarse to fine being filing suit (which involves determination of events called "justiciable controversies" and often a condition called "actual damages" such that there is a threshold aperture of someone actually having hurt another in real life); litigation (which involves the folding of the controversy and damages into the constricted form of "claims for relief" outlining theories of tort and contract); pleadings and motions (which involve challenge to the theories' legal basis); verdict or award (which involve the surviving theories being presented to small exemplar social cohorts for group approval or disapproval); and finally, review (which involves the final survivors of the theories being retested by different, more professional cohorts).

In the common law method, it is relatively easy to identify the number and size of the different apertures. Number equates with venues available to hold such contests (city courts, county courts, state courts, and federal courts), whereas size is congruent to the standard that judges apply in those venues, with the higher the standard the finer the aperture. At the inception or pleading stage, the standard is fairly low, and as standards increase (from "probable cause" to "preponderance of the evidence" to "clear and convincing" to "proof beyond a reasonable doubt"), filtration gets increasingly discriminating. As to other levels, aperture size is congruent to what laypeople (juries in particular jurisdictions and presumably representatives of the public) might feel about the filtrate. The filtrate, "decisional law of the case," seems brutally workable and eventually (albeit clumsily) separable from the particulate, ideas that are simply "not the law of the case." Here, the value of the filtrate *is* partially related to its quantity: the more verdicts that are issued on a certain type of claim, the more that type of claim may be brought by additional litigants and thereby create additional opinions.

Lawyers' epistemological concerns swirl around how to handle the filtrate that they personally and professionally would like to separate out from the great frothy mixture of social and political ideas for good law in which they, their colleagues, and their clients, all sit immersed. The codification method is interesting to those investigators called "politicians," and the common law method interesting to those investigators called "trial lawyers." To add to the strangeness of the experiment, the two sets of investigators can frequently be

a) in different laboratories altogether, b) bumping shoulders inside the same lab, and/or c) the exact same people taking on two different roles depending on when the mood (and fee) strikes.

Science, for its part, involves a mixture with many substances in the form of ideas for what is, and what has historically been, deemed "more explanatory" of observed phenomena, mixed up with what is, and what has historically been, deemed "less explanatory" of those events.[10] Science employs "the scientific method" as its filtration method, and tries to stay sterile from infections by social, political, and religious contaminants (though not always successfully). The apertures used are hypotheses, experiments, statistical analyses, retesting, peer review, and publication, and its investigators occupy one huge laboratory where countless procedures are underway with no clear agreement as to what the filtrates are and what the particulates are other than the passage of time, validity of various experiences, and utility of certain outcomes. Science being a direction, not a destination, there is really no discernible end to the frenetic activity in that lab. The value of the filtrate is intensely related to its quantity: we only learn about nature by studying it more, not by ignoring it more.

It is at the epistemological level that we therefore recognize that lawyers cannot be distanced from the experiment that they are conducting—they are both subject and object at one and the same time. Scientists are (theoretically anyway) not so immersed—while their research and inquiries do affect themselves as individuals, their attempts to discern what proof is sufficient to eventually answer their questions lie on a more abstract and removed plane of existence. Lawyers and scientists can both be good or poor questioners, but the assurances lawyers promote get intensely personal while those scientists develop criteria for and rely upon support for accepting answers to, are assurances that reject social or political answers as "needed" or "approved." In short, the epistemological inquiries of lawyers are necessarily restrained by other people, whereas the epistemological inquiries of scientists are necessarily restrained by a tremendous universe of events and phenomenon of which other people are only a minor, and sometimes insignificant, part. That division then sends the methodological component for both sets of inquisitors spiraling in radically different directions, hence the filtration process and its complications.

The lawyer-scientist therefore does research in dual respects: in one way conducting it (as all lawyers do) by locating and interpreting law others have written out in the form of codes, statutes, rules of court, published appellate opinions, and law review articles, and in a distinct way conducting it (as all scientists do) by proposing original hypotheses, testing original hypotheses, and sifting results through the screen of statistical analysis and peer review. The routes are not clearly complementary or competitive but are necessary to achieving a useful result. Because the core topic of every one of their projects involves animals, however, animal law attorneys find that for their research and conclusions to particularly have value, the sciences dealing with animals cannot be ignored. As a lawyer-scientist, the animal law attorney must strike a bargain in dealing with just what history and pre history draws to their attention. In a crucial sense, the questions posed—and the answers which result—are a product of confronting the past, near and far, and it is far back in time that our ontological, epistemological, and methodological apparatus thus leads us to find where the real significance of laws and animals originates.

NOTES

1. *Rubáiyát* of Omar Khayyám, Quatrain L.
2. Hilary Pepler (1920).
3. Barnes, Barry, David Bloor, and John Henry. *Scientific Knowledge: A Sociological Analysis*. University of Chicago Press, 1996.
4. Mindell, David P. *The Evolving World: Evolution in Everyday Life*. La Editorial, UPR, 2006, 254–55.
5. See *Trust Co. of Georgia v. Kenny*, 3 S.E.2d 553 (Ga. 1939) ("the quantum of precedent is one way; the quality the other").
6. *Kimmel v. Goland*, 51 Cal 3d 202 (1990).
7. See Dennett, Daniel Clement. *Sweet Dreams: Philosophical Obstacles to a Science of Consciousness*. MIT press, 2005, 67–70.
8. Haack, Susan. *Evidence Matters: Science, Proof, and Truth in the Law*. Cambridge University Press, 2014, 35, 55–56.
9. Morgan, David L. "Paradigms Lost and Pragmatism Regained Methodological Implications of Combining Qualitative and Quantitative Methods." *Journal of Mixed Methods Research* 1.1 (2007), 48–76.
10. See Golinski, Jan. *Making Natural Knowledge: Constructivism and the History of Science*. University of Chicago Press, 2008, 103–132:

A lot of what scientists can be observed to do is linguistic behavior. They converse with one another as they work, communicating the details of techniques and observations. They spend long hours drafting and redrafting grant applications. The read at length in the relevant literature, before composing, with great care, the papers in which results are reported.

Chapter 2

The Past as Prologue
and Precedent

"Hidden Far Beneath and Long Ago"[1]

[T]to learn how man and animals live, we cannot avoid seeing great numbers of them die, because the mechanisms of life can be unveiled and proved only by knowledge of the mechanisms of death.[2]

If there was ever to be a lawyer paleontologist, someone whose charge it was to unearth the bones and teeth, shells and footprints, of ancient law and use those vestiges to comprehend the present through the past, then one of their first crucial tasks would be to explain the fossil traces limning the law's treatment of animals.[3] As they would excavate, they would note how curious it was that the law has always classified all animals as property yet has persistently treated a few species as significantly different properties from all others; would find it fairly baffling that the law has baldly ignored the greater part of animals actually in existence; would deem it categorically odd that the majority of courts have traditionally failed to, and still presently cannot, establish a workable test for what constitutes the ownership of any particular animal; and would declare it downright inexplicable that the criteria by which we value individual animals has varied haphazardly over time and from one jurisdiction to the next.

In exhuming those jumbled and confusing remains, our investigator might come to realize that erecting a valuable practice of animal law as a distinct discipline at the very least requires the solid grasp of law and science in equal parts. Exposing the mineralized components of a set of rules from its historical excavation bed is an activity that commands the use of workable tools from both fields, employed in tandem, to comprehend animals as uniquely conflated biological *and* legal objects. Even the shallowest of excavations would reveal that to legislate or litigate any issue involving animals in their various guises—as wildlife, pets, livestock, exotics, or pests—one is going to need to scour channels of legal and scientific information that at times run closely in parallel and at times broadly diverge, that one will need to know as much about exotics versus endemics, vertebrates versus invertebrates, digestion versus excretion, and captivity versus domestication, as one would about compensatory damages versus equitable remedies, partition in kind versus partition in amount, and leases versus bailments.

All lawyers operate under certain conceptual restrictions as they wrangle with the minutiae of their subject, and the harsh constraints under which animal law practitioners work in applying law to animals are no different—an animal law attorney is simultaneously hampered and enlightened by the realities of what animals reflect in both a legal and zoological sense. That tension is not exclusive to the legal profession: well before lawyers came into the picture, people have had tangled thoughts about the conflicting roles animals play in human communities since thought and language first developed to explicate the concern.[4]

The origination and growth of the common law has not necessarily disentangled those threads, and in many cases has knotted them further. The progression of scientific knowledge—particularly our uncovering of the astonishingly explanatory theory, and well-established fact, of evolution by natural selection and of its stunning capacity to reveal the intricacies and mysteries of animal development—has at least equipped us with better field gear with which to try to pierce those complex skeins.

A LAW-ORIENTED EXCAVATION INTO THE PAST, NEAR THEN FAR

Like all good paleontologists, the animal law attorney works backward by starting at the surface of the present and patiently tunneling down. Here, the target objects for scrutiny are the lawyer's analogue to the paleontologist's "transitional" fossils, those remains that exhibit traits common to both an ancestral line and its derived descendant line.[5] To connect "laws" in the large sense with "animals" in the large sense is not to simply locate specific laws about specific animals (of which there are plenty and few that have any overtly fundamental significance), but to locate instead those key transitional areas where some important human practice regarding nonanimals has shared or linked a common trait with some important human practice regarding animals.[6]

We find a recent one straight away in an initial scraping at the topsoil of American history where the phenomenon of dogs being initially treated as market objects is exposed.[7] Shortly after World War II, as part of the

Roosevelt Administration's large-scale push for economic growth, the United States Department of Agriculture introduced an unusual tax incentive program designed to encourage farmers to raise dogs as an "alternative crop"—the idea being that raising dogs might help diversify the type of income arising from struggling farms around the country.[8] Booming suburban families wanted pets, farmers needed additional income, and the happy collision of their tangential market desires seemed ripe to exploit in advancing the health of the national economy. One result of that project was that dogs became a much more established *agricultural* commodity, with economic assessments of the animals showing up on business income tax statements and on farm balance sheets, and with the dogs themselves showing up in livestock barns and at public auctions alongside the more traditional livestock animals.

The specific tax incentives of that program eventually expired, but sociologically at least two interesting phenomena blossomed forth from it. One is the expansion of the "puppy mill," the specific economically motivated pursuit of not just farmers, but all sorts of suburbanites breeding dogs at high volume for quick dollars. The second is the expanding philosophy of treating dogs in general as atypical and distinctive free market goods. While certainly people had bought and sold dogs well before the recovery period after World War II, and had informally considered, indeed over several tens of thousands of years had been quite thoroughly considering, what dogs are "worth" to humans as companions and as goods, still modern concepts of the peculiarities of dogs as legal objects in the guise of trade goods can be clearly discerned in the vagaries of the 1948 U.S. federal tax code.[9]

The next stratigraphic level takes us further down four centuries earlier, just after the earliest published appellate opinions in the United States began around the early 1650s. It is there we can uncover the first legal consideration of animals in general being objects legally distinguishable from other objects, specifically from a 1739 Virginia civil case entitled *The King v. Oldner & Brilehan.* That case held, in part, that a ship could not legally be deemed "a Wreck" (so as to allow goods from it to be forfeited) so long as "a Man Dog or Cat [had] escaped alive" from it.[10] The alliance of dogs and cats alongside men, as members of a joint venture sharing at least one common trait of being sufficiently motivated to independently wish to escape from an area of danger, along with the complementary recognition that deaths of any of the group as living things signified a more complete destruction of an object than were no death at all involved, set a turning point. The disjunctive "or" in that case's holding made such a group legally meaningful in the sense that even a dog or a cat *by itself* being recovered from a foundering ship was an object that ostensibly deserved being treated differently than a keg, lamp, or table being recovered. Our current legislative confusions about animals being legally similar or legally distinct from other inanimate properties all bubble up from the wreckage that created that innocent-looking "or."

The next level down burrows deeper still, three thousand years and more below, into the period of early human social history where both law and property originated and found connection. Here, at the anthropological origins of jurisprudence itself, we can discern one of the most important transitional fossils of all. In early societies without writing at all, everything was orally transmitted such that the precursors to law, the rules of conduct that such groups formulated, disagreed about, or violated, comprised spoken transmissions of what we presently term "folk law."[11] As groups became literate, prime elements of the oral culture were then retained (at times reliably and at others in distorted versions) as recordings of religious ritual, with one result being that the flexibility and anonymity of the oral tradition was vastly reduced.[12]

We can discern "law" peeling away from mere "custom" by the confluence of three epiphenomena coincident with that burgeoning literacy: *force*, *official authority*, and *regularity*.[13] The application of physical force by a party possessing a socially recognized privilege of so acting was important. The application of assigned roles in social groups where one party could assert authority by dictating terms of conduct to another party was important. Finally, the application of regularly sanctioning infraction of a norm by the party in authority was important. A written record of the privilege, the authority, and the sanction was key as well.[14]

At the same time, human social groups were defined by the stark realities of direct animal influences, primarily in the twin forms of having to eat animals in order to live and having to avoid being eaten by animals in order not to die. Force, official authority, and regularity were all intimately tied to those influences, and laws—like the customs from which they arose—hewed closely to what conduct might sustain basic life protections in relation to animal influences.[15] Predation by animals could only be circumvented by force, acquiring animals could only be facilitated by group activity, and parceling out animal resources had to be circumscribed by group sanction.[16] Early laws, as records of those epiphenomena, were the first filtrates and particulates of the mixtures of daily life and death that animals compelled early communities to have to sieve.

ANIMALS AS KEY COMPONENTS OF LAW'S ORIGINS

In the context of hunting, food gathering, animal husbandry, and the avoidance of predation, group members thus constructed the concept of "human accountability" from the consequence of the written law, *lex scripta*, necessarily identifying specifically whom was recording and memorializing the rules, and specifically to whom the recorded and memorialized rules now actually applied with any real effect.[17] What began as a fluid and ever-shifting set of customs about animals cast in a matrix of fluid and ever-shifting inter-personal relationships and human–object relationships, was transformed by the art of "writing things down" into a harsher set of more rigid, more universal, and ultimately consequential set of "laws" about animals. The concept of culpability blossomed forth, and integral to culpability was recognition of the crucial nature of those preexisting relationships between early humans and the manipulation of various nonhuman objects of which their early human environment was composed.[18]

It cannot be denied that animals were the most critical pieces of the inhabitants' immediate daily environment, objects with teeth (to evade), tissue (to ingest), and tempers (to contend with) the attractiveness, danger, and unpredictability of which impacted the tiniest and largest aspects of communal life.[19] Exemplifying great promise and great threat in the same instant, animals had huge technical and economic significance to every member of early human communities in which survival itself hinged on commodifying them; they provided sustenance, multiplied spontaneously, directed the course of human deaths and lives via their activities, and took on religious and spiritual import as models for human conduct.[20]

They were also just one slice of the pie of all natural objects, those things originally held in common, a "negative community" of everything nonhuman that belonged to no one and yet were open to all.[21] The concept of "property" arose as a result of early humans formulating social rules about coveting, obtaining and occupying usable pieces of the world.[22] The basic division of "me" (and "others like me") from "everything else not-me" is a classic adaptation many species have evolved, and the revelation that persons and properties formed exclusive and disparate concepts was fueled by the power to then manipulate the "not-me" parts for personal purposes.[23] As attainments and occupations became enforced socially, laws developed that discriminated between different types of ownership and occupation, and between different types of owners and occupiers.[24] The property concept is intimately tied to entitlements, i.e., the privileges correlative of control, and relationships, i.e., the establishment of person-world connections.

> Whereas ownership represents the functional relationship between a person and a thing, property law represents a particular structure of rights and duties that protects the ownership relationship in a particular way. . . . The entitlement to *possess* an object only enables the right-holder to determine the physical location of the object. . . . The entitlement to *use* an object enables a relationship between 'an owner's set of preferences . . . and the general state of the object owned'. . . . The entitlement to *manage* or *control* an object adds the power to

determine the way that others possess or use an object. . . . The entitlement *to transfer* enables the entitlement-holder to forgo their set entitlements in favor of another person. . . . The entitlement *to profit* enables the entitlement-holder to transfer their entitlements in exchange for monetary gain. . . . Each entitlement therefore represents a distinct functional relationship between the person and object, ranging from the person being able to: determine the physical location of the object, determine the general state of the object, determine how and by whom the object is treated, forgo the entitlements in the object in favor of another person, or financially benefit from (or be compensated for) the transfer of entitlements to another person.[25]

Our past is a complex recording of us learning how to convert the form of natural objects, how to manufacture artificial materials from found ones.[26] To impute value to the work of transforming land and the plants and animals embroidering the land into those materials, property laws worked from an initial distinction of the animate from the inanimate as clearly dissimilar categories.[27] Materials became items of economic exchange, and in those exchanges animate materials were observed to have odd attributes that inanimate materials did not—the two most valuable among them being the ability to form what seemed like intentions (and subsequently manifest those intentions by motion), and the ability to replicate.[28] Our modern laws regulating agriculture, animal domestication, and animal husbandry all owe their genesis to early human communities appreciating that capacity of animals to independently transport themselves over distances and to compound their value over time.[29] Animal movement and animal replication didn't just casually pique our attention—they founded our key interest in exploiting that utility and beget all of our rules governing how to do so.

The deepest layers in our dig into interpolating jurisprudence and zoology carve our way through prehistory into the Neolithic and from there into the Pleistocene and its fauna.[30] There we find that the zoologically impoverished world in which we currently live is our inheritance from a host of dire environmental and social activities in which we were immersed at the wane of the last ice age, 20,000 or so years ago.[31] Our relatively sparse modern interactions with animals are really the tattered rags and remnants of our far more intimate prehistoric interactions with them: killing them, being killed by them, eating them, wearing them, competing with them, fighting them, and, of course, capturing and domesticating them.[32]

Prehistoric fossil assemblages reveal the significant effort and attention our ancestors took with processing and consuming animal bodies as well as with the disposition of carcasses and other remains.[33] Maintaining a constant presence of animals in the local environment required hunting and gathering at a bare minimum; truly effective food production also required controlling and propagating animals after their capture.[34] Small and midsize mammals, fish, and birds were the raw materials at hand that intimately affected Neolithic communities as their members grappled with health, diet, storage, and migration problems.[35] Relationships in death assemblages illustrate our careful commoditization of innumerable species not just as food, but as tools, clothing, and ritual objects as well, and it is clear that among interactions with particular species—especially and including certain hooved mammals (perissodactyls), canids, and felids—advantageous social processes were instigated by which we and them engaged in a delicate ballet of material utilization and mutual domestication.[36] In short, our evolution is their evolution.

THE FORCE AND INFLUENCE OF DOMESTICATION AS A PHENOMENON

Domestication involves three components: a cultural component in which people control the breeding of the animal, a biological component in which an animal becomes different in form as well as behaviorally distinct from its wild ancestor, and a time component, in which a significant period must pass for these things to happen.[37] The exertion of control, the change in form, and the passage of time are all required to fortuitously coordinate for effects to occur.

As to the *cultural* component, for the last 20,000 years people have been artificially selecting the types of animals they like to have around them. Attractiveness, marketability, and risk all play roles in those decisions.[38] We have not domesticated ants because culturally we can't control their breeding, and culturally we don't find any particular traits of theirs desirable to cultivate even if we could. When one thinks of "artificial selection," one doesn't think of ants but does of dogs or cows for the simple reason that human communities obtain no benefits whatsoever from the former yet significant benefits from the latter.

As to the *biological* component, it is only some species that become altered in form and behavior over time due to our efforts. Those alterations are related, in that as the bodies of the individuals change, so do their behaviors. Neoteny is the evolutionary phenomenon by which juvenile characteristics are retained into adulthood, so that the adult animal looks and behaves much more like a juvenile than an adult: snouts are flattened and smaller, eyes are larger, features are softer, teeth are smaller, heads are larger and limbs are shorter relative to each other and to body size, and there is more play-like behavior.[39] In short the puppylike aspect of the animal is conserved, and in addition, docility is increased. Domesticated animals tend to exhibit neoteny.

The biological component has had a remarkable effect as to dogs specifically, where two criteria have made domestication work very well as a social exchange. One is the existence of a well-defined dominance hierarchy.[40] The second is the presence of a high degree of sociality.[41] Wolves, from which dogs developed, exhibit both criteria.[42] Dogs readily transfer over to humans their ranking systems, their docilities, and their inclination for subservience; in addition complex communication and group cooperation are wolf-like traits that have also facilitated long-term human/dog interactions.[43]

> The domesticated dog in the home shows many behaviors that we see in the wolf, such as defense of young and of territory. A dog may be extremely protective of children of its own home, and protect them from neighborhood children. Similarly, a dog on its own territory in the house or garden, or when out on the leash with its owner, is more likely to attack strange dogs and people. Such pack allegiance and defense of territory occurs in dogs well socialized with their owners and with immediate friends of the family. . . . The main point that dog and wolf have in common is that both are socialized, to human beings and to other wolves respectively, and both will immediately accept members of their own pack (the human family and regular acquaintances in the case of the dog).[44]

Finally, as to the *time* component, the effect of evolutionary forces is only seen over innumerable generations of a species' ancestors and descendants genetically passing on certain characteristics as adaptations, while losing others as handicaps. Time is the great crucible in which all physical and behavioral features are charred and converted under the harsh illumination of the immediate (and ever-changing) biotic and abiotic environment. Because generational time spans for many mammals are measured in decades, then significant physical and behavioral changes in mammalian generations will only be observed after the span of millennia.

In total, those particular species that we domesticate become domesticated because our interest and effort is triggered to attempt the project, because the selected targets have the especial types of bodies and brains that actually respond genetically to our efforts, and because sufficient spans of generational time have passed for later humans to discern and benefit from the effects that result. When it does occur, intimate relationships between humans and animals can arise from domestication, but those relationships are not of coequals in any manner.[45] They are highly asymmetrical relationships bordered by need, by resource allocation, by population dynamics, by the exploitation and assimilation of an animal's valuable physical features, and by the reduction or eradication of an animal's harmful attributes.[46] An integral by-product of early humans' artificial selection of animal species with special value, and of those species' reciprocal exploitation of human proclivities for close social relationships, has been the preservation of critical imbalances between "us" and "them," not the fostering or maintenance of any mutuality or respect at all.

We have spent the last 20,000 years manipulating and being manipulated by many animals, including dogs, in an intricate patchwork of commensalism and forced cooperation, an interface that strong evolutionary forces have woven together and that are not easily disentangled.[47] It is easy to confound the beneficial effects of doing so with emotive effects, and even in areas in which we make great efforts to prevent any sensitive relationships with dogs from developing—as with their scientific study—we find it nearly impossible to resist some manner of emotional "bond" as a component of relationship formation.[48] Yet all modern human–animal interactions have their genesis in competition and exploitation, and dogs (along with numerous other species) are what they are today because they evolved in tandem with the artificial selection of desirable characteristics, prime among them being traits involving close-quarter usefulness.

USEFULNESS AS A PARTICULAR FUNCTION IN THE ARTIFICIAL SELECTION OF DOG BREEDS

The phenomenon of "breeds" highlights this observation.[49] The distinctive differences between any two specialized breeds of dog result from the genetic differences created inside their bodies by hundreds of generations of deliberate and restrictive breeding attempts. The equally distinctive stamp of the various personalities belonging to dogs that are members of the different breeds is also a product of the same process of artificial selection. For example, the traits of docility, fear aversion, and general skittishness, are expressed as a function of development of the nervous and endocrine systems in the same way that the traits of a kinked tail, blocked ears, and heavily lidded eyes are expressed as functions of development of the integumentary and skeletal systems.[50]

Usefulness as a controlling factor changes both sides: one by-product of breed selection is that our own behaviors have become interlinked with dog behaviors. As the behavior of a Basenji, for instance, in crouching in response to an upraised hand and using a highly restrained biting method (called "soft mouth") was specifically selected for, selection pressures were correspondingly imposed on those who benefited from use of the method as a consequence.[51] Behavioral change has rippled across human generations due to the selection of desirable suites of animal traits, and our use of animals as beneficial objects follows a prehistoric path we have traversed bounded by our exertion of control, the change in form in both us and them, and the inexorable passage of generations.

In nearly every area of our downward dig, we have noted the repeatedly heightened importance of dogs to human communities. From empirical research programs concerning attachment and separation in dogs and their owners, rigorously controlled isolation studies have determined several inter-related phenomena to occur between dogs and humans whenever they inter-act.[52] One, dogs normally form attachments both to humans and to other dogs as part of their normal serial biological and mental development. Two, site attachment is just as important as is social attachment for dogs, in that part of a dog's individual identity unfolds as an animal that "belongs" to a certain location in space or geographical subarea. Three, changes in social and site attachment are inherently age-related, such that the developmental age of the animal makes a significant difference in what it will eventually become.[53]

In other words, at birth dogs are initially and predominately headed toward becoming collateral members of human society, but that identity can be shifted in either the human or canine direction according to certain conditions themselves shifting during rearing, and themselves depending on specifics as to both time and locale.[54] The longer a dog and an owner interact, the closer in proximity they are, and the richer the number of interactions they have between them, the more the dog's identity becomes wrapped up in the owner's identity, and the greater the reliance on and usefulness of each for the other as keeper and kept object.[55] Of course as cultural animals we have parted ways with dogs as merely social animals at critical junctures before and in the Pleistocene, and have surpassed them beyond recognition in accumulating intricate communal networks across generations, constructs to which dogs have no match. For all the adaptations they have evolved out of the domestication process with us, dogs have not invented forms of govern-ment, defined political roles, developed technology to improve their hunting practices, constructed medical care, or fashioned protective shelters, and, left to their own devices, would undoubtedly live the same today as their progeni-tors, the wolves, lived 100,000 years ago.

Still, physically and physiologically, dogs have evolved to become extraor-dinarily variable animals in all visible respects. Their ranges in size, shape, pelt, proportions, longevity, integument, fertility, fecundity, and even dental apparatus, reflect plasticity uncommon in nearly any other taxon, even at the family level.[56] Physically and physiologically dogs have been valuable to us as rich sources of tools and weapons for a large period of prehistoric and historical time, a mutually beneficial dynamic:

> All wild dogs exhibit the beginnings of a social life, in so far as they associate with each other to form packs for the purpose of hunting as well as for defence.

The individuals of each pack are tied together by bonds of friendship, they help
one another and often, in their operations, work in unison according to what one
might almost call plans designed to meet certain situations. . . . It is therefore not
impossible that young wolves or jackals or other wild dogs, which grew up in
or near the temporary camps of Mesolithic hunters, would quite naturally regard
the men, who provided part of their food supply, as members of their pack, an
association which the hunters would not have failed to turn to their advantage.[57]

The evolution of behavioral suites operate in tandem with the evolution of
structural suites; unquestionably, the physical adaptations that are part of our
evolutionary heritage such as our large cerebral cortexes, upright posture,
opposable thumbs, and capacity for speech, have radically transformed how
we act and how animals around us act.[58] Close attention to the complex effects
of domestication thus pivots the attention of the lawyer-scientist to the bed-
rock significance of "competitive behaviors with other animals across time"
as a source from which all objectification of animals springs.[59] Deciphering
animals as conflated biological and legal objects is a function of identifying
historical and prehistorical bases for our extensive manipulation of them.
Important to grasp is not just that some species adapted well to exploit social
relationships with us and to be exploited by them while others have not, but
that no species, either us or them, has escaped unscathed in the experiment.

TAPHONOMY AS A METAPHOR FOR ALIGNING LAW AND MORALITY

In comprehending the present through the past, we are engaging partly in the
legal version of the science of taphonomy (from the Greek "taphos" meaning
burial and "nomos" meaning law), a discipline that analyzes the peculiar circumstances and events impacting an organism at its death through its burial in
the process of eventually becoming preserved.[60] Since our assigned task is to
explain the past life of legal concepts, not that of actual organisms, we don't
have to delve into the hard details of diagenetic factors that affect the actual
preservation and petrifaction of animal and plant remains; instead we attend
to explaining why and how laws lie adjacent to animals within a conceptual
fossil assemblage. The methodology of thanatocoenosis—mechanically
determining how entities got united in death—becomes an important method
to employ here, since closely observing associations of dead organisms with
other dead organisms winnows out the signals for how past events likely connected the groups together in life.

Lawyers and scientists alike study minutiae in the record of the past to learn about the nature of the present, and thanatocoenosis techniques should be no less part of a lawyer's tool kit than it is a paleoarcheologist's:

> Human society is derived from the society of *Homo erectus*, which is derived from the society of *Australopithecus*, which is derived from the society of a long-extinct missing link between humans and chimps, which in turn was derived from the society of the missing link between apes and monkeys, and so on, back to an eventual beginning as some sort of shrew-like animals that perhaps genuinely lived in Rousseauian solitude. Of course, we cannot go back and examine the societies of *Australopithecus*, but we can make some informed guesses based on anatomy and on modern parallels.[61]

Along with laws and animals, "morality" is also part of the "remains" found closely juxtaposed together in past assemblages. Morality is a human behavioral complex that is cross-cultural for humans (yet absent in animals),[62] and is a mental phenomenon partly derived from phylogenetically recent genetic adaptations in small group behaviors.[63] Value judgments defining a profile of differential approval of a wide range of human behaviors have been subject to communal selection pressures for hundreds of thousands of years of human evolution, and moral codes are the combined result of selection for and against certain patterns of beneficial and detrimental conduct in social settings.[64] In a society of hunter-gatherers who need to punish a member for violating some rule, behaviors that deviate too far from norms end up being sanctioned socially, behaviors that hew closely to norms end up being engulfed socially, and the inhibitions individuals experience via the varying alignments and misalignments help to ultimately produce the mental phenomenon known as conscience, the internal underpinning of morals.[65]

Morality, like law, unsurprisingly arises straight out of adaptive human behaviors.[66] Human behaviors in turn evolved from protohuman ("hominid') behaviors and from vital environmental influences on ancestral populations. The strongest of those influences are ones directly causing deaths, ones directly promoting births, and ones directly hampering or enhancing reproduction efforts.[67] Available and unavailable food sources, high and low predation risks, and the timing and breadth of mating opportunities and restrictions are all specifically key influences on prehistoric human behavior, and are each themselves directly mediated by the presence and absence of animals around prehistoric human populations.[68]

Here is the "just-so" story, then, that the lawyer-scientist considers: Moral actions became initiated by mental theories that prehistoric individuals constructed from their encounters with the physical world ("Avoid stinging things"). In implementing those theories, the associated choices had large adaptive value for individuals whose survival was enhanced inside a group's protections ("Join us—no stinging things here"). The protections, however, came at a price; conformity with group inhibitions and pursuit of group approval were then mandated ("Defiance is punished"). As behaviors and respective sanctions accumulated, the "codes" that resulted imparted fitness to the participants, i.e., reproductive payoffs for adherence. A collective of individual choices about animal-related encounters made across generations therefore distributed advantages about the beneficial ones and eliminated disadvantages about the harmful ones ("Days since last stinging-related death: 100"). Though empirically unverifiable, the story is supported by reason: since natural selection operates on behaviors as well as physical features, moral conduct can therefore be the product of selective forces, and since good and bad encounters with animals had to be an integral component of our Paleolithic ancestors' environment, then strict control of animals as resources and dangers had to be an integral component of the erection of their sociality rules.

Humans have consistently maintained the strategy of adhering rigidly to behavioral patterns that have previously proven successful, patterns that include forming cooperative relationships with certain animal species, and engaging in combat and aggression with others.[69] Segmenting species into comparative slices of useful and harmful objects in the immediate physical environment has been an evolutionarily stable strategy, and in its preservation over generational time has thereby become enfolded into our moral codes.[70] For instance, those early hominids who worked with, not against, wild dogs, secured direct health and longevity benefits, and substantial selection pressure thus favored continuation of that particular suite of preservation-directed behaviors. Respectively, those early hominids who killed, not tolerated, cougars, avoided direct health and longevity detriments, and again substantial selection pressures worked their magic cementing those types of behavior into descendant generations and by extension into the moral codes those generations then fashioned.

The objectification of animals has been a reproductive success story for far too long to ignore its origin, maintenance, or current consequences. A taphonomic viewpoint identifies moral rules about animals as products of our cultural evolution as well as our biological evolution.[71] Unquestionably, evolution has adapted people to anticipate the consequences of individual action, make value judgments, and choose between alternative courses of action, all attributes directly promoted by natural selection pressures. Gaining control of a small mammal, bird, or fish for immediate sustenance was a Paleolithic staple of existence, as was eventually gaining control of larger mammals to cache for lengthier periods.[72] Anticipating the consequences of such control—and choosing among the consequences in light of individual needs and community prohibitions—honed a mindset that needed to enshrine control-based human-animal relationships into code form. Food source, predation risk, and mating opportunities and restrictions were all impacted by those relationships and correspondingly codified. Monitoring expectations about which animals to use and which to destroy also cultivated conscience-based decisions about formalizing that control into the rigidity of legal precepts. That past dictated our future: a thanatocoenotic view unites animal exploitation in our current life with that which had been prehistorically united with us in our previous deaths.

The adaptations that led to "language" were a transcendent elements of that taphonomic assemblage. Unique selection pressures resulted in us creating strange codes that linked peculiar sets of expressive forms to peculiar sets of mutually agreed meanings. Lexical items—wondrous things called "words"—were used to designate concrete objects, then abstract concepts, then logical connections between the two. Morphological forms of the lexical items ushered in the astonishing phenomenon of word combination, and, once propositions could be expressed by one "language-user" to another to attribute aspects of the combinations to aspects of the world, then discourse sparked—and then exploded.[73] The conceptual earth shook and the dust from that global tremor covered all other species and has covered them since.

So: Human-animal relationships arose from exploitation, developed via antagonistic and commensal processes, reflect the tangled outcomes of lengthy evolutionary forces, and were cultivated in the intense illumination of a language use phenomenon. Our next task then is to focus on the defining terms of those relationships in the light of the laws generated from the discourse explosion, and to do so from our side of the yawning chasm that such an explosion then formed.

NOTES

1. *Rubáiyát* of Omar Khayyám, Quatrain XXXIX.
2. Bernard, Claude. *An Introduction to the Study of Experimental Medicine.* Translated into English by Copley Green, with an Introduction by Lawrence J. Henderson and a Foreword by I. Bernard Cohen." (1865).
3. Sections of this chapter are extensions of ideas first articulated in Duckler, G. "The Necessity of Treating Animals as Legal Objects." *J. Animal & Envtl. L.* 7 (2015):1.
4. Chaplin, Raymond E. "Animals in Archaeology." *Antiquity* 39.155 (1965): 204–211.
5. See, e.g., Romer, Alfred Sherwood. *The Vertebrate Story.* No. 596 R65. 1959.

6. As Oliver Wendell Holmes said: "It is perfectly proper to regard and study the law as a great anthropological document." Holmes, Oliver Wendell. "Law in Science and Science in Law." *Brief* 2 (1899): 105.

7. See Schwartz, Marion. *A History of Dogs in the Early Americas.* New Haven, CT: Yale University Press, 1997.

8. Snyder, L. M. and E. A. Moore. *Dogs and People in Social, Working, Economic, and Symbolic Interactions.* Oxbow Books (2006); see also Yates, B. C. and J. Koler-Matznick, *The Evidentiary Dog: A Review of Anthrozoological Cases and Archeological Studies.* (N.Y. 2002).

9. Courts have had difficulty pigeonholing the maintenance and cultivation of dogs into farming and ranching schemas. Raising dogs has not been deemed an "agricultural use" of land. *Weber v. Board of County Com'rs of Franklin County,* 20 Kan. App.2d 152 (Kan. App. 1994). Dog breeding or kennel operations have not been deemed "farming activities." *Development Associates v. Board of Adjustment,* 48 N.C. App. 541 (N. Carolina App. 1980). Dog breeding and dog kennel operations are more likely "animal husbandry" activities (*Harris v. Board,* 44 Ohio St. 2d 144 (Ohio 1975)) (*but cf. City of Beatrice v. Goodenkauf,* 219 Neb. 756 (Neb. 1985)).

10. *The King v. Oldner & Brilehan,* 2 Va. Colonial Dec. B90, 1739 WL 4 (Va. Gen. Ct. 1739).

11. Renteln, Alison Dundes., and Alan Dundes. *Folk Law: Essays in the Theory and Practice of Lex Non Scripta, Vol. I and II.* Madison: University of Wisconsin, 1994.

12. See Maine, Henry Sumner. *On Early Law and Custom.* J. Murray, 1890:
There is no system of recorded law, literally from China to Peru, which, when it first emerges into notice, is not seen to be entangled with religious ritual and observance.

13. Hoebel, Edward Adamson. *Man in the Primitive World: An Introduction to Anthropology.* Vol. 1. New York: McGraw-Hill, 1949.

14. See Maine, Henry Sumner. "Ancient Law." 1861.

15. Vinogradoff, Paul. *Custom and Right.* Vol. 3. The Lawbook Exchange, Ltd., 2000.

16. Malinowski, Bronisław. "Crime and Custom in Savage Society." 1926.

17. Diamond, Arthur Sigismund. *Primitive Law, Past and Present.* New York: Routledge, 2013.

18. Earle, Timothy. "Archaeology, Property, and Prehistory." *Annual Review of Anthropology* 29, no. 1 (2000): 39–60.

19. See Marciniak, Arkadiusz. *Placing Animals in the Neolithic: Social Zooarchaeology of Prehistoric Farming Communities.* Hove, UK: Psychology Press, 2005.

20. Chaplin, Raymond E. "Animals in Archaeology." *Antiquity* 39, no. 155 (1965): 204.

21. See Quiggin, John. "Common Property, Equality, and Development." *World Development* 21.7 (1993): 1123–1138.

22. Holmes, Oliver Wendell. *The Common Law.* Courier Corporation, 1991.

23. Ritchie, David G. *Natural Rights: A Criticism of Some Political and Ethical Conceptions.* New York: Routledge, 2014.

24. See, e.g., Holdsworth, William Searle. *A History of English Law*. Vol. 7. North Yorkshire, UK: Methuen & Company, 1923 at p. 491.

25. Wall, Jesse. *Being and Owning: The Body, Bodily Material, and the Law*. Oxford University Press, USA, 2015 at pp. 24, 27–30.

26. Bates, Marston. *The Nature of Natural History*. Vol. 1138. Princeton University Press, 2014.

27. Srivastava, P. *Economic Zoology: The Role of Animal Life in Human Welfare, Agriculture, and Industry* New Delhi: Discovery House, 2003. *See also* Tattersall, I. *Becoming Human: Evolution and Human Uniqueness*. New York: Harcourt Brace and Co., 1998.

28. See Higgs, E. S. (ed.) Papers in Economic Prehistory. Cambridge University Press, London (1971). *See also* Sparks, John. "Man and Wildlife, by CAW Guggisberg. Evans, Wildlife Preservation, by Philip Street. McGibbon and Kee, Wild Harvest, by Clive Roots. Lutterworth Press." *Oryx* 10.6 (1970): 397–398.

29. See generally Lund, Thomas Alan. *American Wildlife Law*. Diss. University of Oxford, 1978 at pp. 19–34 (University of California Press, Berkeley (1980)). See also Clutton-Brock, J. "Domestic Animals in Zoos: The Historical Background to the Domestication of Animals" in International Zoo Year Book at pp. 240–243 (1976).

30. Zeuner, Frederick Everard. *The Pleistocene Period: Its Climate, Chronology, and Faunal Successions*. No. 130. London: Hutchinson Scientific & Technical, 1959.

31. *See* Martin, Paul S., and Richard G. Klein, eds. *Quaternary Extinctions: A Prehistoric Revolution*. Tucson: University of Arizona Press, 1989; Wallace, Alfred Russel. "The geographical distribution of animals." (1876).

32. *See generally* West, Frederick Hadleigh. "The Antiquity of Man in America." *Late Quaternary Environments of the United States* 1 (1983): 364–382.

33. Marciniak, Arkadiusz. *Placing Animals in the Neolithic: Social Zooarchaeology of Prehistoric Farming Communities*. Hove, UK: Psychology Press, 2005.

34. Megarry, Tim. *Society in Prehistory: The Origins of Human Culture*. New York: NYU Press, 1995 at pp. 260–261.

35. Jarman, M. R. "Prehistoric Animals and Their Hunters. By I. W. Cornwall." at p. 214, *Proceedings of the Prehistoric Society*. Vol. 35. Cambridge University Press, 1970.

36. Yates, B. C. and J. Koler-Matznick, *The Evidentiary Dog: A Review of Anthrozoological Cases and Archeological Studies*. New York: Free, 2002. Zeuner, F. *History of Domesticated Animals*. New York: Harper & Row, 1964.

37. Zeder, Melinda A. "The Domestication of Animals." *Journal of Anthropological Research* 68.2 (2012): 161–190.

38. Akey, Joshua M., et al. "Tracking Footprints of Artificial Selection in the Dog Genome." *Proceedings of the National Academy of Sciences* 107.3 (2010): 1160–1165.

39. Clutton-Brock, Juliet. "The Process of Domestication." *Mammal Review* 22.2 (1992): 79–85.

40. Moosa, Mahdi Muhammad, et. al. "The Role of Dominance Hierarchy in the Evolution of Social Species." *Journal for the Theory of Social Behaviour* 41.2 (2011): 203–208.

41. Coppinger, Raymond, and Lorna Coppinger. *Dogs: A New Understanding of Canine Origin, Behavior, and Evolution.* Chicago: University of Chicago, 2002.

42. Fox, Michael W. *Behaviour of Wolves, Dogs, and Related Canids,* New York: Harper & Row, 1972.

43. Bergler, R. *Man and Dog: The Psychology of a Relationship.* New York: Howell Book House, 1988.

44. Fox, Michael. *Behaviour of Wolves, Dogs, and Related Canids. Supra* at pp. 152–153.

45. Bustad, L. K. "Man and Beast Interface: An Overview of Our Relationships" in *Man and Beast Revisited* (ed. M. H. Robinson and Lionel Tiger). Washington, D.C.: Smithsonian Institution Press, 1991.

46. Franklin, A. *Animals in Modern Cultures: A Sociology of Human–Animal Relations in Modernity.* London: SAGE Publications, 1999.

47. See, e.g., Hyams, E. *Animals in the Service of Man.* at pp. 1–10. Philadelphia: J. B. Lippincott, 1972.

48. See, e.g., Estep, D. Q. and Hetts, S. "Interactions, Relationships, and Bonds: The Conceptual Basis for Scientist–Animal Relations" in *The Inevitable Bond: Examining Scientist–Animal Interactions* at pp. 6–26; Davis, H. and Balfour, D. (eds.) Cambridge, UK: Cambridge University Press, 1992.

49. Vilà, Carles, and J. A. Leonard. "Origin of Dog Breed Diversity." *The Behavioural Biology of Dogs* (2007): 182–206.

50. See Konner, M. *The Tangled Wing: Biological Constraints on the Human Spirit.* New York: Henry Holt and Co., 1982 at p. 84.

51. Scott, John Paul, and John L. Fuller. *Dog Behavior.* Chicago: University of Chicago Press, 1974.

52. Hare, B. et al. "The Domestication of Social Cognition in Dogs." *Science* 298: 1634–36 (2002).

53. Scott, J. P. "The Domestic Dog: A Case of Multiple Identities" at pp. 129–143 in *Species Identity and Attachment* (Roy, M. ed.) New York: Garland STPM Press, 1980.

54. Manning, A. *Animals and Human Society: Changing Perspectives.* London: Routledge, 1994.

55. Beck, Alan M., and Aaron H. Katcher. "Future Directions in Human–Animal Bond Research." *American Behavioral Scientist* 47.1 (2003): 79–93.

56. Scott, John Paul, and John L. Fuller. *Dog Behavior., supra.*

57. Zeuner, F. E., *A History of Domesticated Animals.* New York: Harper & Row, 1963.

58. Foley, Robert. *Humans before Humanity: An Evolutionary Perspective.* Oxford: Blackwell, 1995.

59. Domestication is a dynamic interchange between species, and animals can become undomesticated due to changing environments; ownership rights, also dynamic, are thereby impacted. *See Butler v. City of Palos Verdes Estates*, 135 Cal. App.4th 174 (Cal. App. 2 Dist. 2005) (finding peafowl whose ancestors were released into the wild decades ago by private parties to have become "indisputably feral creatures").

60. Lyman, R. Lee, and Cma Lyman. *Vertebrate Taphonomy*. Cambridge, UK: Cambridge University Press, 1994.

61. Matt, Ridley. *The Origins of Virtue: Human Instincts and the Evolution of Cooperation.* New York: Viking, 1996 at pp. 156–157.

62. See generally Bonner, John Tyler. *The Evolution of Culture in Animals*. Princeton, NJ: Princeton University Press, 1980.

63. Stent, Gunther Siegmund, ed. *Morality as a Biological Phenomenon: The Pre-suppositions of Sociobiological Research*. Berkeley: University of California Press, 1980.

64. Hauser, Marc D. *Moral Minds: The Nature of Right and Wrong*. New York: Harper Perennial, 2007.

65. Black, Donald. "On the Origin of Morality." *Journal of Consciousness Studies* 7, no. 1–2 (2000): 107–119.

66. See Katz, Leonard D., ed. *Evolutionary Origins of Morality: Cross-disciplinary Perspectives*. Vol. 1. Imprint Academic, 2000.

67. Goodman, Alan H., R. Brooke Thomas, Alan C. Swedlund, and George J. Armelagos. "Biocultural Perspectives on Stress in Prehistoric, Historical, and Contemporary Population Research." *American Journal of Physical Anthropology* 31, no. S9 (1988): 169–202.

68. See Pielou, Evelyn C. *After the Ice Age: The Return of Life to Glaciated North America*. Chicago: University of Chicago Press, 2008; Jennings, Jesse D., and Edward Norbeck. *Prehistoric Man in the New World*. No. 571 J4. 1969.

69. Haraway, Donna Jeanne. *When Species Meet*. Minneapolis: University of Minnesota, 2008.

70. Krebs, Dennis L. "Morality: An Evolutionary Account." *Perspectives on Psychological Science* 3, no. 3 (2008): 149–172.

71. Ayala, Francisco J. "The Biological Roots of Morality." *Biology and Philosophy* 2, no. 3 (1987): 235–252.

72. Bulliet, R. W. *Hunters, Herders, and Hamburgers: The Past and Future of Human–Animal Relationships.* New York: Columbia University Press, 2005.

73. See Caplan, David. *Language: Structure, Processing, and Disorders*. Cambridge, MA: The MIT Press, 1992.

Chapter 3

Defining Animals by Relationships and Use

"Who Is the Potter and Who the Pot?"[1]

> What are we first? First, animals; and next
> Intelligences at a leap; on whom
> Pale lies the distant shadow of the tomb,
> And all that draweth on the tomb for text.[2]

Our recent and distant past lay out dense "death assemblages" of rules and benefits for us to consider, rules we constructed to account for what animals do and benefits we gleaned from predicting their behaviors and controlling their bodies. The compartments formed eventually take on the shape of useful categories, laws, by which to make organizational sense of the world within a schema of utility and risk. The definitions of animals we have thereby developed in three broad areas of human endeavor—science, group culture, and law—have developed from prehistoric sources, and as civilization's history has unfolded we have adopted information from those sources to try to make sense of and keep control over a persistently confusing and dangerous world. Relationships with animals, relationships with each other, and our perceptions of the connections comprise the filters and sieves through which we attempt workable definitional and classification projects.

DEFINITIONS OF ANIMALS IN REPRESENTATIONAL AND ILLUSTRATIVE FRAMES

Science defines all living things, animals included, through nested categories, taxa, the only natural one of which is the smallest, "species," those organisms that can interbreed to produce viable young. The other taxonomic categories are primarily linguistic conveniences hoping to make organizational sense of evolution's vast complexity. Taxa reflect evolutionary relationships (links between ancestors and descendants) and the passage of time. Taxa rely on physical characters that persist over lengthy periods, not on behaviors, locations, or human activities. The Linnaean binomial ("two-name") system of a generic and a specific name designates members of groupings in terms of similarities and differences as to certain physical traits, with the most commonly used signifiers being bones and teeth, objects that tend to be fairly permanent and easily measurable.

Cultural and legal classifications are inapposite, using far more fluid and casual categories that don't reflect evolutionary processes, relationships, or time at all, but which rely instead on relatively random behaviors, topical appearances, convenient or fortuitous locations, and emotional effects. Utility, familiarity, comfort, and proximity are emphasized via descriptive modifiers such as "exotic," "tame," "wild," or "dangerous."[3] Names may be one or several words long, and overlap and ambiguity is pronounced, not muted. Legal definitions of animals often exhibit a background flavor of being somewhat arbitrary (if not downright cavalier) because lawyers and language have a complicated history of manipulation and interpretation, and ambiguity is unfortunately a necessity in law, a function of pragmatism, not a defect of semantics. Courts readily accept that "Language is but a means of conveying thought and certainty of its meaning is but relative."[4]

Not only does the pragmatism of legal taxonomies discount facts that zoologists would demand must be accounted for, but compilers of legal taxonomies (primarily lawyers in their role as legislators), hardly bother with consulting zoologists in the first place:

> For 200 years, American courts have called some animals *ferae naturae* (wild animals) and some *Domitae naturae* (domesticated). [T]he determination of the classification belongs to the lawmaking body. Matters of expediency are purely its concern, not that of the courts. When it decides that a class of animals requires regulation, it may then decide, if it so wishes, whether the proper regulation of the class may require regulation of some that might well be excepted from the class if it so desired. The Legislature saw fit to class all foxes as wild animals. Unless we can say that we know as an established, uncontroverted fact that foxes are domestic animals, it is plain that the legislative determination of that fact must stand.[5]

In defining animals, science generally favors *representation*, and culture and law generally favor *illustration*. Representation is expression in the hard sense: technical, objective, informative to others, and of pragmatic benefit to minds in groups and across time. Illustration is expression in the soft sense:

interpretive, subjective, personal, and of visually gratifying benefit to minds in seclusion and at isolated moments in history. The way we personally name the animals around us is a hallmark of the illustrative mode.[6]

In animal representation, what is being defined—that is, the actual objects that zoologists and field biologists hold up, work with, quantify, depict, and assess—are not the living organisms themselves, but instead their extracts, a smattering of residues, matrices, traces, mounts, dimensional models, and recordings of the real-world objects, the "ordered, shaped, and filtered samples" of animals.[7] Cautiously separating "outside observations" from "inside observations," representational acts aspire to stand for the living and the natural, but do not and cannot truly illustrate it. An academic article about an otter is certainly not the otter itself, and even the museum collection drawer containing detailed parts of otter bodies is a simulated compartment of knowledge that sits far removed from what detailed parts of otter bodies in nature either function or look like.

In illustrating animals, what is being defined—that is, the actual objects that lawyers and nonscientists tend to hold up, work with, quantify, depict, and assess—are not of course the living things either.[8] Laypeople define animals through a smattering of literary forms, texts, sensations, colors, connotations, and emotions cultivated from and impressed by a host of more personal experiences—in a sense, the samples of samples. Incautiously blurring together "outside feelings" with "inside feelings," illustrative approaches aspire to exemplify the living entity through a personal psychological lens, but do not truly represent it in actuality.[9] The most beautiful poem about otters does no more service to represent actual otters than does the academic article thick with their measurements, or the museum collection drawer stuffed with their pelts. Nevertheless, it is critical to note that the conventions of representation are at least more useful than artistic devices since they take their authority from previous experience and the state of the academic field to competently build on a body of assumptions about the represented structures. Illustration has neither authority nor collected experience on its side.

State and federal statutes and city and county municipal codes all wrestle with those two versions of expression when defining animals. Legal designations raise a host of problems that highlight the emotive appeal of some species in indifference to their taxonomic status. Legal definitions originally catered to an appreciation of high-aesthetic-utility animals (with terms such as "pets") and a derogation of low-aesthetic-utility animals (with terms such as "pests").[10] As those preferences become ingrained in communal codes, the psychologically intimate relationships people have with pets and the physically sequestered relationships people have with pests are spotlighted. We end up using words to entangle and disentangle ourselves from our surroundings as we approve certain naming schemes and reject others, and criteria for inclusion or exclusion of an animal from various spheres of influence we have over them oftentimes neglects to note their more mundane roles as economic or biological resources.[11]

As a result, some animals are simply deemed, legislatively, to be fundamentally more important than others, and many animals are deemed, legislatively, to not be worthy of mention at all. A legislative ladder of concern is constructed in which the highest rungs are occupied by species we desire to protect, endangered species, domestics, and livestock, and—climbing down through the levels—the lowest rungs offer no protection at all and instead award the destruction of species we desire to eliminate, including game and vermin. We note with such a scale that the rungs stop altogether when it comes to the smallest of animals and has no basis in important biological concepts such as biomass, diversity, population dynamics, or longevity. Upon the closest look, it does not escape notice that within any particular statute the law's ideals about "animals," and the scientific realities about "animals," may pass by each other with leagues of empty space between them. As a hierarchy of "animal-related legal categories" is arranged in the throes of our preferences on use, people are kept off the ladder entirely since we find no "utility" in ourselves at all.

PRACTICALITY IMPOSING A TENSION BETWEEN SCIENTIFIC AND LEGAL DEFINITIONS

In the broadest perspective and given the scope and scale of all natural objects, the lawyer-scientist should start with appreciating how minute the concept of "an animal" really is in the universe. Between the smallest quarks and the largest superclusters, animals occupy the barest sliver of organic space. Being organisms, they fit in the extremely narrow slot of those objects containing the materials and mechanisms required for growth and reproduction; having definite size limits, definite spans of existence, and taking definite forms; having capacities to replicate themselves, take in nutrients, excrete waste, move around independently, and sense and respond to the environment; and revealing an intricate organization of moving parts that change over time in that they are subject to evolutionary forces.

Taxa are tools scientists use to divide and organize organisms with each category nested inside the one preceding: kingdom, phylum, class, order, family, genus, and species. Taxonomic terms primarily position organisms within the kingdoms of *Archebacteria, Eubacteria, Fungi, Plantae,* and *Animalia,* the last of which are those that move independently, respond relatively quickly to external stimuli, possess compact internal organs, and have separate genders. All members of *Animalia* are themselves divided into fourteen phyla, three of the more familiar of which are *Mollusca* (clams, oysters, and octopus), *Arthropoda* (bugs and insects), and *Chordata*, those animals that have notochords, nerve cords and gill slits at some stage in their lives. All chordates are, in turn, divided into four subphyla: *Urochordata, Hemichordata, Cephalochordata*, and *Vertebrata*, the last of which are those chordates that specifically have vertebral columns. All vertebrates, in turn, are divided into seven classes: *Agnathans, Chondrichthyes, Osteichthyes, Aves, Amphibia, Reptilia*, and *Mammalia*, and we have a special affinity for the last, the vertebrates with fur or hair and where the females possess mammary glands.

All mammals, in turn, are divided into nineteen orders. Of those the lawyer-scientist pays special attention to *Primate,* those mammals that are bipedal and that have an opposable thumb, and *Carnivora*, those mammals with four carnassial ("slicing") teeth. All carnivorans, in turn, are divided into seven families. two being quite familiar: *Felidea*, those carnivorans with retractile claws, one genus of which includes *Felis*, and which itself includes the species *domesticus*, the common house cat with well over 100 breeds, and the other *Canidae*, those carnivorans with nonretractile claws, all of which are divided in turn into ten genera, the most familiar to us being genus *Canis* (wolves, coyotes, dogs), and the most familiar species being *familiaris*, domestic dogs with well over 400 breeds currently (and, thanks to the power of artificial selection, more and more on the way each year).

A usable *scientific* classification for a "dog" can thus be fashioned out of that busy, fluctuating, nested hierarchy of observation-based categories and subcategories to define a dog as "A living thing that moves independently, responds relatively quickly to external stimuli, has compact internal organs, separate genders, a notochord, a nerve cord, embryonic gill slits, a vertebral column, fur or hair, mammary glands (in the female), four carnassial teeth, nonretractile claws, and is dissimilar in physical appearance from a wolf, from slightly dissimilar, as in the Akita, to radically dissimilar, as in the teacup poodle."

Such a definition is highly impractical and unwieldy to lawyers and laypeople for numerous reasons, including in its length, hyper-technical listing of features, and awkward-sounding criteria for inclusion and exclusion. It works but at the same time doesn't work at all. Scientific taxonomies of animals beg for distillation down to something utilitarian as well as something linguistically comforting. For that reason, both in parallel with and in rejection of scientific classifications, animals have long been commonly categorized pragmatically, in distinction from the stuffiness of formal taxonomy.

As noted, cultural classifications reject taxonomic rules: they don't reflect evolutionary relationships or a time component, they only partly rely on physical characters (and poorly identified ones at that), and they expend considerable energy attending to the minutiae of superficial appearances, location-typical actions and behaviors, current or historical geographic place-ments, historical fortuities, situational experiences, and the vagaries of rela-tions with human communities. Cultural classifications of animals are but a deformed shadow of scientific ones.

Being nonempirical, some standard cultural definitions include the use of inconsistent terms such as "tame animals," those that breed in liberty but cooperate with humans (such as peacocks); "domestic animals," those that voluntarily associate with humans (such as cats and dogs and mice); "domesticated animals," those whose breeding is controlled by humans (such as livestock, and again cats and dogs); "wild animals," a bewildering and ever-shifting spectrum of animals neither domestic nor domesticated; "endemic animals," ones that regularly live in the place where they are being defined (aka "native animals"); "exotic animals," ones *not* regularly found in the place where they are being defined; and "dangerous or vicious animals," a group whose boundaries vary wildly among every manner of political jurisdiction one can conceive of and sometimes even within the jurisdictions themselves, all depending on just who recently has bitten or attacked whom.

Within the immense *Animalia*, a multitude of taxonomic hierarchies abound depending on the parameters an observer may be examining at any given moment. Body size, anatomical complexity, mass, diet, longev-ity, phyletic history, and utility, among other factors, have all been used to place a wide variety of different members at different locations along a vast number of human-constructed "animal spectra."[12] Described using common names, some spectra overlap while others make any intersection impossible.[13] Mice, mosquitoes, albatross, angelfish, and chimpanzees are all in *Animalia* and may, if necessary, be compared in terms of physical dimensions (e.g., surface area to volume ratio), but could not be constructively compared in terms of their vastly differing social structures. Much has been written about comparisons of animals by diet and habitat, much ignored about how often those factors change from moment to moment depending upon changes in micro-environmental conditions. Animal behavior yields to the dynamism of the local environment, as much as lawyers and laypeople try to pretend that behaviors are permanently fixed species to species.[14]

In spite of legal definitions exempting them, people are in *Animalia* too, of course, and inhabit various positions on the zoological spectrum depending on what's at issue. If locomotory speed is the factor, we occupy an undis-tinguished spot in the crowded middle. If the indicator is mucus secretion, species diversity, or olfactory sensitivity and reception, we have nothing to brag about. As to "communication by complex vocalization" and "ability to manipulate the physical and biological environment," however, we tower mightily; no primate, songbird, beaver, or termite comes close.[15]

At the ontological outset of our inquiries into legal definitions, we find no need to insert ourselves inside classification schemes. It doesn't matter that methodologically there might be some difficulty in comparing our hard skeletal parts, pelt colors, dentition, or geographical distribution of populations (all used to distinguish taxonomic categories in animals) with other species. We don't even get that far in the analysis because we don't start with forming any question in which those factors make a difference as to how we interact with animals, or how animals are treated. Control and utility, in contrast, form the very heart of our past and present relationships with them, so control and utility set the agenda.

Many laws distinguish the commission of certain crimes, the value of certain conveyances, the validity of certain municipal violations, and the responsibilities of certain owners, as hinging on cultural classifications alone. Impaling a dog on a hook is a criminal activity, impaling a cow on a hook is a commercial activity, and impaling a fish on a hook is a recreational activity, with the legal characterization of each spearing satisfied by folk law artifices employing nonspecific terms such as "dog," "cow," or "fish." In short, each spearing's significance is demarked by ideology not zoology. It is through cultural interferences that the legal concept of "animal" meanders far away from the scientific concept of "animal"—our common law is a many-layered network of historical and economic accidents lain upon social conventions, the construction of which science has had little to contribute and been invited to participate in rearranging even less.[16] Ultimately, people don't even want legal concepts to defer to scientific principles where animals are concerned. The utility of our agreements regarding social conduct would be unhelpfully deformed by imposing an empirical net on their depictions. A legal standard that concedes pathogenic microorganisms and large mammalian herbivores, for instance, to be similar natural objects maintaining comparable food chain relationships with humans is a standard under which the practical mechanics of social relations would eventually be badly strained, not pleasantly assisted.

THE CONCEPT OF ANIMAL OWNERSHIP EXPANDS LAW'S CONCERN WITH TAXONOMIES

We certainly understand in principle that humans are aligned closely with all mammals and with primates in particular—but we also understand in practice a social and political need to finesse our taxonomic placement near them.[17] The filtrate of "good" laws maintaining a healthy separation must be strained from the particulate of "bad" laws categorizing participants as a function of whom they are evolutionarily related to. As a result, few cases, over centuries of legal pronouncements, have troubled to acknowledge even fundamental aspects of natural selection, to note shared features between us and animals, or to grasp even basic tenets about animalian evolutionary relationships.[18] Disregarding that the vehicle of taxonomy is driven by the engine of evolution by natural selection, courts deign to even recognize that the transmission of characters through generations has real-world effects:

> Defendant was a farmer and knew the inherent tendency of a horse to shy suddenly when frightened, or was chargeable with such knowledge. Scientists account for this wild trait in the domesticated horse by the tendency of progenitors to shy when in panic from fear of ancient enemies in the native habitat of the aborigines. The rattle of reeds and the swish of long grass, where powerful wild animals waited in ambush to pounce upon their prey, were signals for the wild horse to jump aside and flee for life. The rattle of paper or the sight of a strange object may produce the same fear. This natural tendency to shy, jump aside and run to escape danger as the result of fright has been transmitted through domestication to the remotest progeny of the equine family. Whatever may have been the origin of this wild trait, the fact of it in the domesticated horse is common knowledge chargeable to motorists on the highways.[19]

Legal distinctions between us and animals subsume similarities because legal rationales are based instead on how the two groups relate to each other *socially*. Social distinctions being the linchpin for significance makes it so that rules about animals revolve around a core belief that humans have somehow become free or liberated from certain constraints in a way that animals have not. Karl Marx fostered a great myth in the nonscientific community upholding humans as creatures who, in developing culture and civilization, have thus won some great emancipation from the slavery of being "merely" animals and thus from having to be bound by or responsible to animal instincts and animal concerns.[20] Of course human bodies haven't escaped in the slightest the biological shackles accompanying being a relatively hairless, bipedal, plains-dwelling, gregarious, omnivorous primate, but we have managed to execute a neat escape illusion by using coordinated minds to influence our environments in spite of our bodies' limitations. That influence's most profound effect is the creation of the ownership concept.

Hungrily pacing behind the words of every animal-related definition there prowls the idea of ownership, a seemingly friendly but ultimately troublesome mongrel of a concept best characterized as "the status of exclusive custody and control" of the selected object as well as "the right of its physical possession and enjoyment."[21] As lawyers will attest, the ownership concept is a difficult varmint to subdue—it bites hard at the heels of every litigant claiming to establish how their prevailing interest in a property clearly bests their opponent's.

Animals, as objects, exponentially compound every ownership quarrel. The ability, real and perceived, to control any particular animal is as massive a struggle jurisprudentially as it often is physically—yet it is also of inescapable import to cultural classifications and thus to definitional applications. Scientists don't particularly care about "animal ownership," but both scientists and lawyers care considerably about an animal's "control," and those two concepts are analytically linked.

In dealing with people conveying, exchanging, valuing, or enforcing the use of animals as properties, lawyers are compelled to confront the substantial challenge that animals conduct themselves radically distinct than do all other tangible personal properties, from handbags to hamburgers. Merely having a heightened appreciation of their internal composition as living objects doesn't lead to resolution of the problem, and the attempt some make to treat animals essentially as complex machines with sensitive and intricate moving parts is often a recipe for disaster, an observation Claude Bernard would agree with.

We have noted that prehistory and history are in part a record of people creatively using things they find, transforming natural objects into artificial ones and developing the arts and industries of manufacture and production of materials. That manner of learning conditioned human intellectual processes to change in correlation with changes in the material production. The polar categories of owners and nonowners of the objects made arose as a function of being able to fully control some objects and just not being able to effectively control others.

Where the material object is something as discrete and figuratively infinite in duration as a bowl, or a parcel of land with artificially designated boundaries, the owner of the object can comfortably hold the property in antagonism to the nonowner, i.e., all others. Bowls, parcels of land and the like are primarily static objects and their seeming permanence and attribute of staying put in one place has great appeal to putative owners.

Where the material object is something nebulous, clearly finite, and transitory, as with animals, the feeling of stability is jeopardized and the quality of ownership thereby impacted. In a strange way, the fact that all individual animals necessarily go through two status changes—being born and dying (and many but not all, go through a third change of replicating)—makes their "boundaries" confusingly blurred. When they die their behavioral usefulness zeros out and their structural usefulness plummets (unless they are consumable or aesthetically preservable in the form of taxidermic mounts). When they become able to procreate, their behavioral and functional usefulness accelerates and when they *actually* procreate their desirability either mathematically compounds (for animals such as cows whose usefulness was already established) or erodes even further (for animals such as mosquitoes whose harm was already established).

That animals as personal properties go through these mandatory status transformations emphasizes their uniqueness in comparison to other personal properties and reminds us daily that an ability to produce more things like themselves while *in* the world, and an inevitable disappearance *from* the world, requires a sea change in formulating rules about their possession, control, and value during their short stint of existence in a manner that necessarily distinguishes them from bowls. The industries of livestock farming, agricultural food production, and animal husbandry owe much of their genesis to those transient attributes and to those unyielding and inescapable changes.

Lawyers deal in abstractions and engage regularly in debates on the significance of abstractions as affecting the significance of real-world events. In the illustrative mode, making a rule out of an abstraction about "what is useful" in tandem with the real-world events of "what was just born" or "what just died," is a lawyer's stock in trade:

> In American society, the legal system is the predominant engine of public policy and, perhaps, moral suasion. It is therefore important for all people who are affected by animals—which is, of course, virtually everyone—to know something about how the law treats animals. If the law precludes appropriate ways of thinking about animals, we ought to know about it so that the law can be changed. On the other hand, if the law's general approach to animals is sound, the existing legal apparatus may provide a useful foundation for treating animals fairly.[22]

The translation of usefulness into the doctrine of ownership is then one of law's greatest practical and intellectual achievements, and in the realm of animal-related laws has woven problems and advantages together into the fluctuating spate of "animal" definitions crafted by different legislative bodies.

LESSONS TO LEARN FROM ANIMAL DEATHS

Two cases illuminate the problems of animal usage as shadowed by animal transience. The first is *People v. Shanklin,*[23] which upheld Illinois' Humane Care For Animals Act definition of "animal" as "every living creature, domestic or wild, but does not include man."[24] The *Shanklin* court held that the definition applied to a criminal defendant's acts of cruelty to an animal "regardless of the type of animal." When it issued, *Shanklin*'s unflinching application of the legislature's bizarrely unscientific terminology threatened to brook no legal obstacle to protecting each and every ant, worm, and flea within the geographical boundaries of the entire state of Illinois.

Yet that same year a bracing dose of biological reality then arose in the form of a second case, *LeBlanc v. Hayes*.[25] *LeBlanc* embodies within its four short pages nearly every specter that *Shanklin* both far too casually summoned forth and then far too blithely failed to purge.

In *LeBlanc*, the case's protagonist, Glenn LeBlanc, was a hunter who used hunting dogs to hunt and kill rabbits. Its antagonist, Lod Hayes, was a farmer who used baitfish to trap and kill crawfish that he farmed on his crawfish farm to sell to people for food. Hunter LeBlanc hunted near Farmer Hayes' farm. When Hayes spread out some poison to kill the ants that were ruining the baitfish that he used to harvest his crawfish, LeBlanc's dog, who came on to the farm and ate the poison-laced fish, died miserably as a result. The tort case, in which LeBlanc sued Hayes for monetary compensation for the unhappy loss of his hunting dog, coolly details an orgy of death that puts the grittiest gangster movie to shame: Hayes was deliberately killing ants, fish, and crayfish, and indirectly both killing dogs and protecting rabbits. LeBlanc was deliberately killing rabbits, and indirectly both killing fish and protecting dogs. Hayes' crayfish and LeBlanc's dogs were deliberately killing fish and inadvertently killing ants, while the dogs were also deliberately killing rabbits. No creature came out completely unscathed, especially the poor ants and rabbits, the welfare of which no one (in this case anyway) seemed to give a whit about by any measure.

In brooding over the particular variety of poison that Hayes used, the Court's specific legal holdings in *LeBlanc* ignored the majority of those animals altogether, and instead sought to reconcile concerns for the landowner's property interests with those of harm to the environment. The case's facts, claims, defenses, and ultimate resolution trumpet society's recognition and acceptance of an unshakable truth: that all sorts of animals, from ants to dogs, die on a regular basis for all sorts of biological, economic, and cultural reasons, not the least of which is that we emphatically need them to for society to function. That animals die and that humans work—often eagerly—to kill them with a variety of creative weapons and tools, are historical and prehistorical facts of life on which *Shanklin* turned its back but which *LeBlanc* pragmatically accepted.

Any animal's life is, naturally, a vicious one. Unless forcibly reminded of the cruelty inherent in nature, people tend to heavily romanticize animal life. They daydream that animals—when shielded from human influences—somehow have it pretty good. In the real world, it is an unavoidable fact that evolution by natural selection has permeated life with, and shaped it by, abusive, cruel, predatory, and destructive activities. From birth to death, animals live through a constant stream of relatively brutal experiences: macroscopic predators hunt them; microscopic predators erode them; parasites weaken them; vegetation restricts them; climate degrades them; other animals pirate their resources; toxins invade them; hunger shadows them; their physical environment strains them; their dietary needs burden them; strangers, relatives, mates, and conspecifics exploit them—and farmers farm them and hunters hunt them.

The natural world is, by the necessity of how evolutionary processes work, a world in which competition for resources makes life unrelentingly harsh, grants no permanent relief from pain and decay, terminates early, and is a world in which the careless and intentional acts of other living things in trying to keep their own bodies alive are regularly the genesis of each obstacle encountered. Regardless of the "cruel" nature of their acts or not, humans are part of the natural world, and laws such as the one that *Shanklin* championed—a law that effectively prohibited all intentional killing of all animal life of any type whatsoever—are unsophisticated fantasies that deny the very real role that humans have evolved from and into, participate in, require to exist, and are defined by as "living creatures" themselves, the role that *LeBlanc* acknowledged in spades.

> The natural world as actually constituted is one in which one being lives at the expense of others. Each organism, in Darwin's metaphor, struggles to maintain its own organic integrity. . . . To live is to be anxious about life, to feel pain and pleasure in a fitting mixture, and sooner or later to die. That is the way the system works. *If nature as a whole is good, then pain and death are also good.* . . . People have attempted to exempt themselves from the life/death reciprocities of natural processes and from ecological limitations in the name of prophylactic ethic of maximizing rewards (pleasure) and minimizing unwelcome information (pain). To be fair, the humane moralists seem to suggest that we should attempt to project the same values into the nonhuman animal world and to widen the charmed circle—no matter that it would be biologically unrealistic to do so or biologically ruinous if, per impossible, such an environmental ethic were implemented.[26]

Integral to the social role people have artificially carved out—tempering their physical need to live off the lives of others with their more recent moral need to make themselves feel responsible for doing so—is treating animals as environmental features to be possessed and controlled. In assembling a system of laws and definitions that entrench those activities, it is vital that we acknowledge life's inherent viciousness in the litany recited above. A functioning society, to be preserved, demands the filtrate from our mixture of ideas be those *LeBlanc*-styled rules that acknowledge animal manipulation and death, and the particulate be those *Shanklin*-styled rules that idealize nature into absurdity. A third case, also decided in the same year as *Shanklin* and *LeBlanc, Johnson v. Center for Animal Care and Control, Inc.*,[27] accepted the *LeBlanc* reality of what dogs and rabbits, ants and crayfish, are to us: properties to be necessarily consumed or destroyed as the case may be, with no need to enfold any apology or compunction into the decision being made:

> Property in dogs is of an imperfect or qualified nature and they may be subjected to peculiar and drastic police regulations by the state without depriving their owners of any federal right. Dogs hold their lives at the will of the legislature, are subject to the police power of the state, and 'might be destroyed or otherwise dealt with, as in the judgment of the legislature is necessary for the protection of its citizens.' Here, the defendant seeks only to neuter these animals. However, legislatively mandated actions of an even more drastic nature have been endorsed by our courts. Thus, a statute authorizing the destruction of all untagged dogs found outside their enclosures, even with notice of their ownership, was held to be a valid police regulation.[28]

As one reflection of the adaptions we have evolved to manipulate and control potentially harmful parts of our external environment, not just dogs, rabbits, fish, crawfish, and ants, but *all* animals hold their lives at the will of political bodies from the legislative chamber to the courtroom, all are subject to the police power of the state, and any might need to be destroyed or "dealt with as necessary" for protection of the citizenry—teacup poodle or African elephant.

The lawyer-scientist should not become complacent that the coarse and fine apertures of *Shanklin, LeBlanc*, and *Johnson* somehow have tapered the stream of rules toward generating a higher-quality filtrate—merely two years after *Shanklin*, a New York trial court unblinkingly upheld a cruelty conviction for a defendant killing a goldfish.[29] Whatever additional filtration continues to occur, it is imperative that "criminalizing the intentional destruction of every living creature" be the particulate of that process, since such rules would paralyze us just as surely as would laws prohibiting people from eating, walking around, or sleeping indoors. It isn't just that applying the law of *Shanklin* to the facts of *LeBlanc* would have everybody in that sordid little affair in jail in an instant for the horrific murders of innumerable ants, fish, crawfish, rabbits, and dogs, and it isn't just the liberty rights and ownership rights of an unlucky few that would then be impaired—it is that the very industries of agriculture, hunting, farming, recreation, and construction on which the Glenn LeBlancs and Lod Hayes of the world rely on to live that would be eviscerated were we to reject the authenticity of social and biological relations that *LeBlanc* represents in preference for the invented relationships that *Shanklin* postulates.

Even worse, true animal welfare (in the sense of the welfare of *all* animals) would be as retarded as it would be advanced by rigorous application of *Shanklin*'s rule: for each ant saved, some crawfish's next meal must be placed in jeopardy, and for each crawfish released from captivity in a pond, some dog must apparently go hungry. Yes, *Shanklin* merely substitutes one animal's problem for another's, and yes, we are hard pressed to choose any-one admirable at all, much less a hero, in *LeBlanc*'s storyline. Yes, *Shanklin* turns a dangerously blind eye away from the relativistic nature of law, the fact that every law in some way impacts another, and yes, a slippery slope form of anxiety might develop that until we begin to select which particular species should be more protected, the protection of all species regardless of taxon starts to sound as nonsensical as the protection of none.

Far more importantly, however, is that *Shanklin* averts its gaze from the brutish realization it has taken us millennia to arrive at: that "owning" pieces of the world to the exclusion of other pieces shields us from the chaos and peril of a law-free environment. It isn't just irrational, it is existentially dangerous for us to eject biology-based reason from statutory definitions, to thoughtlessly dismantle property and contract laws, to criminalize every act of an animal's use and cast them anew as the equivalents of murders and thefts. That daydream of protection of *all* animals from designations as property and as objects of contract "saves" animals at the massive expense of destroying valuable concepts, of "property" and "welfare" and "exclusion."

The cognitive scientist Daniel Dennett pensively imagined a "charmed circle" within which we might magically be able to place all organisms finally recognized to be deserving of our moral and legal protection.[30] Legislators who construct definitions such as that in *Shanklin*, rather than deal with the messiness of evolutionary biology, want to jump straight into the comforts of Dennett's charmed circle. Forget science; what is the harm, they muse, in simply legislating out an enormous definitional circle that encompasses *all* entities, "every living creature" regardless of taxonomic type, or economic utility, or evolutionary history, or biological interaction? Theodore Geisel, in his book *The Sneetches*, answered that question by metaphorically illustrat-ing the absurdity in such a project: rules protecting "those with stars on their bellies" *as well as* "those with none upon thars" are antitheses of rules, legal black holes that mercilessly swallow all light and logic, producing voids where none are protected but instead are left exposed and immobilized.[31]

PEOPLE KILLING ANIMALS VERSUS ANIMALS KILLING PEOPLE

As lawyer-scientists, we are compelled to face, not turn away from, the acknowledgment that people kill animals. We have noted they do so for a thousand different reasons, including to eat, to protect themselves, out of pleasure, curiosity, spite, fear, ignorance, or purely to survive. The manner in which they kill may be with or without pause, with or without moral compunction, with or without circumstantial justification, or with or without any objective need to have done so. While there have been, and will continue to be, countless philosophical and academic inquiries into why the rationales for causing animal deaths span such an enormous range—from the metaphysically crucial to the moronically unreasonable—all of those discussions share a collective recognition that animal deaths happen, that they happen frequently, that they have happened historically, and that they comprise a key component of how human lives regularly proceed and have been proceeding since the dawn of human civilization and well before.[32]

Whatever the motivational explanation may be, it is also safe to say that historically the vast majority of animal deaths occur and have occurred entirely without imparting any legal significance to their occurrence. It is unremarkable to note that countless chickens have made their way onto countless dinner plates without a single whit of attention or intervention from a single jurist. Our continued recognition that animal death is an inevitable social and biological phenomenon, and an integral component of human life in general, explains why we don't give legal import to every animal death, for such a legislative project would be no mere pebble, but rather a monumental stone, in the path we traverse in our social lives and daily interactions with the biological world.

Still, we have hobbled ourselves in small part by voluntarily inserting some grit onto that walkway: there are a small number of scattered exceptions to our standard indifference. Where we have assigned jurisprudential import to a few instances of "a person killing an animal," it has been to focus mostly on the killing of livestock, primarily for the nonremarkable reason that livestock, by definition, are fairly valuable market commodities, the destruction of which affects us economically.[33] An even smaller subset of laws has addressed specified domesticated animals, mostly dogs and cats.[34] A neighbor killing a farmer's cow, a trainer killing a competitor's horse, LeBlanc's dogs dying from eating Hayes' crawfish, all exemplify selective animal deaths that we merit warranting a need for civil remedy or criminal prosecution.

Where the law's attention is piqued about an animal's death, the event is analyzed via a single conceptual model: the economic impact of the animal being someone's property. Animals having been legally defined as personal properties in our common law for the last 282 years[35,] that model enables us to weigh their value qua properties and to ponder society's need for economic consequences that might reasonably be predicted to befall the animal's owner by those who, as they kill the animal for whatever reason, may have thereby cost the owner some real loss in value or use.

Over the years, a few select species (primarily *Canis familiaris, Felis domesticus,* and *Pan troglodytes*) have nonetheless been envisioned as people instead of properties, and an insistence championed that they should be granted "personhood"—a call to action that has, so far, failed.[36] Dogs and monkeys not actually *being* either "people" or "persons," the lawyer-scientist notes it as a category error—that is, a mistake where members formally assigned to one group are nonetheless treated as members of an entirely different group—and becomes apprehensive at the real-world legal problems that might branch off the attending confusion.

Among the worrisome consequences of this model (of "animals being people or persons" as opposed to being property), is how the law may then handle the event of "the animal itself killing some other." The jurisprudential and philosophical trouble arising from the collision between that category error and a coming to grips with what to do legally about the act of "animals killing others," is a predicament that must be faced and resolved.[37]

REVIVING THE POTENTIAL FOR ANIMAL
CRIMINAL CULPABILITY AND PUNISHMENT

In a notable historical work, *The Criminal Prosecution and Capital Punishment of Animals* by E. P. Evans—originally published in 1906 as a revision of an earlier journal article entitled "Bugs and Beasts Before The Law"[38]—the author carefully compiled and delineated the various historical curiosities before the Enlightenment when:

> Animals, which were in the service of man, could be arrested, tried, convicted and executed, like any other members of his household; it was, therefore, not necessary to summon them to appear in court at a specified time to answer for their conduct, and thus make them, in the strict sense of the term, a party to the prosecution, for the sheriff had already taken them in charge and consigned them to the custody of the jailer.[39]

During his litany of various "animal crimes" and their historically explanatory (or not so explainable) underpinnings, Evans wrestled with the ideas of two peers, Eduard Osenbruggen (a "Swiss jurist [who] endeavors to explain . . . legal proceedings on the theory of the personification of animals") and Bartholomew Chassenee (a "distinguished French jurist [who] made his reputation at the bar as counsel for some rats . . .").

Evans was adamant that people and animals should not be treated differently under the criminal law. He rejected Osenbruggen's assertion that, "[a]s only a human being can commit crime and thus render himself liable to punishment [since] it is only by an act of personification that the brute can be placed in the same category as man and become subject to the same penalties [and animals cannot be personified]." Unlike Osenbruggen, Evans was positive that animals *could* be personified. He agreed with Chassenee in denying that "animals are incapable of committing crimes because they are not endowed with rational faculties." Like Chassenee, Evans was positive that animals *did* use reason. Convinced that animals embodied key qualities of "persons" and used reason, Evans therefore believed it inarguable that "if crime consists in the commission of deeds hurtful to other sentient beings, knowing such actions to be wrong, then the lower animals are certainly guilty of criminal offenses."

The question arises as to how a thoughtful scholar like Evans, well over a century ago, was so certain that animals could commit crimes as a result of them "knowing" their actions to be wrong. Like many before him,[40] Evans found it appropriate to creatively interpret the expressions of animals by divining the "looks" that animals exhibited subsequent to causing harm as revelations of their "guilty knowledge." The physical appearance of guilt was thus key to his conclusions, and in that way Evans argued subjectively, from the folk wisdom of meaningful expressions and appearances, not objectively, from controlled experiment or the application of logic: "[i]t is . . . undeniable that domestic animals often commit crimes against man and betray a consciousness of the natures of their acts by showing fear of detection or by trying to conceal what they have done."[41]

Evans was also impressed by the personal reactions of people who witnessed the events of animals killing others—and assigned those reactions an epistemological significance as well: "[m]an too recognizes [the animals'] moral responsibility by inflicting chastisement upon them, and sometimes feels justified in putting incorrigible offenders, a vicious bull, a thieving cat or a sheep-killing dog, summarily to death."[42] To Evans, the physical reaction to witnessing harm was of equal weight to the physical appearance of guilt such that animals' legal and moral responsibility for their viciousness was a function of both illustrative forces, of the dramatic brusqueness of feeling that one's observations miraculously revealed.

In short, the source of Evans' conviction that animal minds and human minds were functionally similar was by "reading" their thoughts from their faces. Mind-reading, of course, is risky business and while trial lawyers are often bold enough to attempt it (during jury selection and in energetic cross-examination, to name two places), scientists resist. Their hesitancy to rely on the "personification of animals" (per Osenbruggen) and the "rationality of animals" (per Chassenee) stems from a recognition that those propositions extol anthropomorphism over empiricism. The risk is that with that sort of subjectivity, the mind reader alone becomes the unimpeachable authority for what is being read, and, with no objective protections in place to prevent abuses of self-interest, abuses in "interpretations" then can abound unfettered.

Well over a century after they were first espoused, the conclusion those claims reach—that people's cognitive processes must form a good working model for animal cognitive processes because animal faces appear to reflect human thoughts—have nevertheless been renewed by animal rights advocates. The resultant claim that "animals are people too" and should be treated as such, has some real bitter, however, that necessarily goes with that tempting sweet.

"CRIMINALS" AND "ANIMALS" AND THE CONCEPTUAL GAPS BETWEEN THEM

Consider that, in the criminal context, if one equates an animal with being "a person" then the actor who killed it must have therefore engaged in the functional equivalent of murder, a Class A felony. If one equates an animal with being "a property" on the other hand, then the actor has therefore committed at most the functional equivalent of criminal mischief, a Class C misdemeanor. The model that one adopts, therefore, sets the bar for the interaction's overall legal importance to society: either as the most grievously serious act imaginable to be stopped at all costs, or as a garden-variety bit of misconduct to be sternly but modestly penalized.

Animal rights advocates wield the animals being people or persons model one way only: people have rights, so animals should have rights. Under that rubric they have managed recently to convince at least one court to christen animals as "victims" in the same manner of people being deemed victims of crimes.[43] The focus on the moral "sweet" of "people or person killing an animal" scenarios, however, raises a logical "bitter" that must then be considered: what to do about an animal killing a person. Just as people have killed animals for the six million years of our species' brief existence on this planet,[44] animals have, of course, killed innumerable people throughout that same period. As noted above, historically those events have been thoroughly dealt with in the law solely under the "animals being property" model. Such killing is a phenomenon that has never been assessed legally under the "animals being people or persons" model, yet the proposal for animals to have rights now compels us to shine light upon that omission.

Two consequences initially appear. The first is that the model necessarily requires animals to then be considered also as criminals, i.e., that the axiom of "animals [being people] killing [other] people" necessarily positions animals as themselves subject to the trials, tribulations, and processes that all accused persons are subject to—of formal detention and charge, formal prosecution and proof, public hearing involving confrontation of the accuser, and the imposition of commensurate sanction if convicted. The second consequence is that the first effect, being impossible to support, makes the whole project untenable.

AN ANIMAL'S "GUILTY MIND" AS PREREQUISITE TO CRIMINALIZING ITS CONDUCT

To understand this, we need to thoroughly ponder what "crimes" really entail. In medieval jurisprudence, a person's overt act alone was assumed to constitute the crime; the mental condition or state of the accused was not seriously taken into consideration. Since the Enlightenment, however, the more modern approach has drawn mental states into the equation, and it has increasingly become that "the commission of a crime" is an event that must necessarily presuppose normal freedom of will on the part of the agent.[45] Where sanity, rationality, intent, or attention of the agent as a perpetrator is found wanting, we have come to acknowledge that there really should be no corresponding culpability, regardless of the innocuous or nasty consequences of the act.[46]

In looking primarily to the psychical origin of the deed, and only secondarily to its effects, modern criminal law now fully embraces the concept of the mens rea, the guilty mind, in all its complexities, frustrations, and permutations.[47] The strong light of those two key concepts on which our modern criminal codes are founded—mens rea and free will—reveals the "animals being people or persons" model to be a broken concept and to violate logic and law.

Since the early 1800s, we have come to accept that acts in which certain (but not all) animals are hurt or killed, may be indictable offenses,[48] a proposition now enshrined extensively in our criminal codes (as they have been in our moral codes for far longer). Although a large number of our laws actually provide social approval and moral support to harming and destroying certain types of animals (mostly of feedstock, pests, game, and invertebrates[49]), over the last half century, criminalization of certain domestic and livestock animal-directed behaviors has been on a steady increase, with newly described offenses being added every year.[50] Post-Evans, we have not, on the other hand, accepted the corollary to that precept: whether animals themselves can commit crimes, and thus be accused of and tried for that commission.

In the form of a threshold question—"can animals commit crimes?"—it seems helpful to note first what is *not* being asked. One, it is not a question asking if animals can harm, which in large part is not a legal question at all, but a practical and quasi-scientific one, and one that does not really need much thought or work to answer with a resounding "yes" (to a question, by the way, the legal component of which has been fully explicated ever since the late 1800s).[51] Two, it is not a question asking if animals can be *instrumentalities* in a person's crime, a different question to be answered mostly by criminologists, forensic investigators, law enforcement personnel, fiction writers, and armchair detectives,[52] and again, an uninteresting question for our purposes given that it as well has already been addressed by the common law in the affirmative long ago.[53]

Three and finally, it is not really even a question asking if animals can be prosecuted or sentenced for crimes (events that have in fact happened historically for rather odd socio-political and religious reasons rather than for purely legal ones[54]) and the answers to which may well eventually again become interesting as legal questions, but only after the threshold question here has first been answered. While "can an animal be sentenced for a crime?" will undoubtedly raise an eyebrow-raising and jaw-dropping set of concerns for the future jurist and litigator alike (primarily procedural and practical ones), it is a question that has jumped too far ahead into the future envisioned by our argument, since we both wish and need to know at this juncture how the animal even got to be personally present at the sentencing hearing to begin with.

This question, therefore, is "Can animals commit crimes?" The operative word in the inquiry is the verb, and the focus is on how law perceives what it truly means to "commit" a crime in the first place. It helps to start examining an answer by confronting the visceral, less analytic type of response head on—that is, it isn't that inappropriate to simply start with a pure "gut reaction" rejecting the question right out of the gate: "no, of course animals cannot commit crimes." A very reactionary "No!" answer to the question outright is likely sourced in an underlying (and very human) conception of just what "guilt" and "blame" actually are, an appreciation of just what it truly *means* for one to be "guilty" or "blameworthy."

The law has tried to accommodate that comprehension. Lawyers and lay people alike are familiar with a well-sourced recognition that, at their core, crimes require (for the largest part) some manner of affirmative act that is accompanied by a *mens rea*, as noted, some sort of guilty mental state.[55] Now, hundreds of centuries of interactions with a variety of animals in social contexts have enabled us to become comfortable with casually attributing a whole host of beneficial human qualities to some (primarily to dogs and cats) extolling their imaginary personality traits comparable to ours such as being "brave," "trustworthy," or "noble."[56] Conversely, we are not remiss in also attributing some adverse human qualities to them too (though again mostly to household pets and large-bodied mammals) in semi-equal measure: we may view certain individuals who have personally offended or harmed us as "mean," "vile," "spiteful," or "jealous."[57] Even so, Aesop and Evans notwithstanding, we are hesitant to agree with characterizations where the quality—admirable or pejorative—posits a *moral* basis for its expression. "Guilty" is one we reject in that sense. In normal interactions with animals, we consistently reject an approach of pretending animals somehow operate under the moral guidelines we apply to ourselves.[58]

> Well-trained dogs sometimes let their masters down; they anticipate punishment or other manifestations of displeasure; they grovel and whimper, and they even make crude efforts at redress and reconciliation. But do they feel remorse and bad conscience? They have been conditioned to associated manifestations of displeasure with departures from a norm, and this is a useful way of keeping them in line, but they haven't the slightest inkling of the *reasons* for the norm. They don't *understand* why departures from the norm are wrong, or why their masters become angry or disappointed. They have a concept perhaps of the *mala prohibita*—the act that is wrong because it is prohibited, but they have no notion of the *mala in se*—the act that is prohibited because it is wrong. Even in respect to the *mala prohibita* their understanding is grossly deficient, for they have no conception of rightful authority. For dogs, the only basis of their master's "right" to be obeyed is his *de facto* power over them. Even when one master steals a beast from another, or when an original owner deprives it of its natural freedom in the wild, the animal will feel no moralized emotion, such as outraged propriety or indignation. These complex feelings involve cognitive elements beyond an animal's ken. Similarly, to suffer a guilty conscience is to be more than merely unhappy or anxious; it is to be in such a state because one has violated an "internalized standard," a principle of one's own, the rationale of which one can fully appreciate and the correctness of which one can, but in fact does not, doubt.[59]

In the criminal context, our refusal doesn't involve the "affirmative act" of the putative crime, since we are fine with accepting that animals engage in all sorts of affirmative acts that are clearly harmful or dangerous to others.[60] It is a refusal that instead derives from the obvious absence of the mens rea component, since even if one accepts that some animals do have minds at all (a perfectly acceptable premise under an "animals being people or persons" approach), it seems empirically invalid to identify or recognize their "*guilty* minds."[61] It is nearly impossible to support a determination that animals share the peculiar human mental state of experiencing guilt about anything at all, much less about the sharp consequences of some particular piece of socially reprehensible conduct.

> Whatever the original foundations of delictual liability, the fact is that by the nineteenth century it had firmly come to rest upon the notion of fault. The moral and logical attractions of the proposition that a human being should make good the harm caused by his fault were (and still are) very great. But the converse of this principle, namely that there can be no liability where there is no fault,

offered an additional attraction to an era which was more concerned in *not* making *certain* people liable than in compensating every loss (even of the most eccentric nature) at the drop of a hat. So in this sense fault, like *culpa* in earlier times, could be seen as a corrective device which could help retain the boundaries of liability within manageable proportions. It is, no doubt, due to this rather unusual coincidence of morality and economic expediency that the notion of fault owes so much of its aura of soundness and inevitability.[62]

Lawyers and scientists also cast off any presumption that animals—regardless of mental states—can feel guilt in a core sense, even where their body language or facial expressions might be anthropomorphically interpreted to express something that looks superficially similar to our own expressions of guilt, abjectness, or remorse.[63] Not just self-awareness, but self-evaluation and self-criticism would have to be acknowledged to justify such a presumption, yet none of those states manifest in animals in any conceivable manner. If animals can't experience guilt as a moral imperative, then, the requisite mental state cannot be shown and they can't legally be considered to have committed the mental state component of a crime at all, regardless of what they actually did, who they hurt or how, or what their faces or bodies might look like right before, during, or subsequent to the act. It is their incapacity to articulate any comprehension of accepting the social compact that criminal responsibility requires that lies at the heart of our conclusion:

> The syntactic structure of human language, its capacity to multiply symbols and meanings without limit, and its integral relationship with the institutions of human social life might make one think that there is a radical difference between the world experienced by a language user and that of any other creature. So it would surely be a mistake to confuse acting on purpose (intentional animal behavior) with other, *intellectual* activities, such as reflecting on, or analyzing, the reason for acting so (various kinds of reflective evaluation of one's own decisions and actions, or of the actions of others), or deliberating about the correct evaluation of competing options (various kinds of practical deliberation about one's own best course or the options open to others whom one is advising).[64]

Knowing what we know in the law about the existence of legal rights necessarily being tied to the corresponding existence of legal responsibilities that impart value to those rights,[65] it would be a legally impossible world in which an entity could have a right, say as a victim, but not have any accompanying responsibility whatsoever, say as a potential perpetrator themselves. We simply don't allow for the existence of "specially privileged" classes of people who get to have rights but who themselves cannot be held responsible for their own actions potentially affecting the rights of others.[66] The one status is necessarily tied to the other status. Our emphatic gut-level "No!" response to the "can animals commit crimes?" question then, in that sense, necessarily shuts the door on any other concern in this area since it therefore demands an acceptance in parallel that animals cannot then have legal rights either, whether as "victims" or otherwise. Case, therefore, closed.

APPLYING RULES ON THE COMMISSION OF, AND PUNISHMENT FOR, CRIMES TO ANIMALS

Or is it? Envision instead answering "Yes" to our central question, i.e., positing that "yes, animals can commit crimes." What really is it to commit a crime? What is actually involved in the analysis? As Evans lamented a century ago:

> [W]hy should not animals be held penally responsible for their conduct as well as human beings? There are men apparently less intelligent than apes. Why then should the man be capitally punished and the ape not brought to trial? And if the ape be made responsible and punishable, why not the dog, the horse, the pig, and the cat?[67]

Evans' questions form a set of solid, emotionally appealing puzzles to solve, and answering them in the affirmative does not seem that reckless. Evans felt that the "guilty mind" issue was easily disposed of since he decried that animals' sense of guilt was plainly manifest in their looks and deeds, and thus the only real obstacle to making criminals out of animals was practical, specifically, that their prison sentences wouldn't accomplish the preventive social purpose we normally expect should stem from such punishment:

> [I]t is undeniable that animal intelligence is capable of distinguishing between right and wrong and of comprehending what is punishable and what is not punishable. In general when a dog does wrong, he knows that he is doing wrong; and a monkey often takes delight in doing what is wrong simply because he knows it is wrong. If a monkey gets angry and kills a child, he obeys the same vicious propensity that impels a brutal man to commit murder. There is no greater 'defect of reason' in one case than in the other. Why then should the monkey be summarily shot or knocked on the head, and the man arrested, tried, convicted, and hanged by the constituted authorities? Simply because such a public prosecution and execution would not exert any influence whatever in preventing infanticide on the part of other monkeys; if it could be shown that a formal trial would produce this salutary effect, then it certainly ought not to be omitted.[68]

Had we some reliable signal from the animal world that the participants truly grasped the larger significance of their punishment, he argued, then we would be obligated to punish them as criminals—it was only their failed comprehension of punitive seriousness that was the sticking point and better communication with them about what really deterred them could fill the gap. He noted, "If it could be conclusively proved or even rendered highly probable that the capital punishment of an ox, which had gored a man to death, deterred other oxen from pushing with their horns, it would be the unquestionable right and imperative duty of our legislatures and tribunals to reenact and execute the old Mosaic law on this subject."[69]

For deterrence to work as a mechanism, an entire population of subjects must participate. All to be deterred must grasp that certain actions connect to certain consequences—that is, the target of the deterrence proposal has to be able to conceive of a spectrum of likely futures and then tailor their present conduct in anticipation of avoiding the bad and facilitating the good.[70] The population's members simply being able to generically plan for the future isn't by itself sufficient for deterrence to work; they also have to envision hypotheticals and then use their predictive powers and deliberate action in combination to construct a desirable reality from the hypothetical.

That project demands the transmission of information in the form of abstract concepts conveyed across and throughout population segments. It also demands the comprehension of, and desire to maneuver around, morally good and morally bad outcomes. What it doesn't entail is measures of intelligence or of communicative ability. Undeniably, many animals, can be "deterred" from acting by all sorts of triggering phenomena such as the posturing and alarm calls of potential prey.[71] The leopards in the referenced study are highly intelligent and highly communicative, and are plainly well deterred from attacking chimpanzees in future predation projects as a function of employing both qualities. But they are making such decisions via the balancing of *biological* imperatives, not *moral* ones. The difference is crucial.

DEFENSES TO CRIMES ENMESH THE IDEA OF RIGHTS IN APPLYING CRIMINAL RULES TO THE ACCUSED

Evans' wish to prosecute rats is crushed not just by what rats are compared to humans, but also by how prosecution itself "works" with its targets. Historically, our legal taxonomy of crimes has been extensive, creative, and ever-changing, and one can leisurely peruse the myriad, jurisdiction-specific lists, sub-lists, and sub-sub-lists of "crimes against the person," "crimes against the State," "computer-related crimes," "crimes of immorality" and, of course, "crimes of animal cruelty," these last also known as "animal-related crimes." Ask a lawyer what an "animal-related crime" is, and they will list the parade of proscriptions encompassing the traditional person killing (or hurting) an animal scenario. Advocates in particular will spotlight sociological explanations for the genesis of such events[72] and the appropriateness of the punishments and prohibitions against human perpetrators.[73] It engenders confusion, on the other hand, to tender the parallel "animal killing (or hurting) a person" scenarios as another example, and most would exhort that acts by an animal can't comprise crimes.

Certainly, if they were, two additional jurisprudential questions would arise. The first is: to which crimes are animals then exposed? The second is: what are the defenses then available to them in being accused of doing so? Criminal codes encompass a large (and ever-expanding) set of defined bad acts, and all have defenses associated with them, with the picky details of the defenses depending somewhat on within which category the crime itself falls, and somewhat on the essential elements of the crime itself.

In short, "crimes" as a category jurisprudentially require "defenses" as a comparable category, and the two concepts are thus fundamentally intertwined.[74] For instance, there is a solid reason why the defense of "lack of criminal intent" to have even committed the crime charged may not be allowed to be combined with "self-defense" as a justification for committing the crime charged, which is that it devalues the impact of criminalizing the conduct in the first place and raises inherent inconsistencies in allowing such competing defenses.[75]

As to which crimes animals would be exposed, a handful comfortably fit. Assault, mischief, and theft type offenses seem like reasonable, non-radical choices, since many accept that a dog or cat, for instance, can "steal" a chicken, "trespass" onto private property, or "assault" a child. Courts have not been hesitant to consider that such occurs:

> The degree of the imminence of danger to chickens to justify the killing of a chicken stealing dog and the degree of the imminence of danger to sheep from a sheep-stealing dog are not the same.[76] That the plaintiff's dog on one occasion stole an egg, and afterwards snapped at the heel of the man who had hotly pursued him *flagrant delicto*—that on another occasion he barked at the Doctor's horse, and that he was shrewdly suspected in early life to have worried a sheep—make up a catalogue of offences not very numerous nor of a very heinous character. If such deflections as these from strict propriety be sufficient to give a dog a bad name and kill him, the entire race of these faithful and useful animals might be rightfully extirpated.[77]

Accusations of animals "stealing," or "trespassing" or "assaulting" embrace thoughts that have their origins in the messiness of common parlance and how we express ourselves outside of the law's peculiar verbiage. For instance, as to an animal's "trespass," uncertainty arises via two very different uses of the word. There is the term's colloquial definition as a verb meaning "any wrongful entry onto another's real property," an activity in which even inanimate objects such as tree branches and tennis balls engage. The law certainly recognizes "trespass" in its verb form involving wrongful entries, and it is commonplace for a court to consider that an animal may thus "trespass" onto another's property.[78] The legal usage of the verb form reflects the idea that the owners of such objects—in their role as defendants—may be held legally responsible for damage caused by their owned objects even if they themselves did not personally make any actual entry.[79]

In distinction, there is also the term's legal use as a noun in premises liability law defining who is a "trespasser," a different word referring to the specialized legal "status" of certain litigants in civil actions against landowners for negligence.[80] Courts regularly compartmentalize those disparate uses, such that, with the latter, the plaintiff's "status" as a trespasser is analyzed as a condition dependent a) on the specific type of conduct the plaintiff might have been engaging in as an actor, b) on just what manner of knowledge or awareness the plaintiff may have had about the property on which they entered, and c) on exactly what sort of particular uses the plaintiff might have been making of the property at the time of entry.[81]

Under *that* use of the term (as the specialized noun), however, courts do not deem animals to have any legal status at all.[82] "Persons" alone—in their role as plaintiffs—have that legal status, as "trespassers." Animals cannot enjoy such a status since requisite tests of knowledge or awareness simply cannot be applied to them.

Saying a dog "stole a chicken" then, is one thing. Saying that in doing so the dog then "committed the crime of theft of poultry," however, is analytically different, in large part because it imbues the dog as an actor with a legal status that dogs have never been cloaked with—as "criminals"—and presupposes that the dog could then manifest the requisite mental state for theft, intentionally, knowingly, recklessly, or negligently. It is that imposition of status and presupposition of mental state that draws the real concern and to their credit some animal rights advocates work diligently with this almost intractable issue.[83]

Continuing with the "which crimes make sense to apply" question, other choices become quickly comical: crimes involving firearms or any weapons, the manufacture or distribution of narcotics, the misuse of motor vehicles, acts of fraud or deceit such as forgery or counterfeiting, constructing impersonations, or planning conspiracies or premeditated homicides, to identify just a few. For those examples, we don't worry about the animal's status or mental state since we are stopped cold at the outset in envisioning the animal's actual physical capability to even execute the act in the first place, Planet of the Apes–type fantasies notwithstanding.

IMBALANCES SUGGEST A COMPARISON OF ANIMALS WITH CHILDREN

Both the physical incapability obstacle and the status obstacle illuminate an additional distinction between animals and people: that our extensive manipulation of the current environment has made them far more situationally vulnerable to us than we had ever been to them in the past. Teeth and claws hardly impress a species that can wield automatic weapons, and from the lawnmower to the long-range missile, our eruption of tool usage has exposed animals to persistent and unescapable harm across the fences and at the doorways in every human community. As a microcosm of organic life susceptible to abuse without special protection, authors more and more frequently envision animals as children.

Certainly in making that comparison, we easily notice that both groups lack the complex coordinated movements and the sophisticated neural equipment to adequately respond to the contingencies we call "responsibility." Is a solution then to say that animals cannot be criminals in the same way that children cannot be criminals—an argument that sticks with attending solely to the physical incapability and status hang-ups and that avoids altogether worrying about the mens rea issue? For the lawyer-scientist, however, the analogy becomes confounded at a rather basic conceptual level.

The concern is the disparate trajectories each is following. Human infants begin as creatures of natural impulses with severely constricted physical capabilities and no control over themselves and no concept of self, much less of responsibility or punishment.[84] As the infant learns to control its movements and its body, nevertheless, it slowly begins to attain physical maturity and construct its "self."[85] Only as it develops into the critical stages of producing and comprehending language does it then become social in the sense that it becomes free to act independent of its environment, to make choices, to mold and affect the behaviors of others by acts of will—and to comprehend being punished for transgressions against those parameters.[86] Children mature—animals don't. The status of "being responsible" is a function of a necessary coordinated interplay between and among a) the passage of developmental time, b) the effect of certain evolutionary adaptations being expressed, and c) the alteration of the subject's mind in the appropriate manner. Among other effects, deterrence can then be used as a device effective against children but not against animals.

Responsibility arises directly from that interplay and is buttressed and enhanced by an intricate network of human sociality, and we do not expect animals to experience that interplay or develop as members of any organized communal network, social or otherwise, as they get older.[87] Maturity also embraces an awareness of one's own mortality, an important component of making the acceptance of responsibility truly hit home. As Desmond Manderson poetically put it, for animals "the waters of experience are not stained by the prospective loss which death threatens, or the retrospective loss which time accomplishes."[88] That distinction is crucial to a comparison of animals with children, and an ontological and epistemological set of inquiries makes it fitting that we reject the idea that neither group can commit crimes simply because of a superficially shared vulnerability.

> True morality, in the highest human sense of the word, presupposes a mental capacity no animal possesses, and conversely, human responsibility would itself be impossible without a definite foundation of sentiment. Even in man, the feeling of responsibility has its roots in the deep instinctive "layers" of his mind and he may not do with impunity all that cold reason affirms. While ethical motives may amply justify a certain action, inner feeling may rebel against it, and woe betide the man who in such a case listens to reason rather than to sentiment.[89]

If the mens rea problem is our first hard obstacle to justifying animal rights in this "killing and harming model" that we have posited for animals, then it is in the area of "defenses to crimes" that our analysis of animal rights hits its second, almost equally insurmountable, impediment. To get to it, consider that criminal defenses have substantive components and they have procedural components. While we would start with the substantive, to do so, a short detour into the nature of free will is necessary.

HOW FREE WILL INSERTS INTO THE APPLICATION OF CRIMINAL DEFENSES

We identify "free will" in several different ways. One is the recognition that "we could have done otherwise," or in other words come to the understanding that external possibilities in the world exist and that choosing among them reflects an act of will.[90] Another is that "we act for understandable reasons," i.e., the acceptance that internal explanations for our conduct exist and that articulating those reasons reflect an act of will.[91] A third is the idea that "we originate our own actions," rejecting the excuse that our acts are controlled by biological, physiological, or mechanical explanations, and conceding that transcending those explanations reflects an act of will.[92] All of these descriptions of free will require the posing of alternatives to any claim that the conduct in question was the act of an automaton, a being without choice or explanation, or someone crucially tainted by an outside interference that could not be evaded.[93]

Now apply all this to "substantive defenses to crimes." All criminal defenses require that the accused's free will have been in play or involved in some manner.[94] Conceptually, self defense and the defense of others and of property are justification defenses where the accused's free will is overtly expressed, for example, in "I chose to protect myself (or this other) by choosing to harm another." Conceptually, entrapment and duress defenses are those defenses where the accused's free will was deceived or overcome by the stronger free will of another, as in "I was enticed (or physically forced) into choosing to commit the act by another choosing to tempt or lure me (or force me) to do so." Conceptually, excuse and choice of evils defenses are those defenses where the accused's free will has been embraced as a moral or social strength: "I chose to commit this crime instead of this other crime because it was the more moral or socially acceptable choice of two required or mandatory paths."[95] Overall, will is a paramount ingredient in any defense recipe.

As to procedural defenses to crimes, we focus on the idea that criminal defendants have constitutional rights affecting the nature and progress of their prosecution: rights about the presumption of innocence, rights against self-incrimination, rights against unreasonable searches and seizures, and rights to confront their accusers and of due process. All involve certain mechanical steps between arrest and incarceration, but more importantly, all enshrine our ideals as to what we think socially about ourselves as agents with free will—that we all start off on an equal footing as blameless actors and that others have to make a public, and specifically extremely strong "no doubt"–type showing that we have voluntarily chosen to harm, as well as that it is unfair to take advantage of temporary weaknesses in will that coercive situations may often create resulting in our harming others.[96] Overall, rights are also a paramount ingredient in any defense recipe.

Were we to grant rights to animals, and in turn therefore step down the methodologically troublesome path of charging and prosecuting animals for crimes, we could perhaps get past some of the initial mechanical problems—for instance as to that of confronting the accuser by, say, assigning a spokesperson to "confront" on behalf of the animal, or as to the more flexible social policy type problems of appropriate punishment perhaps by, say, detailing physically appropriate restraint conditions as functional analogues for incarceration. Even so, the free will problem remains absolutely insoluble.

If, on the other hand, in order to affix procedural defenses to animal actors, animals are technically to be considered as having free will, then these corollaries must apply to them by fiat. One is that "they could have done otherwise," that is, we would have to presume that all animals can freely choose from external possibilities in the world; a second is that "they act for understandable reasons," that is, we would have to presume that internal explanations direct their conduct and that the animals themselves can readily articulate those reasons; and a third is that "they originate their own actions," that is, we would have to presume that no biological, physiological, or mechanical explanation for an animal's conduct alone will ever be sufficient.

Modern scientific studies, however, inform us that all those things are in fact empirically untrue about animals: all the empirical data generated to date indicates that, to a beast, animals collectively could not have cognitively weighed hypothetical options and spontaneously selected to have "done otherwise," and that their conduct in the world is radically far from being freely chosen but is instead almost universally behaviorally compelled at some level.[97]

Similarly, the data indicates that they don't often act "for understandable reasons" at all, and their absolute inability to articulate any reason whatsoever thus dooms any rational conclusion that they are in "complete and independent control" of their own conduct.[98] Moreover, the data indicates that they don't tend to spontaneously "originate their own actions" given that external biological, physiological, and mechanical explanations (particularly as suites of complex evolutionary adaptations) for their conduct are far more sufficient to explain the gist of what they are doing and why.[99]

Were we to reject all of that data and blindly embrace those presumptions as some sort of moral imperative, a tectonic paradigm shift would occur, one spelling the end of the animal sciences, the end of animal behavior as a field of study, the end of the use of animals as objects—and not just the end of breeding them, raising them, killing them, eating them, riding them, wearing them, owning them, training them, selling them, or displaying them, but the end of all socially consequential interactions with them altogether. *LeBlanc* is the warning bell loudly ringing out that doing so would be a massive step backward, not forward, in truly understanding the world, the basic task of the scientist and lawyer.

The various links in the tangled chains of science, law, and logic enable us to track this analytic route: to decide that animals can commit crimes is to decide that animals can present defenses, and to decide that animals can present defenses is to decide that animals have free will and rights. The conclusion however is unyielding: as animals are not found to have free will and rights, then they cannot display guilty minds or use defenses attendant to guilty minds, thus cannot "commit" crimes, and thus cannot be deemed the functional equivalent of people in any role, victim or otherwise.

That aperture of applying criminal defenses realistically cannot be closed. Our animal-related crimes are garnished with exceptions to culpability in the cloth of statutory and common law defenses, among them, the common law defense of protecting other property.[100] We absolve many forms of animal harm and destruction as a nod to the necessity and reasonableness of protecting other things we own or use that we want to make sure don't get ruined or deprived of value. The eradication of the weevil and the vole to save the cotton field and the rice paddy is a crucial component of daily agricultural life. The mens rea factor in the criminal law, along with the social value and biological realities of protecting people and property in general, together encompass a principled recognition that weevils and voles should not be deemed our legal counterparts.

The bitter with the sweet also command this: If animals are "people or persons," and thus by mandatory and logical extension in turn rights-holders, then animal cruelty laws should apply to them exactly like such laws apply to all people. Yet truly adjudicating competing rights among all rights-holders as an intrinsically defined group requires administration among all of concepts of "culpability," "responsibility," "malfeasance," "guilt," "negligence," and "duty," each layered only on the shoulders of those with free will. Vessels of will that they are, people can be deemed negligent, or reckless, or deliberate and pay prices for being so; animals cannot be. People can have legal responsibilities; animals cannot. People can have duties of care imposed on them; animals cannot. It could be no other way.

> What is important is that the insistence on importance or seriousness of social pressure behind the rules is the primary factor determining whether they are thought of as giving rise to obligations. Two other characteristics of obligation go naturally together with this primary one. The rules supported by this serious pressure are thought important because they are believed to be necessary to the maintenance of social life or some highly prized feature of it. Characteristically, rules so obviously essential as those which restrict the free use of violence are thought of in terms of obligation. So too rules which require honesty or truth or require the keeping of promises, or specify what is to be done by one who performs a distinctive role or function in the social group are thought of in terms of either "obligation" or perhaps more often "duty." Secondly, it is generally recognized that the conduct required by these rules may, while benefiting others, conflict with what the person who owes the duty may wish to do. Hence obligations and duties are thought of as characteristically involving sacrifice or renunciation, and the standing possibility of conflict between obligation or duty and interest is, in all societies, among the truisms of both the lawyer and the moralist.[101]

In the available roles of members and participants in the overall system that initiates, decides, administers, and enforces justice and law, we easily note that animals cannot be lawyers, or legislators, or prosecutors, or fact finders, or neutrals, or jurists, or victims—and by the same logic and for the same logical reasons, neither can they then be criminals. In the illustrative frame, "criminal" or "perpetrator" or "the accused" all circumscribe a particular type of role we construct for ourselves to play inside the law game, one not really conceptually different than the role of "witness" or "judge." To inhabit any of those roles, one dons a costume, in this instance, the heavy cloak of socially mandated and agreed-upon responsibility for the affirmative and mentally cognizable behavior of oneself toward others. To obtain the benefits of, and suffer the burdens on, any legal role, the description and application of legal responsibilities is a crucial component of dressing the part, getting on the stage, and engaging in the serious theater of social participation.

People alone play those roles in the "rights" game, a game created by people only for people. All are roles that require acts of the expression of free will, admixed with impositions of acknowledged (or imputed) responsibility, and all emanate at the core from a willing participation in an integral social network of others as they, in turn, express acts of their free will or shoulder their responsibility accordingly. Animals have no will to express, have no responsibilities imposed on them or imposable in any sane sense, belong to no truly social networks—and thus don't get to play.

Calling animals "criminals" is a logician's "category error" in the same sense that it is flatly erroneous for the Oregon Supreme Court to call animals "victims" or for advocates to call them "rights-holders,"[102] a rejection of definitions and logic in favor of putting on a form of theater couched to impress an easily impressionable audience with rhetoric that broadcasts drama and rejects reason. The seemingly small and emotionally appealing mental leap that the animal rights advocate tempts with is this: from the syllogism "[a] person who kills a dog destroys property," jump straight across to that of "a person who kills a dog destroys another person." In landing, however, the leaper will undeniably find themselves at the crumbling edge of a much more dangerous chasm: the gulf from the syllogism of "a person who kills a dog destroys another person" to "a dog who kills a dog destroys another person." While logic and law compel that second jump, it is a traverse fatal to both.

Animal-related charges against a person for engaging in animal abuse, animal neglect, or animal abandonment often are proven in courts to be serious or mild forms of human misconduct, as the case may be, but that is not because the object, the "victim," of the misconduct is a human superficially trapped in an animal costume. Relying on how our laws are written and the complicated manner in which we involve animals in our lives, the act of "animals killing others" is a phenomenon that should halt, not incite, the thoughtless rush to make animals into our social colleagues, our relational associates, and our jurisprudential equals.

From their genesis in prehistorical relationships to their immersion in historical narratives, legal taxonomies reflect the softness, the plasticity, of how people tinker with illustrative expression, and the result is that the lawyer and layperson alike *objectify* animals as non-equals, as "things owned." Exactly what types of owned objects they are comparatively, and the peculiarities of how that ownership functionally operates with things so weirdly feral yet civilized, so curiously mute yet expressive, and so puzzlingly here-today-yet-gone-tomorrow, is now our next topic to explore.

NOTES

1. *Rubáiyát* of Omar Khayyám, Quatrain LXXXVI.

2. George Meredith. *Modern Love* (1862).

3. Kellert, S. "Urban American Perception of Animals and the Natural Environment" *Urban Ecology* 8: 209–228 (1984).

4. *Cox v. Tyrone Power Enterprises*, 49 Cal. App. 2d 383 (1942).

5. *State v. Miller*, 149 Wash. 545 (Wash. 1928).

6. Room, Adrian. *The Naming of Animals: An Appellative Reference to Domestic, Work, and Show Animals, Real and Fictional*. Jefferson, NC: McFarland, 1993. Rothfels, Nigel. *Representing Animals*. Bloomington: Indiana University Press, 2002.

7. Lynch, Michael, and Steve Woolgar. "Representation in Scientific Practice." (1990) at p. 5.

8. Baker, Steve. *Picturing the Beast: Animals, Identity, and Representation*. Urbana: University of Illinois, 2001.

9. Akhtar, Salman, and Vamik D. Volkan, eds. *Cultural Zoo: Animals in the Human Mind and its Sublimation*. Abingdon, UK: Routledge, 2018.

10. See, e.g., Parson, Glenn. "The Aesthetic Value of Animals." *Environmental Ethics* 29, no. 2 (2007): 151–169.

11. Hearne, Vicki. *Adam's Task: Calling Animals by Name*. New York: Knopf, 1986.

12. Duckler, G. "The Economic Value of Companion Animals: A Legal and Anthropological Argument for Special Valuation." *Animal L.* 8 (2002): 199.

13. The use of common names is for convenience. Cougars, panthers, mountain lions, and pumas, for instance, are all the same species described under different names due to regional and cultural histories.

14. Claude Bernard discerned as much in his experimental work turning rabbits temporarily carnivorous. See Bernard, Claude. *An Introduction to the Study of Experimental Medicine*. Translated into English by Copley Green, with an introduction by Lawrence J. Henderson and a foreword by I. Bernard Cohen (1865).

15. Duckler, G. "The Economic Value of Companion Animals: A Legal and Anthropological Argument for Special Valuation." *Animal L.* 8 (2002): 199.

16. Holmes, Oliver Wendell. *The Common Law*. Cambridge, MA: Belknap of Harvard University Press, 2009.

17. Scientists are not immune to partiality in this area:

The peculiar fascination of the primates and their publicity value have almost taken the order out of the hands of sober and conservative mammologists and have kept, and do keep, its taxonomy in a turmoil. Moreover, even mammologists who might be entirely conservative in dealing, say, with rats are likely to lose a sense of perspective when they come to the primates, and many studies of this order are covertly or overtly emotional.

Simpson, George Gaylord. "The Principles of Classification and a Classification of Mammals." *Bull. Amer. Museum Nat. History.* 85 (1945) at p. 181.

18. Darwin's influence on case law addressing human–animal relationships has been negligble. Only a handful of cases even cite Darwin as authority for a scientific proposition, and those all post-2004: one begrudged Darwin's work as support for the idea that behavioral, genetic, and phenotypic differences occur between hatchery and natural fish (*Trout Unlimited v. Lohn*, CV06–0483-JCC, 2007 WL 1795036, at 1 (WD Wash June 13, 2007), *aff'd in part, rev'd in part*, 559 F3d 946 (9th Cir 2009)); a second acknowledged that "disease, degeneration and death" are "normal," and "may even benefit some species" (*In re Union Pacific R.R. Employment Practices Litigation*, 378 F.Supp.2d 1139 (D. Neb. 2005); and a third noted that many "life forms" are threatened by loss of ozone since "all species apparently evolved with ozone cover" (*Covington v. Jefferson County*, 358 F.3d 626 (9th Cir. 2004)).

19. *Meyers v. Neeld*, 137 Neb. 428 (Neb. 1940).

20. See Marx, Karl (trans. E. & C. Paul) *Collected Works.* Vol. 3. London: Lawrence & Wishart, 1975..

21. *Wisbey v. Nationwide Mut. Ins. Co.*, 507 P.2d 17 (Or. 1973).

22. Mack, Arien. "Humans and Other Animals." (1999).

23. *People v. Shanklin*, 769 N.E. 2d 547 (Ill. App. 2002).

24. 510 ILCS 70, Section 16(c)(1).

25. *LeBlanc v. Hayes*, 827 So. 2d 611 (La. App. 2002).

26. Norton, Bryan G. "Conservation and Preservation: A Conceptual Rehabilitation." *Environmental Ethics* 8.3 (1986): 195–220 at pp. 181, 197, 198–99.

27. *Johnson v. Center for Animal Care and Control, Inc.*, 192 Misc. 2d 210 (2002 N.Y. slip op.).

28. *Blair v. DuMond*, 280 A.D. 1021 (3d Dept. 1952) (authorizing peace officer to kill on sight any dog at large in violation of a curfew order).

29. *State v. Garcia*, 3 Misc. 3d 699 (2004 N.Y. slip op.).

30. Dennett, Daniel C. *Kinds of Minds: Toward an Understanding of Consciousness.* New York: Basic Books, 2008.

31. Geisel, Theodor. *The Sneetches.* New York: Random House, 1961.

32. See, e.g., Nurse, Angus. *Animal Harm: Perspectives on Why People Harm and Kill Animals.* Abingdon, UK: Routledge, 2016.

33. See, e.g., *State v. Klein,* 98 Or 116 (1920) (reversal of conviction for wantonly and maliciously killing a cow).

34. See, e.g., *State v. Pinard,* 255 Or. App. 417 (2013) (conviction for maliciously killing a dog).

35. *The King v. Oldner & Brilehan*, 2 Va. Colonial Dec. B90, 1739 WL 4 (Va. Gen. Ct. 1739).

36. See Taimie L. Bryant, *Sacrificing the Sacrifice of Animals: Legal Personhood for Animals, the Status of Animals as Property, and the Presumed Primacy of Humans*, 39 *Rutgers L. J.* 247 (2008); Tom L. Beauchamp, *The Failure of Theories of Personhood, Personhood and Health Care* 59, 59–69 (1999).

37. Sections of this chapter are extensions of ideas first articulated in Duckler, Geordie. "Animals as Criminals." *J. Animal & Envtl. L.* 10 (2018): 20.

38. Evans, Edward Payson. *The Criminal Prosecution and Capital Punishment of Animals*. London: W. Heinemann, 1906.

39. Id. at 10.

40. See, e.g., Topsell, E. *The Historie of Four-Footed Beastes.* London: E. Coates, 1607.

41. Id. at 34–35.

42. Evans, Edward Payson. *The Criminal Prosecution and Capital Punishment of Animals*. London: W. Heinemann, 1906.

43. *State v. Nix*, 283 P.3d 442 (Or. Ct. App. 2012), *aff'd*, 355 Or. 777 (2014), *vac'd,* 356 Or 768 (2015), and *vac'd,* 356 Or. 768 (2015).

44. A rough calculation currently accepted by paleontologists from the basis of the molecular evidence for when the human lineage departed company from the other African apes.

45. Cf. David G. Ritchie, *"Free-Will and Responsibility,"* 5:4 *The International Journal of Ethics* 409, 409–31 (1985); Robert E. Gahringer, *"Punishment and Responsibility,"* 66:10 *The Journal of Philosophy* 291, 291–306 (1969).

46. Mackay, Ronald D. *Mental Condition Defences in the Criminal Law*. Oxford, UK: Oxford University Press, 1995.

47. Francis Bowes Sayre, *"Mens rea,"* 45:6 *Harv. L. Rev.* 974–1026 (1932).

48. *Commonwealth v. Leach*, 1 Mass. 59 (1804) (regarding the poisoning of cattle).

49. Under Washington law, for example, RCW 16.08.030 makes it a crime to *not* kill some animals: "It shall be the duty of any person owning or keeping any dog or dogs which shall be found killing any domestic animal to kill such dog or dogs within forty-eight hours after being notified of that fact, and any person failing or neglecting to comply with the provisions of this section shall be deemed guilty of a misdemeanor. . . ."

50. See, e.g., *State v. Rawson*, 62 N.E. 3d 880 (Ohio Ct. App. 2016) (criminalizing the tormenting of a dog).

51. See Robson, William Newby. *The Principles of Legal Liability for Trespasses and Injuries by Animals*. Cambridge University Press, 2014.

52. See, e.g., Poe, Edgar Allen. *The Murders in the Rue Morgue* in Bell, HW, *Tales of Mystery and Imagination* (1904) (where a sailor's recklessness in allowing a murderous orangutan to run free effectively comprises a form of manslaughter).

53. See, e.g., *State v. Bodoh*, 595 N.W.2d 330 (Wis. 1999) (dogs can be considered "dangerous weapon"); See generally Fern L. Kletter, Annotation, *Dogs as Deadly or Dangerous Weapon for Purposes of Statutes Aggravating Offenses Such as Assault and Robbery*, 124 A.L.R.5th 657 (2017).

54. This topic has been extensively examined by historians. *See*, Walter Woodburn Hyde, "The Prosecution and Punishment of Animals and Lifeless Things in the

Middle Ages and Modern Times," 64 *U. Pa. L. Rev.* 696, 706–07 (1916); Jen Girgen, "The Historical and Contemporary Prosecution and Punishment of Animals," 9 *Animal L.* 97, 101 (2003); Paul Schiff Berman, "Rats, Pigs, and Statues on Trial: The Creation of Cultural Narratives in the Prosecution of Animals and Inanimate Objects," 69 *N.Y.U. L. Rev.* 288, 290 (1994).

55. See, e.g., *People v. Lawson*, 215 Cal App. 4th 108 (2013).

56. Fox, Harold Munro. *The Personality of Animals.* Melbourne: Penguin, 1952.

57. Hornaday, William Temple. *The Minds and Manners of Wild Animals: A Book of Personal Observations.* New York: C. Scribner's Sons, 1923 at p. 75.

58. See Buck, Frank, and Edward Anthony. *Bring 'em Back Alive.* Simon and Schuster, 1930 at pg. 291: "I was once asked to write a story of the jungle in which the animals had a 'code.' I had to refuse, not knowing anything about this phenomenon. If there is such a thing it has escaped me. Life in the jungle is a free-for-all fight, no fouls recognized, and no weight limits."

59. Mitchell, Robert W., Nicholas S. Thompson, and H. Lyn Miles, eds. *Anthropomorphism, Anecdotes, and Animals.* Suny Press, 1997 at pp. 48–49.

60. Mary Coate McNeely, "A Footnote on Dangerous Animals," 37:8 *Michigan L. Rev.* 1181–1208 (1939).

61. See *People v. Frazier*, 92 Cal. Rptr. 3d 794 (Cal. App. 3d. Dist. 2009) ("Despite the physical ability to commit vicious and violent acts, dogs do not possess the legal ability to commit crimes. As a consequence, a dog cannot be a principal to a crime.").

62. Lawson, Frederick Henry, and Basil S. Markesinis. *Tortious Liability for Unintentional Harm in the Common Law and the Civil Law: Volume II, Materials.* Vol. 120. CUP Archive, 1982 at pp. 42–143.

63. Darwin, Charles. *The Expression of the Emotions in Man and Animals.* Kartindo. com, 1948.

64. Osborne, Catherine, and Catherine Rowett. *Dumb Beasts and Dead Philosophers: Humanity and the Humane in Ancient Philosophy and Literature.* Oxford, UK: Oxford University Press, 2007 at pp. 64–65, 74.

65. Duckler, G. "The Necessity of Treating Animals as Legal Objects" 7(2): 1, 5 *University of Louisville Louis D. Brandeis School of Law Journal of Animal and Environmental Law* 45 (2016).

66. See, e.g., *Rhodes v. Walsh*, 55 Minn 542 (1893) ("All citizens should be deemed to stand equal in their rights before the law. This country recognizes no special privileged class . . .").

67. Evans, Edward Payson. *The Criminal Prosecution and Capital Punishment of Animals.* London: W. Heinemann (1906) at p. 236.

68. Id. at 247.

69. Id. at 249.

70. Kennedy, David M. *Deterrence and Crime Prevention: Reconsidering the Prospect of Sanction.* Abingdon, UK: Routledge, 2012.

71. See Zuberbühler, Klaus, David Jenny, and Redouan Bshary. "The Predator Deterrence Function of Primate Alarm Calls." *Ethology* 105, no. 6 (1999): 477–490.

72. The prevailing belief in this area, termed "the progression thesis" or the "violence graduation hypothesis," claims that people who harm animals must be people

who a) historically have themselves been harmed, b) presently harm in general, and c) prospectively are likely to harm people in future scenarios. *See,* ORS 609.650 "The Legislative Assembly finds that . . . there is a clear link between animal cruelty and crimes of domestic violence, including child abuse . . ." Sociological and statistical research on the thesis, however, reveals there is no objectively established causal correlation between cruelty to animals and the impulse to violence to any person or group. See Felthous, Alan R. & Stephen R. Kellert, *"Childhood Cruelty to Animals and Later Aggression Against People: A Review," The American Journal of Psychiatry* (1987); Arluke, Arnold, et al., *"The Relationship of Animal Abuse to Violence and Other Forms of Antisocial Behavior,"* 14:9 *Journal of Interpersonal Violence* 963, 975 (1999); Stephen R. Kellert & Alan R. Felthous, *"Childhood Cruelty Toward Animals among Criminals and Noncriminals,"* 18 *Human Relations* 1113, 1129 (1985); Karla S. Miller & John F. Knutson, *"Reports of Severe Physical Punishment and Exposure to Animal Cruelty by Inmates Convicted of Felonies and by University Students,"* 21 *Child Abuse & Neglect* 59, 82 (1997); Suzanne E. Tallichet & Christopher Hensley, *"Exploring the Link Between Recurrent Acts of Childhood and Adolescent Animal Cruelty and Subsequent Violent Crime,"* 29:2 *Criminal Justice Review* 304, 316 (2004); Piers Beirne, *"From Animal Abuse to Interhuman Violence? A Critical Review of the Progression Thesis,"* 12:1 *Society & Animals* 39, 65 (2004): Glenn D. Walters, "Testing the Specificity Postulate of the Violence Graduation Hypothesis: Meta-analyses of the Animal Cruelty–Offending Relationship," 18.6 *Aggression and Violent Behavior* 797, 802 (2013).

73. See, e.g., Flynn, Clifton P. *Social Creatures: A Human and Animal Studies Reader.* Brooklyn, NY: Lantern Books, 2008 at pp. 169–230. Under the heading "Criminology and Deviance," that volume lists articles addressing cruelty and violence to animals by people, not the other way around.

74. See Robinson, Paul H., and Jane A. Grall. "Element Analysis in Defining Criminal Liability: The Model Penal Code and Beyond." *Stanford Law Review* (1983): 681–762.

75. See *State v. Kiehl,* 78 N.E.3d 1226 (Ohio Ct. App. 2016).

76. *Granier v. Chagnon,* 122 Mont. 327 (1949).

77. *Dodson v. Mock,* 20 N.C. 282 (1838).

78. See, e.g., ORS 608.015 "Civil liability for animals trespassing on adequately fenced land situated on open range."

79. See, e.g., ORS 608.015(2).

80. See *Towe v. Sacagawea, Inc.,* 347 P.3d 766 (Or. 2015).

81. See, e.g., *Stewart ex rel. Hill v. Kralman,* 248 P.3d 6 (Or. App. 2011) (referring to "trespassers" in terms of recreational lands immunity statutes).

82. See, e.g., *D.E. v. Com.,* 271 S.W.3d 539 (Ky. App. 2008) (referring to trespassers).

83. See Rowlands, Mark. *Animals Like Us.* Brooklyn, NY: Verso, 2002; Mack, Arien. *Humans and Other Animals.* Columbus, OH: Ohio State University Press, 1999.

84. Philippe Rochat & Susan J. Hespos, "Differential Rooting Response by Neonates: Evidence for an Early Sense of Self," 6.3:4 *Early Development and Parenting* (1997): 105–112.

85. Id.

86. Id.

87. See, e.g., *Giles v. Russell*, 180 S.E.2d 201 (S.C. 1971) ("It is not likely that the traits of an animal will change rapidly").

88. Manderson, Desmond. *Courting Death*. London: Pluto Press, 1999. p. 1. ("But the human animal, at least, is different. The shadow of time past and the darkness of death to come fall over and structure our lives"). Manderson's view of the sense of mortality as unique to the human experience summons forth Omar Khayyam.

89. Lorenz, Konrad. *Man Meets Dog*. New York: Kodansha America, 1994 at p. 195.

90. Randolph Clarke & Justin Capes, "Incompatibilist (nondeterministic) Theories of Free Will." *Stanford Encyclopedia of Philosophy* (2000): 1, 214.

91. Id.

92. Walter, Henrik. *Neurophilosophy of Free Will: From Libertarian Illusions to a Concept of Natural Autonomy*. Cambridge, MA: MIT Press, 2009.

93. Zaibert, Leo. *Five Ways Patricia Can Kill Her Husband: A Theory of Intentionality and Blame*. Chicago: Open Court Publishing Company, 2005.

94. See generally Joseph D. Grano, "Voluntariness, Free Will, and the Law of Confessions," 65 *Va. L. Rev.* 859–945 (1979).

95. Edward B. Arnolds & Norman F. Garland, "The Defense of Necessity in Criminal Law: The Right to Choose the Lesser Evil," 65 *J. Crim. L. & Criminology* 289, 289–301 (1974).

96. See *Williams v. State*, 2016-KA-00552-SCT (Miss. 2017) (explaining duress defense).

97. See generally Hinde, Robert A. *Animal Behavior: A Synthesis of Ethology and Comparative Psychology,* New York: McGraw-Hill, 1966, for a comprehensive survey.

98. Strawson, Galen. *Freedom and Belief: Revised Edition*. Oxford, UK: Oxford University Press, 2010.

99. That is not to say animal behavior is simplistic for universally the opposite is true; it is just to say that it is mechanistic, albeit complex. See, e.g., Ewer, Rosalie Francis. *Ethology of Mammals*. New York: Springer, 2013:

Observation of an animal's behavior can distinguish between motivations produced by external stimuli and by changes occurring within the organism, but cannot tell where inside it the latter takes place. . . . Selection must operate to produce an animal that behaves appropriately and does the right thing at the right time, but there is no *a priori* reason why all motivational systems should function identically. Indeed, one might well expect the reverse: considerable diversity in the detailed manner in which internal changes affect the performance of different activities.

100. See, e.g., *State v. Jones*, 229 Kan. 528 (1981).

101. Hart, Herbert Lionel Adolphus. "The Concept of Law by HLA Hart." (1961) at pp. 84–85.

102. *State v. Nix*, 356 Or. 758 (2015).

Chapter 4

Property, Ownership, and Control

"The Worldly Hope Men Set Their Hearts Upon"[1]

> Pet keeping, virtually a civilized institution, is an abyss of covert and unconscious uses of animals in the service of psychological needs, glossed over as play and companionship.[2]

In law's recitation of their use and ownership, animals are "tangible personal properties," i.e., physically movable objects capable of being possessed and conveyed to others.[3] Property laws revolve around ideas of care, custody and control of all sorts of objects, and they impose very distinct burdens and constrain very distinct freedoms on human behavior. In law, all property must have some owner somewhere, either privately or by the state. Some properties have their own legal identities and accumulate explicit rules that adhere to their use (e.g., motor vehicles), while others are deemed to be merely the mechanisms, infrastructure, or superstructure that make other properties socially or economically interesting, yet themselves have no special rules applicable to them (e.g., the component parts of a motor vehicle).

THE DISTINCTIVE COMPARTMENTS OF "PERSONAL PROPERTIES" AND HOW ANIMALS FIT INSIDE

The division of property into real and personal creates a functionally significant test as to whether an object's value derives from being easily manipulated. That benefit of being easily detachable from the land, however, carries with it the corollary detriment of having its attainment and control made more difficult. Control also affects whether the personal property is natural or manufactured, the latter being those items, products, and goods intentionally modified by people. A lump of clay is thus jurisprudentially distinct from a vase solely because of what someone has done to the clay to make it into the vase as a product. Manufactured personal property takes as its presumption that the manufacturing itself, that is, the human manipulation of the natural object, has been engaged in for a reasonable use or to facilitate consumption in some sense, for food perhaps, clothing, or aesthetic enjoyment.[4]

As natural personal properties, animals are connected to their owners in usual and in unusual ways. Governmental ownership of animals relies on the concept of them being deemed "*ferae naturae*": as long as an animal remains wild, unconfined and undomesticated, no individual property rights can exist in the animal and it belongs to the state alone.[5] Qualified private property rights only arise in animals when they are legally removed from their natural liberty and made subject to a person's control. The qualified private right is lost and reverts to the state if the animal regains its natural liberty.

The private ownership of animals is therefore a reward one earns for undergoing the risks involved with restraint and confinement and for assuming the cloak of responsibility that the state sheds at the moment of confinement.[6] Animals are proprietary trade goods in that their use and enjoyment has been bought and paid for in three respects: the wresting of control away from implied state control, the manual labor of capture and confinement, and the acceptance of personal liability for social problems arising later with their use once they have been captured and confined:

> Fault as understood in the nineteenth century clearly 'presupposed free will . . . and beyond that also the notions that the actor had a choice in the conduct in question between doing it in a perceptibly dangerous way and doing it in some feasible, safer way. Holmes emphasizes this element of choice and reminds us that "a choice which entails a concealed consequence is, as to that consequence, no choice". Thus, legal negligence involved something of personal moral shortcoming; the man who was held liable had been guilty of ethical as well as legal wrong. And since fault involved a more or less informed choice, it was possible to see how the prospect of liability could influence the choice for the better. This last sentence underlines the social utility of the concept. For in addition to keeping liability under control, it also helped edify potential defendants by encouraging them to behave more carefully.[7]

Codes from all manner of jurisdictions create further subdivisions of animals as personal properties under schema in which the designations track the animals' guises as either local trade items or as nonlocal objects potentially injurious to trade or to people. Through the lens of the lawyer-scientist, we can fashion the most pragmatic of those definitions by collating legal and economic terms:

Domestic (or pet) animals are defined as a) domesticated animals, b) with no commercial value, c) kept inside of or around a private residence, d) which are indigenous to the jurisdiction defining them, and e) the utility of which is almost exclusively aesthetic and symbolic (e.g., dogs and cats). A subcategory is *assistance animals*, often defined as domestics specially trained to assist persons with disabilities, with their utility being as the functional replacements of devices designed to enhance a person's mobility and/ or sensory perceptions.[8]

Livestock animals are defined as a) domesticated animals, b) with potential commercial value, c) kept outside of or around a private residence and d) the utility of which is primarily for transport, entertainment, and/or consumption (e.g., horses, mules, cattle, sheep, pigs, and fowl).

Wildlife animals are defined as a) undomesticated animals, b) with no commercial value, c) which are indigenous to the jurisdiction defining them, and d) the utility of which is aesthetic and ecological (e.g., wolves and bears). A subcategory is *game* animals, often defined as wildlife with potential commercial value and with their utility being for entertainment and consumption (e.g., detailed lists of certain birds, fish and mammals commonly hunted for sport or food).[9]

Predatory (or pest) animals are defined as a) undomesticated animals, b) potentially destructive to agricultural crops or to game animals, c) which are indigenous to the jurisdiction defining them, and d) which have either no utility at all (e.g., weevils) or have very limited utility for their pelts or plumage (e.g., coyotes, rabbits, rodents and certain birds).

Exotic animals are defined as a) undomesticated animals, b) with no commercial value, c) which are *not* indigenous to the jurisdiction defining them, and d) the utility of which is almost exclusively as educational or entertainment devices (e.g., primates, large felids, and many perissodactyls).

The designations of all the groupings filter neatly around their utility and location in comparison to people, and for that reason have an artificial narrowness in the context of biology. To the scientist, the baffling exclusion of a massive span of other animal life is jarring—there is no place within any of those categories for earthworms or blue whales or much that is in between. To the lawyer, the exclusions don't matter much but the inclusions raise the worry of behaviors that have a deleterious effect on workable regulation. The question of how property rules as to non-animate properties work in conjunction with what the listed animals actually do in real life becomes problematic. While a substantial list could be compiled itemizing the myriad ways in which animals as tangible natural objects are distinct from tangible manufactured or nonanimal objects, lawyers are most intrigued by three, each being some enigmatic expression of independence that no bowl or handbag has ever exhibited:

1. The ability to manifest some form of intent to make independent decisions.
2. The ability to move themselves about independently.
3. The ability to independently compound their value over time.

Why the significance of these phenomena, as opposed, say, to observations that dogs, but not handbags or hand grenades, can bark or dig or whine or scratch or breathe or eat? For one, those three behaviors seem to strike a serious blow to the proclamation above that they don't have free will, and observing their spontaneous motions persistently tempts the lawyer to want to infer human-like underpinnings to why they are doing so. Two, it is those particular behaviors that dramatically impact our effective control of them, and if they are to be truly usable objects, then those events need to somehow be legally accounted for.

OWNERSHIP OF OBJECTS AND ITS INTIMATE RELATION TO PRACTICALITIES OF CONTROL AND EXCLUSION

Let's begin by comparing animals to another set of objects that wiggle all around the place: stars. There is a business entity called the International Star Registry where one can "buy" a star and name it after a person, all for about $50.00. Ostensibly it is the purchaser's star and no one else's, and for their money they get a nice certificate memorializing the purchase. There is no exclusivity at all to that ownership of course—buyers certainly can't possess what they bought in the sense that one can with most other purchased objects. Buyers can't restrict another's access to the star, or even prevent them from renaming it after a different person, buyers can't enjoy (or prevent others from enjoying) its attributes based on any manipulation of it, and buyers certainly can't derive any real financial or utilitarian value out of being the star's declared "owner." Because of the nature of what stars actually are, ownership rights in stars are entirely illusory.

On the other hand, there is no International Ant Registry, where one can purchase an ant, and name it, and get a gold-embossed certificate about their ant. Entomologists estimate somewhere around one quadrillion (one with 15 zeros after it) ants doing their thing on every continent in the world at any given moment, so lack of a registry is certainly not based on any concerns of supply shortages—there are plenty of ants everywhere for everyone to have by simply looking down at their feet. Knowing what we know about the eccentricities of consumers, there is also probably no shortage of people willing to buy one, if only for the novelty of the experience. Finally, the characteristics among and between all the ants *in* the world are about as negligible (to anyone other than an entomologist) as are the characteristics among and between all the stars *out of* the world (to anyone other than an astronomer), so some special physical quality of what makes up each individual ant is not a decisive difference either, at least to the lay public.

Yet ants are treated quite differently than stars in the way the law considers them as legal objects. This is because the common law memorializes the historical understanding that people can physically obtain, manipulate, corral, control, and thus own animals, a group of which ants are definitely a part, and thus allows people to assert exclusionary rights in animals to run to their personal benefit and to the detriment of others even in spite of the complications created by independent motions. The stars versus ants example tells us this: ownership rights in animals are real legal constructs and are not illusory, that motion and replication effects are snags in the mill but not rejections of the overall capacity to run the mill, and they all begin with the putative owner having to take real steps to do a real something. So, what is it the prospective animal owner must do?

THE PURSUIT AND CAPTURE OF "BEASTS" AS A MANDATE FOR THEIR OWNERSHIP

Well, for one thing, to become an animal owner, one must first wrestle physical control of the animal away from everybody else, run away from them or run toward them as it might. One can't just "register" an ant and thereby become its owner, a person has to go out into the wild and capture one. Two hundred years ago, the law accepted that if it was in a person's interests to try to kill some wild thing and that person was pretty good at it, then they'd be assumed to have succeeded in being its owner—or at least of what was left of it after "mortally wounding" it. The classic case of *Pierson v. Post* states the curiously phrased rule:

> The mortal wounding of such beasts, by one not abandoning his pursuit, may, with the utmost propriety, be deemed possession of him; since, thereby, the pursuer manifests an unequivocal intention of appropriating the animal to his individual use, has deprived him of his natural liberty, and brought him within his certain control.[10]

Primitive and historically distant it may be, but the *Pierson v. Post* rule haunts us every day. We "reduce to our actual possession and control" tens of thousands of wild animals over the course of our lifetimes, mostly bugs, mosquitoes, flies, and ants. The fact that they aren't very likable, or very big, or very dangerous "wild" animals changes nothing—the fact is they are animals, were in the wild, we did pursue and mortally wound them, and thus took the time and the effort to deprive them of their natural liberty (while then probably disposing them moments later). The human effort, not the animal targeted, is what conceptually matters:

> There is a famous saying in the Laws of Manu that a ploughed strip of reclaimed land belongs as much to the tiller as the deer brought down by an arrow belongs to the hunter. [I]t is neither land as such nor the animal as such that is claimed as property, but the result of the personal exertion of the tiller and of the hunter.[11]

Now, some legal categories of animals that we take the time to "reduce to actual possession and control" we value higher than others, such as domestic, livestock, and game animals since once we attain them there is a concrete benefit to consuming, riding, or wearing them. Chasing, capturing, and confining animals spans a wide range of effort, from slight to nearly impossible. A lynx, a mosquito, and an oyster each offer a unique challenge within that range, and while the value of the animal captured may reflect the varying level of effort and risk, the ownership right that results remains relatively constant:

> The owner [of oysters] has the same absolute property in them that he has in inanimate things or in domestic animals. Like domestic animals, they continue perpetually in his occupation, and will not stray from his house or person. Unlike animals *feræ naturæ*, they do not require to be reclaimed and made tame by art, industry, or education; nor to be confined, in order to be within the immediate power of the owner. If at liberty, they have neither the inclination nor the power to escape. For the purposes of the present inquiry, they are obviously more nearly assimilated to tame animals than to wild ones, and, perhaps, more nearly to inanimate objects than to animals of either description. The indictment could not aver that the oysters were dead, for they would then be of no value; nor that they were reclaimed or tamed, for in this sense they were never wild, and were not capable of domestication; nor that they were confined, for that would be absurd.[12]

We haven't domesticated lynx or mosquitoes, nor are we ever likely to,[13] but we have domesticated dogs and cats, and even though we may become their owners in the same *Pierson v. Post* manner just explained, we give an additional beneficial significance to dogs and cats in a way that legally distinguishes them from lynx, mosquitoes, oysters, ants, or stars for that matter.

What is transformative with dogs and cats is how the establishment of owner-ship rights is so tangled up in their own mutualistic, reciprocal, and socially interactive conduct with us.

Formally establishing ownership is another matter. With either personal properties, such as cars, or with real properties, such as houses, there are socially and legally approved indicia reflecting who the owner is. For one thing, owners of those objects possess a title (as with a car) or a deed (as with a house) formally documenting its purchase, the "official" memorialization of an exclusive right to control from one to another for consideration. There is no "pursuing, capturing, and appropriating" houses and cars in order to own them and, sit in rust or go up in flames, an owner preserves their status as long as their name is on the right piece of paper.

HOW THE CONCEPTUAL CAPTURE OF A DOG ESTABLISHES ITS OWNERSHIP

No formal document attends ownership of a dog, on the other hand, as far as the common law is concerned. One may have an invoice from a pet store, vet record from an animal hospital, AKC registration paper, ribbon from a dog show, or photograph of the puppy being whelped, all indicating aspects of exclusive ownership, yet all are just that: indicia (weak or strong) of owner-ship, not legally dispositive articles.

With properties such as cars and houses, the transactions conveying them between people rely on the existence of a reliable market for such items. We feel comfortable using financial documents that reflect the objective value of the house or car to other consumers in the market as proof, but with ani-mals, especially dogs, the existence of a uniformly agreed-upon market is not certain; although animals are bought and sold privately and publicly, their indeterminable yet finite lifespans and radically changing behaviors moment by moment turns their initial purchase price inconsequential. The dog bought at one date is a different dog later depending on what one has been doing with it in the interim, and dogs tend to appreciate, not depreciate, in value in light of an owner's investment and involvement.

Stranger still, and inapposite as to how we treat other tangible personal properties, is the idea that, as a dog's value increases, its owner becomes *less* willing to either accept value for the animal or impart monetary value to the animal at all. The St. Bernard embedded inside a family home for a decade is found to have eerily changed to become "priceless" compared to the very pricey St. Bernard that was not a day ago coaxed out of the pet store window.

We will address economic factors in closer detail in the next chapter, but for now consider the cartoon dog Scooby-Doo as an illustration whose distinctive qualities and behaviors offer insight on ownership indicia. What does the law say about who owns Scooby-Doo? Is it the person who fashioned his collar or tag, who purchased or carries the snacks, who walks next to him, or who converses with him? The cartoon offers a host of potential candidates to the lawyer interested in discerning whose claim is strongest. Who initially bought the dog or who publicly claims to be his owner are, as with real world dogs, not nearly as significant as the "actions and activities" of those interacting with him.[14] Reciprocally benefiting behaviors means that exchanges of conduct between people and dogs imparts discrete legal burdens and discrete legal benefits from one to the other, Scooby-Doo and his gang included. The exchanges have civil and criminal effects: we impose civil liability and criminal responsibility on the putative owner for lack of care for or harm to the dog, as well as for the dog's own harmful acts against others. The benefits in turn are a bevy of genuine advantages, emotive and otherwise, including an ability to recoup compensation for its injury or destruction by another.[15]

The *Pierson v. Post* capture of Scooby-Doo is magnitudes more complex than the swatting of a bee. It is a maelstrom of behavioral interchanges among him and those people around him—forces pulling the participants hither and yon via cavalier disregards of command by the dog, earnest proffers of food by people, or the evasion of hostile influences by both. Ownership tests account for actions a dog engages in as property that the law does not take into account with respect to any other object, and folds into the equation the consideration that whatever a person may have themselves decided about an animal, the animal may have decided something contrary about the person, and the current actions and activity of people competing in maintaining control set the stage.

In looking to *what* the potential owner is doing, not necessarily *who* the potential owner is, animal ownership reduces the importance of status or position and increases the importance of behavior, specifically animal control-related conduct exchanges. "Actions, attitude and understanding" are vitally important to our concerns over animal ownership. Holding yourself out to the world as the owner of a handbag or a hamburger does not require the participation of either handbag or hamburger—but doing so with a dog does. That a dog may have several owners in its lifetime is no more remarkable a statement than that a car may have several owners in its lifetime. But you do not have to alter what you physically do and who you personally are to become and remain a car owner, as you do with being an animal owner. While an owner does not lose their rights to an animal just because the animal leaves their premises, an owner may lose their rights if they lose their care, custody or control of the animal—regardless of where that animal is. Even then it may not be enough since the animal may make independent decisions that are adverse to an owner's own desires to remain its owner.

ANIMAL OWNERSHIP AS A SHIFTING FORCE

In the horror movie *Fallen*, the antagonist is an invisible demon who moves from one character to the next, taking over a person's body for a brief period before moving on to inhabit whomever is nearby (the movie ends with the demon possessing a cat, to the chagrin or satisfaction of the viewer depending on one's feelings about cats).[16] "*Fallen*'s" theme is a common one in science fiction and horror movies—this idea that possession of the inner interests of a person may be at one and the same time both real and phantom-like: *The Thing*, *Invasion of the Body Snatchers*, and a hundred other similarly creepy tales prey on threats we may feel to our preservation of innate personhood or identity.

The legal recognition of animal ownership accomplishes much the same thing but with a difference: not just as a weight, but also in part as a reward, does animal ownership possess a person, that is, inhabit them (thematically) like a demon. Legal ownership in animals reveals itself as an apparition, a specter granted temporary legitimacy by the interaction of the animal and the person—not by the solidity of a formal title, deed, invoice, or statement, but by the flimsiness of present interactions alone. If one rests or pauses in asserting their interest, ownership may flit off them and onto the next vessel. One is not cloaked with animal ownership as a landed privilege because of who one is—a child, a spouse, a consumer—but is cloaked with it as a reminder of what one does instead—and more importantly what one has done lately.

Pierson v. Post is over two centuries old and counting, and the solidity of rules on who owns animals and exactly how they own them is situated close by a chasm between "us" and "them," a tremendous gap created and maintained by the exploitation of usage through domestication, by that developed sociality, by the unique evolutionary adaptation called language, and by our historical construction of morality, none of which animals manifest and all of which separate us[17]:

> One of the central and fundamental motivations for human action is to act out and sustain moral order, which helps constitute, directs, and makes significant human life itself. Human persons nearly universally live in social worlds that are thickly webbed with moral assumptions, beliefs, commitments, and obligations. The relational ties that hold human lives together, the conversations that occupy people's mental lives, the routines and intentions that shape their actions, the institutions within which they live and work, the emotions they feel

every day—all of these and more are drenched in, patterned by, glued together with moral premises, convictions, and obligations. These morally constituted and permeated worlds exist outside of people, in structured social practices and relationships within which people's lives are embedded. They also exist "inside" of people, in their assumptions, expectations, beliefs, aspirations, thoughts, judgments, and feelings. There is nowhere a human can go to escape moral order; there is no way to be human except through moral order. Human animals are moral animals in that we possess a capacity and propensity unique among all animals: we not only have desires, beliefs, and feelings, (which often have strong moral qualities) but also the ability and disposition to form strong evaluations about our desires, beliefs, and feelings that hold the potential to transform them.[18]

Smith's words above about our morality being inherent in our sociality apply in spades to animal ownership; our exploitation of animals, our social interactions with them are equally "drenched in, patterned by, glued together with" moral premises, convictions, and obligations about them. Concerns about another wishing to treat an animal like a car, a toy, a buddy, or a child, are universally couched in terms of the "morality" of doing so where answers formulated about the propriety of a proposed model are invariably phrased in the language of right and wrong, decency and indecency, what's fair or unfair to the animal and to other people. As cartoons are designed to do, the world of Scooby-Doo glosses over notions of morality and fairness in owner–animal relations, but it, like its protagonist, never strays too far from its loyalties to and intimate connections with people as those in charge.

ANIMALS BEING NEITHER CHILDREN TO A PARENT NOR WARDS TO A GUARDIAN

Were dogs to truly be just like cars, then we would treat their ownership and regulation similarly, requiring they be tattooed with a Very Important Number (VIN), accompanied by a title certificate, and supervised by a Department of Mangy Vertebrates (DMV) that would issue licenses, record VINs and titles as public documents, track mileage, monitor emissions, register claims about them, and impound and sell at auction those that are found abandoned or unlicensed. That they are not, and that there are no plans in the works for an International Dog Registry is not a comment on the impracticality or economics of such a project as with ants, but an acknowledgment of the emotional anxiety likely to issue over such "unfeeling" treatment of the target object.

VINs and DMVs for dogs[19] trigger a host of concerns, among them the morality of constructing such institutions given the complexities of our social relationships. Many of those tensions infect legal dispositions in court cases where a decision must be made regarding responsibility. One set of cases involve who is to be granted ownership of a dog that two parties previously co-owned together.[20] There, the "best interests" test (which courts regularly apply in family law custody cases in determining steps to take to protect the interests of a child affected by a dissolution) has been rejected as applying to animals. The highly subjective factors that are key to a best interests analysis concerning a child's feelings or perceptions as evidenced by statements, conduct, and evaluations, are "unascertainable" with animals.[21]

Another set of cases involve "protecting" an animal from a person or a person from an animal and include proposals to replace "owner" with "guardian." Linguistically emancipating dogs and cats from "ownership" doesn't prevent courts from still imposing liability on someone being legally responsible for their harmful acts, in spite of how "freed" the animal has ostensibly become from the ignominy of titles and deeds. Laws addressing daily concerns communities have about biting, noise, filth, and running at large are not restricted to "owners" in the first place since codes regularly impose legal obligations on those who "keep," "have custody of," "are responsible for," "care for," "harbor," "exercise control over," "permit to reside on property with," "are in charge of," or even "have the ultimate right to make decisions regarding disposition of," dogs and cats.

Neither type of case can ultimately avoid grappling with the concept of "animal control." In part, the "control" refers to controlling *people*: outlining the common law test, local ordinance, or administrative regulation that must be imposed regarding what can and can't be done with the animal someone must be in charge of. In part, the "control" equally refers to controlling *animals*: accounting for the technical restraints of leashes and fences with which people are obligated to corral animals as part of their compliance with obligations. A fretful optimism underlies both interpretations in the form of the panicky confidence we have that either animals or people can somehow *be* effectively controlled in the throes of their complex interactions.

At a base level, control of an animal involves a person being able to dictate the animal's physical location and to some extent the animal's generic state of health. Doing so isn't just because our large cerebral cortexes and opposable thumbs make it that we can, it is also because our complex social networks make it that we *must*: the manufacture and use of leashes, collars, muzzles, tethers, halters, saddles, fences, gates, and harnesses are as crucial as brakes are on cars: without them, a potentially dangerous object is transformed into an actually dangerous object. Restraint isn't limited to keeping locomotory movements in check, but includes limiting entire body systems as well, primarily excretory and reproduction systems. Until animals can voluntarily control their own bowels, bladders, sexual conduct, and procreation in the same manner that humans do, then restraint as to those functions is mandated by precepts devoted toward protecting communal safety and communal health. This comes clear in noting that dog owners, cattle ranchers, and zoo vets all often force severe restraints, including contraceptive measures on potentially breeding pairs to prevent surplus animals from being born.[22]

Beyond that, however, "control" gets dicey and, at a more philosophical level, can go off the rails entirely. Our rules about responsibility for animals flow from a premise that we have the ability and the interest to control not just animal bodies, but also animal behaviors. Rules about the use of other types of personal properties, from automobiles to antiques, hinge not on behavioral manipulation but on economic assessment and physical possession. The true "control" of a dog's behavior, as Scooby-Doo might himself articulate, is strikingly unattainable. Behavioral studies affirm that substantial control exerted over any species more complicated than a worm can permanently compromise physiological and psychological health.[23] Because animals are dynamic and change radically over time, then control tracks those changes, being situational and temporally specific throughout the life of each animal; just because control may be established at one moment in time does not mean that it is always in place under all circumstances.

Saying that we *can't* rigorously control all animal behaviors of course is not the same as saying that we don't *wish* to: In the tiny subset of *Animalia* we find encircling us daily, there are definitely behaviors we desire and behaviors we abhor, from poodles parading to pigeons pooping. In between those extremes, there is a dizzying span of complicated animal behaviors, however, that we are often in dispute with each other as to both their appeal and their effective regulation. The social and legal acceptability of a small wiener dog's behavior in the form of yelping, for instance, is a "relative measure" in that it may hinge on location (at a park versus on an airplane): on frequency (once versus 20 times); on circumstance (at noon on a summer's day versus at 3 am on a stormy night), or on a thousand other factors that both yelping and dogs tend to invoke in those people around them.

In that sense, then, definitional emphases such as "foster" or "guardian" are resolutely ineffectual in catapulting over the obstacle that we have designated *all* animals, not just horses, cows, pigs, sheep, dogs, and cats, but *all* as objects extractable from the natural world that can be and are obtained, restrained, marked out and specially identified, and for which remedies for loss have been carefully constructed. Within that vast pen, we have also designated dogs and cats as our "belongings," giving equal weight to the two primary connotations that that term evokes: first, the practical phenomenon of physically possessing them as tangible objects that can be conveyed and transferred among ourselves, manipulated by each individual owner, and eventually disposed of with whatever attendant consequences, and second, the psychological phenomenon of mentally desiring ("longing") for private enjoyment of something. In the case of pets, the "thing" turns out to be an object that transcends bare economic identity, and that cleverly parallels qualities cultivated in ourselves of being loved, appreciated, and providing a sense of personal emotional satisfaction.

THE VETERINARIAN-PATIENT RELATIONSHIP MODELS THE PERSON–OBJECT DICHOTOMY OF ANIMALS

Much about considerations of control and ownership come to a head in the practice of veterinary medicine. Veterinarians may employ emotionally assuaging strategies, but in reality they nonetheless treat the animal akin to a favorite but broken appliance to be fixed depending on model, parts availability, and price. The disparity between the veterinarian's kind words and their stark conduct is a function of veterinarians finding themselves enclosed by conceptual cages where they operate as garage mechanics, family therapists, and medical health professionals all rolled into one.

When one takes their child to a pediatrician, three roles develop: doctor, patient, and patient's parent. Since the patient is, by definition, a minor, the doctor must rely on the parent to consent to decisions about the child's health, and the parent must rely on the doctor explaining the propriety of a proposed course of treatment. Every state has healthcare laws specifically supporting that arrangement and outlining particular duties among those roles.

When one takes their dog to a veterinarian, three similar roles arise—doctor, patient, and patient's owner—and, as a practical matter, much of the same drama is played out in that, with the veterinarian's input, the owner parentally make the core decisions about what is ultimately done to the patient at what cost. No battery of heavily regulated healthcare laws apply to that interaction, however, and what is a legitimate medical practice in the veterinarian's office derives, not from healthcare statutes at all, but from laws on contract and sale regarding the ownership and conveyance of personal properties between market participants, as well as from administrative regulations regarding good animal husbandry practices intermixed with a bevy of tort rules regarding what the reasonable standard is for preventing or repairing damage to personal property.[24] Purely as a custom we tend to describe the dog as the "patient" but as a legal matter dogs do not have any status or rights that patients enjoy.

Viewing them in those respective roles, one again confronts that vast legal and moral chasm separating dogs from children, and nothing reveals that gulf better than pondering the possible range of decisions to be made in the respective examination rooms. One *cannot* contract with a doctor to euthanize their child, to destroy or remove parts of his body for sale to others, compel one kid to become pregnant or another to be rendered infertile.[25] One *cannot* employ a doctor to brand or mark their child for identification or tracking purposes, or pay them to license the child with a government agency. One *can* prevent a doctor from disclosing personal information about their child. One *can* recover for the grief experienced as a result of a doctor causing the wrongful death of the child. A doctor *cannot* hold one's child hostage until the medical bill is paid. Were a person to select a less effective treatment for their child or decline treatment altogether solely to save the expense, while they might or might not technically violate a local law, they would at least be universally abhorred for such a decision. The opposite of all of those things are true with veterinarians and animals.

Much less of a gap divides doctors from veterinarians in their particular roles even though such large ideological distances separate their patients. Both doctors and veterinarians are subject to statutes regarding neglect and abuse, and both are held to a comparable standard of reasonable skill and care for diagnosis of conditions, performance of procedures, administration of medications, supervision of assistants, and provision of treatment.[26] As with a doctor, a financial relationship with a veterinarian is not a threshold requirement for action against them as both professionals may be held liable for negligence even where the services are gratuitous.[27] Mere proof of an unfavorable result, without more, does not establish liability as to either, nor does an honest error in judgment made in the course of pursuing acceptable practices by either.[28] Where alternate procedures are available, neither can be found liable for malpractice when employing medically acceptable techniques.[29]

An expert witness is crucial to prove that either negligently treated or cared for a patient (however, with veterinarian malpractice claims, plenty of non-veterinarians who routinely tend to and treat animals, such as farmers, ranchers, breeders, stable workers, ferriers, zoologists, and even pet owners, qualify to set the standard of care). Finally, if either a doctor or veterinarian's conduct is wanton, malicious, grossly negligent, or in reckless disregard of others, punitive damages may be awarded against either, such as when either falsely claims to have performed a procedure, charged for a procedure that was never conducted at all, performed a completely unnecessary procedure, or misinterpreted patently obvious symptoms of dog *or* child.

Because disparate laws impose burdens on dog owners differently than on parents, open and frequent communication between veterinarians and owners is almost more critical than it is between doctor and patient. In both sets of relationships, emotions can and do run hot; in both examination rooms a human-oriented susceptibility to panic over the unknown and a human-oriented weakness for assigning blame frequently interfere with the use of plain reason or plain talk; and correspondence between both sets finds unequal levels of education between the parties frequently unweaving the fabric of what had otherwise been a carefully woven understanding about reasonable treatment. Knowing that there is an imbalance of power, of knowledge, *and* of the application of law against the dog owner should make owners particularly sensitive to engaging in more talk, not less, about what has been, is to be, or could be done.

Ignoring, for a moment, the varying social skills employed by veterinarians where some simply have developed a better "bedside manner" than others, veterinarians can thus treat an owner's animal as a machine to be repaired to the extent that all of the following conditions are true: a) that animals physiologically are comparable to machines, b) that the law allows veterinarians to do so, and c) that the animal's owner continues to employ them when they do so. Owners being consumers in the marketplace, and veterinarians being merchants in the marketplace, it is not unusual to acknowledge that the "dog as machine" model is regularly employed, in no small part because it is rational and economically effective to do so.

The lawyer-scientist recognizes that (a) is a poor assumption based on what science has uncovered about the complexity of living as opposed to nonliving things, even extremely complicated ones; that (b) is clearly correct for historical reasons, and that economic factors of tradeoff, incentive, and frugality have long combined to convince owners as consumers that (c) is a condition within every client's theoretical power to change but not within every client's actual pocketbook to change very freely. The market of available veterinarians is shaped by the clients' use of their actual, not theoretical, pocketbooks, and the market of veterinary treatment of animals is shaped by the actual, not theoretical, laws and market relations between owners and owned objects.

We are remiss as lawyers, as scientists, as consumers, as citizens, and as economic participants, if we do not continually assess the complicated impacts that animals have on their owners as well as on those with whom those owners come into contact, from what goes into them to what comes out:

Our environment has many unpleasant features. One is dog excrement. Piles and pats of it abound, waiting to slip up the inattentive pedestrian. But what do we do if we see a squatting dog? We either express haughty contempt, turn away, or blame the owner. Would any of us kick or punch the dog? Probably not; instead we are more likely to shout at the person holding the lead. On the one hand we seem to believe that the dog is not entirely responsible for its actions, on the other we feel that it should not be deliberately hurt simply because it is doing what it must. We are not certain what we should do about the dog that fouls our front garden; indeed we are not sure we can rightly do anything. Our treatment of the animal is difficult. Animals present society with ambiguities;

with companionship, food, clothing, fun, but also with demands for compassion, abstinence and kindness. They disgust and please us; we can do with them what we will yet pull back with horror from open cruelty. The dog makes claims upon us, although we are not entirely sure what those claims are. But they still profoundly influence our treatment of the animal.[30]

Tester's observation above that "the dog makes claims upon us, although we are not entirely sure what those claims are" acknowledges the dog as both a market object and as a belonging, a companion. To the dog's owner, those are vital, albeit diverging, relationships to preserve and protect. Though nonowners should ostensibly have little effect on decisions made about the dog in either relationship, as community members in general they nevertheless contribute to formation and implementation of rules surrounding ownership and treatment of the dog and thereby have significant influence.

When we ask what is the benefit and what is the cost, such questions require that we engage in two further analyses. One is an economic assessment, the second is an inquiry into the effect of "rights." Both community dollars and community demands become inserted into the equation. In Tester's example, he seeks an answer to whether the nonowner kicks the squatting dog or shouts at the person holding the lead. If the hesitation to kick and the inclination to shout is claimed to stem from a concern over loss of value or from personal feelings of one action simply being "not right" and the other simply being "right," then other actors appear to project requirements of obligation and protection onto the animal's use. The desire is to have the object protected either in the market or from the adverse actions of others, or both, and we find that responsibility, like kicking and shouting, has its payment as a function of ownership having its price. To account for that, we must turn to economic principles for assistance.

NOTES

1. *Rubáiyát* of Omar Khayyám, Quatrain XVI.

2. Shepard, Paul, ed. *The Only World We've Got: A Paul Shepard Reader*. San Francisco: Sierra Club Books, 1996.

3. Brown, Ray Andrews. *The Law of Personal Property*, Callaghan, 1975.

4. Penner, James E. *The Idea of Property in Law*. Oxford, UK: Oxford University Press, 1997.

5. See *Emans v. Turnbull*, 1807 WL 886 (NY Sup Ct 1807): ("Animals *feræ naturæ* belong to nobody; but if they make nests or burrow in my land, and have young ones there, I have a property in them, *ex ratione soli,* until they fly or run away").

6. See Veblen, Thorstein. "The Beginnings of Ownership." *American Journal of Sociology* 4.3 (1898) at p. 353:
The "natural" owner is the person who has "produced" an article, or who, by a constructively equivalent expenditure of productive force, has found and appropriated an object. It is conceived that such a person becomes the owner of the article by virtue of the immediate logical inclusion of the idea of ownership under the idea of creative industry.

7. Lawson, Frederick Henry, and Basil S. Markesinis. *Tortious Liability for Unintentional Harm in the Common Law and the Civil Law: Volume II, Materials.* Vol. 120. CUP Archive, 1982 at pp. 42–143.

8. Mason, I. (ed.) *The Evolution of Domesticated Animals.* London: Longman Press, 1984.

9. Decker, A. and G. Goff. *Valuing Wildlife: Economic and Social Perspectives.* Boulder: Westview, 1987.

10. *Pierson v. Post*, 3 Cai. R. 175 (N.Y. Sup. 1805).

11. Hoebel, E. Adamson. "Anthropology and Early Law: Selected from the Writings of Paul Vinogradoff, Frederic W. Maitland, Frederick Pollock, Maxime Kovalevsky, Rudolf Huebner, Frederic Seebohm, Lawrence Krader, ed." (1968): 767–768, at p. 122.

12. *State v. Taylor*, 27 N.J.L. 117, 1858 WL 5022 (N.J. Sup.), 72 Am. Dec. 347, 3 Dutch. 117 (N.J. 1858).

13. Shepard, P. *The Only World We've Got.* New York: Vintage Books, 1996:
Among animals, suitable candidates for domestication are social, herd-oriented, leader-or dominance-recognizing forms . . . Individual wild creatures brought into the house, no matter how much they are loved or how long they are kept, do not become domesticated. If they live they may not thrive as well as in the wild; if they thrive they still may not reproduce or generate a lineage; and if they breed the offspring may still prefer to go free if they can escape. There is an inborn difference between domesticates and all other animals.

14. *Pippin v. Funk*, 794 A.2d 893 (N.J. App. 2002).

15. See Duckler, G. "Between Price and Pricelessness: Calculating the Specific Monetary Value of a Dog Intentionally Harmed by Another." *J. Animal L. & Ethics* 3 (2009): 121.

16. See *Smith v. Steineauf*, 140 Kan 407 (1934):
From deification in Egypt, the cat fell in the Middle Ages to the lowest depths of superstitious disrepute. The cat was the consort and agent of witches, and sometimes Satan himself took the form of a cat. Accounts of the cat's weird wickedness are found in the folklore of all the countries of Europe. That was natural enough when belief in association and compact with the Prince of the Power of Darkness was part of the common culture. But the astounding thing is that superstitions regarding the cat and its potency for evil persist and govern human conduct to this day. Woe to the cat thath must be dealt with by some court or legislative body, with this survival lurking in the back of its mind.

17. Deacon, Terrence William. *The Symbolic Species: the Co-evolution of Language and the Brain.* New York: W. W. Norton, 1997.

18. Smith, Christian. *Moral, Believing Animals: Human Personhood and Culture.* Oxford, UK: Oxford University Press, 2003 at pp. 8–9.

19. Though not for cows; *See* Pendell, Dustin L., Gary W. Brester, Ted C. Schroeder, Kevin C. Dhuyvetter, and Glynn T. Tonsor. "Animal Identification and Tracing in the United States." *American Journal of Agricultural Economics* 92, no. 4 (2010): 927–40.

20. *Akers v. Sellers*, 54 N.E.2d 779 (Ind. App. 1944) (dog "gifted" to a spouse during the course of the marriage confers ownership); *Ballas v. Ballas*, 178 Cal.App.2d 570 (Cal. App. 1960) (dog registered to spouse during marriage treated same as car also registered to spouse during marriage); *Arrington v. Arrington,* 613 S.W. 2d 565 (Tex. App. 1981) (dog can be treated as a financial asset by spouse during course of marriage); *In re Marriage of Stewart*, 356 N.W.2d 611 (Iowa App. 1984) ("A dog is personal property and while courts should not put a family pet in a position of being abused or uncared for, we do not have to determine the best interests of a pet."); *Jett v. Municipal Court*, 177 Cal. App. 3d 664 (Cal. App. 1986); *Nuzzaci v. Nuzzaci*, Not Reported in A.2d, 1995 WL 783006 (Del. Fam. Ct. 1995) (court only has jurisdiction to award dog to one spouse or the other); *Bennett v. Bennett*, 655 So. 2d 109 (Fla. App. Dist. 1, 1995) (dog properly dealt with through equitable distribution process); *Raymond v. Lachmann*, 695 N.Y.S. 2d 308 (N.Y. App. Div. 1999) ("best interests of the cat" considered); *See* also, *Leconte v. Kyungmi Lee*, 35 Misc.3d 286 (N.Y. City Civ. Ct. 2011); *Juelfs v. Gough*, 41 P.3d 593 (Alaska 2002) (enforcement problems supersede personal interests in pet); *DeSanctis v. Pritchard*, 803 A.2d 230 (Pa. Super. 2002) (dogs more like household items than people); *Green v. Shall*, N.E.2d, 2004 WL 628649 (Ohio App. 6 Dist. 2004) (regarding who cares for the dog during course of marriage); *Conahan-Baltzelle v. Baltzelle*, 2004 WL 1959486 (Va. App. 2004) ("although both parties clearly have affection for the family dog, only one party could be awarded the dog"); *Wolf and Taylor*, 224 Or. App. 245 (Or. App. 2008) (agreement regarding visitation of a dog is illegal); *Whitmore v. Whitmore*, Not Reported in S.E.2d, 2011 WL 588497 (Va. App. 2011) (declining to establish visitation or shared custody schedule with dog similar to that ordered in child custody cases).

21. See *Finn v. Anderson*, 64 Misc 3d 273 (NY City Ct 2019):
[It is] difficult if not impossible to truly determine what is in a pet's best interests as there is no proven or practical means of gauging an animal's happiness or "its feelings about a person or a place other than, perhaps, resorting to the entirely unscientific method of watching its tail wag." [E]ven if it were possible to ascertain a pet's feelings, and even if a Court could make a finding of a pet's best interests, it is "highly questionable whether significant resources should be expended and substantial time spent on such endeavors . . . [t]o allow full-blown dog custody cases, complete with canine forensics and attorneys representing not only the parties but the dog itself, would further burden the courts to the detriment of children." The "best interests" of the child standard is based on the implicit understanding that the ultimate goal of the Courts is to ensure that the child is nurtured into independent adulthood. It is the future adult that must be the Court's primary consideration, and not the interests of the father or mother. However, in the case of a pet cat or dog, the pet never becomes an independent being apart from the owner.

22. Such actions would undoubtedly violate a human's personal right to be free from unwanted interference with bodily functions, and in fact, forced contraception has been proscribed when proposed, for example, as sentencing alternatives for human prisoners. The ability to test the effects of various immobilizing drugs on animals, such as the use of dart tranquilizers, would also be impaired by a right against undue restraint.

23. Franklin, Adrian. *Animals and Modern Cultures: A Sociology of Human-Animal Relations in Modernity*. Thousand Oaks, CA: SAGE, 1999.

24. See Kay, William J. *Euthanasia of the Companion Animal*. Philadelphia: Charles Press, 1988.

25. Kay, William J., et al. *Euthanasia of the Companion Animal: The Impact on Pet Owners, Veterinarians, and Society*. Philadelphia: Charles Press, 1988 at pp. 44–45:

Consciousness of self and the ability to understand and choose between alternatives is crucial in the dialectic concerning the justification of euthanasia for any animal whose future existence is likely to be pathetic. If an animal is not conscious of self and its future appears miserably wretched, then the only humane, compassionate course is to alleviate the creature's suffering by euthanasia. The issue is not one of diminishing happiness, but of eradicating further suffering through death. Even when consciousness of self is present, the animal is not capable of understanding its future prospects or of choosing whether to live or die; it should be deemed morally right and necessary for others to make this choice for the animal. This choice, however, is justifiable only if it is truly made out of compassionate interest for the being who is absolutely incapable of making the choice for itself. Whatever we choose, we are responsible for the foreseeable consequences that result, just as we are equally responsible for the fate of an animal we allow to continue to exist in a miserable state.

26. *Quigley v. McClellan*, 214 Cal App 4th 1276 (2013).

27. *Latham v. Elrod*, 6 Ala App 456 (Ala Ct App 1912).

28. *Brockett v. Abbe*, 3 Conn Cir Ct 12 (1964).

29. *Williams v. Midland Acres, Inc.*, 77 NE3d 583 (Ohio Ct App 2017).

30. Tester, Keith. *Animals and Society (RLE Social Theory): The Humanity of Animal Rights*. Abingdon, UK: Routledge, 2014.

Chapter 5

The Economics of
Animals as Objects

"Take the Cash and Let the Credit Go"[1]

A huge, well-fed human population, sustained by global manipulation of our island planet, cannot afford animals—not unless they are essential to us.[2]

Animals are, when viewed in perhaps the coldest light, simply biological resources. The condition that makes biological resources so valuable—their limited but unlimited potential to support humans—becomes problematic when defending them strictly in financial terms alone. How do you evaluate them as empirically worthwhile if each one is unique or indistinguishable from one another, i.e., irreplaceable? One piece to that puzzle is grasping the concept that biological resources increase in value as they increase in rarity. Where a steady demand exists, decreasing supply creates increasing worth. Contrasted with the phenomenon of "temporal discounting," that issue tends to create the question of how to determine decreased availability of any particular resource.

ANIMALS AS ECONOMIC RESOURCES
EMBODYING EMOTIONAL CONSEQUENCES

Where the biological resource is an animal, and where the animal is specifically a person's pet, a suite of psychological factors both anchor and interfere with the forces driving standard economic preferences. Innumerable animals have the capacity to provide food, clothing, or transport, but only a peculiar set of species have the capacity to provide entertainment, comfort, or recreation. Anthropomorphic factors include perceptions about the animal's ability to experience pain; account for aesthetic appeal such as cuteness, size, phyletic similarity to humans, human-like appearance, mental similarity, and hygiene and regular habits; and entangle consumer-type decisions in the brambles of religious belief.[3] The use and ownership of dogs and cats specifically, more than with any other type of market object, raise considerations of quasi-religious and spiritual associations, public historical acceptances and private historical rejections of previous communal uses, the lure of behavioral plasticity, the oddness of habituating capacity, and the swirl of symbolic associations connected to the purchase or sale decision for any object containing an emotional component.[4] In short, we find that a bevy of inexplicable subjective feelings about living things have invaded our processing of what should be a normal objective transaction:

> Dogs regularly tend to be anthropomorphized. A dog's expression and behavior may be used to attribute to it such human qualities as sympathy, kindness, and love, or, less commonly, neglect, selfishness, and hostility. This is beautifully illustrated in the comedy *Sylvia*, by Albert Gurney. An actress assumes the role and behavior of a dog. Conflicts develop with a couple, and the husband, a Manhattan investment banker, becomes more and more attached to his dog, eventually falling in love with it. The man begins to favor the dog over his wife, and he assumes aspects of the dog. Later on, his wife, to a lesser degree, begins to do this also. In this situation the humans take on the traits of the dogs. The dog, in turn, begins to assume some human qualities. Through projection, dogs can represent for humans aspects of the unconscious that are warded off, such as aggressivity, hostility, and sexuality.[5]

Still, emotion aside for a moment, animals as goods have price tags, and if myriad individuals make choices in an environment where efficient markets accurately signal the cost of alternative choices, then the prices that emerge should reflect true economic values. Animals fall within the category of market object that involves not just "rival goods," but exclusive goods and goods that encompass decisions with relatively short time horizons. Those three aspects can be translated as saying, respectively, that a) a given level of output more for one person means less than for others; b) that there are meaningful ways in which some consumers can be excluded from enjoying the ownership or use of the good; and c) that losses are not irreversible, since over time new goods in the form of offspring as new or replacement goods, can be produced.

Owners like to imagine, as people invested in the aesthetic appeal of an animal such as their pet, that their dog or cat is unique—and in a strict biological sense they are correct. Sexually reproducing animals are unique and irreplaceable objects by definition since genetics dictate that each individual is an expression of a gene complex as distinct as human fingerprints, each unlike that of any other, each having never arisen before or likely ever to be repeated again. That inimitability is reflected in the fact that simply as to mammals alone, the number of potentially genetically different individuals for a given mammal species exceeds a decadillion, a nearly inconceivable figure with 30 zeros attached to it, itself reflecting the awesome power of genetic variation to construct a singular object in the universe, and a process that cannot be applied in any comparison to inanimate properties.[6] In an economic sense, however, pet owners are at the same time quite wrong, and effective replacement of their animal as a good is a market reality. The owner treats the animal as if it were the only one of its kind in the world. The world, however, treats the animal as if it were fungible, that is, replaceable by another of like "kind" or at least functionally equal among all other animals of the same "type."

Separations of domestics from livestock from wildlife from pests and so on remind us that lawyers limn out a host of crucial differences between "kinds" and "types," investing legal meaning within the socially and culturally derived categories under which they irrationally pigeonhole animals. We have seen previously that those are epistemologically antagonistic to the carefully constructed taxonomies that scientists employ, but we haven't yet fully considered the economic effect of what happens when lawyers do so.

DOG OWNER AND PIG FARMER, CONSUMERS AND MERCHANTS IN PARALLEL AND IN CONTRAST

It is unremarkable to note that people who manage and trade in livestock such as cattle ranchers, sheepherders, and goat, chicken, and pig farmers, regularly play market roles, as well as that pet owners, on the other hand, seem distinct. Economically, however, key similarities exist between dog owners and pig farmers. One, both groups use tools of *restraint* to exert an effective control over their animal that signals to every outsider that the animal has a significant location (and thus value) worth protecting, the field fence used by the former and the nylon collar used by the latter. Two, both groups use tools of *special identification* to exert an effective claim over their animal that signals to every outsider that the animal has an exclusive owner whose interests are personal to them, the brand, ear tag, or tattoo used by the former, and the microchip or identification tag used by the latter. Three, both groups use tools of *remedy* to exert an effective consequence over their animal that signals to the outsider that the animal has a significant value worth protecting, demands for compensation used by both as to another's careless or intentional destruction of their animal.

Those unversed in economics highlight the distinctions as if social comparisons were all that really mattered: pet-owning, many say, is not a vocation but an avocation, and pet-owners just aren't in the "business" of owning their animals as pig farmers are. Yet the conduct of pet owners runs counter to their proclamations of not playing the market game. Pet-owning embraces a set of curious economic entanglements, a prime one of which is the idea of "price." Price is the economic form of value, and when applied to the attainment and disposition of pets and other animals in the marketplace is confounded by a suite of "psychological desires, cultural demands, and social constraints peculiar to a time, a place, and even an individual."[7] All sorts of attributes make an animal desirable to a potential purchaser, and price is a distorted reflection of certain interplays between those attributes:

> When considering animals, the case for understanding how sociocultural values are reflected in price is particularly urgent. During the colonial days of English common law, and codified since by the laws of the United States, animals were legally categorized as chattel, or property. Because of this characterization, money has been perhaps the most common mediator of Americans' relationships with their domestic animals. . . . Understanding this aspect of animals' economic value is the only way that characteristics such as affectionate disposition, health, strength, or pedigree can become part of their official (economic) worth and identity.[8]

To appreciate a few of those entanglements and their significance to the law on animals as objects and thus animal value, a clear understanding of what the majority of normal market participants act like in the market will help.[9]

With a normal market good that becomes completely or partially consumed when used, a rational purchaser will buy the good at a price that is generally commensurate with the level of satisfaction expected to be obtained from the fullest use of the good. The purchaser's determination of value is, in a very real sense, a function of their best predictions about likely usefulness or enjoyment. With those types of goods, what, if anything, is left of the good is discarded at the end of its useful life since by definition it has been "used up"—and the term "consumer" seems to be an appropriate description of what the purchaser is actually doing. Satisfied consumers are those whose predictions have been met, while dissatisfied consumers are those whose predictions have been unfulfilled.

The law considers the purchaser to also be the good's legal "owner," and all the rights and privileges that accompany the condition of ownership are bestowed on the purchaser. Those rights and privileges that have to do with the good's conveyance, that is, with the legal transfer of the good to another, are not triggered, however, since the definition of a consumable good is that its value is not in being conveyed but is in being consumed instead.

Some market goods are not "consumed," in the technical sense in that their use does not actually use them up—they remain intact for the most part regardless of use. A rational purchaser will buy those types of goods at a price that is still generally commensurate with the level of satisfaction expected to be obtained from the fullest use of the good, but that additionally takes into account the prospective economic benefit that might be obtained if the good is later conveyed away—since by definition it still is "useful." In those scenarios, a rational consumer might invest time, dollars, and/or energy into the good in order to obtain satisfaction from it *and* in order to eventually sell it (albeit for a reduced value, recognizing depreciation of the good due to time and use).

The law still considers the purchaser to be the good's "owner" just as with the first category, but now the term "consumer" does not seem to be as appropriate a description of what the purchaser is actually doing with the good, and we tend to characterize these people simply as "owners" alone, rather than as owners and consumers. This phenomenon is partly why it appears humorous to refer to someone holding a hot dog as the hot dog's "owner" even though the description is legally correct, while it similarly appears unfeeling to refer to someone holding a wiener dog as the wiener dog's "purchaser," even though that description is equally legally correct.

[A]s far as pets are concerned, the simple rules which normally govern our treatment of domestic animals no longer apply. Instead of maximizing productivity, minimizing costs, and turning a blind eye to the welfare of the animals involved, we do exactly the opposite. The economic benefits of pet-keeping are negligible at best. Yet the majority of pet owners spare no expense to ensure that their animals are as happy, contented and secure as they possible can be. [T]he majority of pet-owners are normal rational people who make use of animals to augment their existing social relationships, and so enhance their own psychological and physical welfare. Thought of in these terms, keeping a dog, say, for companionship is no more outlandish or profligate than wearing an overcoat to keep out of the cold. Indeed, it would be fair to argue that pet-keeping is genuinely 'adaptive' in the evolutionary sense of the word, since it contributes to individual health and survival by ameliorating the stresses and strains of everyday life. Pets, according to this view, are as useful in their way as domestic pigs or poultry. The only difference being that one cannot easily measure their usefulness using a conventional economic yardstick, any more than one can attach a precise value to friendship.[10]

A rational "owner's" determination of value is still a function of their best predictions about likely usefulness or enjoyment of the good but is complicated by the need to also predict both cost of its upkeep and potential profit from its resale. With inconsumable goods, the good is not discarded at all since it does not get "used up," and the idea of value is not nearly so fixed or concrete; as time passes and events occur involving the good, the owner's assessment of its resale value as high or low fluctuates, and the owner tends to often reflect back on whether the initial purchase price was wise or foolish. No matter what, the rational owner should eventually attempt to recover some dollars for the good in an eventual resale, albeit with the realistic caveat that purchasers of all types, being human, don't always act purely rationally anyway.[11]

CONTRIBUTION, INVESTMENT, ENJOYMENT, AND RETURN OF AN ANIMAL AS A GOOD

From a larger perspective, the process from initial attainment to ultimate divestment of all market goods—consumable or not—can be modeled in four basic steps: contribution, investment, enjoyment, and return. "Contribution" comprises the dollars put into the good's purchase at the beginning, "investment" comprises the effort put into the good's maintenance, "enjoyment" comprises the benefit received in the good's use, and "return" comprises the dollars recovered from the good at the end, taking into account investment and enjoyment.[12]

For instance, a visitor to the ballpark makes a contribution of five dollars to purchasing the hot dog, makes an investment of zero dollars in its maintenance, gets perhaps one dollar worth of enjoyment in its use, and receives a return of zero dollars for it after use. A visitor to the car lot makes a contribution of twenty thousand dollars to purchasing the car, makes an investment of five thousand dollars in its maintenance, gets a few thousand dollars of use out of it, and receives a return of few thousand dollars for it in a later conveyance. Substitute "pig" for "car" and massage the dollar amounts a bit and the same model works (for the most part).

With animals as pets, however, the model becomes perverted. A visitor to the dog kennel makes a contribution of one hundred dollars to purchasing the dog, makes an investment of ten thousand dollars in its maintenance, gets an undeterminable amount of use of the dog—and then refuses to seek any return for it. This is curious to the non dog-owner (and pig farmer), since dogs, as inconsumable goods, should ideally have some return value.

The economist Richard Posner has described economics as "the science of rational choice in a world . . . in which resources are limited in relation to human wants."[13] As economists are wont to do, Posner assumes that people are "rational maximizers of their ends in life," a concept that is synonymous with satisfaction and self-interest (although not selfishness). As long as normal consumers make rational decisions, normal consumer markets have some predictive power in relying on assumptions about maximizing self-interest. In parallel, as long as normal property owners make rational decisions, normal property ownership arrangements and relationships have some predictive power in the same way.

Dog and cat owners should, ideally, be making rational choices in a world in which dogs and cats are limited in relation to human desires for dogs and cats. Were they to do so, we could make some stabs at predicting their influences in the market (subtle and overt) as participants including as consumers. Dog and cat owners however tend to be irrational market participants, in part because real costs and benefits to them regarding animals don't necessarily correlate with quantity as costs and benefits regularly do with other market items. Pets generate "shadow prices," i.e., social opportunity costs, which expand the real factors at play in their decisions.[14]

Some of this finds an explanation in another economic concept called "temporal discounting," the idea that the longer the delay in accessing a resource, the lower its perceived value. Studies illustrate that the value of an item decreases exponentially as a function of time in which the decay appears to be a measure of risk by the consumer: the longer it might take to be able to get the resource, the more likely the resource might be lost, degraded, damaged, or unavailable in the interim, and therefore the less effort devoted to obtaining it even if it is the larger reward than the currently available one.[15]

The relationship between value and time falls under the general topic of temporal discounting: the longer the delay to accessing the resource, the lower its value. There is a vast literature on discounting in rats and pigeons, and a smaller set of studies in less traditional laboratory animals, such as starlings, jays, tamarins, marmosets, and macaques. Paralleling studies in humans, the central question is: How does the value of an item or action change as a function of time? Economists tend to think of the relationship between value and time as an exponential curve: The subjective value of a reward sometime in the future decreases at a constant rate. The decay is therefore a measure of risk, of potentially losing everything by waiting for the larger reward. In contrast, students of human psychology and animal behavior tend to think of this relationship as a hyperbolic curve. Like the exponential model, there is a trade-off between subjective value and time, but with two distinctive differences: value is inversely proportional to time delay, and preference reversals arise when the time delay to both rewards stretches out into the future. Preference reversals are real in humans, a fact that annoys economists with a bent toward rational choice, but delights psychologists interested in the basis of subjective preferences.[16]

Preference reversals will sometimes arise when the delay is substantial as in the reward being offered well into the far future, and economists are annoyed at such reversals since they do not reflect rational decision-making by consumers consistent with expectations.[17] Similarly, preference reversals appear to be the order of the day when the resource is a pet as consumers often overvalue pets when they are more inaccessible than when they are readily available, again, an economically irrational mode of behavior.[18] Dishwasher buyers engage in temporal discounting; dog buyers engage in temporal expensing.

When we fold into the equation laws that affect dog and cat owners—for instance, laws regarding contracts about, ownership of, injuries to, injuries by, and conveyances of dogs and cats—things get awry. Laws impose social costs, and laws about animals dutifully follow that rule. A social cost is one that diminishes the wealth of a society (such as what happens with a "right"), whereas a private cost rearranges that wealth but doesn't increase or reduce it. In criminalizing aspects of animal ownership in ways we haven't criminalized dishwasher ownership, we impose social costs, those "shadow prices" we noted above, on animal owners. Conveyances of animals from one person to another, the private costs that have no social effect, don't actually create market effects—they are just ways of using animals in the way we use money, as a medium of exchange, and simply rearrange resources without altering their amount. Criminal laws proscribing and penalizing the inadequate care of certain domesticated animals, the possession of certain exotic animals, and the failure to control certain livestock animals, do create genuine changes in wealth, albeit subtle ones nestled inside of inflated sale prices and restricted purchase opportunities. These effects create black market economies and impair the free flow of animals as goods.[19]

Pigs and dogs are not the only animals assessed for value in markets, of course—we ponder the incentives and the detriments of every animal in determining their relative worth to putative owners and their effect on distributions of wealth. Those animals that substantially decrease other resources are considered pests, e.g., the weevils or locusts of the agricultural world and the fleas and ticks of the urban world, and economic effort is expended to eradicate them. Wild animals are a wash: being functionally neutral to us economically they have no value; as Posner puts it "there is nothing to be gained from creating incentives to invest in them."[20] Those animals that increase other resources after accounting for the resources they use, e.g., horses, cows, chickens, sheep, goats, and pigs in the agricultural world, and dogs and cats in the urban world are beneficial, and economic effort is expended to promote and produce them. We can "afford" them in the economic sense because they are essential commodities to pig farmer and cat lady alike as valuable objects whose restraint and housing yields benefits. Since tracking their whereabouts and remedying their loss are crucial features of our economic environment, our laws reflect that input and output.

Pets have value not because they tend to themselves generate other resources—they don't—but because indirectly they make existing resources, such as homes, workplaces, and personal environments, themselves more desirable and thus more valuable:

> The term *value* has had very different meanings in different intellectual contexts. Nineteenth and twentieth-century political economists, including Karl Marx and Georg Simmel, probed the social relations inherent in the value of everything from labor to the purchase of objects (and even the value of humans). Philosophers and historians (Friedrich Nietzsche most prominently) insisted that value also encoded the ideals and motivations of individuals and the telos of a whole culture. Combining these two characterizations of value suggests a fruitful way of studying human-animal relationships [such that animal value] focuses on the attributes of the animals themselves—their health, behavior, strength, speed, rarity, loyalty, and so on—as factors in their perceived worth.[21]

Two other economic principles that alter valuations of personal properties are tradeoff and incentive. As to the first, tradeoff, lawyers appreciate the economist's observation that many decisions are the result of forgoing some potential outcomes in favor of obtaining alternatives—voluntarily exchanging costs for costs or benefits for benefits. Our legal and economic history is replete with scenarios in which rational actors assess potential exchanges and then reevaluate to engage in those that the actor reasonably believes will result in some net increase in the benefit, or some net decrease in the cost, of the action.

As to the second, incentive, lawyers also recognize the economist's insistence that people will tend to generally respond favorably to even modest rewards to act in a certain way and will usually (though the lawyer hurriedly interjects "not always") alter their behavior accordingly. Rational people tend to be stimulated by the promise of a favorable return on any given recognizable pattern of conduct, and human behavior can be predicted to change—albeit often in a quite complicated fashion after being buffeted about by a bevy of competing influences—when costs or benefits change in light of encouragements to do so. The interjection arises because lawyers not infrequently deal with deviations from the principle in the form of clients (and jurists and jurors) who irrationally reject reasonable incentives in favor of making decisions solely based on emotion alone.

At the same time, larger economic considerations dictate that no actor truly acts alone, that is, acts freely and without influence in an economic vacuum—all economic actors must be deemed part of a coterie of players striding about and colliding on a larger stage, dictating lines to others as they move around the set, at times front and center, at others standing in the wings, shouting

stage directions to others waiting their turn, or sitting in the theater pondering personal reactions to the performance, all during a play in which a host
of obvert and discrete social forces and communal forces extract a variety
of payments for any beneficial exchange of which they have formed a part.

As that drama plays out locally, regionally, and globally, benefits and detriments to each player are weighed depending on their unique circumstances.
Not just lawyers, but all market participants consider a concept such as
"ownership" to be a benefit in the economic sense, but it is lawyers who more
particularly note that acceptance of the fact that we live socially demands
acceptance of the fact that detriments are always lurking about, i.e., that some
payment somewhere must then attend that benefit and eventually come due.
The economic concept of ownership raises the economic concept of rights
(rights, for instance, to control the good, to exclude others from using or
harming the good, to profit off the good, to dispose of or waste the good, and/
or to repurpose or resell the good) as mixed bags of benefits and detriments.
As a result, in the same mode that owning goods has cost and value, then the
rights in those goods must have cost and value as well.

So lawyers consider a concept such as a "right" to be a benefit in one economic sense, and since benefits are intimately tied to burdens in another, then
the lawyer broadcasts the hoary precept that "with rights come responsibilities" as the concession that rights-holders "pay" for the privilege.[22] All the
various social mandates that allow us to exercise rights to engage in certain
activities, at the same time impose on us obligations to not engage in others
and to comport ourselves with innumerable social mores. The physical confinement of a prison, the financial confinement of a contract, the imposition
of a debt, and the burden of spousal and parental responsibilities all weigh
heavy on us on account of, not in spite of, the freedoms we enjoy in our roles
as citizens, as consumers, as parents, as spouses, as owners, and so on.[23]

In this part of the play, those who don't own animals and those who rally
to eradicate the private ownership of animals create their own entangled role
on the free market stage by such a stance. At an initial glance it seems like
a role that should not have any economic ramifications whatsoever, since
these aren't actors engaging in direct transactions involving animals, such as
purchasing them. Yet by creating substantial market forces on those who do,
they stand on the stage along with the others subtly inserting indirect benefits
and indirect costs into the tradeoff and incentive equations.

VALUING ANIMALS AS PROPERTIES,
BOTH GENERALLY AND SPECIALLY

In placing the background scenery of "people's belongings" with which the stage of economic interaction is set, courts struggle with the phenomenon that animal "value' is massively problematic in comparison to the value of other personal properties. Complications arise in aligning dog value with cow value since we treat the value of our meals and the value of our friends differently— yet "relationships" flower with both:

> This testimony does not help to establish a *monetary* amount for the "intrinsic" value of [the injured dog] Tucker. On the one hand, the cost of neutering and adoption seems too low a reflection of its intrinsic value. Conversely, Tucker's relationship to plaintiff and members of his family does have value separate and distinct from sentiment, an element which the law precludes from consideration in ascertaining damages. . . . However, it is impossible to reduce to monetary terms the bond between man and dog, a relationship which has been more elo- quently memorialized in literature and depicted on the motion picture screen.[24]

Person-car "relationships" are different still.[25] As people "rationally maxi- mize their self-interest" with cars, car values rise and fall in correlation with car quantity, car quality, the presence of other car purchasers, and the relative absence of social costs to owning and using cars. Car consum- ers take an *ex ante* perspective about cars—a "before the fact" process of decision-engaging where the decisions are based on expectations of the future rather than on regrets about the past (as Posner poetically puts it "they treat bygones as bygones").[26] People can't be presumed to rationally maximize their self-interest with animals since an *ex post* perspective frequently inter- feres—an "after the fact" process of decision-making in reassessing purchase of a dog not as a purchase at all but as the addition of a family member or the initiation of a romantic relationship: "my dog is my child," "I love my dog." It is for that reason that judges will bandy about market terms in cases about the "value" of dogs but end up conflating emotive and social terms instead, such as "special value" rules:

> The owner of a dog wrongfully killed is not circumscribed in his proof to its market value, for, if it has no market value, he may prove its special value to him by showing its qualities, characteristics, and pedigree.[27]

An economist's view of a "special value" rule interprets "special" narrowly, to mean "specialized use," couches the phrase as synonymous with utility applying only where the dog replaces a special instrument like an alarm sys- tem or newspaper delivery machine, and assessing value as the comparable cost of such devices.[28] Under that rubric, messier concepts, such as a dog's "personality" or "companionship," are refuted. A competing version interprets "special" far more broadly to mean "unique to that particular owner" where the interaction with it is intensely personal.[29] The differing approaches shine a bright light on how relative the value concept is for cow, dog, or car:

> Presumably we are neither dismayed nor perplexed by the discovery that there are no natural, universal units of economic value. What is a live goat worth? Well, where and when? In rural France today it has considerable value, but is it more or less than its current value in China, or the value of a secondhand Chevy pickup in Louisiana in 1972? What is the same live goat worth today, delivered to the private office of a Wall Street broker? One can work out an estimate of "the value" of the goat (in 1968 dollars, let us say) at various times and places, to various people, by working through the exchange rates, inflation rates, market prices, etc. Who earned more in an average year: one of Caesar's generals or a Supreme Court Justice? I take it no one supposes such exercises home in on unique, real economic values.[30]

In considering how to "hone in on unique, real economic" animal values, the lawyer-scientist acknowledges that value is rooted in the notion that some animals have universal economic effects and others don't, a position reflected in the term "intrinsic value."[31] Blackstone distinguished between animals raised for food and those that are "only kept for pleasure, curiosity, or whim, [such] as dogs . . .; because their value is not intrinsic, but depending on the caprice of the owners."[32] Companion animal loss has not always been remediable; for much of our history animals were felt to lack intrinsic value to communities and courts would not recognize their loss as "valuable" (e.g., no cause of action for larceny when they were stolen).[33] That has changed in modern times and criminal laws, integrating the morality of individual responsibility, mix together the *ex ante* and *ex post* perspectives on animal loss and penalize it, while the promotion of animals as enhancements to private life has catapulted civil assessments of value into a "blooming, buzzing confusion"; as "undefined,"[34] as "fair market value,"[35] as the "cost to replace,"[36] and as an amalgam of those acknowledging that relationships with people are influential.[37]

WRONGFUL DEATH LAW AS A TEMPLATE
FOR DEAD ANIMAL VALUE

Arguments aimed at increasing economic damages awards in companion animal loss cases frequently reject statistical data in favor of anecdote and sympathy alone to convince jurists and fact finders that animals are more akin to family members than to personal properties and that some special animals (but of course not pests or wild animals) significantly improve peoples' quality of life and have beneficial effects on human health.[38]

> Talking to oneself, which must be how our behavior would appear to many a non-owner, is a thoroughly depressing thing to do; in fact so lowering of mood and self-esteem and enhancing of confusion and of anger that it's linked to mental disorders of all types. Talking to an animal, however, is profoundly mood-enhancing—the description of a minor triumph, the sharing of a personal blow, even the everyday running commentary upon our and our animals doing feels *good*; and it does so because of our conviction as owners that the animal both listens and understands; that it enters our experience in turn—and more, that it empathizes with us. "Something to talk to" is still one of the most important reasons given for owning a pet in the first place. Talking to an animal has been likened to the experience of Rogerian therapy, where it's the perceived empathy and non-interventionist behavior of the listener that makes the therapy work. Such "talking" has also been linked to the experience of prayer—another act of faith with no tangible evidence of a comprehending audience, and engaged or interventionist listener at all, but does that stop us from doing it? Hardly.[39]

The lawyer-scientist notices that the "beneficial aspect" door swings both ways: dogs and cats, as intensely social organisms, themselves *require* companionship from humans, an unusual type of reciprocal obligation imposed by our interactions in both domesticating them and being domesticated by them.[40] The legal landscape of available remedies in companion animal death cases is therefore bounded by considerations of how *each* of the participants, animal and person, engage tradeoffs and incentives.

Tort law—which "adjusts losses among society's members and affords compensation for injuries sustained by one person as a result of the conduct of another"[41] proffers both. The incentive that an animal's "special value" may be informed by the civil law on wrongful death (where people are compensated for another relationally close to them having been wrongfully killed) carries with it the tradeoff that subjective factors get eliminated. People value human life, and wrongful death rules compel juries to translate lives into dollars methodologically, inserting and eliminating, as the equation may require, factors ranging from the banality of employment history all the way to the ire of good old moral outrage.

Oregon's wrongful death statute, for example, sets forth four specific categories of compensation available for a wrongful death that primarily posit valuation as a function of utility:

1. Medical and funeral expenses: that is, the cost of burying the body;

2. Any disability, pain, suffering or loss of income suffered by the dead person between the time of the injury and death: the cost of suffering while still alive;
3. Pecuniary loss to the estate: that is, the cost to others of losing their economic services; and,
4. Loss of companionship by a spouse, children, and parents: that is, the cost of losing their relationship services.[42]

The United States Supreme Court in *Sea-Land Services, Inc. v. Gaudet* [43] examined eight criteria to be considered in determining both a right to, and an amount of recovery for, the loss of one wrongfully killed, criteria that have been used multiple times since then[44], and which contemplate dynamics people find both economically and socially essential:

1. Relationship of husband and wife, or of parent and child (or similar relationship between collateral relatives);
2. Continuous living together of parties at and prior to time of wrongful death;
3. Lack of absence of deceased or beneficiary for extended periods of time;
4. Harmonious marital or family relations;
5. Common interest in hobbies, scholarship, art, religion, or social activities;
6. Participation of deceased in family activities;
7. Disposition and habit of deceased to tender aid, solace and comfort when required; and,
8. Ability and habit of deceased to render advice and assistance in financial matters, business activities, and the like.

The categories are at one and the same time pragmatic and emotive, and ponder the confluence of utility, the economic cost that a community bears for doing without a member, and amorphous aspects of love and affection. Trying to tailor the eight *Gaudet* factors to animals is a good litmus test for delineating just what animals are to people in contrast to what people are to themselves.[45] Not just prices, but connections, are pulled out of the shadows in such an analysis.

For instance, the second, third, fourth, sixth, and seventh factors have a ready connection to the types of interactions in which a dog "does things" functionally for a human.[46] The first, fifth, and eighth factors, on the other hand, illustrate real constraints and limitations on how dogs and humans can and ever will interact.[47] In essence, our prehistorical objectifications of animals, and our anthropological heritage as animal owners and users who developed laws about animals, may be directly inserted between the lines of

Gaudet, addressing crucial historical and prehistorical relational constraints. Those constraints mandate acceptance of biological and cognitive separations in life that cannot be ignored, and correspondingly reject pretenses of equality in death: "*La vie, c'est la mort*"—"such is life, such is death."

The statutory criteria for valuation in wrongful death cases rely upon some universal postulates, basic themes about people and their respective worth in relation with each other, all of which revolve around the following ideas:

1. *No single human life can ever be scientifically converted into an exact value:* there is no mathematical formula and one will never ever see an expert testify as to what humans are worth.
2. *There is no recognized "market" for human life:* it is not a matter of the lack of buyers, fluctuation in prices, or seasonal supply—there simply is no "market" at all.
3. *All lives must be valued differently based upon who is being evaluated:* every person must be considered to be an individual with their own unique value.
4. *Each life has high value:* that is, no life, no matter how mean, is considered either cheap or without value altogether.

With animals, on the other hand, the universal postulates seem to be polar opposites with applying the list:

1. Single lives *can* be very easily converted into exact market values and often are.
2. There *is* an obvious market for animal life.
3. Particularities have no place, and all animals of the same "type" are easily treated as if each individual animal was in fact identical.
4. Each animal life seems to have low value and primarily as food or commodities so that they frequently have more value dead than alive.

THE TAPHONOMY OF WRONGFUL DEATH ANALYSES

In a sense, wrongful death analyses are legal analogues of yet another form of taphonomy, analyzing the peculiar circumstances and events impacting an organism, here a person, at its death to discern its greater significance to the overall environment in which it resided in life. The assemblage is examined not for its organic signatures or mineralized components, but there is still chemistry of a sort being used to decipher what beneficial interactions in life are preserved in death and need to be disinterred and made significant. A result of that taphonomy is not a reconstruction of an extinct community, but compensation for the sad truth that no reconstruction can be accomplished.

A comparison of compensatory damage awards in human wrongful death cases, ranging anywhere in the tens of thousands to the millions of dollars, with those damage awards obtained in companion animal death cases, is a telling one taphonomically: animal cases, unsurprisingly, result in awards barely in the hundreds of dollars (if awards are received at all). A small sample from appellate opinions over the last century reflects that economically there is no match whatsoever between a dead human and a dead pet, and their valuation as bodies do not mimic in the slightest their biologic and evolutionary similarities in life, only their vast social and cultural differences.[48]

Accepting that dead animals are not the functional equivalents of dead people, then exactly *how* may an interference between an owner and their animal nevertheless be quantifiable in a supportive sense, i.e., specifically translatable into a dollar value that embraces love for dogs? The tripartite nature of the question creates difficulty for both lawyers and scientists. While psychologists, for instance, embrace the "wrongful interference" concept well enough, they generally consider the activity of pricing animals to be distasteful. Economists, on the other hand, accept that legal rules penalize property interferences, and are devotees of valuation schemes, but rail at a suggestion that animals are entitled to special treatment, and dispute that it is valid to economically value emotional attachments to them. Lawyers, in contrast to those groups, must dovetail legal, psychological, and economic components: they must consider levels of culpable behavior, the change in value of owned objects both natural and artificial, and the tangible effects that people's emotional expressions have on those around them as a result of altering or impairing certain objects.

All three areas come to a head when the topic is dogs or cats. As emotions go, the love of an owner for their pet dog or cat can range from mild affection to near-pathological psychosis.[49] Should personal appeal or distaste for one end of that spectrum over the other alone govern our legal decisions about a proper award for the owner's loss of a pet? As market prices go, the cost of a puppy or kitten can range from free to tens of thousands of dollars. Should expense analysis alone govern our legal decisions about a proper remedy for a pet's death? Answers circle back to the theme that for hundreds of thousands of years, our social relations have developed in intimate connection with our evolution. For thousands of years, our laws—those social relations we have taken the trouble to dress up in formal wear—have also developed in association with our evolution. For the last couple of centuries, the means by which we propose, interpret, and enforce our laws, that is, legislation and litigation, have become more and more sophisticated—yet still are not magically extricable from the twenty to thirty thousand years or so of human social history that have preceded them. Our laws, especially about animals, are an inescapable and integral part of our human nature.[50]

SINCE RELATIONSHIPS ARE AFFECTED BY BIOLOGY, VALUATIONS PIVOT WITH SERVICE ANIMALS

In that sense, lawyers—even as economists assessing values to be compensated—have spent much time hanging onto (and being hung up by) the foibles and fortuities of how humans have actually evolved and developed. From the length of a human life to the length of a human foot, our organic attributes are regularly reflected in a hodge-podge of legal entitlements and restrictions. Whether one is supposed to stay 100 yards away from another, to whether one is presumed dead if they are missing longer than seven years, qualities surrounding our manual dexterity, bipedal and upright posture, developmental timing, three-dimensional color vision, capacity for language, and very flexible life spans all can help (partially, anyway) explain why so many of our laws seem odd, unscientific, inconsistent, and plain old irrational.[51]

> [H]uman evolution was shaped by an increasing dependence on nurturing and affectionate interchanges, initially between humans and later between humans and other animals. The incipient domestication of animals and plants was probably facilitated by the physiological and psychological rewards of nurturing as well as by economic gain. From the time that animals were first domesticated until the massive urbanization that followed the industrial revolution, most people had rewarding and clearly defined social relationships with the animals that provided the material benefits.[52]

One area of inquiry in animal behavior science today consists of studies examining how long-term relationships between people and animals developed and became established.[53] A parallel pressing question in law is how long-term relationships between humans and animals are monetarily valued. An answer to the legal question entails incorporating what we know of the scientific question and examining which human–animal relationships in general the law cares about and why. Nowhere is the relationship interplay made more vivid than with animal ownership by the disabled.

The tensions in this area begin with the innocuous observation that equal opportunity is an overarching principle that society values highly, and thus dictates that access to educational, employment, and other important societal benefits should not be based on an individual's immutable traits, on stereotypes, or on irrelevant characteristics. Over time, commonplace devices such as canes and wheelchairs have come to be considered in the law simply another part of a person and thus deemed to be irrelevant characteristics that would not support a valid basis on which to deny any person equal access to services or goods available to the abled.

Since assistance or service animals are functionally similar to those devices, the same reasoning is applied, and the dog is made a tradeoff and incentive at the same time. Because canes and wheelchairs don't independently transport themselves from place to place, manifest intent, or miraculously duplicate themselves, then service animals add an extra layer of complexity to the business of accessing social utilities—yet navigation of the moral and legal problems with equal protection for the disabled means their status as tools must remain.[54]

The constitutionalist Ronald Dworkin wrote that the distinctions between legal and moral obligations "are not puzzles for the cupboard, to be taken down on rainy days for fun. They are sources of continuing embarrassment, and they nag at our attention."[55] People needing equal access to services but also needing assistance from animals to benefit from that access have warranted our attention for decades, and nearly every person's request to employ an animal as a medical or therapeutic aid is met by another's competing call for restraint; even those who wish dogs to be our equals have some discomfort with them being our replacements. Underlying resistance to social policies that have animals swap in for people as well as for mechanical devices raise moral concerns, and the most carefully formulated regulations on service animals nevertheless make neighbors and peers bristle, officials and charities beseech, bosses and teachers compromise, politicians and lawyers maneuver, and strangers and victims opine on a grand scale.

Under the American with Disabilities Act (ADA), the benefits service animals provide to the disabled are balanced against the hardship that disruptions might impose upon others around the animal, the public, patrons, colleagues, customers, and coworkers. Assessments must be made on the premise that the service animal takes the place of a therapeutic tool that ameliorates stress or allows one to perform a certain task better, and require proof that the animal has particular qualities—mechanical or medically salutary—enabling it to do so, akin to the utilitarian version of "special value." Vague endorsements of effectiveness as an overall source of good feelings are insufficient; instead, a solid empirically based conclusion that specific targeted problems are being solved that a person needs solved in order to live are mandated. In other words, we are reluctant to give legal significance to the pedestrian observation that "dogs make people feel better," since the worry is that every mental state or condition that stirs feelings of depression or low self-esteem would entitle its expression to heightened statutory protection, thereby diluting the strength such protections are supposed to provide. Once we disregard targeted tasks, professional behavioral training, and true educational utility, there would be no logical reason to not accommodate those who wished to use cats, fish, reptiles, or birds instead. Underlying our anxiety over such a dilution is the popular perception that animals in general tend to subtract from human productivity far more than contribute to it.[56]

The valid use of an animal as a tool for the disabled is a small piece to the larger puzzle of what valid use is as to *any* living thing as an object, and the complex suite of actions involved when humans employ objects reflect a host of dynamic and competing biotic and abiotic forces. Among them, principles of animal biology and rules on ownership rights jointly contribute to an epistemology of how animals might best interact with people in a way that avoids harm and abuse in both directions. Examining their application as unique tools in a legal setting is simply one more method by which society generally examines itself—appreciating not just fundamental similarities and ideals between people and animals, but fundamental distinctions and realities as well.

So economically, dogs and cats affect their own intrinsic value to society, to specific communal groups, and to their owners in a manner fundamentally distinct from the way in which values are assigned by people to other tangible personal properties such as handbags and hamburgers, objects that we also own and enjoy, but which do not interact with us in any of the unique ways in which pets do.[57] While eating a hamburger or wearing a handbag can and does affect personal psychological states sufficient to alter decisions we make about ourselves and others, those behaviors do not truly influence the economic value of the handbag or hamburger itself—that is, the market for those types of goods is not seriously impacted by how much any particular individual might or might not have "loved" a particular member of the group. Buying and selling personal properties may well be a standard form of social exchange—a variety of cooperation between two or more individuals for a unique mutual benefit—but emotional factors in the exchange are discounted, not dispositive.[58]

At the same time, psychological studies have shown that the lengthy exposure to any stimulus is itself often an adequate condition for a person to form an attachment to an object sufficient to give the object some personal "intrinsic" value.[59] Exhortations such as "I love hamburgers" or "I love my handbag" are sentiments reflecting the personal rewards we tend to manufacture for ourselves out of recurring associations we sometimes exploit with close quarter objects over time, from food preferences to clothing accessories. While it is nothing new to observe that familiarity arising out of a repeated stimulus frequently creates the psychological state we call "love," it *is* novel to ask if dogs are sufficiently comparable to handbags and hamburgers such that the same rationalization—simple sensory reinforcement through constant exposure—similarly explains the common refrain "I love my dog."

While time by itself helps create that manner of attachment as well, emotional bond formation between owners and their dogs, in distinction, supports an adaptive explanation. Courts have recognized the existence of attachment bonds between an owner and a pet,[60] but remain oblivious to the idea that domestication demands that natural history, geographical location, and mutual conduct are also crucial factors that must be taken into account as well. Dog owners have, over tens of thousands of years, performed acts of a self-reinforcing nature with dogs, while dogs, over the same period, have reciprocated with roughly similar acts.[61] Both participants have required close temporal and spatial proximity to each other for the exchange to persist and to take on a social meaning. Different than they have done with any other owned objects, dog owners gain love or affection from close, serial interactions with their dogs (or lose the same through disruption of the interactions) based on selection pressures in the owner's biological environment including of the dog's own conduct as much as of their own.[62]

Asking the ontological question if the wrongful interference with an owner's love for their dog is compensable, i.e., even a legitimate category of recoverable damage, therefore requires attending to an evolutionary path leading to developments in the common law marshaling together a platoon of concepts: one, that dogs are personal properties subject to the police power of the state; two, that owning a dog is a protected social privilege but certainly not an absolute one; three, that the act of keeping a dog directly affects the keeper's immediate and nearby social community; four, that keeping a dog confers a personal benefit and personal detriment on the keeper; five, that destroying another's dog is a form of social injury, a tort for which some remedy exists; and six, that the remedy can include financial recovery for the value of a lost relationship (if the destruction can be shown to be intentionally inflicted).[63]

Dogs are subjects of our emotional attachments primarily because they and we have worked quite hard over the millennia to manufacture both dogs and ourselves to be that way.[64] At heart, there is nothing "mysterious," "accidental," or "deeply spiritual" about the love of a dog for an owner or the love of an owner for a dog; the relationship is most easily explained by the same remarkable mechanism that has unveiled hundreds of thousands of other interactions between interacting species: pair bond formation or reciprocal environmental benefits engineered by evolution by natural selection and hamstrung by local environmental pressures.[65] There is also little that is mysterious or inexplicable about us as socially increasing the value of dead dogs in lawsuits: as economists, lawyers have been steadily digesting, applying, and benefiting from a quasi-scientific awareness of the monetary significance of certain local community interactions, owner–dog interactions included, and then folding into those observations arguments regarding maximizing economic benefits from market-related losses.

All animals are and have been objects, are and have had value, and are and have been market goods, and by definition all then position people—whether by chance or design—as object holders who manipulate the objects, as persons interested in preserving the value of such manipulations, and as market participants where the manipulations affect trade and exchange with others.

What we next need to consider is that the animal rights advocates' economic participation in these themes is just as irrational as that of their animal-owning counterparts, and that irrationality stems from a demand for a benefit without a concession of making any corresponding payment. Simply as to the economic tool of a "right" alone, animal rights advocates clamor for their slice of the rights cake, but have remained mute about the more distasteful obligations with which such a treat must by necessity be served, the animal debts, animal jails, animal accountability mechanisms, or animal obligations that would mandatorily accompany the bestowment of animal freedoms.

With animal rights come animal responsibilities, QED. What those burdens mean legally is a question to be confronted at the outset, not ignored, and to be addressed now, not later on when inconsistencies have arisen in the form of insurmountable difficulties in application and enforcement. Thus, the junction where animals and rights meet and part ways is at the crucial event of their capture and retention, and so to get there we have to take a stroll through the zoo.

NOTES

1. *Rubáiyát* of Omar Khayyám, Quatrain XIII.
2. Shephard, P., *The Only World We've Got*, Sierra Club Books, San Francisco, 1996.
3. Crist, Eileen. *Images of Animals: Anthropomorphism and Animal Mind.* Philadelphia: Temple University Press, 2000.
4. Akhtar, Salman, and Vamik D. Volkan, eds. *Cultural Zoo: Animals in the Human Mind and Its Sublimation.* Abingdon, UK: Routledge, 2018.
5. Akhtar, Salman, and Vamik D. Volkan, eds. *Mental Zoo: Animals in the Human Mind and Its Pathology.* Abingdon, UK: Routledge, 2018 at p. 128.
6. Hilbish, Thomas J., and Richard K. Koehn. "The Adaptive Importance of Genetic Variation." *American Scientist* 75.2 (1987): 134–141.
7. Simmel, Georg. *The Philosophy of Money*, 1900.
8. Jones, Susan D. *Valuing Animals: Veterinarians and Their Patients in Modern America.* Baltimore: Johns Hopkins University Press, 2003.
9. This section is taken from ideas first articulated in Duckler, G. "The Necessity of Treating Animals as Legal Objects." *J. Animal & Envtl. L.* 7 (2015): 1.

10. Serpell, James. *In the Company of Animals: A Study of Human-Animal Relationships*. London: Cambridge University Press, 1996 at pp. 14, 119–120.

11. *Hollywood National v. IBM*, 38 Cal.App. 3d 607, 614 (1974) ("Were bona fide purchasers or holders in due course, required to act reasonably, the argument goes, the fabric of negotiability, the flak suit of commercial life, would be torn to shreds.")

12. See Deaton, Angus, and John Muellbauer. *Economics and Consumer Behavior*. London: Cambridge University Press, 1980.

13. Posner, Richard A. *Economic Analysis of Law*. Philadelphia: Wolters Kluwer, 2014.

14. See, e.g., Drèze, Jean, and Nicholas Stern. "Policy Reform, Shadow Prices, and Market Prices." *Journal of Public Economics* 42.1 (1990): 1–45.

15. Hauser, Marc. *Moral Minds: How Nature Designed Our Universal Sense of Right and Wrong*. New York: HarperCollins Publishers, 2006 at pp. 143–144.

16. Id. at p. 343.

17. See, e.g., Slovic, Paul, and Sarah Lichtenstein. "Preference Reversals: A Broader Perspective." *The American Economic Review* 73.4 (1983): 596–605.

18. Katcher, A. H. and A. Beck, "Animal Companions: More Companion Than Animal" in *Man and Beast Revisited*. Washington, D.C.; Smithsonian Institution Press (eds. M. H. Robinson and Lionel Tiger), 1991.

19. See, e.g., Hobson, Kersty. "Political Animals? On Animals as Subjects in an Enlarged Political Geography." *Political Geography* 26.3 (2007): 250–267.

20. Posner, Richard A. *Economic Analysis of Law*. Philadelphia: Wolters Kluwer, 2014 at p. 34.

21. Jones, Susan D. *Valuing Animals: Veterinarians and Their Patients in Modern America*. Baltimore: Johns Hopkins University Press, 2003.

22. See Deign, John. "On Rights and Responsibilities." *Law and Philosophy* 7.2 (1988): 147–178.

23. See generally Duckler, G. "Animal Wrongs: On Holding Animals to (and Excusing Them from) Legal Responsibility for Their Intentional Acts." *J. Animal L. & Ethics* 2 (2007): 91.

24. *Zager v. Dimilia*, 138 Misc.2d 448 (N.Y.Vill.Ct. 1988).

25. Well, most. Cf. Roger Taylor's romantic ode "I'm in Love with My Car" (Queen 1975).

26. Posner, Richard A. *Economic Analysis of Law*. Philadelphia: Wolters Kluwer, 2014.

27. The phrase was taken from *Hodges v. Causey*, 77 Miss. 353 (Miss. 1900).

28. See, e.g., *Carbasho v. Musulin*, 217 W.Va. 359 (W.Va. 2005); *Petco Animal Supplies, Inc. v. Schuster*, 144 S.W.3d 554 (Tex. App. 2004).

29. See Duckler, G. "Between Price and Pricelessness: Calculating the Specific Monetary Value of a Dog Intentionally Harmed by Another." *J. Animal L. & Ethics* 3 (2009): 121.

30. Dennett, Daniel Clement. *The Intentional Stance*. Cambridge, MA: MIT Press, 1989 at pp. 208, 276.

31. See, e.g., *Sentell v. New Orleans and Carrollton Railroad Co.*, 166 U.S. 698, 701 (1897); *Livingston, supra* at p. 233, n. 30.

32. William Blackstone, 2 *Commentaries* 393.

33. *Commonwealth v. Massini*, 188 A.2d 816 (Pa. Super. Ct. 1963) (noting that at common law, a cat could not be the subject of larceny); *Citizens' Rapid Transit Co. v. Dew*, 45 S.W. 790 (Tenn. 1898) (rejecting the common law view that a cause of action for larceny of a living dog will not lie because they are not considered property).

34. See, e.g., *Duff v. Louisville & N.R. Co.*, 292 S.W. 814 (Ky. Ct. App. 1927).

35. *Livingston, supra* at 787–88 (looking to numerous jurisdictions to derive a general definition of fair market value); See also *McCallister v. Sappingfield*, 144 P. 432 (Or. 1914).

36. *Nichols v. Sukaro Kennels*, 555 N.W.2d 689 (Iowa 1996).

37. *Morgan v. Kroupa*, 702 A.2d 630 (Vt. 1997) (stating that for most pets, "[their] worth is not primarily financial, but emotional; . . . value derives from the animal's *relationship* with its human companions"); See C. Oxford, UK: Oxford University Press, 1988 at 30–31.

38. Alan Beck & Aaron Katcher, *Between Pets and People: The Importance of Animal Companionship* 4–6 (1996).

39. Harvey, Jacky Colliss. *The Animal's Companion: People and Their Pets, a 26,000-Year Love Story*. London: Atlantic Books, 2019 at pp. 149–150.

40. See Rowlands, Mark. *Animals Like Us.* London: Verso, 2002 at pp. 171.

41. Cecil A. Wright, "Introduction to the Law of Torts," 8 *Cambridge L.J.* 238, 238 (1944).

42. ORS 30.020 et. seq.

43. 414 U.S. 573, 94 S.Ct. 806, 39 L.Ed. 2d 9 (1974).

44. See *Thompson v. Offshore Company*, 440 F. Supp. 752 (S. D. Texas 1977); *Voelker v. Frederick Business Properties Co.*, 465 SE 2d 246 (W. Va. 1995).

45. Duckler, G. "The Economic Value of Companion Animals: A Legal and Anthropological Argument for Special Valuation." *Animal L.* 8 (2002): 199.

46. See generally Richard and Alice Fiennes, *The Natural History of Dogs*. New York: Bonanza Books, 1968.

47. See generally Rowan, A. (ed.) *Animals and People Sharing the World*. Hanover, NH: University Press of New England, 1988; Mason, I. (ed.) *The Evolution of Domesticated Animals*. London: Longman Press, 1984.

48. Sick German shepherd carelessly euthanized by vet: value awarded $500.00 (*Fredeen v. Stride*, 269 Or. 369 (Or. 1974)); Collie intentionally shot while chasing a deer: value awarded $125.00 (*Stull v. Porter*, 100 Or. 514 (Or. 1921)); German shepherd intentionally shot while chasing chickens: value awarded: $250.00 (*Green v. Leckington*, 192 Or. 601 (1951)); Scotch collie intentionally shot in confrontation with horse: value awarded $200.00 (*McCallister v. Sappingfield*, 72 Or. 422 (1914)); Boxer intentionally shot by policeman: value awarded $300.00 (*City of Garland v. White* 368 S.W.2d 12 (Tex. Civ. App.1963)); Toy fox terrier killed by another dog: value awarded $100.00 (*Kling v. US Fire Ins. Co.* 146 So.2d 635 (La. App. 1962)); Mixed breed carelessly struck by motorist: value awarded: $100.00 (*Griffin v. Fancher* 20 A.2d 95 (Conn. 1941)); Shi Tzu killed by another dog: value awarded $500.00 (*Hyland v. Borras* 719 A.2d 662 (NJ Super AD 1998)); Sick Pekingese puppy carelessly euthanized by vet: value awarded $50.00 (*Lincecum v. Smith* 287 So.2d

625 (La. App. 1973)); German shepherd carelessly lost by kennel: value awarded: $1,000.00 (*Wertman v. Tipping* 166 So.2d 666 (Fla. App. 1964)).

49. Coren, Stanley. *The Intelligence of Dogs: A Guide to the Thoughts, Emotions, and Inner Lives or Our Canine Companions*. New York: Free, 2006.

50. Malik, Kenan. *Man, Beast and Zombie: What Science Can and Cannot Tell Us about Human Nature*. London: Weidenfeld & Nicolson, 2000.

51. Duckler, G. "Between Price and Pricelessness: Calculating the Specific Monetary Value of a Dog Intentionally Harmed by Another." *J. Animal L. & Ethics* 3 (2009): 121.

52. Katcher, A. H. and Beck, A. *Animal Companions: More Companion Than Animal*. In, *Man and Beast Revisited*, ed. Robinson, M. H. and Tiger, L. Washington, D.C.; Smithsonian Institution Press (1991).

53. Zajonc, R. B. "Attraction, Affiliation and Attachment." In *Man and Beast: Comparative Social Behavior*, ed. J. F. Eisenberg and W. S. Dillon. Washington, D.C.; Smithsonian Institution Press (1971).

54. Hyams, E. *Animals in the Service of Man*. Philadelphia: J. B. Lippincott Company, 1972.

55. Dworkin, R. *Taking Rights Seriously*. Harvard University Press, 1978.

56. Hoage, R. J. *Perceptions of Animals in American Culture*. Washington, D.C.: Smithsonian Institution, 1989.

57. See Duckler, G. 2004. "On Redefining the Boundaries of Animal Ownership: Burdens and Benefits to Evidencing Animals' Personalities." *Animal Law Journal 10:63*.

58. See Duckler, G. "Between Price and Pricelessness: Calculating the Specific Monetary Value of a Dog Intentionally Harmed by Another." *J. Animal L. & Ethics* 3 (2009): 121.

59. For an overview, see Bornstein, Robert F. "Exposure and Affect: Overview and Meta-Analysis of Research, 1968–1987." *Psychological Bulletin* 106.2 (1989): 265.

60. See *San Vicente Villas Homeowners Ass'n, Inc. v. Cohen*, Not Reported in Cal. Rptr.3d, 2003 WL 22962813 (Cal.App. 2 Dist.), Not Officially Published (Cal. Rules of Court, Rules 976, 977) (Cal. App. 2 Dist. 2003); *Triangle Management Corp. v. Inniss*, 62 Misc.2d 1095 (N.Y. City Civ. Ct. 1970); *Schnapp v. Lefkowitz*, 101 Misc.2d 1075 (N.Y. Sup. 1979); *Daughen v. Fox*, 372 Pa. Super. 405 (Pa. Super. 1988); *State v. Cowan*, 103 Ohio St.3d 144 (Ohio 2004); *Toledo v. Tellings*, Slip Copy, 2006 WL 513946 (Ohio App. 6 Dist. 2006).

61. See Harris, M. *Cannibals and Kings: The Origins of Cultures*. New York: Vintage Books 1977. "Domestication [of animals is] the greatest conservation movement of all times."

62. Serpell, J. *In The Company of Animals*. Oxford: Basil Blackwell Ltd., 1986. See also Rowlands, Mark. *Animals like Us*. London: Verso, 2002. Snyder, L. M. and E. A. Moore, *Dogs and People in Social, Working, Economic, and Symbolic Interactions*. London: Oxbow Books, 2006.

63. Schaffner, Joan. *An Introduction to Animals and the Law*. Houndmills, Basingstoke, Hampshire: Palgrave Macmillan, 2011. See also Robson, William Newby. *The Principles of Legal Liability for Trespasses and Injuries by Animals*.

Cambridge: University, 1915. Zajonc, R. B. "Attraction, Affiliation and Attachment" in *Man and Beast: Comparative Social Behavior*. Washington, D.C.; Smithsonian Institution Press (eds. J. F. Eisenberg and W. S. Dillon), 1971.

64. Robinson, Michael H., and Lionel Tiger. *Man & Beast Revisited*. Washington: Smithsonian Institution, 1991. Rowan, A. (ed.) *Animals and People Sharing the World*. Hanover, NH: University Press of New England, 1988.

65. See generally Lorenz, Konrad. *Man Meets Dog*. Hove, UK: Psychology Press, 2002.

Chapter 6

Animals in Zoos

"The Lion and the Lizard Keep the Courts"[1]

The head of a one-horned ram was brought to Pericles from his country-place, and Lampon the seer, when he saw how the horn grew strong and solid from the middle of the forehead, declared that, whereas there were two powerful parties in the city, that of Thucydides and that of Pericles, the mastery would finally devolve upon the man to whom this sign had been given. Anaxagoras, however, had the skull cut in two, and showed that the brain had not filled out its position, but had drawn together to a point, like an egg, at that particular spot in the entire cavity where the root of the horn began. Now there was nothing, in my opinion, to prevent both of them, the naturalist and the seer, from being in the right of the matter; the one correctly divined the cause, the other the object or purpose. It was the proper province of the one to observe why anything happens, and how it comes to be what it is; of the other to declare for what purpose anything happens, and what it means.[2]

Consider the visitor at the zoo in front of the polar bear exhibit. They see the bear pacing, turning, pacing, and turning. To a friend, they might comment critically on the stereotyped behavior: it is sad, it is disturbing, it is not natural, it is cruel to make the polar bear behave so erratically within the small confines imposed by an artificial environment. They might observe that were that particular bear to be in the wild it would almost certainly be "happier," "running free," and not pacing neurotically on a small patch of painted cement. They might even extrapolate from there, that the same would go for "all the bears in the exhibit," or "all polar bears in zoos everywhere," or "all animals in all zoos"—but they would start to find each level of that expansion tamped down in turn by private hesitations, nagging concerns that the picture is cloudier than they are proposing. Those pauses concede that human-animal

115

dynamics are unavoidably complex, and it is not lost on the visitor that they are here at the zoo voluntarily, and perhaps thus complicit in some fashion in whatever is happening both behind and in front of the bars. Saving face, they likely impart a scornful glance toward no one in particular and move a few yards down to go look at the next exhibit.

Privately, the visitor might feel the very human emotion of guilt. While they know rationally that *they* didn't cause this unhappy situation to come about, nonetheless, where they are standing seems to be a location intimately collaborative with a community that has facilitated the bear's capture, maintenance, and care, i.e., as a direct contributor to the disturbing result of a neurotic animal trapped in a cage. The discomfort perhaps shares a tone with a semireligious belief about, or a personal experience with, restrained animals in other walks of life, and is disconcerting enough to maybe thwart a return visit for some time—but eventually, on a date, for a class, as a parent or grandparent, they return.

The bear's pacing and the visitor's anxiety are connected at a deep level. Because they don't grasp abstractions, or manipulate symbols, or keep records, animals don't have their own historic or cultural processes, but since we do all those things, we tend to include animals as part of our own historical and cultural interests and worries, expending substantial time and energy trying to "interpret" for ourselves just what they are all about. The interpretation engenders as much confusion as it does enlightenment since there is no clear path as to "what an animal means" external to its simple fact of existence. It causes us in our group form to place the animal in a cage while simultaneously wishing, in our individual form, for its release.

Much of that paradox, and our confusion, stems from the disconnect we experience when comparing a) our own biological status as animals, b) our constructed religious beliefs about certain animals, c) our personal preferences for certain animals, and d) our amassed scientific knowledge about certain animals.[3] It is very hard to reconcile themes in which animals were somehow created for us, themes in which nature created both us and them, themes in which we need to handle them effectively as threats, and themes in which we impose obligations on ourselves to respect them as economically valuable. We certainly can't turn to religion for assistance: what religions are great at doing is using animals symbolically, often in rituals, to exemplify human neuroses and human fantasies. What religions *don't* do of course is take any sort of effort to mark out sensible, working definitions of what animals themselves actually are, their evolutionary origins and trajectories, or how they actually operate in the real world, a project that we are personally urged to attend to:

The true character of animals and their meaning in the world, once common knowledge to the humans whose lives intertwined with theirs, is today lost in a miasma of human fantasies. If the Industrial Revolution made animals into mere objects to be used as man saw fit, the nature worshiping counterrevolution that followed made them into objects of adoration to be revered. Wolves, the favorite villains of fairy tales, are now ecological heroes; but in transforming them into majestic symbols of the wild and free, today's nature enthusiast is no closer to understanding their true nature than were the brothers Grimm. The favorite animal in a survey of visitors to the National Zoo in Washington, D.C., was the giant panda, typically described by zoogoers as "cute, cuddly, and adorable." It actually is solitary, ill-tempered, and aggressive, but never mind.[4]

With zoo animals, lawyers adopt the cultural, not the taxonomic, stance, and treat zoo animals as "types." Scientists adopt the taxonomic stance, discerning, measuring, recording, and marking various attributes to flush out "species." No bright lines of demarcation are found by either discipline, including any clear lines dividing "us" from "them" even though biology focuses on the proximities while law focuses on the gaps. Both fields of inquiry take a thoughtful pause when noting the ferocity with which all the other animals engage in the most brutal and un-humanlike behaviors imaginable: predation, parasitism, exploitation of the infirm, the young and the old, the manipulation of every weakness by every strength possible. It befuddles lawyers and scientists alike that cooperation, altruism, and symbiosis are the exceptions in animal behavior, not the norm.

Both scientists and lawyers therefore question how we can be so like them yet not like them at all, with the former turning to analogue and the latter turning to morality on the paths toward their respective answers. These are inquiries started at childhood and interweave accumulated knowledge and firsthand observation with religious instruction and a flurry of messages from parents, teachers, and peers about decency, respect, and compassion. Science remains silent about proposing courses of conduct; biology and zoology predict and explain, but do not offer advice. Both lawyer and scientist, for their part, find that as they mature into their professions choosing what one is to do about any given animal at any given moment is the most challenging part of developing one's moral code about selecting research proposals and clients, resolving studies and cases, and presenting arguments on theories and effects back to the community.

ANIMAL-RELATED RITUALS CONNECT
MORAL COMMANDS AND PROSCRIPTIONS
TO LAWS ON CONFINEMENT

Morality twists and untwists itself around each thread of the common law in that the construction of any given set of rules is laced tightly by communal sentiments about the rightness and wrongness of who in the group has been harmed and who (or what) is the harm's source.

> Rules are conceived and spoken of as imposing obligations when the general demand for conformity is insistent and the social pressure brought to bear upon those who deviate or threaten to deviate is great. Such rules may be wholly customary in origin: there may be no centrally organized system of punishments for breach of the rules; the social pressure may take only the form of a general diffused hostile or critical reaction which may stop short of physical sanctions. It may be limited to verbal manifestations of disapproval or of appeals to the individuals' respect for the rule violated; it may depend heavily on the operation of feelings of shame, remorse, and guilt. When the pressure is of this last-mentioned kind we may be inclined to classify the rules as part of the morality of the social group and the obligation under the rules as moral obligation.[5]

Moral codes regarding animal restraint and display trace their group origin back to prehistoric concerns over personal harm and in the remains examined in our thanatocoenotic assemblage we discern the outlines of ritual, a classic component of how human nature privately and publicly expresses itself. What particular rituals we each have learned and use personally depend in large part on the fortuities of our upbringing and of geography, but the fact *that* all people learn and use them at all does not. There is huge variation in the rituals people have developed about manners, clothes, ornaments, praise, blame, sexual conduct, fidelity, homes, property, humor, storytelling, mourning of the dead, entry into adult life, trading, marriage, work, and friendship. What each ritual may be called from group to group and how each operates in its picky details varies depending on the local population, divvying up into the quaint niceties we call "customs." Nevertheless, that all these things are and have been present in every human community in some socially accepted format—that fact does not vary. Rituals—and animal-related rituals in particular—have been an integral part of human nature since before the earliest civilizations arose.

WHAT RITUALS ARE AND WHAT THEY ARE NOT
IN RELATION TO FORMS OF HUMAN CONDUCT

As "a fairly rigid set of repeated movements, fixed in order and sequence, the core gestures of which are primarily symbolic, in which the symbol is itself natural, not arrived at by convention, and often typical of a certain emotional state," real rituals are far narrower than the use of the term casually implies.[6] Simple repetition alone is not enough; there are many things we call "rituals" that don't fit the relevant definition. One's "morning ritual" of pouring and drinking of a cup of coffee—while certainly a very patterned activity that happens with regularity in pretty much the same way at the same time each day, is not a genuine ritual since the pouring and drinking have no external symbolic content—the pouring and drinking as movements are not representations or illustrations of larger concepts but are simply the combined functional method to get a desired substance into the body that, as a regimented set of steps, has slowly turned into a noteworthy habit.

Rituals in religious contexts tend to be easier to recognize. Under our definition, for example, given the assumption that many religions consider a dove to represent peace (or at least the general condition of peacefulness), then the quaint performance of publicly releasing a flock of doves whenever one wishes to make a certain political or public statement, as a symbolic act attuned to generic peacefulness, would readily be called a ritual. The gesture triggers a peculiar emotional state resulting from the aesthetic satisfaction we experience through seeing what a swath of birds looks like escaping confinement and crossing against the open sky. There is no internal content to the act—releasing those types of animals isn't an imperative since we are the ones who confined them in the first place—there is only external symbolic content and nothing more.

Rituals in cultural contexts are messier. Consider the classic childhood games of follow the leader, hide-and-seek, tag, leapfrog, and king-of-the-castle. Each one of these activities mimics crucial patterns that all living organisms confront in every community, yet all are expressed as a form of play with considerable symbolic content. Each game is a ritualized version of a basic animal drive or need that primarily has to do with harm and restraint: hiding from predators, chasing prey, demonstrating dominance over subordinates, and excluding competitors from coveted resources. By their stylized rules, however, all the steps in the games are really working hard as signals for something beyond the playful movements themselves, and all have a lot to do with recognizing and attending to the power all animals feel when in control of another's confinement and release.

In hide-and-seek, for instance, were a finder to *truly* want to find someone or a hider to *truly* want to hide from another, the devices and tools available to do so are nearly limitless and the outcome possibly fatal. The game as played, however, puts extremely artificial constraints on participants—none are allowed to go outside a certain area, finders must provide sufficient time for hiders to secrete themselves, being caught means being physically touched or observed in some special fashion, and once caught, hiders usually restrict themselves to a certain location or position. No actual harm or threat to harm is involved at all. All these constraints reflect a peculiar interest in a) confining and releasing others as a means of control and b) avoiding actual harm, all while the playing proceeds.

The confinement is symbolic, and its expression exaggerated; no animals are hurt in the making of the entertainment. Many rituals employ pageantry, costume, and a lexicon by the participants that is not easily understood by outsiders, all in order to either laud or obfuscate the symbolism. Take foxhunting for example. As an animal-related ritual of confinement, it has several core elements. One, to join requires a rather restrictive costume in the form of dress according to certain traditions. Two, full participation requires knowledge of an elaborate language code with descriptions of animals and hunting practices constructed in highly specific terms and phrases. Three, when put into motion as a practice, foxhunting for the human participants doesn't really even involve the actual hunting of foxes.[7]

From a step back, it is apparent that the dogs do all the work, and the "hunters" are barely hunting at all but are instead focused on the rote expression of a formalized set of actions by directing the dogs to engage in a predator-prey relationship with the foxes—actions artificially constrained through a mix of natural and constructed symbols in regularly repeated and stylized patterns of capture and release. Weighty prehistorical forces are at play in this odd game. Although foxes are killed as an end result of the hunt, their *being* killed is really not the hunt's central concern—as with bearbaiting and bullfighting, the particular *way* in which the animal's quite controlled death is brought about is far more the key symbolic point instead.

In previous incarnations in prehistory, the foxhunt has its parallels in the superstitious practices associated with our ancestors chasing and killing, and being chased and killed by, animals.[8] Participants would put on animal masks, execute animal-mimicking dances, and use animal components such as pelts and bones to exaggerate animalistic movements. Ritual dances associated with animal hunting and predation avoidance spotlight the desire by the participants to transfer the animals' identities to themselves and to facilitate an ability to "take on" the power or attributes of the animals. This desire created complicated attitudes: one needed to interfere with and harm the animal to accomplish it, by trapping, killing, or dismembering the animal, but one also needed to preserve the power or attributes it had so that the core desired object—the animal's strength as opposed to the animal itself—was not destroyed in the process.

Terms involving "respect" and "reverence" for the animal seem incongruous with the brutal and bare acts of evading, hiding, stabbing, piercing, flaying, and dismantling, but certain rites to ensure that the animal would not harbor animosity to the slayer built up over time, and certain aspects of how the attributes were to be transmitted developed as well, such that eating and drinking parts of the animal were believed to impart the attributes, while acting like the animal, having the animal in close proximity, or dominating the animal in some fashion, would all impart the strengths in a different manner.[9]

Not only were certain organs considered sources of power, but certain species deemed more suitable as conduits than others. Not only was the act of destruction ritualized, but so were the acts preceding and following: ceremonies of purification and absolution often accompany ritual killings, and the anatomical components that remain after the killing often provided special treatment. Animal-related rituals sometimes even forego physical acts and involve language games alone. Depictions of the quarry as having human qualities, penance by the hunter recited as a reflection of personal deprivation, the ritual rendering of the quarry's image in a variety of media is presented, and characterizations about the animal's incorporation into the human body is ritualized in group performances involving standing, chanting, and close quarter interactions with animals in confined spaces.[10]

Though the heart of all ritual has had an evolutionary function, many rituals have become so attenuated in time and space from their prehistoric origins that the initiating motivations have become overwhelmed by, and lost within, the swirling and degrading patterns. Rituals involving the confinement and release of animals can nevertheless be found everywhere you look: in prose and poetry and in artistic productions such as dance performance and film, from putting a rat in a maze to eating a chocolate rabbit to the nearly inscrutable version reflected in sports team mascots. The same elements are all there: the promise of interspecies transformation, the mimicking of the natural object, the repeated and methodical activity in a series of formal motions, the attempt to incite an emotional response in the participating community, and the pre- and post-ceremonial treatment of the venerated object.

This is all traceable to the development of religious belief at prehistorical stages when a god, worshippers, and the sacrificial victim, were all deemed members of the same prehistoric tribe; the animal being killed "belonged" to the people doing the killing as their owned or possessed object, and it was critical that the direct connection and relationship between the one who sacrifices and the sacrificial object was memorialized.[11] It isn't really that the worshipper of the sports team who clothes themselves in the pelt of the

team's mascot seeks to invest themselves with the totemic power of the particular animal, it is simply that they want themselves, the animal, and their
tribe to all be recognized as one singular community. It isn't unfair to claim
that sport team mascot garments are sacred in the manner that tassels and
fringes prescribed by Jewish law are sacred, or that the thongs of goatskin
used by ancient Libyans were sacred. Assyrians who worshipped fish gods
wrapped themselves in fish skins, Cyprians who worshipped sheep gods
wrapped themselves in sheepskins, and Chicagoans who worship Bears wrap
themselves in (fake) bearskins—and all find their rationale for doing so to be
shaded under the same original canopy of a communal desire to acknowledge
communal values and the power imbued in the capture and retention of a
beast feared, needed, and controlled.

In a sense, ritual games, ritual sacrifice, ritual observation, and ritual displays all have parallels among them that predate religious belief and stem
directly from our evolutionary interactions with other animals as potential
predators, potential prey, and potential competitors for resources. What was
once of the greatest importance in trying to assess that competition—the
entire assimilation of the personality into that of the animal by covering the
whole body in the animal skin, by ingesting the animal's blood, by attaching
the bones and hooves, by committing oneself to a hallucinogenic trance and
becoming the animal with all its muscles and joints and senses—over time all
that has been reduced to the extremes in all dimensions.[12] All that is outfitted
now is a single feather, or a single totemic image, or a single tooth or claw
as a trivialized amulet. All that is acted out is a simple pattern or a single ste-
reotypical motion. All that is displayed now is the animal with the cage bars
in front and the informational placard aside. The actual horns and charge and
smell and violence of the bull or lion merely have their faint allusions now,
but the allusions remark the source as a life-or-death concern over the capture
and confinement and use of an animal as a means of assuring the sanctity, the
safety and preservation, of one's own individual and group life.

The observation of animals in confined spaces therefore has a massive
cultural impetus to be maintained as a modernized ritual in all human populations. We are not talking about what occurs on the other side of the bars
where the animals sit in their pens. Certainly, on that side there is behaviorally
"ritualized" mating and behaviorally "ritualized" competition of animals in
captivity—every head butt to an intruder and groin thrust to a potential mate,
every menacing rush at a potential prey object, and every deflective cower in
retreat from a likely superior all have their place, and signals back and forth
from dominants to subordinates are fraught with an ethological import that
might well be called "symbolic" to some very limited extent.[13] There are far
more significant rituals to attend to however on the human side of the bars

of any animal cage, from the hamster in the bedroom to the elephant in the sanctuary.

ANIMAL DISPLAYS AND ARTIFACT DISPLAYS DIVERGE IN THEMES OF INFORMATION AND EXPERIENCE

Elaborate rituals tend to enable their participants to cope with deep anxieties, both physical and emotional, about the dynamic between the ritual object and the participant, and it is no different with people and animals. It is simply not that mysterious then, that our largest feelings of guilt, and our most elaborate customs about animals, all involve public captivity—particularly in zoos that we have deliberately constructed to observe animals in close confinement with ourselves in the form of aesthetically pleasing and morally assuaging collections and exhibits. Superficially similar to the way that we collect and exhibit books and art, we do collect and exhibit animals, but animal collections are very unlike other types of "serious" collections, including of human-made objects, literature, or art. Zoos as animal collections are also fundamentally unlike libraries or general compilations of accumulated items or information about the world such as libraries represent.

One reason for this is that living animals on display are not valued anything like original works of art or books. In addition, those who visit zoos don't go there to learn about humans or glean information, even zoological information, as one would with a research library, a museum, or school. Museums and libraries are associated with learning, are quiet and relatively reverential locales, invite lengthy periods of contemplation, encourage private experiences, and overall have the tradition of being adult-oriented institutions. Zoos, in contrast, are associated with popular entertainment, are much more social and shared public experiences, encourage shorter periods of observation and limited intellectual participation, do not lend themselves to enhancing aesthetic or intellectual experiences, and overall are much more child-oriented institutions.

Part of why zoos are popular in fact is that they are *not* academically intimidating—visitors don't need to have a high level of knowledge or really *any* knowledge in order to still have an enjoyable experience. Zoos are never organized as "systematic collections"—ones organized according to a specific scientific scheme—because zoo visitors don't particularly care about the niceties or utility of systematic presentations. Five minutes of eavesdropping on remarks made at the bars of any cage swiftly substantiate that the requirements of the public inside zoos are achingly marginal: patrons want to, one, confirm the common name of the animal they are looking at, two, obtain some assurance it is okay, and a distant third, pocket a few trivial facts about where it "normally" lives and what it "normally" eats. Beyond that, they are simply not interested, and untold hundreds of thousands of dollars have been wasted by zoos learning the hard way that accurate, information-packed, "educational" placards about the animals on display are consistently passed by unnoticed, unread, and unappreciated.

That "limited information" model is a reflection of two tangled ideas that angle back to our thoughts on value: one, that visually and tactically animals have a *high* emotional significance to people in general as a byproduct of our evolutionary heritage, and two, that intellectually and situationally animals have a *low* situational significance to people who actually visit zoos, since the average zoo visitor is a highly urbanized city-dweller who will encounter, at the most, a few dogs, cats, mice, and pigeons in the course of their entire lives. While the aim of most zoo directors is to try to make the exotic animals on display personally significant, success in that area is hard to come by, and creates an inherently contradictory quality to the experience. Sliding "views" into the slot of "hot dogs" from our earlier example derives an equation where modest monetary amounts on contribution and investment yield larger emotive amounts in enjoyment and return of the purchased experience.

Monkeys, of course, are not Monets. Individual items in museum collections and in art galleries are unique and irreplaceable at an easily recognizable level, from the Mona Lisa on down. Cute names notwithstanding, no individual animal in a zoo collection, on the other hand, is objectively considered unique, and the patent interchangeability of one zebra for another makes it that visitors just don't consider any particular resident to attain any special status as a general principle. Historically, captive animals have had no intrinsic worth, even though they've had plenty of extrinsic appeal, nor can they be deemed part of a historical cultural process such as with machines, inventions, or written or spoken ideas, since we did not "make" them and since they themselves do not reflect any genesis, thoughtful step, or endpoint in our own cultural development.

As the zoo gift shop brusquely reminds us, artistic *representations* of animals—in the countless drawings, paintings, engravings, and sculptures one sees regarding animal forms—are different since they require transforming the literal image of the animal into something new that required effort, creativity, imagination, and technical skill. For that reason, a Henri Rousseau painting of a tiger is deemed much more valuable to us than the actual tiger that the painting was based on.[14] Animals, not being man-made, require no interpretation, but being alive, active, and ultimately unpredictable, nevertheless require significant amounts of direct concern in the form of pragmatic (and symbolic) control and care.

Zoos often try, in vain, to increase the intellectual worthiness of their residents by explaining how the animal is representative of a certain species with certain characteristics that become ecologically compelling when placed in a certain setting. Still, the individual animals on display pay the price of being of little individual account, since the story of their exact lives in that setting and their relations with others living in the zoo is really not the story that the zoos want to tell—it is far too limited in scope and interest. For that reason, one finds that the information provided in every captive display is usually about how the *species* would or should live in the wild, not how the individual sitting right there actually lived before capture or lives in captivity at all:

> Should one really learn that the chimpanzee, for example, is a neurotic humanoid that cadges food from humans and throws tantrums and excreta should this not materialize? Or that the orang-utan which by nature seldom descends to the soft forest floor, is a pathetic bundle of matted red fur in the corner of a tiled cell?[15]

A PLAY IN ANIMAL FORM

The standard zoo visitor does not really want to be reminded of what they actually witness, a scene that uncomfortably reminds them of an all-too-familiar experience: their own close-quarter housing made from industrial materials with all the accoutrements of the domestic residence that they just recently left, replete with dishes and drains, doors and artificial lights. They would much rather be prompted to use their imagination to put the animal in a wildly different context, a natural habitat of which they have absolutely no firsthand experience whatsoever and most likely never will. Rather than be goaded to form abstract concepts of distant places and circumstances, zoo visitors simply wish to be effortlessly transported to a foreign locale using that particular animal in that particular cage as the vehicle to do so. What they truly seek is theater and what they have really come to see is a play.

Theater is what one encounters at the zoo. An animal in a cage is an actor, acting out the ages-old drama of wildness and capture, tameness and release, and the viewer wishes to be entertained by its activity as if all those things had already occurred and already been overcome, and that the animal had already been released and its geographical and evolutionary remoteness or proximity to the observer afforded no real immediate impact. In zoos, the idea of an animal as an actor blind to its own blind audience is an accepted one, but it is complex. We want the acting to consist of an animal's natural actions as if it was in the wild, not its unnatural actions in response to its captivity.

"Activity" is really the key; a classic sociology study of zoo visitors made the famous observation: "Where there is no movement, there is no fun."[16] The study revealed that while visitors don't really like seeing stereotyped, begging, sexual, aggressive, predatory, or excretory actions by animals, they sure like seeing any or all those things a lot more than seeing simply no action at all.

The zoo is a theater of inauthenticity attempting to tell a story of authenticity. Visitors want a very peculiar show—one of generic contentment, nonthreatening visual interest, and some mild, but not radical, novelty. In basic ways, pet owners want much of the same thing and pet store inventories crassly cater to that very aim. Exotics in zoos, however, are not so compliant, and tend to not act in the way that the public either wishes or is told that they really do act. Moreover, their environments have to be intricately manipulated to make it seem that the behaviors, if they ever occurred, would be occurring in the right place for them to do so were they to do so.[17] Here is a recitation of what one is really experiencing in the "Asian forest" section of the Bronx Zoo:

> Obviously this is not an Asian forest, since Asian forests do not grow in New York, yet it is almost impossible to remember that one is in fact in a building. It is a man-made forest not just in the sense that trees and plants have been put in a particular location by man, but in the more profound sense that many of the trees are actually manufactured by man. The huge tree which dominates one of the areas is actually made out of steel tubing over which there is metal cloth which is itself covered by an epoxy resin textured and painted so carefully that most people would never guess that it is fake. The vines that climb around it are real vines. Some vines however are not, and those which are provided for the gibbons to swing on are fiberglass. The mist which envelopes the tree tops is real mist but it is produced not by natural conditions, but by the sort of machine commonly used in commercial citrus groves. The rockwork is artificial but it is a base on which real peat moss and algae grow. Here one can see animals which actually do live in Asian forests, but what one does not see is the animals living as they would do in that forest. The sound of the cooing of the forest dove is real, but it was recorded in Thailand. It needed architects, zoologists, botanists, graphic designers, construction workers, welders, carpenters, painters, electricians, plumbers, audio specialists, gardeners, muralists, cabinetmakers, and glaziers to build a jungle to human specifications in New York. All this then is man-made space, a human interpretation of a jungle world designed, constructed and managed by human effort in order to generate a particular experience of the natural world.[18]

We need ritual confinement and we take great pains and expense to continually maintain it. Modern human communities don't engage in ritual animal

sacrifice anymore, but all modern human communities have zoos and the phenomena are intimately connected in that zoos are the modern perturbations
of what animal sacrifices initially aimed to produce as an initially functional,
and then consequently emotive, payoff. The payoff attained by the zoo never
quite succeeds, and attempts by zoos to give a full impression of a species'
natural behavior, natural relationships, and natural surroundings must always
fail in several senses, the largest being that since the artificial environment
utilized is but a minute part of a radically different actual environment,
our intense evolutionary need to memorialize the control of other animals
remains unsatisfied, and sits as a detraction and distraction from fulfilling
core desires.

So, the zoological theater is what first were terrifying life-or-death chases,
then were cleverly constructed traps, then were elaborate animal sacrificial
altars, and eventually were pig pens, chicken coops, and dog kennels now all
roiled together in a high-production-value format. Commercial and public
pressure constantly exists to provide each new generation of actors a slightly
better stage than the one before, and with more complex scenery and props
to make the illusion of naturalness more visually satisfactory, or at least as
satisfactory as biologically possible.

BEHAVIORS IN CAPTIVITY AS NECESSARILY
AND ARTIFICIALLY CONSTRAINED

So: zoos are institutions established for human pleasure, but it is a pleasure
then that is morally convoluted. One complication involves the realities of
animal behaviors as they occur in non-captive "natural" environments. Not
just the standard acts of predation, but carcass scavenging, consumption of
the young, exclusion of the weak, despoliation of micro and macro environments, and a brutal mortality in all its myriad forms, are all areas of animal
conduct that humane concerns would press us to prevent no differently than
us preventing a pet dog from eating a pet cat. Zoos must comport with those
same outwardly imposed moral guidelines no differently than when we
tamp down and impose strictures on animal behaviors in our homes and on
our streets.

Because true life-in-the-wild-type acts would be far too distasteful for any
visitor to actually observe, moral attitudes therefore cause us to engage in a
constant "ethical restructuring" of the stage, scenery, and props on and with
which animal actors are allowed, quite restrictively, to put on their plays
while in captivity. In maintaining organized exotic animal collections for the
last four thousand years, we have been dabbling in an artistic medium that has
very close connections to the medieval morality play, the religious pageant,

and the Victorian drama, and we have done so through manipulating a company of strange actors we have had the chance or skill to capture and exhibit, but with whom we share uncomfortably close ties as evolutionary colleagues and whom have not developed their own culture, morality, or responsibility in any fashion. Neither, of course, do they grasp the import of what we have done to them—and guiltily we note that obliviousness as well. Turning away while the bear paces exacts a hard price.

Zoos are institutions for human entertainment, although our enjoyment of what they exhibit is more elaborate than even the most intricately nested film or play. Prehistorically, we tended to place other animals in confinement as an evolutionary adaptation to protection and competition, part and parcel of a practical strategy to deal with them effectively as threats and as competitors. With the threat mostly removed, historically we continue to place animals in confinement, now more to be entertained by our ability to confine and their activities in confinement, and their utility to us regularly includes a mix of their aesthetic appeal along with their ceremonial value as captives. Moral attitudes about what is appealing in animals stem from sources independent of the attitudes we have developed culturally as to what is appealing in human-constructed objects, i.e., artifacts. Our captivity rituals make us continually reassess and restructure the stage, scenery, and conditions under which we require confinement tales to be told.

The visitor to the zoo acts out their own pattern, tracing a series of symbolic steps that others have trod before them and will likely trod after. They are the trappers and the trapped, seeking out ritualized observations of confined animals in order to reconcile conflicting thoughts regarding control and use that have been transmitted from their ancestors across generations and entrenched as evolutionary adaptations to the local environment. Visiting a zoo is an exercise in assessing zoological self-knowledge, an ontological parsing out of what do we truly know or not know of the shifting roles people can play in eluding or embracing the more unfamiliar animals they might encounter.

ANALYZING WHAT "RIGHTS" MIGHT BENEFIT
OR BURDEN ANIMALS IN CONFINEMENT

Here, the lawyer-scientist pauses to contemplate in what manner laws link up with biology regarding animals maintained inside discrete boundaries. Folding the natural history of captive animals into their regulation returns us to what legal rights are and how they are employed regarding the concept of captivity. With captive animals, the most applicable rights to confront are substantive rights of freedom from undue restraint and the ownership of private property, and our death assemblages disclose two skeletons lain out side by side in every excavation we examine: threats to communal safety and freedom from restraint.

> I desired, above all things, to give the animals the maximum of liberty. I wished to exhibit them not as captives, confined to narrow spaces, and looked at between bars, but as free to wander from place to place within as large limits as possible, and with no bar to obstruct the view and serve as a reminder of captivity.[19]

The zoologist Carl Hagenbeck spent a good deal of his professional life occupied with proving the assertion that captive animals, even and especially dangerous ones, deserved the benefits of certain liberties, including the liberty to not be enclosed in what he recognized and despised to be animal prisons. Hagenbeck never felt, however, that animals should be completely liberated; a zookeeper above all else, keeping, not releasing, animals was his occupation.[20] Hagenbeck labored under the common misconception people have that humans have become liberated from certain constraints in a way that animals have not. It is a misconception that the lawyer-scientist is in a unique position to tackle head-on.

In thinking about the strata of legal rights, starting with rights to "freely move about" and to "own property" and moving toward more esoteric types of rights, lawyers confront three predicate questions: What are rights in the first place, to whom do those rights apply, and how are the rights actually given effect? With zoo animals, the first question asks: What is meant when we talk about a zoo animal possessing a legal right to move freely or to own objects as humans do? The second asks: What type of legal objects might zoo animals be considered given that they could be rights holders under the law? The third asks: What legal procedures would enable us to enforce, or restrict us from altering, the legal status of zoo animals were they to be rights holders? It is readily apparent that these questions track our epistemological, ontological, and methodological pathways of inquiry, and it is appropriate that we do our best to objectively apply those tools in the answers.

Every "right" is composed of three connected pieces. One is that it must include the privilege of having something done for the holder (or not done against them). A second is that it must include the holder's acknowledgment that an action runs to their benefit and to another's detriment. The third is that there must be some social contract describing it and providing some penalty for its violation. To posit an *animal* as the holder conjures up a host of odd images with the first two pieces, in part because acts of will seem to be implicated. Can animals appreciate the privilege of having something done for them? Can animals acknowledge benefits or detriments? With privileges such as obtaining a driver's license or executing a will, why would an animal even *care* to do those things, and what would be the point of pretending that they should?

An animal's privilege in applying for or receiving a driver's license is conceptually and practically foolish, but the privilege of being free from being tortured to death in scientific experimentation, on the other hand, does not seem absurd at all. The privilege of being free from undue restraint and receiving basic necessities appear to be appropriately vested in animals. The modifier "undue," by the way, is crucial: the existence of devices such as traffic lights, door locks, and prison cells should make it very clear that the right of humans to be free from restraint has itself historically been a *qualified*, not an absolute right, stemming originally from a privilege humans grant to themselves that is inherently constrained by the worrying presence and potentially harmful activity of other humans around them. From John Locke to Sigmund Freud, it has been well recognized that our very sociality hampers true freedoms of mobility and private ownership. It is our historical agreement among ourselves to recognize that sociality, moreover, that details the qualifications in law. Alone on a desert island, one has no "right" to be free at all, being that the right's assertion, whatever form that could be, would be purely abstract and the conduct of enforcing it an act of nonsense.

Imagine a set of laws granting animals in general the first right, a right to freedom from undue restraint. How might such laws then affect zoo animals? At first glance, it might seem that the very premise could not hold—zoo animals are by definition restrained organisms and applying a right to *not* be restrained would be a logical inconsistency, eliminating the category "zoo animal" (and the cages) altogether. The word "undue," however, resolves inconsistency since the right could survive and be given force if the captivity of animals in zoos were allowed as a general circumstance but in such a way so that the captive animal benefited from the proscription of true abuse or mistreatment while captive, or from the prevention of captivity within an inherently abusive environment. That benefit, of course, then requires that the animal at the very least comprehend and at the very most themselves employ abilities to open locks, access enclosed and open areas voluntarily, and voluntarily submit to, or voluntarily decline, the fastening of some manner of restraint. The privilege of possessing, including possessing basic necessities of life, has separate considerations. Humans have it (in most circumstances), while animals do not since animals are not rational agents who can cognitively appreciate the benefits and detriments of exclusivity or possession.

All rights are dynamic, that is, by their nature they change over time as ideas and policies about their particular utility change. For that reason, they are often conceptually divided into those that attach to the person, and those that attach to the situation, so that who one is and in what situation they may find themselves eventually will affect the viability of the right itself. One's right to vote "at all" goes with them wherever they go (except to jail), but their right to vote "in a certain jurisdiction" may very well end the moment they cross that jurisdiction's borders. One's right to vote "now," may have only recently come into existence historically, or, on the opposite side of that coin, may perhaps be abridged in the future depending on status and conduct.[21]

The right of humans to be free from undue restraint is an odd mixture of both types of attachment: in general it has historically attached to the holder, and seems to be given value no matter what part of the country people find themselves in (although its enforcement certainly changes with the jurisdiction). The right of humans to be free of particular undue restraints, on the other hand, often attaches to the situation: it may well be that by political fortuity alone the same defendant being prosecuted for the same type of crime would stand shackled in a Texas courtroom but unshackled in a Washington courtroom.

Would a zoo animal's general privilege to not be unduly restrained necessarily be tied to its physically being inside a zoo's boundaries? By necessity, it would have to be as zoos are places of restraint by their nature, restraints that don't occur nor make sense to be imposed outside of zoos. While domestic animals can be left free to roam, once they are removed from their native surroundings, they by necessity must be more strictly confined—and we regularly define zoo animals in general as animals that are exotic to the place of confinement. It is mandatory then that a good working definition of the right therefore will be intrinsically dependent on the definition of what is a zoo animal at all.

Even as attaching to the situation, an animal's "right" prohibiting undue restraint inside a zoo is problematic. Zoo vets, for example, often force contraceptive measures on potentially breeding pairs to prevent surplus animals from being born. Such actions would undoubtedly violate a person's right to be free from unwanted interference with bodily functions, and in fact forced contraception has been proscribed when proposed, for example, as sentencing alternatives for prisoners. The ability to test the effects of various immobilizing drugs on animals, such as the use of tranquilizers, would also be impaired by a privilege to not be unduly restrained. Rights, like measurements of time and space, are relative, and all rights are definitively relative to each other; thus, the expansion of certain rights for zoo animals inevitably commands the contraction of certain rights for others.

The expression 'free as a bird' is misleading: animals in the wild are prisoners of space and time.[22]

The image of the zoo animal as a prisoner is commonly tendered among social scientists and animal rights advocates, due in part to the numerous superficial similarities between the two groups.[23] Zoo animals regularly find themselves in prison-like conditions, surrounded by people who appear to act much like wardens, guards, and visitors. Bars and security measures are prevalent, and substantial effort is expended to prevent escape and harm to those on the outside. There is a general feeling inside most zoos that the visitor stands on the margins of a minimum- or maximum-security environment looking in from a safe distance at the daily life of a prison community whose wardens are concerned about the physical and psychological welfare (or at least the appearance of the physical and psychological welfare) of the workers and the visitors above that of the inmates.

While the similarities between exotics and prisoners may therefore seem sociologically apropos, the comparison is a poor one in a legal sense given how rights and penalties apply. For one thing, we must look at the basis for the rights that real prisoners themselves have (and don't have) and ask if zoo animals are truly comparable in ways that the law holds to be fundamental to prisoners in being socially penalized for socially disapproved misconduct.

Jurisprudentially, zoo animals are not prisoners at all. They were not incarcerated in order to be explicitly punished, to be rehabilitated, or as a deterrent to others seeking to engage in similar conduct, nor are zoo animals promised under some social contract to be eventually released when a certain condition, such as a specified period of time or the payment of a fine, has passed.[24] Zoo animals are instead confined under conceptually different guidelines than are prisoners due to the absence of any social obligations to conduct themselves in a special manner to either avoid or complete the "incarceration" that has been imposed. In other words, humans reside in prisons exclusively *on account of* behaviors and *in spite of* their biological status, whereas animals reside in zoos *in spite of* behaviors and *on account of* their biological status. The contrast is fundamental.

When people talk about rights, they work from the premise that rights affect people *on account of* behaviors and *in spite of* biological status, and when people talk about rights they therefore cannot help but be driven toward a discussion of moral principles derived from behavior not biology, since rights often stem directly from moral propositions about behavioral similarities among people and in rejection of biological distinctions.[25] The right to be free is based in part on a moral belief that freedom is good and absolute restraint (like slavery) is bad regardless of what "biological type" of person is being restrained.

While the moral reasons may be muddled up with one another, it is inescapable that prisoners are kept in prisons on moral grounds even if the legal terms slightly vary in their moral presumptions from jurisdiction to jurisdiction. Animals in zoos, to the contrary, are not kept in captivity under any moral presumption whatsoever (certainly not explicit, documented ones), and are both placed in and remain in captivity without any contractual or social relationship to refer to that might justify either their removal from the wild or their reintroduction back into it.

THE DAY CARE AS A FUNCTIONAL MODEL FOR ANIMAL CAPTIVITY

Consider instead a zoo animal to be on par with an infant or child—not in terms of mind, behavior, or appearance, but solely in terms of social status. In one sense, infants and children are conceptually akin to animate personal properties, being movable objects controlled primarily by the one who bred them in which specific ways of treating, disposing, and conveying them are respectively approved and prohibited. Under the model, their own behavior is irrelevant. Children are placed in and stay in day care facilities regardless of (and sometimes in absolute antagonism to) any social obligation to conduct themselves in a particular fashion.

Children in day cares may not be relieved of the restraint simply because they comport themselves differently over time, or because time passes (other than that they eventually get too old to be in the day care). They are not in any sense prisoners, and they are "confined" *on account of* their biological status and *in spite of* their behaviors, like animals. As with animals placed in zoos, children in day cares are there because a responsible person has recognized it beneficial to other people to place them there, sometimes even if it is not entirely beneficial to the child. As with animals placed in zoos, children in day cares have their daily needs met with or without their assistance or even their knowledge.

Like zoo animals, children barely comprehend, and are expressly barred from employing, abilities to open locks, access enclosed and open areas voluntarily, and voluntarily submit to, or voluntarily decline, the fastening of some manner of restraint. The stay is indefinite, regimented, and primarily for ulterior purposes. We do use, with infants, bars (of a sort), and security devices, and escape prevention measures, all to a lesser degree than with prisoners obviously, but our attitudes towards why we do so is entirely reversed from the penal model, it is (hopefully) fiduciary and beneficial, not adversarial and punitive.

Restraint isn't just physical, it is proprietary as well; children certainly do not "own" their sneakers, toys, and blankies in the sense that it would violate a law or right to take those items away from them, but they also certainly do seem to "own" the parts of their own bodies and the food that they have acquired in that same sense. Neither zoo animals nor children in day cares can effectively communicate with anything near the sophistication and understanding of adults, thereby making it impractical for each to personally assert any rights that might benefit them. The concept of parent and guardian carries with it the concept that a human is protecting privileges that the child has but cannot even identify or appreciate, much less demand or assert. So it may be with zookeepers and their furry and scaly charges.

Who would assert a right on behalf of either a child in a day care or an animal in a zoo? The list of possible candidates to be the child's protector is a slim and sensible list—the natural or adoptive parent most easily comes to mind. The list of possible candidates to be the animal's protector, on the other hand, is awe-inspiring—zookeepers, animal trainers, administrators, visitors, the American Zoo and Aquarium Association, the American Wildlife Federation, knowledgeable research scientists, the ASPCA, and the interested general public all might vie for the position, with none demonstrating a clear claim to priority. Depending on who is selected as the "spokesperson," outcomes would vary drastically in the definition, prosecution, and vindication of whatever is the perceived "violated" right.[26]

Even with the zoo animal's right asserted by someone reasonable and responsible, the right must be memorialized in or taken from a formal legal document. The easiest method for doing so is to utilize an already existing document outlining other primary rights, such as a statute or constitution. Given the use of the word "person" throughout those documents, the definition of "person" would either have to be expanded considerably, risking making the word into nonsense, or the documents themselves would have to be drastically revamped to replace the term, with the attendant consequences.

The rule in *Pierson v. Post* reminds us that animal possession, including of exotics, as a reward earned for undergoing the risks involved with the animal's restraint and confinement, and for assuming the cloak of responsibility society sheds at the moment of confinement. Transforming products of nature into products of the marketplace has been a relatively straightforward and somewhat unremarkable process for humans; transforming animals as proprietary trade goods, whose rights in their use and enjoyment have been bought and paid for in labor as well as in the acceptance of personal liability, into rights-possessing objects themselves is, to the contrary, an immense paradigm shift.

RIGHTS CONFINE, NOT UNSHACKLE,
BEHAVIORS FROM RESPONSIBILITIES

Law embraces written works transmitted across generations, which are the bars on our own cages, rules that *constrain*, not liberate, a plethora of human activities. Laws change as human behaviors change, but don't truly *create* freedoms, instead reflecting the compulsion on humans to impose burdens on freedoms that already had been recognized and enjoyed in nature. The "moral" document called the federal Constitution was constructed to memorialize the obvious idea that absolute restraint is bad but that limited restraints are necessary for all to enjoy the benefits of liberty. While "person" is not defined in that document, it is implied that it is species-specific and that the freedoms delineated have intrinsic value only for Homo sapiens. The reference to "life" in our historical declaration of our independence from England, and upon which the intrinsic value of the Constitution is thereby based, is solely "human life," not any other life. We have made a historical, although not necessarily a logical or scientific, decision to legally trod that path:

> Laws of societies, unlike laws of nature, of course, can be violated and can be changed. They are transient, rather than permanent, properties of a population, which may or may not be subject to revision by reform as opposed to alteration by revolution. It depends upon historical conditions, including the customs, traditions, and practices of that society. Thus, the proclamation that all men are endowed with certain *inalienable rights* represents a conception of how a society ought to be organized as a normative ideal. It reflects a commitment to conduct that society (through the adoption of suitable policies, procedures, and laws) in such a fashion as to promote those aims for the members of that society, not just for *some* of its members, moreover, but for *all* of them-although at the time slaves were not citizens and women not allowed to vote![27]

The distinction renews the issue of classification; ultimately what objects have been placed in zoos, and what criteria are used to justify distinctions among the residents of zoos, are questions that, tempered by preference and prejudice, are accountable to useful taxonomies, scientific, cultural, legal, or otherwise. Zoos may often list taxonomic classifications on informational materials and displays associated with their residents, yet rarely do they use taxonomic classifications to select and manage the residents. Zoos are hardly concerned with taxonomy, since taxonomy interferes with the economics and the cultural underpinnings to what zoos are all about.[28] Zoos, whether viewed as small arks or large coffins, carry inside them a skewed and illogical variety of oddly selected mishmash assemblages of evolving animals.[29] Though bars have been placed between the observer and the observed, they circumscribe areas candidly reflecting the evolution of the common law far more than of the organic evolution of animals.

> The origin of menageries dates from the most remote antiquity. Their existence may be traced even in the obscure traditions of the fabulous ages, when the contests of the barbarian leader with his fellow-men were relieved by exploits in the chase scarcely less adventurous, and when the monster-queller was held in equal estimation with the warrior-chief. The spoils of the chase were treasured up in common with the trophies of the fight; and the captive brute occupied his station by the side of the vanquished hero. It was soon discovered that the den and the dungeon were not the only places this link of connection might be advantageously preserved, and the strength and ferocity of the forest beast were found to be available as useful auxiliaries. . . .[30]

DISTINGUISHING ZOO ANIMALS FROM OTHER COMMERCIAL OBJECTS

Economically, we can recognize, as rational consumers seeking to maximize self-interest, this compelling insight: the animals that compose a zoo's mandatory guest list must be a function of the marketplace and of people's views on animal value in all its symbolic and pragmatic permutations. When considered as objects of value alone, zoo animals find themselves to be fundamentally distinct from other commercial objects in at least three ways.

First, zoo animals by nature are unique and irreplaceable objects. The biology of modern genetics commands even the legal recognition that every animal is a distinct fingerprint of nature, each unlike that of any other, each having never arisen before or likely ever to be repeated in nature's pattern. We have remarked that genetic variation has the clout to construct a singular object in the universe, a status inapplicable to non-living commercial properties, even hand-crafted ones, since any artificially manufactured object can be replaced given enough time, money, and interest in doing so.

The contrast between the fundamental composition of zoo animals and of other personal properties is a crucial one, given that nested deep within each animal, be it mite or moose, rests an organic trademark for that entity constructed of an astonishingly complex chains of nucleic acids and describing (in the language of molecular compounds) an astonishingly specific natural object.[31] Should the article of trade with which one is bargaining happen to be a living creature, the trader is compelled to live with the fact, good or bad as it may be, that it is the only one of such kind in the entire world that has been or ever will be.[32] By that fact, the condition of inherent irreplaceability, the opposite of fungibility, must be incorporated into the legal status of zoo animals as material objects.

Second, zoo animals are much more noticeable and much more public commercial items than the vast majority of commercial objects. As with works of art, certain market transactions involving zoo animals are especially vulnerable to public scrutiny and under such scrutiny often become cloaked with a notoriety not accompanying non-living goods. That those transactions engage the emotions and strident opinions of the communities in which they occur, suggests that the items in the exchanges are worthy of more sensitive treatment than that given standard trade goods.

Third and finally, zoo animals, similar to livestock and dissimilar to pets and pests, form an integral part of the ecological health of every community in which they reside, a community composed of owners and nonowners.[33] In recognizing that overall biological and cultural health and diversity is increased by the presence, and damaged by the absence, of zoo animals, we find that oscillations in that health and diversity transcend the maximizing self-interest of just the owner and the buyers in the marketplace.[34] In other words, more interests than purely economic ones are at stake in the ownership of zoo animals as properties. As an aspect of their relativity to environmental laws, laws regulating animals as properties encroach hard upon the protection and enforcement of communal and environmental health.

Zoos preserve and keep captive what they and the paying public like— primarily large and unusual-looking terrestrial mammals. On that account, zoo animals are not representative of *Animalia*, and collections are instead (poorly) representative of minor subdivisions of *Mammalia* alone. Were there to be laws directly ensconcing zoo animals as special properties, they would need to enfold inside of them realistic, legal, and scientific distinctions between the large mammals and all others. Economics notwithstanding, there are animals it simply makes no sense to enclose—technologically, it is possible to keep whales captive for short periods of time, but doing so would be disastrous on several levels. Genetically bottlenecked species, abused animals, truly nomadic animals with no specific home range, all defy the need or logic for extensive captivity.

Zoo animals may be at one and the same time entertainment devices, educational displays, museum curiosities, research subjects, dangerous instruments, pets on their way to being domesticated, or wild things simply passing through an artificial enclosure soon on their way to being wild once more. To lawyers, nevertheless, zoo animals are foremost the personal and business properties of other people, and our current myopia about the potential sophistication of such a role carries with it great risks.

ENVISIONING A FUTURE FOR ZOOS
AND THEIR INHABITANTS

Some animal advocates have commented that the social compact to treat zoo animals as properties betrays the callousness of social compacts in general. But it can also be appropriately said that at the prehistorically ancient moment humans evolved an ability to subject other animals to captivity, the course toward the circumstances of the present day was unavoidable. It is naïve to think that the social compacts that developed in the past can now be abrogated merely by appeals to humans to start being less callous. The better aspects of human nature are rarely brought forth by pleas for their appearance, Hollywood movies notwithstanding. The hard fact is that social costs and private costs combine to enable good human qualities to be brought forward much more readily by the prospect of a substantial reward for displaying them in social situations. The drive not to be better, but to be better than the other person, is an evolutionary phenomenon with as much applicability to modern human activities as it has had to ancient transformations of long-extinct animals millions of years ago.

> To choose what is best for the near future is easy. To choose what is best for the distant future is also easy. But to choose what is best for the near future and the distant future is a hard task, often internally contradictory, and requiring ethical codes yet to be formulated.[35]

The future for zoos is inextricably linked to our own past. From the Egyptian stage through the Roman, European, and to the American stage, a zoological menagerie, whatever its physical form, has been primarily intertwined with the symbolic role of animals within the culture that maintains it. No one eats, harvests, or employs the animals in zoos; they are mostly urban luxuries, representing the city dweller's aesthetic perception of and romantic nostalgia for the wild. Objects of awe and ridicule simultaneously, zoo animals carry on their backs the pomp and circumstance of evolution's majesty, and on their faces the poignant look of the circus clown. Past and present, risk and reward, coalesce with each exhibit in the park.

In turn, from its inception in prehistory, the law has been primarily concerned with the symbolic role of human interactions within each culture that maintains it. No one physically creates or destroys those relationships—they are either recognized or ignored, caringly recorded and attended to, or carelessly forgotten and abandoned. Symbolic values thus permeate our concept of how we perceive ourselves (via law) and our concept of how we perceive other animals around us (via zoos). To envision a captive animal as a child in a daycare or as a historical monument is a thought experiment that reflects on both perceptions and embraces concerns that laws and zoological parks regularly touch on, among them communal welfare, human compassion, and environmental health. Justifications for confinement spark hosts of questions, among them whether the entity would be better off a) left to its own devices or b) under some restraint, whether the entity would be better off c) if objects around it were controlled by others or d) if it retained full control, and whether the entity would be better off e) under a written document outlining rules for its maintenance, or f) where regulation is circumstantial or by informal consensus.

A DEMOGRAPHIC WINTER APPROACHES FOR ANIMALS IN AND OUT OF CAPTIVITY

Are zoos arks or prisons, asylums or sanctuaries, classrooms or theaters? People use animals for all sorts of things, but one thing that people do not use animals for is for making cultural distinctions among themselves. Animals are not used as objects that readily divide or demarcate one human community or one civilization from another. Artifacts, that is, man-made objects, are and have been used in very sophisticated ways to help us understand ourselves and our complex social histories—the sciences of archeology and of cultural anthropology are entire disciplines centered around unearthing, recovering, and interpreting the real meaning of our past through artifacts.

Animals travel on a coextensive trajectory with artifacts. As we now are keenly aware, due to our commercial and agricultural activities of the last four centuries or so, humans have been heading toward a "demographic winter," a period of time over the next two to four hundred years in which most of the habitat for animal wildlife in the tropics will be eliminated.[36] There is no question that the species currently living in those habitats will die out as a mandatory result of that loss of space. As that winter approaches, the only possible way those species might be saved from extinction by a mushrooming human population is by being captively bred. There is no such thing as a "witness relocation program" for displaced species due to human interference—either they are put in captivity or they become extinct.

In addition, breeding too small a number creates the potential for a "genetic bottleneck," that is, the loss of genetic variation in a population that will also eventually cause the extinction of the species. To prevent a second zoologically impoverished world, therefore, sufficient numbers of animals need to be maintained in captive environments. In turn, to maintain the necessary genetic variation in a source population for a period of roughly three hundred years, captive groups will have to be maintained at certain minimum population sizes. Minimum population size (a number dependent on the species), translates into minimum space, food, and resource requirements. Even with those in place, by the time the full demographic winter has descended, we will still most likely lose about half of the current species on the planet. While most of those are insects, we will also lose most primates, most large carnivores, and most perissodactyls and artiodactyls, the hooved mammals. Animal diversity is simply on the downhill slope, like it or not, and not having zoos is not going to stop the decrease one inch.

Employing a large enough time scale as a ruler, this fact rears up: not only are zoos the stewards of all viable animal populations for the foreseeable future, but despite our hardest efforts, the animals that will eventually be saved from extinction on this planet and placed in zoos are going to be a small, select group of midsize mammals radically unrepresentative of either species currently in the wild or species that have been wild in the past.

Second to their use as food items, the next greatest economic value of most animal species for humans is their aesthetic use by zoos. At the basest level of analyzing human–animal interactions, people truly do two core things with other animals more than any other activity: we enjoy eating them and we enjoy looking at them. Purely as an economic decision, the captive propagation of animals inside of zoos is more appealing financially to those that run zoos than are the much more expensive, much less financially rewarding, and ultimately fruitless, tasks of habitat preservation and reintroduction.

It is a free market reality that zoos lose money and funding if they give all their animals away, or if all their animals die off, or if all their animals are too expensive or difficult to maintain. Significant market forces therefore put enormous pressure on zoos to have their populations do better in captivity than they would in the wild. Although certainly not all species do well in captivity, the ones that do tend to have longer individual life spans and larger numbers of viable young, due to the directed absence of predators and pests.

The phenomenon of evolution by natural selection operates inside of zoos no differently than it operates outside of zoos. The biological rules about what a "selection pressure" is and what an "adaptation" is aren't magically abated at the park's entrance. The very same external and internal pressures of food supply, climate, potential mates, and potential predators operating on the squirrels right outside the park gates are also operating on the zebras and giraffes inside the gates.[37] The very enclosures themselves act as selection pressures. Evolution by natural selection is a treadmill and there is no place in the world in which one can get off to rest and let the rest of the world go by.

Zoo animals are evolving just as inexorably within zoos as without. Studies conducted on large felids in captivity, for instance, show that the articulation point between the skulls and bodies of tigers from zoo collections has become anatomically and functionally different than in wild specimens, and that the difference could be attributed directly to the result of unnatural diets and specialized behaviors in captivity.[38] If the bodies of captive tigers are physically changing in relation to their captive environment, their behaviors can be presumed to change alongside: the tigers we see today in the zoo, being third, fourth and fifth generation tigers from those ancestors living in the wild, are different *types* of tigers then we might have encountered in the wild three or more centuries ago.

These findings reflect changes occurring slowly but inexorably toward a calmer, more docile and sedentary lifestyle. It is inevitable that selection in captive populations is for tameness and for general adaptability to confined environments. Ever since zoos were first constructed, we have been actively selecting against species that are capable of self-sustaining reproduction only in the wild, as well as species with nomadic, isolationist, secretive, aggressive, or destructive behaviors. The gene pool of captive populations is substantially changing such that wild animals are being set on a path to one end, and that is domestication. In a sense, the very concept of "wild animals" is a concept on its way toward extinction itself.

With zoos, the market forces that most impact their success as business ventures include visitors' perceptions and desires. Based on what it is that visitors perceive zoos should be, if the desires of visitors become fulfilled, then attendance increases, revenues increase, and there is a market incentive to increase either the number of zoos or their size and scope. If those desires are *not* fulfilled, zoos fail as businesses and will not maintain captive populations even if it is a strategically wise idea to do so.

Based on sociological research studies, zoo visitors' fundamental perceptions of what a good zoo is, as well as what the real value of zoos and zoo animals themselves are, translate into four critical requirements. The first is the necessity of close-range observation and interaction. There has to be a physical proximity between the animals and the visitors or people will simply not go to the zoo. There is such a strong correlation between visitor satisfaction and proximity that you can literally measure happiness with a yardstick. The second is the apparent "comfort" of the animals. The animals require an environment that looks and seems comfortable *to people* in terms of what people feel *they* would like to have. This is true regardless of whether the animals themselves actually experience the perceived comfort or discomfort. The third is the expectation of some manner of entertainment. It has to be enjoyable for visitors to watch the animals at some basic level. Zoo exhibits that are too serious about strong topics such as conservation or extinction are universally rated more poorly than those that emphasize "fun facts" or interactive experiences. Finally, there is the need to anthropomorphize the animals being viewed. The visitors have to identify with and project onto the animals in some substitution of identity. Visitors want to be included, not excluded, emotionally from the animals' lives.

Taking those factors into account explains why in zoos we see such phenomena as animals being given comforting names; exhibits and displays
that promise or attempt to "immerse" the visitor into the animal's environment; the use of humor, electronics, and modern graphics as advertising
techniques; and, most subtly, substrates and atmospheres directed toward
the human-centric perception of "cleanliness" and organizational order in
the animal's environment, places where defecation, aggression, exploitation,
and sexual activity are downplayed, and where "naturalistic" foliage, back-
grounds, behaviors, and interactive objects are highlighted.

For example, the slow loris is a tropical mammal that has adapted over
evolutionary time to a habitat in which it regularly covers its nesting and
feeding area with its own urine in order to both ward off potential predators
and mark its territory.[39] Although the animal literally cannot stand to be in an
area not soaked in urine (developing a syndrome in captivity known as "floor
fear"), zoos that try to maintain lorises refuse to accommodate the species
in such habits due to keeper, visitor, and FDA concerns over cleanliness and
odor. Lorises simply don't make it in captivity. Solely due to the imposition
of human standards associated with being a business that relies on customer
comfort levels, lorises are on their way out. The slow loris and its aversion
behavior is a good example of free market criteria overruling a decidedly
non-marketable problem. In short, it isn't just that economics drives the fact
that the tigers we see today in the zoo are different types of tigers then we
would have encountered in the wild, it is also that economics drives the fact
that we see tigers *at all* as opposed to, say, lorises or red river hogs.

The potential for feeling good about close associations with and the entertainment value of tigers is much larger than the same potential might be with
these other, less appealing animals. Again, human history is, in large part, the
history of the manufacture of artificial objects from nature. Human beings are
very creative animals and material production has never really been limited
to some strict ethical guidelines about what can be fooled with and what
cannot—people fool with everything they can get their hands on, including,
recently, with their own underlying genetic structure.

To that end, we have ended up designing and fashioning animals no differently than we have clothes or jewelry or cars. We have given a special name
to the design and fashioning of animals, that is, artificial selection, but the
open-ended rules are the same: what we like, what is useful, what sells, what
is novel, what is sensual, what is funny, what is exciting—those hallmark
questions reveal the criteria that we subtly but persistently employ in choosing the actors for our entertainments. Normally, the free market sets the tone
oddly similar to the forces of natural selection: objects that don't sell or are
too expensive to produce for what they might eventually be worth, or are not
enjoyable and useful, tend to vanish from the market. With animals, it means

some types are simply not bred. Supply and demand form certain parameters with the animals we have placed around us as entertainment devices and market objects.

A LIMITED MENU OF OBJECTS FROM
WHICH TO SELECT SETS THE STAGE
FOR PRESERVATION ATTEMPTS

There has been a myopia for some time that artificial selection of animals has only been engaged in with respect to those animals that have become what we *call* domesticated species—dogs, cats, horses, cows, sheep, goats, and chickens, and the like—where we have deliberately bred and crossbred such animals to produce strains or breeds that are either economically, personally, or culturally useful or interesting to us.

But that restriction is of course false at a core level: we have also been artificially selecting all sorts of animals for more than 4,000 years in another way: by artificially enclosing them in restricted areas and keeping them separate from native or wild populations. The actors grow up on the stage and their shows play without curtains or intermissions, splayed dramatically and mundanely against strange and leafy green screens, where visitors as roving audience members "pick and choose" as to which presentations (and which cast members) do well and which "bomb at the box office."

Aggregates of captive animals thus must take into account the animals' value as devices for entertainment. As with movies and plays, animals do not compose a completely wide-open creative universe: there is by necessity a limited field of forms from which to pick out the eventual winners and losers. As to animal "genres," those who maintain captive populations work from an ingredients chart of already domesticated or tamed animals. The difference between what is a domesticated animal and a tame animal in turn rests on certain factors that impact the resulting concoction.[40]

True domestication of dogs and cats has taken place through changes in hereditary characteristics over time, not through nonhereditary activities such as putting them in captivity. The fact that you can enclose, care for, and even train, a turtle or goldfish doesn't mean that you can form a relationship with it in the sense that humans can and have formed with relationships with domesticated animals such as dogs. A relationship implies communication and an interchange of emotions in both directions. There is nothing in the evolutionary development of a turtle or goldfish that allow it to engage in bond forming with a human no matter how much the person capturing, owning, and confining it may project feelings onto it.[41]

In distinction, the difference between what is an endemic animal and what is an exotic animal rests on two different factors: one, their natural habitat and range, and two, biogeography in particular (aka zoogeography). The second factor translates roughly into "where did the animal use to be found before people interfered with its habitat and range." In asking the question "Where are they found?" the focus is on the animals' original location in the world, regardless of their behavior or their interactions with us.

The phenomenon of domestication is always of endemics by definition since it is animals that are naturally around human communities that start off becoming selected for and end up being domesticated. Captives, therefore, may be and often are, either domesticated, tame, endemic or exotic species, as long as they meet two fundamental criteria: there is an available supply, and they are financially smart objects to display.

Captive animals are merchandise from a restricted pool of potential merchandise, in other words, and are subject to the rules of the free market whenever a market is confronted with a restricted supply. Where the merchandise might have come from is subsumed by what type of merchandise it is. If humans find certain animals aesthetically desirable to pay to see, then those animals will become captives. If humans find them unappealing, or too risky, or too expensive in their upkeep, they will not become captives. Across time, our assessments have transformed from concerns of security into concerns of finance. While already domesticated animals could certainly be made captives, there is little point to doing so, since there is little appeal to pay to see something you can see in public for free. The "petting zoo" is the semipermeable membrane situated halfway between the closed "cell walls" of the zoological park and the open field "cytoplasm" of the dog park. Supply and demand control the channels through which the residents of each area flow.

In a sense, captive animal populations will always be protected by laws and always be defended from loss, not out of high-minded environmental protection concern, but because they comprise a subset of specially manufactured personal properties that have been intentionally modified by humans to serve as workable economic investments. We don't need to increase laws regulating zoo animals, because the market forces that indirectly regulate them as products are already overwhelming. As with movie theaters, unless and until a reasonable technological alternative is developed that satisfies the same needs in the same manner, their market is protected over the long haul even if the prices and availability fluctuate over the short period.

Here is how the "demographic winter," then, finally fits in. As mentioned, the problem that is inexorably approaching is that the available stock of entertaining items of property is dwindling. Animals being malleable in an evolutionary sense, we might be able to continue to fashion a new stock for the coming drought period, as long as we aren't too hellbent on pretending that the external world, the wild world, will be able to stay the same while we do so. Reintroduction of wild animals back into the wild is an expensive folly, an ultimately useless exercise. Zoos need to stop trying to recreate a natural paradise for captives that a) never did exist, b) does not now exist, and c) never will in the future exist. Zoos need to stop trying to act as false arks, theme parks, or temporary way stations for wild animals that are somehow magically and momentarily passing through a human enclosure on their way to the wild once more. Zoos need to start creating the same type of permanent and human-oriented environments our standard domesticated animals currently experience and benefit from.

As the demographic winter approaches, we are being presented with options as to what to do with the animals we have placed around us. We could conceptually "hibernate" for a long while about the issue—that is, close our eyes to the real problem, go to sleep and wake up to see what the changed world holds for us in the realm of species diversity when, and if, the winter ever ends. An insistence on extensive and complex reintroduction programs, on the preservation of animals in wildlife refuges, and on the temporary nature of zoo enclosures, is a refusal to open our eyes to what changes are truly occurring, and it only delays the inevitable decrease. Alternatively, we could do our best to prepare for the lack of resources, i.e., wild populations and the natural habitats in which they live, by stocking up on and artificially developing such "supplies" as we might need to survive such a winter. We cannot bring the entire world into our homes, nor can we have the world outside our homes stop changing. But we can secure ourselves in some respects against a culturally undesirable change by increasing and expanding our zoos and our captives with our eyes wide open to the evolutionary path that is being developed.

While we have been displaying animals, the demographic winter has been increasingly approaching in which their previous habitats will be too sparse to reuse, and likely become completely eradicated. To prevent that zoologically impoverished world and the loss of the aesthetic value of displaying exotics, sufficient numbers of certain exotic animals need to be maintained in even more complex captive environments. The disappearance of "wild animals" tracks an inevitable consequence of the tangled effect of shifting moral attitudes about captivity in general, an inexorable rise in human habitation of formerly wild environments, a poorly balanced social and political dynamic about what to do about animal habitat loss, and of course a perennial desire for distraction and entertainment and the enjoyment of symbols in all their ritualistic glory.

Gaining animals and losing animals in the world correlates not just with our desires for their futures but also with our comprehension of their "desires" for their own futures. There is another task now ahead of us—peering somehow right into their very skulls to try to locate what they need, what they intend, what promises they hold, and what risks they pose.

NOTES

1. *Rubáiyát* of Omar Khayyám, Quatrain XVIII.
2. Plutarch. *The Parallel Lives (The Life of Pericles)*. Vol. III of the Loeb Classical Library Edition 1916 at p. 17.
3. Waldau, P. and K. Patton (eds). *A Communion of Subjects: Animals in Religion, Science and Ethics*. New York: Columbia University Press, 2006.
4. Budiansky, Stephen. *The Covenant of the Wild: Why Animals Chose Domestication: With a New Preface*. New Haven, CT: Yale University Press, 1992 at pp. 1–2.
5. Hart, Herbert Lionel Adolphus. *The Concept of Law.* Postscript edited by Penelope A. Bulloch and Joseph Raz and with an introduction and notes by Leslie Green. Oxford, UK: Oxford University Press, 2012 at pp. 84–85.
6. Bell, Catherine M. *Ritual: Perspectives and Dimensions*. Oxford, UK: Oxford University Press on Demand, 1997.
7. Howe, James. "Fox Hunting as Ritual." *American Ethnologist* 8, no. 2 (1981): 278–300.
8. Ekroth, Gunnel. "Animal Sacrifice in Antiquity." *The Oxford Handbook of Animals in Classical Thought and Life* (2014): 324–54.
9. See, e.g., Conneller, Chantal. "Becoming Deer. Corporeal Transformations at Star Carr." *Archaeological Dialogues* 11, no. 1 (2004): 37; Hallowell, A. Irving. "Bear Ceremonialism in the Northern Hemisphere." *American Anthropologist* 28, no. 1 (1926): 1–175.
10. Schwartz, Glenn M. "The Archaeological Study of Sacrifice." *Annual Review of Anthropology* 46 (2017): 223–240. *See also* McClymond, Kathryn. *Beyond Sacred Violence: A Comparative Study of Sacrifice*. Baltimore: Johns Hopkins University Press, 2008.
11. Ekroth, Gunnel. "Animal Sacrifice in Antiquity." *The Oxford Handbook of Animals in Classical Thought and Life* (2014): 324–54.
12. See, e.g., Russell, Nerissa. *Social Zooarchaeology: Humans and Animals in Prehistory*. Cambridge, UK: Cambridge University Press, 2011.
13. Hediger, Heini. *The Psychology and Behaviour of Animals in Zoos and Circuses*. No. 591.52 HED. 1968.
14. See generally Mandel, Igor. "Aesthetic, Art-Historical and Economic Values in Painting: Empirical Study." *Available at SSRN 3160419* (2018).
15. Batten, Peter. *Living Trophies*. Springfield, OH: Crowell, 1976.
16. Mullan, Robert, Bob Mullan, and Garry Marvin. *Zoo Culture*. Urbana: University of Illinois Press, 1999.
17. Hediger, Heini. *Man and Animal in the Zoo*. New York: Delacorte Press, 1969.
18. Mullan, Robert, Bob Mullan, and Garry Marvin. *Zoo Culture, Supra*.

19. Hagenbeck, Carl. *Beasts and Men*. London: Longmans, Green, and Company, 1909.

20. Id.

21. It is not unusual to hear the drive to establish rights for animals compared to that for suffrage, since the comparison appeals to the idea that many class distinctions in certain large groups are artificial that historical prejudices have maintained and that could be overcome by a more enlightened viewpoint. Animals as a "class" being an appropriate analogue for subdivisions of humans as "classes" is one of many problems with such a comparison.

22. Hancocks, David, and Richard Farinato. "Is There a Place in the World for Zoos?/Another View of Zoos." (2001).

23. Bostock, Stephen St C. *Zoos and Animal Rights*. London: Routledge, 2003.

24. Duckler, G. "The Economic Value of Companion Animals: A Legal and Anthropological Argument for Special Valuation." *Animal L.* 8 (2002): 199.

25. *See*, Melden, Abraham Irving. *Rights and Persons*. Berkeley, CA: University of California Press, 1980.

26. As to court-appointed guardians, the court makes determinations about the ward's interests, special needs and circumstances. *State ex rel. Juvenile Dep't of Multnomah Cty. v. Burke*, 170 Or App 644 (2000), *rev den*, 331 Or 583 (2001) (to approve plan for guardianship, court must determine child's interests and find that the "special needs or circumstances" of child support decision). *See* ORS 125.010(1) or ORS 419B.366 as to court-appointed guardians, making the court the arbiter of who the guardian is and who is suitable to protect the ward. *Windishar v. Windishar*, 83 Or App 162 (1986), *opinion adh'd to on recons*, 84 Or App 580 (1987) (proposed guardian deemed unsuitable where he was geographically and emotionally remote from protected person and was uninformed about and insensitive to protected person's needs, and where his outlook and manner of controlling protected person's affairs was detrimental to protected person).

27. Fetzer, James H. *The Evolution of Intelligence: Are Humans the Only Animals with Minds?* Chicago: Open Court Publishing, 2005 at p. 204.

28. Norton, Bryan G., et al., eds. *Ethics on the Ark: Zoos, Animal Welfare, and Wildlife Conservation*. Washington, DC: Smithsonian Institution, 2012.

29. Many menageries in the past displayed humans, usually natives who accompanied acquisitions of animals during wartime or military expeditions. Laplanders, Nubians, Pacific Islanders, and Eskimos composed the most common groups, and often served as the animal's trainers after capture. The mentally disturbed and physically disabled have been displayed as well. As late as 1906, the New York Zoological Park exhibited an African "pygmy" as a playmate for a chimpanzee with information on both individuals displayed on the front of the cage.

30. Bennett, Edward-Turner. *The Tower Menagerie: Comprising the Natural History of the Animals Contained in that Establishment (etc.)*. Jennings, 1829.

31. Our newfound ability to clone living creatures hardly changes either the specificity of that biochemical trademark or its larger legal significance. For one thing, the process of cloning does not enable the biologist to construct animals from scratch. Cloning still relies on the preexistence of the unique genetic directive initially

constructed by nature. Additionally, cloning at most simply increases the quantity of natural objects. For that reason, it may be best to think of cloning primarily as a heightened increase in the possibility of identical twins, an event that formerly had to wait for natural happenstance to occur in animals, as well as humans, but which occurred nonetheless.

32. Duckler, G. "The Economic Value of Companion Animals: A Legal and Anthropological Argument for Special Valuation." *Animal L.* 8 (2002): 199.

33. Budiansky, S. *The Covenant of the Wild.* New Haven: Yale University Press, 1992.

34. Colinvaux, Paul A. *Why Big Fierce Animals are Rare: An Ecologist's Perspective.* Princeton, NJ: Princeton University Press, 1979.

35. Norton, Bryan G., et al., eds. *Ethics on the Ark: Zoos, Animal Welfare, and Wildlife Conservation.* Washington, DC: Smithsonian Institution, 2012.

36. Soulé, Michael, et al. "The Millenium Ark: How Long a Voyage, How Many Staterooms, How Many Passengers?" *Zoo Biology* 5.2 (1986): 101–113.

37. Endler, John A. *Natural Selection in the Wild. (MPB-21), Volume 21.* Princeton, NJ: Princeton University Press, 2020.

38. Duckler, G. "An Unusual Osteological Formation in the Posterior Skulls of Captive Tigers (*Panthera tigris*)." *Zoo Biology: Published in Affiliation with the American Zoo and Aquarium Association* 17.2 (1998): 135–142.

39. See, e.g., Nekaris, K. A. I., and Carly R. Starr. "Conservation and Ecology of the Neglected Slow Loris: Priorities and Prospects." *Endangered Species Research* 28.1 (2015): 87–95.

40. Redding, Richard W. "A General Explanation of Subsistence Change: From Hunting and Gathering to Food Production." *Journal of Anthropological Archaeology* 7.1 (1988): 56–97. Taming an animal does not make it domesticated and most wild animals raised as pets either do not reproduce in captivity or become unmanageable and unbreedable as adults.

41. See, e.g., Nagasawa, Miho, Kazutaka Mogi, and Takefumi Kikusui. "Attachment Between Humans and Dogs." *Japanese Psychological Research* 51.3 (2009): 209–221. Again, animal scientists are not immune:

I literally did not understand Lorenz's writings until their meaning was patiently explained to me, over and over again, by the meerkats to whom, in gratitude, I have dedicated this book.

Ewer, Rosalie Francis. *Ethology of Mammals.* New York: Springer, 2013 at p. xiii.

Chapter 7

Problems with Animal Intent

"To Provoke a Conscious Something"[1]

I can not resist the temptation to assert my belief that an elephant can be taught to read written characters, and also to express some of his own thoughts or states of feeling in writing. It would be a perfectly simple matter to prepare suitable appliances by which the sagacious animal could hold a crayon in his trunk, and mark upon a surface adapted to his convenience. . . . I can conceive how an elephant may be taught that certain characters represent certain ideas, and that they are capable of intelligent combinations. The system and judgment and patient effort which developed an active, educated, and even refined intellect in [a person] deaf, dumb, and blind from birth ought certainly be able to teach a clear-headed, intelligent elephant to express at least some of his thoughts in writing.[2]

Animals—lacking the capacity for speech—cannot obviously explain in words what they mean or intend by their actions. There is a consensus nevertheless, that, whatever the behavior in fact is, it is the animal's owner who is in the best position to decipher the behavior's meaning. Being the one assumed to be most closely acquainted with the animal's general qualities, it is reasonable to expect the owner to be especially attuned to an animal's past, present, and likely future actions; is likely the most familiar with repetitive behavioral patterns and inconsistent behavioral anomalies; and is probably keenest on what it takes to gain or distract the animal's interest, what it has taken in the past to tamp down the animal's less desirable conduct, instincts, and propensities, and what it might take in the future to raise up the animal's more desirable and valuable traits and prospects.[3]

QUANTIFYING, QUALIFYING, AND
EVIDENCING INTENTIONAL ACTS

The scientist approaches deciphering animal intent mostly through measurement of the temporal proximity between discrete facial changes and bodily movements.[4] The lawyer's approach is through analogues with human nonverbal conduct, the "actions speak louder than words" argument which the law often finds useful to contend with the untruthful witness. Lying and deceit, however, are primarily motivated behaviors,[5] and we don't have a rational basis to assume that animals are motivated to "lie" about anything so it quickly becomes problematic to analogize "why the dog really did that" with "why the recalcitrant witness really did that." Deceptive or innocent, human intentional states are heavily mixed up with human emotional complexes, and in that respect analogue is unserviceable—though Evans would disagree, even the most ostensibly indicative nonverbal expressions traceable in an animal's look don't truly reveal the internal states that we readily acknowledge in ourselves; we cannot deny that in their comparison physical appearances are superficial and cognitive states are profound. In short, while animals present all manner of appearance, a foundational predicate is absent on which to base genuine determinations of what is internally truly in play:

> [Grief] is a sophisticated emotion and the grasp of language is certainly a necessary, if not perhaps sufficient, a condition of it. Animals can, of course, manifest relatively short-term distress at, say, the loss of a mate, but it shows itself only in a disruption of behavior. Without language it cannot *consider* its plights. Furthermore, as with hope and remorse, there are not characteristic prototypes: pulling a long face or weeping frenziedly would be inadequate simulations of grief.[6]

Still, physical expression—and what that expression means—is undeniably the lawyer's stock-in-trade. Supposedly adept at both decoding as well as eliciting the expressions of witnesses, lawyers work with their own theatrical-based tool kit to glean what advantages they can within the prickly confines of evidentiary and procedural rules. Forces pull in myriad directions to inflame or not inflame a jury, badger or not badger a witness, and influence or not influence a judge, and the "true" emotive signifier behind the "facile" physical expression (in the courtroom anyway) is supposedly something well under their control.[7]

When that game involves presenting another's intent through their expression, one of the limitations lawyers bump up against in evidencing any actor's intent are not solely perception-based and descriptive constraints, but rule-based limitations as well: evidence codes restrict what is available in a dispute to use in divining an actor's psychological state as expressed in the form of their "understanding," "desiring," or "rejecting" propositions. In contrast to people, goods or products don't have psychological states, so the law and evidence rules about determining their intent is simply nonexistent.

It is a commonplace in and out of the courtroom that intent isn't exclusively tied to words: defense counsel, prosecutors, parents, and psychologists, are all acutely aware that a hidden agenda can be expressed physically. Subtleties in pupil dilation and fist clenching offer windows into the mind, and where species present physical equivalents via broad and nuanced movements of paws, tails, and the like, then it is an available argument that dogs, for example, unlike dishwashers likely possess internal preferences and dislikes, interests and disinterests, assertions and hesitancies, attentions and distractions, dispositions and desires. Even the nonscientist is confident that dogs are far more complicated than dishwashers, so the attempt to use dog faces and dog body language as signifiers of *some* certain mental state is then engaged.

Nevertheless, because people remain uncomfortable in a formal legal setting suggesting they share generalized mental experiences with any group other than themselves, unease makes judges and legislators resistant to proffering the same rules to animal owners that enable witnesses to speak of other people's internal experiences. At present, the real "meaning" of an animal's present acts remains confined to a limited extrapolation of the animal's past conduct, i.e., animal minds are read, at the most, as signifying only a "propensity" for engaging in similar actions into the future. [8] While the term "propensity" is defined as "an often intense natural inclination or preference," the common law plays freely with the intonation in that definition as to what is "natural": "It is the act of the animal and not the state of mind of the animal from which the effects of a dangerous propensity must be determined." [9] Thus to courts anyway, "proof of habitual acts of ferocity or mischief is proof of a ferocious or mischievous nature." [10] In short, actions don't speak *louder* than words for dogs, they speak in place of words.

LIMITATIONS ON THE MANIFESTATION OF ANIMAL "PERSONALITIES"

Discussion in cases about animal intent is also limited to the discussion of "traits," one or two particularly distinguishing behavioral features about an animal that are uniquely identifiable through recounting the animal's especial conduct in especial circumstances. Courts are comfortable with allowing owners to generalize experiences and there is no real surprise in courtroom or backyard to hear owners proclaim as to their dog, cat, or horse that some conduct shows that the animal "is fond of X," "really hates it when you do Y," or "will always come whenever I do Z."

Even that litany, however, is abbreviated. The largest reason that even the most loquacious of owner/narrators tend to run out of descriptors fast is because animals' daily lives are thematically boring. Dogs and cats eat and drink, urinate and defecate, and sleep and move around when not sleeping. In the broadest strokes that is it, and though the "moving around" contains repetitive and semi-varied acts of copulation, running, playing, fighting, licking, chewing, and biting, given that dogs and other animals lack opposable thumbs, bipedal posture, large frontal lobes, and the ability to speak or write, then ultimately that day's fascinating story is going to have to necessarily be curbed within a highly restrictive suite of available tetrapod behaviors.

It is a biological truism that such a repertoire cannot change much regardless of distinctions as to owner, age, upbringing, or environment. There are no educational, scholarly, intellectual, artistic, religious, political, financial, spiritual, sensual, poetic, creative, workplace, criminal, travel-related, relationship-oriented, mystically transformative, or mundanely vocational experiences for an animal's owner to point to in description since those things are not and cannot be part of any animal's day, history, life, or community.

As a result, testimony on animal traits, even when couched as a purported presentation of an animal's true "personality," is simply about the animal's temporally particular physical acts framed inside of the narrow range of its other physical acts, rather than about what any of those acts might illustrate as to larger aspects of how a mind is somehow manifesting complex thought processes. This deep-level recognition of a disconnect between people and animals becomes an area in which the lawyer and the biologist share common ground as to why the rules are so restrictive and why propensity is the order of the day:

> It might seem necessary to suppose that some animals have minds if we had no other explanation for their flexible, adaptive behavior. But there is another explanation, namely the power of natural selection to optimize behavior along with the other features of organisms. A large segment of the public knows what it thinks about the mental life of familiar animals, hence laws and societies to prevent abuse. It is incumbent on minorities in a democracy to respect laws that enshrine the perceptions of the majority, be these perceptions true or false. Scientists who think that there is inadequate evidence that animals suffer constitute such a minority; in any case that is a conclusion they reach with their "heads" while their "hearts" are mostly with the majority. Of course one cannot rule out the possibility that one day someone will devise a satisfactory test for feeling in animals. But there is none in sight and meanwhile it requires an anthropomorphic bias to be convinced they have feelings.[11]

Out of an abundance of caution, courts allow consideration of an animal's basic traits and past history but are loath to consider anything further afield.[12] The range of cases in which that consideration arises is also narrow: where the presence or absence of an owner's control of their own animal is at issue is normally where courts have allowed the "habits, characteristics, and instincts" of the animal to be judicially determined.[13] Even then, domestic animals are the only group on which evidentiary light is shined—no extension of that theme has ever been made in case law as to someone deciphering intent for livestock, wildlife, pests, or exotics. The niceties of how a particular animal may behave or manifest whatever might be construed as its basic character has developed strictly from adjudicating municipal ordinance violations involving control issues with dogs and cats. In that area, owner and expert witnesses have been allowed to testify about a dog's "dominant personality," for instance, and to opine that when the owner fails to show dominance, the dog may view the owner as subservient.[14] The general nature of dog behaviors as meaningful predictors of a future course of conduct has been held to even be in the realm of judicial notice as well.[15]

In civil cases, witnesses have been allowed to describe the personality of a dog at the time it was sold, solely to adjudicate whether a seller can warranty changes in a dog's future personality. In doing so, it has been noted that such a warranty would be inappropriate given that "animals are exposed to an ever-changing environment and may also change, themselves, accordingly."[16] The recognition is that if it is appropriate to characterize dogs as having personalities, then like human personalities they must at least be dynamic in the same manner. Courts also impose certain status boundaries on who gets to opine: while the observer doesn't have to be the owner, they at least must be sufficiently acquainted with the animal to be able to testify as to particular qualities.[17] Only with that limitation do factual disputes as to the "playfulness" and "maliciousness" of dogs get to proceed to the fact finder.[18]

BREED PROFILING IN DOGS AS AFFECTING DETERMINATIONS OF INTENT

The relational closeness of witness to animal as the object of the testimony is important, but the recognition that dogs have been artificially selected to act differently than other animals is equally so. What a certain dog intended or is like in character, for example, is crucially influenced by what people overall feel that the dog's *breed* must relegate it to be like. The inclination to assign general behaviors to domestic animals based on their breed has been a human predilection since breeds were initially developed, indeed, was one of the prime reasons *that* breeds were initially developed. Opponents of breed profiling claim it reduces dog status to that of automatons, and they assert that individual personalities transcend breed lines, while proponents attest there is solid historical and observational support for noticing how similarities in conduct consistently track across lineages.[19]

Where applied, such profiling can affect the manner in which evidence about dog intent is presented. There is a common law presumption about dog behavior that all dogs are presumptively good dogs,[20] a rule most jurisdictions hold fast to as reasonable and unassailable: "Dogs as a class are not considered dangerous to humans." "It is not a common trait of dogs to run into people." "Activities commonly expected of dogs are defecating, urinating, digging, and harassing other animals."[21] In other words, as a presumption, a normal case about whatever a dog did or didn't do can at least begin with simply accepting that it must have been a good dog to start with in spite of what then may have transpired even moments later.[22]

Some forays have been made into shifting the burden such a rule imposes so that the "innate viciousness" of certain breeds is the threshold presumption.[23] In other words, rather than the complaining party having to meet the burden of production on whether a specific dog was dangerous, the owner of the targeted breed instead is the one who has the burden to prove that their dog was *not* dangerous. Crucial to note is that both the common law and burden-shifting presumption share an important human-animal-distinction theme, which is that we feel comfortable presuming something behaviorally basic about "all dogs of a certain type" in a way that we would never do with people. That dogs (and all animals) come in "types," but that people don't, is a *feature* of law, not a bug.[24] Our previous taphonomic analysis of animal rule origins confirms this.

As to terminology, the definitions that courts use both overlap and fail to intersect at crucial junctures.[25] For example, after a veterinarian held an "evaluation session" with a Rottweiler and its offspring, he testified that "[t]he pair had a predatory aggression . . . toward other animals, but did not have an aggression or vicious disposition toward humans."[26] The court accepted his observations that the two dogs were respectively "dominant" and "a follower," that one was "sweet and docile," and that one was "tougher" whereas the other was "readier to back off." The terms blended human psychology phrases and colloquialisms neither internally consistent with each other nor externally consistent with the expert's own limited determination. The confusion engendered in the result is a product of the laxity with which intentionality terms are often applied to animals.

The laxity is ever-present: jurists consistently pride themselves on their folk wisdom about animals eclipsing a behaviorist's observations. In another case, judicial notice of animal habits was allowed under the reasoning that "Courts will take judicial notice of the habits and instincts of domestic animals because the impulses and peculiarities of nature of these creatures are supposed to be generally known."[27] The court relied on a) a tautology ("we will presume we know, because it is supposed that we know"), b) a pair of cultural classifications indecently folded together (domestic animals and the quasi-religious term "creatures"), c) a creative transposition of the contextually fluid terms of "habit" and "impulse" as if they were synonyms, and d) a simplistic portrayal of a very real and complicated interactions between people and animals. That approach is the rule, not the exception.

WHAT WE CAN KNOW AND WHAT WE CANNOT KNOW ABOUT ANIMAL MINDS

It is the rule because all people—judges and owners—grapple problematically with what any animal's "habits," "instincts," or "impulses" truly reveal, even with animals situationally close to them, animals they have closely studied, or animals the laws on which presume there should be basic things already known about them.[28] A legal guidebook called the *Restatement (Second) of Torts* unequivocally presumes that people are knowledgeable in exactly the manner that lawyers need but that zoologists reject:

> Knowledge of habits of animals. A reasonable man is required to have such knowledge of the habits of animals as is customary in his community. Thus, he should know that certain objects are likely to frighten horses and that frightened horses are likely to run away. He should know that cattle, sheep and horses are likely to get into all kinds of danger unless guarded by a human being, that bulls and stallions are prone to attack human beings and that even a gentle bitch, nursing her pups, is likely to bite if disturbed by strangers.[29]

The zoologist contests the presumption's accuracy, but the lawyer has a different problem—figuring out how to connect the presumption with vesting the attendant responsibility. Pretending that people must generally be familiar with what any feature of the landscape is "really like" is all in a day's work for the litigator but linking some person's responsibility for that feature occurring is a far thornier matter. Lawyers don't just ask "*Cui bono?*"—who benefits?—they also ask "*Cui pecunia?*"—who pays? The Restatement is doing what laws frequently do: pontificating on conduct and chiding those members of the community who don't pay attention to harmful consequences of that conduct. But in doing so it uses the word "habits," an acceptable category for the conduct of persons, but an unusual category for the conduct of personal and real properties. Of course people can and should "pay"—be responsible for—their own conduct, but can or should animals do so?

Two scenarios arise where this potential confusion becomes important. One is in code violation and criminal cases where a defendant is proposed to be liable or culpable for what an animal under their control has done to a person (or to an animal that a person owns), i.e., where the owner of a German shepherd has been cited by the local county agency for his dog killing a neighbor's horse. The other is in civil cases where an animal someone owns is itself harmed or killed and the owner seeks compensation for the loss, i.e., in the same circumstances where the German shepherd owner is being sued civilly by the neighbor horse owner for their horse's value.

In the first category of cases, the imagined mental state of the defendant's German shepherd in the form of its presumed "habits" is important since it reflects, roughly, whether that dog was or was not under the defendant's control. In the second category of cases, the imagined mental state of the German shepherd is not important but the mental state of the plaintiff horse owner as to what the horse's "habits" may have reasonably signaled to them becomes significant instead.

Both categories raise the specter of intent, human and animal, and both point up why people and animals are so difficult to compare mentally. The second category in particular embroils us in the concept of animal value, particularly the entanglement of what value animals provide to us as market objects and as accoutrements we keep in our homes. The "value" of some animals—a trout, for example—has objective significance only in the marketplace but not personal significance in someone's mind. The "value" of other animals—a horse, German shepherd, or Siamese cat, for example—has significance in minds of others and in spite of any marketplace. Though neither the trout nor the Siamese are comparable to a person, the latter's relational connection to its owner (a quality the trout doesn't share) invests it with a different value. The criteria for the Siamese's value gets swirled up in calculations and extrapolations about its "habits," "instincts," and "impulses," that is its perceived cognitive state in conjunction with how we feel generally about benefits and costs of personal properties, how cat owners feel generally about cats' conduct, and how the particular Siamese owner particularly felt about that Siamese as an item of value.

The existence of possible relationships underscores the confusion engendered in animal valuations, possibilities concrete as to Siamese and make-believe as to trout. The surest relationships people have is with each other, so a standard instruction to a jury on how to assess the value of someone whom a plaintiff was "related to" in a wrongful death suit, might be repurposed to apply to the Siamese:

"In determining the value of an animal, you may consider factors that include, but are not limited to:

a. any love, affection, guidance, or assistance the animal might reasonably have been expected to provide to its owner;
b. any services the animal customarily performed for its owner in the past;
c. any services the animal might reasonably have been expected to perform for its owner in the future;
d. the animal's age, breed, abilities, life expectancy, health, habits, and character.
e. In determining the character of an animal, you may consider factors that include, but are not limited to:
f. lay or expert witness testimony on the animal's intent, instincts, and general demeanor;
g. your own observations of specific conduct and disposition."[30]

The reformation meshes well with legal rules on permissible testimony and evidence, as well as with acceptable presumptions on "laws of nature" as to animals in general.[31] The evidentiary factors referenced in the instruction don't demand that the animal have a "good" personality or a "high" price; they are nondirectional such that viciousness, stupidity, or uselessness of an animal may be considered and weighed just as well as their antitheses.

The instruction also draws us closer to a fair contrast between the rules on animal personality evidence and the rules on evidencing similar traits regarding people. Unsurprisingly, evidence of a person's character is not admissible at all to prove that they engaged in certain conduct on a certain occasion.[32] The minor exceptions to this rule that are limited to evidence of habit, plan, or scheme take pains to be identified as exceptions, not as revisions of the prohibition.[33] "Propensity" evidence of a person's history of bad acts is normally excluded due to the high danger of unfair prejudice, confusion of issues, and potential for misleading the jury such a proposition would invite.[34] Evidence laws disclose that we don't cavalierly reject what we know about key differences between people and animals in the way that "minds" are manifestations of expression. Realities about what the conduct of each actually expresses, and what the expression of each actually must mean, support divisions in the form of rejecting propensity evidence for the one and demanding it for the other.

Within that rubric then, courts historically have forbidden parties from assessing animal intentionality, with the concern that any attempt to determine a dog's present intent would mire decision-makers in a "morass of subjectivity."[35] People, to the contrary, are *not* assumed to be "naturally good," and certainly do not appear to have a judicially determined propensity for anything at all, much less for activities as straightforward as digging or running. Human intent is such a tangled web that we back off from employing universals in any manner and just accept it as whatever the actor says it is—and what the actor's conforming or nonconforming conduct might reveal could support or challenge the validity of its assertion.

Human intent is divorced from human character. The law uses the concept of a person's character is if it is a given and has never identified what character is truly composed of or unquestionably excludes. "Propensity," while the rule for dogs, is not the rule for people nor could it be given the historical existence of, and extraordinary fluidity regarding, people's minds, and the plasticity of their innumerable and nearly undecipherable mental states. Animal behaviorists recognize that anticipatory activities, being adaptive, don't necessarily imply intentional processes that are phenomena requiring "special forms of social exchanges" where the sender of a message controls its content and its consequences on the receiver.[36] "Propensity" accommodates anticipatory conduct; "character" demands the presence of that special exchange.

Of what ultimate legal significance is the determination of any animal's intent, and why should we care how it is determined? Well, could it be ascertained, an animal's intent could "sub in" for the owner's intent in one of two distinct ways: either to *excuse* owner liability (if we assume animals have free will and are thus independently responsible for their own actions), or, alternatively, to *cement* owner liability (if we assume animals are automatons and their intents are simply the owner's intent one step removed). The former approach is contrary to how we conceive free will operates and leads to the unhappy result of "animal jails"; the latter approach is contrary to how we conceive "animal minds" in fact operate and leads to the slightly less unhappy result of a momentous and unacceptable increase in exposure to criminal and civil liability for animal owners. The unpleasantness that looms in both models makes courts strike a cautious stance in adopting a theory of animal intent.

History and prehistory again and again tie an object and its owner together in a tightly bound web of adaptively significant interactions. Levels of dangerousness of an animal—the picky distinctions between a harmful dog, dangerous dog, vicious dog, or aggressive dog—all involve compartmentalizing individualized dog behavior in relation to the generalities of people's behaviors, adjudging what certain individual dogs might do in the future based on what they have already done with certain individual people in the past. What particular past conduct they have engaged in as to any person, in turn, is deemed a reflection of what the past or present owner allowed or enabled them to do. Again, control is essential.

Moreover, human intent and animal intent are not analogous. Because human social relations are light-years distant from animal "social" relations, proposals that animal traits are analogous to human traits are irrational:

Ants are described as making "slaves" and having "queens." But the slavery of ants knows nothing of the auction block, of the buying and selling, of the essentially commodity nature of the slave relations of human society. . . . Nor do ants have "queens." The force-fed egg factory encased in a special chamber in the middle of an ant colony that is called a queen has no resemblance to the life of either Elizabeth I or Elizabeth II or of their different political roles in society . . . What happens is that human categories are laid on animals by analogy, partly as a matter of convenience of language, and then these traits are "discovered" in animals and laid back on humans as if they had a common origin. There is in fact not a shred of evidence that the anatomical, physiological, and genetic basis of what is called aggression in rats has anything in common with the German invasion of Poland in 1939.[37]

Workable laws reject analogy, and indeed demand that people and animals are *not* analogous. The inequity is absolutely necessary; a dog isn't required to know its owner, but an owner is required to know their dog since failure to do so has substantial social consequences: "The principal danger of [an animal's] escape comes from human error."[38] Social protections mandate that animal conduct be controllable.[39]

None of this requires rejecting basic behavioral precepts—it isn't antagonistic to our observations to note animal instincts akin to those humans have.[40] As we have seen, though, one of the fundamental distinctions the law employs to separate people from animals is that people can voluntarily restrain their instinctual behaviors, whereas animals seem compelled to involuntarily express (and act subservient to) such behaviors.[41] We can break free from our habits and thereby change the consequences. A complementary distinction is that we use language to ascertain that others will voluntarily restrain *their* instinctual behaviors in exchange for us restraining ours; in contrast, spoken or written promises are simply not available from animals.[42] The prison of habitual conduct is one to which we have constructed a key.

PACTS MADE *WITH* ANIMALS AND PACTS MADE *ABOUT* ANIMALS AND THEIR DISTINCTIONS

Part of our unlocking mechanism is this: the "agreement" is an exclusively human invention. Laws, also an exclusively human invention, both arise from and give richness to the core idea of what an "agreement" is. Our twin capacities for self-imposed restraint, and the means to broadcast that we are engaging in such restraint, are weighty foundations underlying our rapacity for mutually negotiated rules of performance, the *aqua vitae* of agreements. Your "agreement" with your neighbor about your dog is critically different, in the eyes of the law, from your "agreement" with your dog about your neighbor.[43]

Being involved with others socially is not merely a question of mutual coordi-
nations of behavior. Social relations involve enlisting others in one's projects,
being enlisted, and attempting to keep one another in line. Moral standing is
a general concept for one's position that is at the same time constantly being
modified by these shifting arrangements. Moral standing is not something that
is merely assigned. Rather, as a general form of social status, *it is negotiated*,
and *negotiation is part of its very meaning*. It is a general term of basic social
status that is constantly being negotiated with, by and on behalf of others. This
is simply another way of saying that moral standing occurs within networks of
social relations that are fluid, not static.[44]

From *The Prince*[45] to "the prisoner's dilemma,"[46] sociologists have appreciated the fact that "playing by the rules" confers a greater advantage on the
player than does violating the rules. What those rules are, and just how to
play, are in turn transmitted from one person to the next, as well as from one
generation to the next, by language—the rich and complicated acts of speech
and writing. Our past is, in large part, a game that has lasted for millennia,
the players being people socially obligating themselves to other people in
a world where self-interest supports the practice and biology provides the
vehicle: evolution by natural selection has fashioned both the ability to use,
and the interest in using, mutually fashioned symbols and concepts to control
the content and consequences of our interactions with those around us.

Words are at best a loose cargo net of labels that we throw over our wild and
woolly perceptions, hoping to catch and observe some of our thoughts and
feelings. Words are sketches of the real thing, and some sketches capture a better likeness than others. Can you describe the feeling of an itch with the label
"itch"? Neither can a dog, but the dog scratches, so we know it, too, itches. Can
you describe the wetness of water? Or how love feels, or sadness, or the smell
of snow or how an apple tastes ? No words equal the experience. Speech is a
slippery grip for measuring thoughts. People might lie. We sometimes ignore
what someone is saying and use body language as a more truthful guide to what
they're *really* feeling. Sometimes words fail us. And the fact that we learn different languages shows that words are rather arbitrary: that authentic thoughts
arise first; then we paste words onto them. Words interpret thoughts. Thoughts
come first.[47]

Our procedural rules, evidence codes, jury instructions, and appellate opinions all reflect those immutable contrasts of people with animals, because
they are in reaction to our prehistorical and historical social interactions with
animals, interactions across the millennia that account for our developed
disconnection from them. Animals do not make recognizable "deals" and do
not have social obligations no matter how complex their social organization.
Not only are they unable to truly restrain their instinctual conduct, but our

lack of real communication with them makes it nearly impossible for us to ascertain their intent to bargain or restrain themselves even if they could.[48] Animals, like people, can be taught of course by other animals (particularly people) to do certain things, and we have investigated a rich variety of species, from earthworms to elephants, that can be observed to manipulate or restrain *some* behaviors through what they have learned (or at least what we think they have learned).[49]

The true scope of the learned restraints, however, depends heavily on the species of animal, the type of learning, who or what is doing the teaching, the motivations of the teacher and the student, and a variety of very specific environmental circumstances affecting the efficacy of the lesson.[50] Out of caution and experience, even our expectation that *some* few highly domesticated animals can control *some* small range of learned behaviors has so far not been nearly enough to justify inclusion of them, much less any animal in general, within the intricate and special rules of social conduct, deal making, and predicates of reason that we currently impose upon ourselves.[51]

> The bird that flies wherever it wants is voluntarily wheeling this way and that, voluntarily moving its wings, and it does this without benefit of language. This distinction embodied in anatomy between what it can do voluntarily (by moving its striated muscles) and what happens autonomically, moved by smooth muscle and controlled by the autonomic nervous system, is not at issue. We have added a layer on top of the bird's (and the ape's and the dolphin's) capacity to decide what to do next. It is not an anatomical layer in the brain, but a functional layer, a virtual layer composed somehow in the micro-details of the brain's anatomy: We can ask each other to do things, and we can ask ourselves to do things. And at least sometimes we readily comply with these requests. Yes, your dog can be "asked" to do a variety of voluntary things, but it can't ask why you make these requests. A male baboon can "ask" a nearby female for some grooming, but neither of them can discuss the likely outcome of compliance with this request, which might have serious consequences for both of them, especially if the male is not the alpha male of the troop. We human beings not only can do things when requested to do them; we can answer inquiries about what we are doing and why. We can engage in the practice of asking, and giving, reasons.[52]

RESTRAINT AND ITS SIGNIFICANCE

The empirical fact that many animals can learn is, in general, primarily of interest to the ethologist and the zoologist, those who study just what it is that animals actively do during their day.[53] The fact that only a very few animals can learn what we would call "self-restraint," on the other hand, is of interest to the lawyer and the sociologist as well, those nonscientists who study the roles and interplay of social relations and of what people actively do with each other during their day.

We must not overlook the fact that the foundational trick—i.e., voluntarily restraining one's own behaviors—made its appearance due only to the pressures of millions of years of natural selection by which it was slowly accomplished. Human evolution has excluded animals from the entire panoply of human social expectations as to conduct.[54] As we recognize how rights arise from formalized social expectations, we can then start to appreciate why animals are necessarily excluded from the expectations of rights as well.

Why is self-regulated conduct (and the capacity to communicate about what the regulations are) such an important predicate to legal rights? Well, as noted, the benefits of social relations arise straight out of the burdens created by voluntarily engaging in them; rights are tightly welded to responsibilities because responsibilities define rights. Of what value is a victim's right to participate in the sentencing of a convicted perpetrator, if non-victims are not restrained from participating? Of what value are bankruptcy protections to a debtor, if the financially solvent are not laden with duties to creditors? A person's right to rely on and enjoy the use of private property without unreasonable interference, for example, has value by virtue of society's imposition on them of a need to recognize and respect the concept of "boundary lines" in general. Similarly, a person's right to not be unjustly harmed has value by virtue of agreeing to a social compact; the understanding in place that they will be held physically or financially accountable when they unjustly harm others.[55] Those speech acts have a fundamental value to people distinct from the communicative acts of even the most gregarious of animal species:

> A man who makes a statement does more than let it be known that he believes something, a man who makes a request does more than let it be known that he wants something, a man who makes a promise does more than let it be known that he intends something. But again, what more? Each of the speech act categories, even the expressive category, serves social purposes that go beyond just the expression of a sincerity condition. For example, the primary extralinguistic purpose of directives is to get people to do things; a primary extra-linguistic purpose of assertives is to convey information; a primary purpose of commissives is to create stable expectations of people's behavior.[56]

We have noted previously that a legitimate investigation into a worthwhile subject employs the ontological, epistemological, and methodological levels of analysis, and a legitimate investigation into rights should do the same. We are aware that we want to define them, we are aware that they are valuable things that are somewhat ineffable among different social cohorts, and we know that it is important to secure them and to not degrade them. With that, we tend to get most invested in asserting and enforcing them through methodology.

THE CONNECTIONS BETWEEN RESTRAINT AND RIGHTS AND THE SIGNIFICANCE OF PROCEDURES

We tend to express the value of rights (which themselves arise from the genesis and use of those unique speech acts) through legal procedures. The Fourth Amendment to the U.S. Constitution's right to be secure in our homes and persons is given its most concrete expression primarily through the machinations of the motion *in limine*, a procedure used to exclude certain types of evidence. The First Amendment's right to freely express ourselves and freely associate with others is given its most concrete expression through the intricacies of the restraining order and the absolute and qualified privileges, procedures used to protect and constrain witnesses. It makes sense that we could therefore only impart value to "animal rights" by giving them expression through procedure as well; to the extent that it is not self-evident, the rule of law mandates that animals would have to labor under some manner of procedurally defined obligation were they to obtain similar constitutional or statutory privileges.[57]

An ability to communicate conceptually with each other is absolutely essential to giving life to the concept of a "privilege," or a "motion," or a "witness." The immense, manipulative power of speech and writing, in turn, is what gives our enjoyment of any freedoms, and our displeasure at any restraints, true meaning. Conceptual and symbolic speech, in all its permutations, invests our enforcement mechanisms with far greater persuasive power than a club or a rock ever could—speech acts can traverse time and distances in a manner that is orders of magnitude above the nonspeech threat of the most expressive of physical displays or postures.[58]

Take the right not to be harmed: Those who stump for the right for animals not to be harmed look expectantly to a bevy of protections from injury or death being granted directly to animals but tend to ignore that fundamental fairness to "rights-holders" in general would require three obligations being imposed in conjunction with each protection. Those obligations arise in terms of conduct and are embraced in the class of acts that require the intensely creative power of linguistic communication to give them effect. These obligations are the formal, public assertion of the right by the act of *pleading*; the formal, public uncovering of the right by the act of *discovery*; and the formal, public presentation of the right by the act of *trial*.[59]

Pleading is a very stylized form of written communication that frames a factual problem in the accoutrements of a legal terminology. *Discovery* is a very stylized form of oral and written communication that marshals the evidence necessary and sufficient for resolving the problem. *Trial* is a very stylized form of oral and written communication that marries the pleading to the facts to the evidence to the law in order to ultimately resolve the problem in a public forum. There is not a single step on that staircase that does not impart both a burden and a benefit on any participant who wishes to resolve concerns through the application of law.

Of the three, the most powerful form of showing how social and legal obligations are imposed is the trial. Cultural images and perceptions associated with the courtroom trial reflect the fact that trials are one of the most commanding and authoritative ways we have of projecting the legal concepts we set down on the printed page into the public mind. Yet what role could rights-bearing animals play in a courtroom trial?

> If the animals had in any proper sense rights, we should no more be entitled
> to put them to death without a fair trial, unless in strict self-defen[s]e, than to
> torture them for our own amusement.[60]

The casual oddity of that image, of animals standing trial, reveals a serious intrinsic problem with the pragmatism of a right, for instance, that to not be harmed. It stands to reason that animals that possess their own tort claims as to harm, just like humans, would be expected to "tame their passions to suit the condition assigned," as it were, to restrain their instinctual behaviors and propensities to harm, and to be socially obligated to control themselves in the same public aspects that humans control themselves. Animals extended that manner of recognition would then suffer under (and be granted defenses against) the possibility of incarceration, punishment, or loss of some privilege, for violating those social obligations.[61]

The scenarios of harming and being harmed arise frequently in discussions of animals, obligations, and the law that addresses both. Many of our legislated and litigated rules affecting animals revolve around incidents of attack, physical confrontation, and personal injury. For that reason, incidents of personal and physical harm seem to be a fruitful area in which we might assess how fashioning any "animal right" could ever be procedurally viable. Under such an analysis, and as with people currently, it is rational to require that animals, as beings protected against assault, battery, and the like, would shoulder procedural obligations for themselves intentionally assaulting or battering others, as well as be relieved of some of the sting of such procedural obligations for engaging in harmful acts in circumstances where the acts are considered socially justified.

For purposes of most criminal codes, people are held to have acted intentionally whenever they act with a conscious objective to cause the result or to engage in the conduct with which they have been charged.[62] The focus of those statutes is the extent to which the defendant subjectively intends the result, as opposed to merely intending the act that caused the result.[63] If animals are granted the right to not be harmed, and if they are to be held responsible for engaging in their own intentional misconduct, then we need to get a firm grip on just what their intentional conduct encompasses. We would need to examine how animals could subjectively intend the result of their directed conduct. In that sense we need to revisit intent with the version in which we should be most interested being that where the consequences of the actions are intended, not just the actions themselves.

At the threshold of such an analysis is our previous recognition that intentionality in that sense requires the existence of mind, and some lawyers have familiarity with that first delicate step into the deep waters of animal psychology. Courts have occasionally incorporated into their decisions acknowledgment that at least some animals do have minds.[64] Examples of jurists' recognition of the phenomenon appear sprinkled throughout the common law—albeit more with the flourish of the romantic novelist than with the dryness of the field biologist:

> Even a human being, under a railroad bridge when a train thunders over it, will instinctively seek a place of greater security elsewhere; and if this feeling exists in the human breast, what must the effect of such an experience be upon the mind of an animal?[65]

> As the complaint fails to allege that the cow had an evil disposition, such as would lead her to attack human beings, necessarily there is no charge that the appellant had notice of any such evil disposition; and as the willful conduct of the animal in attacking the appellee was not such as the appellant had a right to expect, or might anticipate, he is not responsible for the injury caused by such unexpected and willful conduct.[66]

> It was on a zero night in February, at a time when all good and valuable horses should have been at home and in bed, that the poor, senseless animals were killed. And, under the circumstances, who will blame the animals or reflect on their intelligence if they deliberately committed suicide by running across the railway in front of a train running at 50 miles an hour? All their troubles and starvation was ended in a moment.[67]

> While we do not pretend to read the mind of a bovine animal, it seems apparent that these animals do not want to be lassoed, thrown to the ground and tied up so that their horns and other anatomical parts can be severed. The prospect that "muggers" will not be gentle certainly must loom on the animal's horizon.[68]

Legal opinions reflect (occasionally) our common sense and our common consensus about what is socially acceptable, and we certainly don't need judges to tell us what we know in our bones and what we have already discerned above—that intentionality is one of the key distinctions between dogs and dishwashers and people.[69] What does a dog, for instance, subjectively intend in the sense that it would be legally held to "know" that its acts would cause injury?[70] We tend to generally refrain from extrapolating ultimate goals out of immediate actions, and we have seen that we aren't keen on making such projections with animals. To be fair, there really has been no need to do so: our legal concerns have always been about *owner* responsibility, not about animal responsibility, and so our rules have developed accordingly.

PROBLEMS IN DECIPHERING ANIMAL INTENT
IN ORDER TO APPLY PROCEDURAL BENEFITS

In other contexts though, we find that the general rule courts currently apply is that the intent of an animal is simply immaterial to a determination of owner responsibility for animal actions.[71] It is in that "morass of subjectivity"[72] that we find ourselves surrounded by the problems and promises of what language actually reflects. Owners can at least verbally and graphically explain their intentions and their knowledge of consequences, but animals cannot. The subjectivity morass is a natural byproduct of two discrete and organic limitations: the absence in animals of a spoken language, and the vast breadth of animal species in which unspoken intent would have to be deciphered from within a vast array of questionable nonlinguistic animal acts.

> Consider Amos, the mouse, there on my kitchen floor. He runs in the opposite direction from the waiting cat. In the same motion, he runs toward the waiting broom. He also runs between a black square on the linoleum and a tomato stain, towards the kitchen clock and towards London, away from magnetic north, thirteen times as fast as the clock's second hand swings, five seconds after the last perceptible motion on my part, 0.05 seconds after the last agitated flick of the cat's tail. Clearly this list of descriptions of Amos's running could be extended indefinitely. And wait; is his behavior even a running? Perhaps Amos's motion should be described merely as a rhythmic beating of the paws, which happens to carry Amos across the floor, just as it happens to carry him toward London. Nor will it help to relativize Amos's motions to his own body. Notice Amos as he blinks. Are his eyelids momentarily covering his eyes? Or are his eyelashes being disentangled momentarily from his eyebrows? Or do the eyelashes point momentarily to the navel, or is it to the toes? Perhaps all that occurs is a rotation of the eyelids. Do they rotate at an angular velocity of 1000 degrees/sec, or is the rate equal to three revolutions per mouse heartbeat? Nor are motions

in any way peculiar with regard to the infinity of their possible descriptions. Amos can make squeaks, chattering sounds, sneezes, coughs, choking sounds, or he can be silent—silent except that, if you listen closely, he makes breathing sounds, and little thumping sounds with his feet (danger signals, or just foot patter?), and also with his heart. Which of these sounds, and which silences, are subject matter for behavioral science and which are not? How should the sounds be described? By pitch, or inflection, duration, periodicity, harmonic structure, rhythmic structure, amplitude, pattern of repetitions? Consider the sounds that a human makes. Some of these, such as screams and laughs, can be described relatively crudely. Others, the speech sounds, need to be described in great detail, and in accordance with principles of such subtlety that these are not yet fully understood. Still other sounds, such as sounds made while choking or urinating, sounds made by the heart and, normally, those made in breathing, do not need to be described at all. Sometimes silences need to be described and sometimes they do not.[73]

Ontologically, the first limitation may be phrased: If they cannot talk, then how do we know what they mean?[74] If our answer demands a reference to nonverbal conduct, then the second limitation kicks in, and methodologically posits: If we are to substitute meaningful behaviors for meaningful speech, then *which* behaviors of *which* animals qualify in *which* circumstances and under *which* interpretations? At the very outset of addressing both limitations, we return again and again to the truism that animals themselves cannot tell us these things directly:

Most animal research [regarding animal personality] has focused on traits, behaviors, and abilities, but no research has examined personal projects, identity, attitudes, and life stories. Presumably, this discrepancy between the domains of human and animal personality is largely driven by the nature of the latter concepts, which require participants to articulate their internal motives, feelings, and beliefs. Clearly, any phenomena dependent on self-reports by the research participants cannot be examined in nonhuman populations.[75]

A reliance on behavior alone spells huge trouble. The rule-making opportunities inherent in sifting through the repertoire of animal behaviors are daunting to say the least: with tens of millions of species to work with,[76] with tens of thousands of individual behavioral "acts" to consider from the tip of the nose (Amos' flaring of the nasal membranes), to the tips of the toes (Amos' curling of the lateral digits), with an uncountable number of environmental circumstances to confound an interpretation, and with potentially six billion plus human-oriented personal opinions and ideas on what *that motion the animal engaged in right then* truly meant, the explosion of interpretation possibilities would keep lawyers, not to mention evidence code writers, occupied for a ridiculous period of time.[77]

If we really are the most intelligent species on Earth—and I believe we are—why didn't science approach this from the other direction a long time ago? Why are years spent painstakingly teaching lab animals sign language if modern researchers believe that their capacity to learn is less than ours? Wouldn't it be much easier if we finally began to learn the language of animals? We have many more opportunities now than we had a few years ago, when it would not have been possible to produce sounds at, say, horse level because we lacked the ability to whinny at two different frequencies. Today, a computer could do a reasonable job of translating what we wanted to say into the appropriate animal vocabulary. Unfortunately, I don't know of any serious attempts to do this. There are certainly people who can imitate animal voices, for example the calls of different species of birds. However, people who can imitate a blackbird or a chickadee can do no more than pipe "this spot's already taken" in bird language. That's all that the beautiful song trilled by the males sitting up there in the tree-tops means. What sounds so delightful to our ears serves within the species to scare off competitors. That would be like having a parrot that kept saying, "Go away." Unfortunately, that's as far as we've got with our ability to communicate with our fellow creatures.[78]

Courts have struggled with deciding what behaviors by what animals have meant and to whom, and the combination of judicial conservatism and folk psychology has resulted in assigning animals to a quasi-human, quasi-machine middle ground where self-preservation is accepted and self-awareness rejected often in the same sentence:

[The] presumption that [a] dog will get out of the way [of a train] in time to avoid injury or not move into danger exists only where there is nothing in the circumstances of its approach or manner of its being upon the track to indicate to a reasonably prudent operator that the animal is helpless, or indifferent to its surroundings and danger . . . [A] dog must be placed on the same footing with that of a man walking upon or near a railroad track apparently in possession of all his faculties, and that the presumption would not apply to a dog near or upon the track in a position which showed that he was helpless, or totally oblivious of his surroundings. [It is] reasonable to place a dog on somewhat the same footing as a human being when in the possession of all his faculties and capable of seeing the danger and escaping from it.[79]

There was nothing unnatural about the action of these two old mules. It is the natural instinct of all animals to shy away from danger when they see it. We might excuse from this class the bovine species which apparently relies upon the judgment or instinct of man to save himself when they are in the way. The two mules in this case were old, one sixteen years of age, and the other much older. They were gentle and unafraid of automobiles and other motor vehicles. This is proved by the fact that they displayed no fear of this big truck and two graders, which certainly are much noisier than a car or a light truck, such as did frighten them. It is further demonstrated that they were gentle by the fact that they did not run away after jumping off the road, and were brought to a stop within ten or twelve feet, pulled the wagon back up on the road, and quietly went on their way. It appears to us that the mules used good judgment in jumping off the road.[80]

Courts, unable to fully reconcile a philosophical refusal to treat animals solely as machines with a competing philosophical refusal to treat them identically to humans, have created the jerry-rigged solution of propensity as the concession that present instincts and past behaviors mesh together to at least circumscribe the possible range of the animal's otherwise undecipherable intent.[81] The combination of an absence of human propensity and a presence of the phenomenon of human language together support the notion that appreciation of past and current histories is mandatory in locating a foundational difference betwixt animal minds and the minds of people:

> The lower courts held that the dog did not "attack" the child since its act of lunging for the chicken was merely instinctual. In a similar fashion, Appellees assert that because the dog was attempting to recover a piece of chicken, the dog did not possess "the obvious intent to destroy, kill, wound, injure or otherwise harm the object of its action." We disagree. Although we cannot ascertain the intent of the animal, we presume that because the dog in fact severely injured the child, it intended to do so in order to recover the chicken she was attempting to eat.[82]

We have been conflicted over assertions about animal intentions for centuries. In applying the topic to people, we haven't bothered with propensity; we rail at incorporating "human nature" into our rules, and prohibit attempts to evidence what nature emboldens, shames, or commands us to do as individuals. With some exceptions, the defense of "it was just in my nature to do that" has never been accepted in our courtrooms, and no witness is usually allowed to testify that the reason a person engaged in a certain act was due to their temperament.[83] We are not automatons and we know it. No judge would allow a behaviorist to testify as to the cultural "meaning" of a person's peculiar acts or an anthropologist to testify as to how humans as a "type" truly operate—those proposals would be struck as impermissible character evidence.[84]

In contrast, it is not uncommon for courts in cases concerning animal owners to enlist animal behaviorists to help extricate the fact finder from the sorry tangle of deciding whether the propensity that certain animals might or might not have had to act in a certain manner was due to their genetics, their circumstantial upbringing, their immediate physical environment, human influences, the effect of "inner nature," or some filtered combination thereof.[85] No matter how experienced and sophisticated the behaviorist might be, they are not the functional equivalent of courtroom translators under the pretense that they are simply taking another's "language" and reconveying it to an audience in different words:

> Dressing a chimpanzee in diapers, sending him to a good school, and bribing him with cartloads of bananas and M&Ms still doesn't make him into a chimpanzee who can use language the way we do. [T]he circumstantial evidence from studies of language development suggests that this difference is a fundamental one, having to do with a unique human awareness of self and other. Animals use communication in a fashion that appears to seek influence over the behavior of others, but not the thoughts or knowledge of others. Humans, by contrast, from infancy show an understanding that other humans have minds that work roughly the same way their own do, and whose knowledge can be altered by words and actions.[86]

To be on the safe side, most animal behavior experts simply coalesce a plethora of factors together as if each could not be safely winnowed out, and then justify the result by using the vagaries of multi-factorial causation. For example, in a criminal case against the owner of two Rottweilers that had mauled a young child, a trial court accepted a behaviorist's personal premise that the animals were mere mechanisms, constrained to act the way they did regardless of whatever their actual intent may have been:

> An expert opined that, based on the two dogs' breed, lack of training, and how they were raised and maintained, they had a strong propensity toward aggressive behavioral responses. He testified that if a dog is aggressive in a particular situation, the dog "becomes pretty consistent and regular" in displaying such behavior in the same context and with the same stimuli.[87]

The concepts employed such as "stimuli" and "behavioral responses," are derived from the long-outdated science of behaviorism[88]—a theory that posited animals at the best as complicated organic machines with readily predictable responses to specific inducements, and at the worst as inanimate objects altogether.[89] The underlying premises of the behaviorist model—and the prevailing judicial viewpoint—have been expressed by the sociobiologist J. F. Wittenberger:

> We cannot assume that animals make conscious decisions because we cannot monitor what goes on inside their heads. Nevertheless, it really does not matter what the proximate bases of those decisions are when evolutionary reasons underlying their behavior are our principal concern. . . . Particular stimuli or contexts elicit particular behaviors. An animal need not know why those

stimulus-response relationships exist. It need only know what the relationships are. This knowing need not involve conscious awareness, though in many cases animals are undoubtedly conscious of what they are doing; it need only involve the appropriate neurological connections. . . . Animals can be goal-directed without being purposeful, and they can behave appropriately without knowing why.[90]

Among other concerns, including as to whether behaviorism is even appropriate for the law to employ, is a critical evidentiary problem for the courtroom lawyer: What are consistently acceptable and usable "units" of behavior? Physical-style units—i.e., anatomical traits—are relatively easy to define; one can count feet, parts of bodies, or even whole lives. The very concreteness of the (comparatively) discrete nature of anatomical traits points up the trouble in which fact finders find themselves when asked to determine the proof of a behavioral trait: behaviors in general simply "do not come already carved up into distinct chunks like cuts of meat in a butcher's window."[91] In a tape of a dog barking, even the ability to say specifically what one "bark" is from another gets lost in semantics. As noted, animals have a relatively restricted repertoire of behaviors and most repertoires seem relatively constant across species.[92] Even within those parameters, however, which movements are and are not signifiers of which mental states is resolutely undeterminable.

The invisible yet obvious fact to which I direct your attention is that there is a literal infinity of different possible descriptions that might be given of any animal's behavior at any given time, only a tiny few of which descriptions have any relevance for behavioral science. These are the descriptions that connect in a pertinent way with function. Consider, for example, the various motions that animal makes. A good portion of the behaviors of animals are motions of one kind or another. But motions can only be described relationally. Relative to what do we describe the animal's motions?[93]

Common sense initially aids the carving up of animal actions, and courts take a sort of folk wisdom comfort in accepting that pigs root,[94] dogs whine and howl,[95] horses lunge,[96] cats wander,[97] cattle roam,[98] and mules are stubborn.[99] Nevertheless even that "pedestrian's guide to ethology" quickly morphs into anthropomorphism with episodic descriptions in which arbitrarily selected vignettes of animal life are enthusiastically equated with the full panoply of human experience, events personally divined by the observer and couched in the pleasure of narrative as opposed to the bother of measurement.[100]

It is unclear at present if animal "personality" manifests through animal activity, whether exciting or boring.[101] Among the concerns is that the way animals grasp and utilize sensory stimuli is not even remotely near the way in which people transform those stimuli into formed social concepts:

Animals struggle with each other for food or for leadership, but they do not, like human beings, struggle with each other for that that stands for food or leadership: such things as our paper symbols of wealth (money, bonds, titles), badges of rank to wear on our clothes, or low-number license plates, supposed by some people to stand for social precedence. For animals the relationship in which one thing stands for something else does not appear to exist except in very rudimentary form.[102]

Animal incapacities in recognizing symbols at all, much less in manipulating symbols, do not just present minor hurdles toward us understanding their intent clearly—such incapacities reveal the complete absence of what we would call intent at all. It is true that there are animal rights advocates putting hard work into analyzing that issue but the empirical pitfalls are perilous.[103] The anthropologist Alan Barnard draws an evolutionary line from our origins to our development of the manner of symbolic manipulation needed to construct intentionality in all its nested levels and he identifies the product as a core distinction between us and animals: "Symbolic thought entails a consciousness of the aesthetic. It also entails the wish to communicate this, one would imagine, to someone else, with the view to influencing that person's perceptions."[104] Even with domesticated animal minds—intimately "designed" as those features have been via processes of commensalism, domestication, and artificial selection to favorably react to people—the result has not been an entity that then conducts itself specifically in order to influence others' perceptions about it. The absence of symbolic thought dooms any evaluation of intent in spite of complex learning and the overtly socialized behaviors many species exemplify.

> There is a fundamental distinction between a process by which certain chimpanzees have learnt to crack open palm nuts using two stones a hammer and anvil, and a process through which humans have created the Industrial Revolution, unraveled the secrets of their own genome, developed the concept of universal rights—and come to debate the distinction between humans and other animals.[105]

That knowledge eschews rights. To invest animals with rights would require holding animals responsible for intentional acts. To determine which animal acts are those in which the consequences were subjectively intended would require: a) communicating with animals without a common language or the use of symbolic communication; and b) agreeing upon *which* acts of *which* species mean *what*. For lawyers, trouble ensues at both steps.

THE USE OF PRESUMPTION AND INFERENCE IN
EVIDENCING BEHAVIOR AND INTENTION

Part of the trouble is that the methodology to do those things is unformed. If a broad description of a lawyer's methods includes use of the rules of evidence, then narrowing down the methods means wielding two important but problematic tools in that evidentiary tool kit: the (sometimes) sharp scalpel and (frequently) blunt probe of "presumptions" and "inferences." Inferences are instruments based on logic and are not relegated strictly to the courtroom but pepper all cognitive activities; presumptions, in contrast, are legal-oriented devices based on the shifting of evidentiary burdens and the allocation of fairness within the requisites of a formal contest. As to many facts of nature, geographical depictions, historical occurrences, and certain mental activities, courts have been willing to both infer and presume that certain facts demand only slight proof as to their existence.

Presumptions are formal and inherently judicial. They comprise the set of specific propositions that can be both initially accepted and subsequently rebutted. A presumption begins life as something accepted as true. If its rebuttal is successful, then the presumption is overcome and considered to not be true anymore—it dies an ignoble death as an incorrect assumption whose falsity had been hidden but was eventually revealed. If its rebuttal is unsuccessful, however, then the presumption is imposed and rejuvenated with life—it is considered to be as true for the future as it first was. A judge decides which "life path" the presumption traverses and pronounces its demise or reanimation accordingly. Presumptions can be timeless or they can be *recherché* to the point of obsolescence: the presumption in 1891 that married women must own no property for themselves was once an unremarkable, accepted legal premise but has since suffered a lengthy and embarrassing death as a judicial truism.[106]

Inferences, for their part, are informal and inherently nonjudicial tools. They are simply part of the apparatus of logic, not necessarily tied to the fate of any particular proposition. Inferences are given "weight" in the law and fact finders can have significant agreements or disagreements about just what that weight is. Judges can generally claim to allow or disallow certain inferences to be made to begin with, but fact finders are those who rely on the use of inferences in their determinations: it is a jury, not a judge, who decides which "life path" the inference traverses and it is the jury, not any lawyer, who pronounces the demise or reanimation of each accordingly.[107]

For example, in distinction from our earlier presumption that "all dogs are presumed to be good," more subtly there is also a classic *inference* about dog behavior often raised by parties in civil animal law cases that a jury is encouraged to rely on: that all dogs generally possess an alertness, agility, and fairly well-recognized ability to avoid danger and to take care of protecting themselves when faced with some danger—an almost automatic inclination to self-preservation that is a recognizable and familiar behavior pattern in nearly all normal living things.[108] No judge can take that exercise in reason, experience, and folk wisdom away from the jury and no jury instruction can command a jury to disregard their gut level awareness that nearly all dogs will likely run *away* from speeding cars and trains, not run toward or under them, when given any sort of even basic choice about it.

The ideological contrast is this: a dog is "dangerous" as long as the law says it is, even if in normal life one might not consider it to truly be so, but a dog is not "suicidal" even if a lawyer or judge wishes to describe it as so, because the experiences of normal life allow for the former designation as a social convention but reject the latter designation as not having empirical support.[109] Lawyer methodology therefore places *some* constraints on our reasoning, those that society demands for legal systems to operate on a core level, but not full-on constraints that fly in the face of common sense type reasoning altogether.

To be fair, of course, objectivity in the methodology arena is not easily come by: as to the study of animals specifically, all sorts of cultural, political, and religious agendas arise (and are vehemently invoked) that impede what would otherwise be an impartial inquiry as to what animals are, how animals are treated, or what laws should apply to them—especially in comparison to people.[110] While evolution by natural selection has engineered people to act fundamentally distinct from all other animals in a way that makes legal distinctions between them and the other animals crucial,[111] the *reasons* as to why both law and science treat animals differently than people are reasons steeped in prehistoric and historic events and concepts, not just in practical observations.

If the technique of the lawyer—aimed as it is toward competent legal analysis—is not truly the technique of the scientist, close though they might be in intellectual spirit, still, the rational inquiry into the possible answer of any answerable question for the lawyer-scientist is wrapped up in both true and false divisions between people and animals. The ultimate division is that of subject and object. In the law, a "subject" is a person who understands something, where that thing is the "object" of his or her understanding. A "legal subject" therefore is a person who attempts to understand the law, the application of legal doctrines, and the workings of the legal system, and "legal objects" are those items or things that he or she then apprehends in doing so.[112] A threshold precept in employing such terminology is that the act of "apprehending objects" equates roughly with the act of "*using*" the objects, albeit use for a multitude of disparate purposes.

A primary goal of the law is to grasp hold of and explicate a variety of intellectual concepts about all objects in terms of their potential uses, animals included, uses valued through their evolving roles as first, raw organic components of a community's local environment, and second, malleable and consumable detachments from that environment.[113] Animals, as they transform into legal objects, are interesting for the very reason that they have such hugely flexible utility, and humans currently utilize them (and have utilized them) in myriad ways, including as food, vehicles, weapons and poisons, protections, amusements, construction materials, medicines and health aids, trade goods and market commodities, currencies, clothing, and components of shelters.[114]

In contrast, the law does *not* treat animals as personal subjects of "self" in the way we have always treated ourselves. The law does not adopt a stance of considering animals to be like ourselves in the form of "others," "our kin," "our brethren," or "our equals"[115]; rather than forging personal relationships with them that would require shared mental experiences, we instead forge functional relationships that require sharp attention to their interferences with our health, safety, and public activities. It is their adaptive conduct and replication we are reacting to in forming our laws, not their insertion into our social networks.[116]

When it comes to effective legal procedure to deal with rights determinations, how minds work makes all the difference between separating subject from object. Courts will (cautiously) peer into human minds because judges, being humans themselves, accept the predicate that a mind similar to the judge's exists to be read and that the message divined requires a social consequence to its holder. It is for that reason that courts might infer one's subjective intent to cause harm simply because it seems reasonable,[117] or because others in the community demand it (as in criminal[118] or sexual abuse[119] scenarios).

There are no reasonable inferences to rationally rely on from animal conduct, on the other hand, and their object status is a corollary of the fact that no "mind-reading" feature is available for us to access. Judges confronted with an animal's pattern of conduct risk basing decisions on pure speculation were they to start down the road of interpreting meaning from action.[120] The rational route is to equate the animal with any other object and forgo interpretation altogether.

Take, for example, the act of an animal biting, something most animals quite commonly do and something that lawsuits commonly present.[121] Is there any reasonable inference to glean from a bite occurring? Is it legitimate to presume that when an animal bites it has a specific state of mind in doing so? Since people also bite, are bites animal-specific or can they be animal-independent? Is the inferential significance of an act of biting dependent on the species, breed, gender, age, health, personal history, or lineage history of the animal engaging in the bite? None of those questions can be answered objectively. If we do not infer or presume facts about the mindset of a biting animal, on the other hand, and if we do not have the animal's own voice to tell us what they were thinking as they bit, we become pushed to use more attenuated tricks of proof, or, perhaps, to accept no proof at all, and we end up merely speculating about what state of mind, if any, may have existed.

Even were there somehow to be a broad public policy instituted against biting sufficient to justify an initial inference for social reasons (that harm by any biter was presumptively intended, say), the situational complexity of any given biting incident makes us sensitive to the fact that, without language, we are truly only guessing at explanations beneath the surface. The speculation isn't simply the one we are already nervous to make, that another has a mind that has decided to express itself through a particular pattern of physical conduct, it is also that specific thoughts themselves must be both in existence and manifested, i.e., "in mind," at the moment the conduct occurs.

With people we defer to the sophistication of minds with the rule that witnesses cannot speculate on the thought processes, including the intent, of another person. It is recognized generally that the mental status of another is solely a matter of opinion (and thus inadmissible) rather than fact. Witnesses are precluded under the opinion rule from testifying that another did or did not know a certain thing or feel a certain way, and the appropriate procedure for examining such a witness is to have them detail the facts from which such a conclusion of knowledge or feeling could be drawn by the trier of fact.[122]

THE ART OF INQUIRY AND THE INSERTION OF RELIABILITY AS A CONCERN

This brings up the topic of inquiries, something that people, not animals, make, and the most effective of which are those that begin broadly and then quickly home in on the minutiae. Our past experiences (and present suspicions) about what people use the sophistication in their minds to do, make lawyers and scientists eventually turn their real focus on the particulars of exactly how people are going about doing it. For lawyers as well as for scientists, specifying the facts of a course of conduct is a key task to discerning the real forces going on behind the conduct—and creating such detail through the rigors and formalities of observation and language in the form of writing thus becomes paramount in both disciplines. For lawyers as well as scientists, it is the picky details that are the highest prized parts of the flower blossoming from language's stem, and again how and what people write out is instrumental in setting forth those details.

The central target that such inquiries aim for is reliability. How dependable and trustworthy, in other words, are words? Sworn oaths are all well and good, but cynics are quick to note that oaths are often broken or disrespected depending on what the speaker's private agendas might be and how far they are willing to pursue them. It might seem like we need something more substantial than only a promise to "tell the truth, the whole truth, and nothing but the truth," which at times can just seem like the piling of additional untrustworthy words on top of the original ones, but what is that additional "thing"?

We need, and have, shared experience. We best assess a witness as reliable when we compare what they are saying and doing with words and deeds we ourselves have either benefited from or been harmed by in our own histories. That comparison, that connection, is unavailable with animals, and the unfamiliarity with the background experience inherent in what they are possibly "saying" dashes any hope of connecting animal expressions to human goals. Several factors regarding that reliability absolutely crush proposals to have people speak for animals.

One, the translator's acquaintance with the one being spoken for influences the resulting interpretation: the better the observer knows them and the lengthier the ties between the two, the more subjective the observation. Owners know their animals well, and the acquaintance angle taints reliability when it is the owner "discovering" intent.

Two, communication among translators often inflates, deflates, or conflates agreements about what is meant: competing shared opinions as to meaning create competing interpretations. Testimony about animal intent seems to encourage duplicative witnesses, which in turn fosters unreliability.

Three, differential exposure to the animal alters opinions: in the temporal sense, a single instance is likely to be interpreted differently than a series of multiple occasions. In the categorical sense, some "groups" of animals (dogs, for example) are simply going to be easier to interpret than others. Testimony about a single squeal, compared to testimony about a week full of squealing, is going to raise a host of divergent opinions complicated when the squeal arises from a pig as opposed to a dog.

Finally, some peculiarly human-oriented states (jealousy or disgust, for example) are undoubtedly going to be significantly harder to interpret than others. Their manifest expression may well be physical, but their genesis and repression are intimately psychological acts, and one treads precariously to assign specific meaning to the strong kick of a leg that is one solitary image in an entire tapestry of historical events between the kicker and the kickee: "With respect to both their detection and ascription, mental phenomena tend to be heterogeneous and complex and thus they can be neither off-handedly denied nor simply attributed to animals; their credible ascription, or, obversely, their justified deletion requires solid grounds."[123]

Any translation attempt is going to have to take place in the courtroom, festooned as those locales are with the stagecraft of respect, formality, and security. Yet animals are universally kept out of courtrooms, and that so far only the state of Washington has held specifically that physical observation of an animal inside a courtroom is even partially allowed.[124] Of course, even were the animal in the room, the procedural arsenal we would need to account for all contingencies is imposing, and would have to be stocked with a whole new common language to utilize that borrows creatively from biology, psychology, ethology, and sociology; a standardized set of characteristics translated into species-typical behaviors; and a new set of independent experts in animal communication to rely upon to opine about them.

A judge will have to subject each proffered assertion to the fire of the evidentiary crucible, assessing the relevance and materiality of each exhibit or testimony offered into evidence ranging from classical operant conditioning lab tests of domestic dogs to straight-faced scientific claims of observing anxiety in worms.[125] Those whom are sensitive to what intrusive uses we already put animals to currently will likely be displeased that all this effort will necessarily increase, not decrease, animal-based scientific research.

Numerous impediments to this project exist. A towering one is that we just don't find in animals the subtle psychological clues that people, talkative or mute, invariably provide us illustrating that they truly do recognize the import of their actions:

> [R]emorse or guilt requires a grasp of wrongdoing and the need for reparation. Clearly a being unable to learn to talk of the past, to know what the past is and that it can be atoned for, ought not to be said to be remorseful. What seems to be important . . . in the case of remorse, like that of hope also, but unlike that of fear, is that there is an absence of characteristic prelinguistic prototypes which would provide grounds for attributing remorse or hope to creatures that do not use language . . . [I]t is the only possible area in which these feelings operate.[126]

The phenomenon of being wordless is a superficial similarity between animals and the mute or children; the core dissimilarities are far deeper. "Personhood" is in fact a vast and critical distinction between what people are and what animals are, and our evidentiary rules and our justice system work well in recognizing the gap as a legally critical one.[127] There is no doubt that many animals are individuals in the very rough sense that they have distinct character-related suites of conduct; domesticated animals such as dogs and cats in particular can act *as if they were* playful, or suspicious, or aggressive, or mischievous,[128] or ridiculous in the sense that we intuitively know humans can be. But cognitive scientists recognize that our inter-specific differences go far, far beyond those in outward appearances or inner structures; humans are individuals in a fundamentally different sense. To be a "person" requires possession of all the necessary and sufficient conditions of intelligence, affectivity, agency, rationality, self-understanding, self-esteem, and mutual recognizance.[129]

> [W]e are self-created beings who realize ourselves through our relations with other such beings. Humans are persons, not simply individuals, because we are capable of being agents responsible for our actions. We are individuals with rights, duties, and obligations, individuals who have control over our actions, and not simply conduits for natural impulses.[130]

Animals also lack the ability to control themselves for the long-term future, to forestall that moment's gratification, to constrain a present inclination because of a future need. It is true that animals, in their psychological makeup, and in our interpretation of what their nonverbal behaviors might "mean," are certainly and superficially like human infants. Yet it is "superficial" in that even then the comparison is fundamentally invalid, given the progression of animals from infancy to adulthood in comparison with the progression of humans along the same trajectory:

> Think of how a child becomes an adult. To begin with an infant has no control over itself; it is a creature of natural impulse. At this point it is simply an object, not a subject. As it develops, an infant learns first to gain control over its bodily functions, to control its gaze, its movements, to learn to crawl and then to walk, to manipulate objects, to be toilet trained. Control of its behavioral impulses takes longer. A child that can walk, talk and is manually adept may nevertheless throw temper tantrums if it cannot immediately satisfy its desires. Children can be unbelievably cruel, to each other and to other creatures; they take a delight in being shocking for the sake of it, and crave instant sensual pleasure. That is why we often describe as 'childish' behavior that is not under control. The process by which a child learns to control its natural impulses is also the process through which it comes to construct its self. The 'self' is not something that is innate or pre-exists; nor is it a thing to be found in a particular part of the brain, or the body. Rather it is a description of the capacity to control oneself.[131]

We have already noted that only as the infant develops into the child and then into the adult in producing and comprehending language does it form that capacity for control and become truly social in the sense that it becomes free to act independent of its environment, to make choices, to mold and affect the behaviors of others by acts of will.

THE DEVELOPMENT OF FREE WILL AND
THE EVOLUTION OF RIGHTS

Free will is an offshoot of an ancient evolutionary path millennia in the forging. Animals are not on any trajectory toward personhood as they develop; they are, in a real sense, unusual organic automatons, entities without free will. Their conduct occurs in the glaring absence of their own choice or of self-constructed internal reasons, and is ultimately explainable entirely by biomechanical, physiological, adaptive, environmental, and mechanical forces and effects. It is conduct that is precursor to, and galaxies distant from, the manner of freedom, the capacity to act rationally in a social milieu, the type of autonomy we evolved, and which in the light of prehistory and history enabled us to construct legal rights:

> Our minds have been built by selfish genes, but they have been built to be social, trustworthy, and cooperative. . . . Human beings have social instincts. They come into the world equipped with predispositions to learn how to cooperate, to discriminate the trustworthy from the treacherous, to commit themselves to be trustworthy, to earn good reputations, to exchange goods and information, and to divide labour. In this we are on our own. No other species has been so far down this evolutionary path before us, for no species has built a truly integrated society [such as ours].[132]

A substantial body of academic work on human developmental processes has revealed that from what we learn in our own childhood, and from our close observations of others, we naturally expect that, over time, a human infant will change and, as it develops a "self" with advancing age, become slowly enmeshed in the complex web of rules with which adults embroider their lives.[133] We do not naturally expect, in marked contrast, that animals would mature intellectually as they get older, to become possessed of any more recognition of self than they ever had at any age.[134] That distinction, and the disparity of language capacity between children and animals, is crucial to relying upon a comparison:

> Young chimpanzees have a drive to communicate, but it is of a special, limited kind. They engage in what psychologists call gestural babbling, a freewheeling invention and testing of body postures, hand signals, and facial expressions, along with some use of sound. Over a period of months this chaotic mixture grows into the characteristic adult repertory, plus a few personal idiosyncrasies. Human children, in contrast, engage in *verbal* babbling. From an early age they seem driven from within to create and test new words, meanings, and sentences. So characteristic is this inventive stage that its product is recognized as a special child's language, with peculiar qualities of rhythm and syntax. Even the mere

beginnings of the child's language pushes far beyond the mature ape's ultimate capacity. And where the ape must be urged and guided into the use of language, the human child often must be forced to shut up. Furthermore, the child's mind is equipped with epigenetic rules that lead it quickly to the choice of certain grammatic rules over others. They guide the mind to the more complex operations of sentence formation and thought. Thus the child's language matures easily into the adult tongue.[135]

Some time during the stages of this progression, at meteoric speed relative to the timescale of biological evolution, the capacity of symbolic expression—language—was written into the genes that dictate the organization of the brain. That is, there is a genetic capacity for language, an inborn propensity to learn language. The developing child uses words and then goes on to develop syntax or grammar without any formal learning. This seems to occur universally over the same age span in all children and with all tongues. Apes can learn a sign language used by the deaf and string several signs together. They can even use these to cooperate for immediate needs, but it is a vast gap to the remarkable interweaving of the knowledge function and symbolic language as seen in the human child and adult.[136]

Even could the rules regarding discerning the intent of infants or of the mute somehow be applied to animals, we would still be treating them as personal property objects but with the minds of children. That poorly constructed machine would be broken from the moment it was turned on. Animals are not treated as children under the law,[137] again because we excuse children from their own voluntary acts due to the fact that they are still only children, and in acceptance of the rule that all changes as they swim upstream into adulthood:

Minors under the age of 5 are, as a matter of law, deemed incapable of negligent acts, i.e., failing to exercise reasonable care under the circumstances. "The proposition that 'An infant may be so very young that no negligence may legally be imputed to him' is predicated on the principle that a child of very early years is 'incapable of realizing that his heedless conduct might foreseeably lead to injury to another which is the essential capacity of mind to create liability for negligence." Given the legal incapacity of minors under the age of five to act with reasonable care, the sole factual issue in this case concerning the victim was his age: was he under the age of five and, therefore, excused due to incapacity from taking reasonable precautions against the attack that killed him.[138]

We don't legally, scientifically, or logically treat animals as children since not only does no reasonably useful change in an animal occur as a function of ontological time, but no change will ever occur as a function of neurology either—the "essential capacity of mind" needed to create personal liability, whether for negligent, reckless, or deliberate conduct, does not exist at any stage nor ever will.

> [We have an] understanding that other human beings may have other values, profess other systems of belief, and form ideas of life and mental models of the world that differ from one's own. And this understanding opens out a new stage in human mental development: namely, the realization that each individual has a distinct 'inner' life which is distinct from one's own. This in turn is a prerequisite for recognizing, and focusing on, the fact that such a thing as the inner exists at all, and that, in so far as the other has a unique inner life, this is true of oneself as well. It is thus now, and only now, that a real, fully developed self-consciousness emerges—in the form of a phenomenological model of one's own 'inner' mental life and that of others.[139]

THE DOCTRINE OF "PROVOCATION" AS A PROCEDURAL COROLLARY TO THE ASSERTION OF RIGHTS

Darker clouds still loom on the horizon for the procedural treatment of animals as humans, children or otherwise. Were animals bestowed with a procedural right not to be harmed and cloaked with the accompanying legal responsibility to themselves abstain from harmful acts, then common law requires that, as with people, they must then also be exempted from responsibility in circumstances in which they have been provoked. Restraint and provocation are two sides of a single coin.[140] The concept of provocation is founded upon the understanding from psychological studies that an actor can be stirred to an action they otherwise would have refrained from or would have not intended were it not for a driving or compelling force directing them to so act.[141] Provoked actions, therefore, occur in spite of the best efforts one puts forward to curb themselves from acting, and it is the best efforts that justify the protection.

Whether animals can be "stirred to an action they otherwise would not intend" depends, of course, on what it is they intend and we have seen that a morass awaits those who venture too far in that regard. In addition, the premise is required that animals initially make best efforts to not be stirred—and we have found that premise faulty. However, courts have not had great difficulty in applying provocation rules to animals, again, primarily dogs. In doing so, human psychology seems to transfer over in part to animal psychology:

> The statute also requires that the dog [which bit a child] acted without provocation. Although the Dog Act does not define the term "provocation," "to

provoke" has been defined . . . as to "arouse to a feeling or action; to incite to anger; to call forth; to stir up purposely." A child attempting to eat a piece of chicken clearly does not fall within such definition.[142]

It should trouble the scientist that the lawyer augurs an animal's provocation out of what is "expected" will trigger a reaction in a like animal. "Provocation means any action or activity, whether intentional or unintentional, which would reasonably be expected to cause a normal dog in similar circumstances to react in a manner similar to that shown by the evidence."[143] "Any action by a person which causes the dog to immediately engage in a response that is motivationally different from the response it was engaged in just prior to the action of the person."[144] As innumerable bite victims will confirm, reactivity and response do not signal clearly from "normal" or "similar" behaviors, even of the same animal only a day or minute before. To account for the unexpected snap, causation is primarily inferred by the temporal and spatial immediacy of the change—in our example, the closer and quicker a dog goes from point A (behaviorally) to point B, the more likely the change was caused by an incited act. The animal's motivation, however, is also still measured by using a work shed full of mixed legal and factual factors, including an assessment of its temperament and behavior immediately before the incident, the context of the incident, the animal's past behaviors, and even its current medical condition.[145] Nevertheless, under no legally derived circumstances is motivation ever predicated on an assumption that the animal had self-control that simply had been overcome by an act of pure will.

Animal owners, i.e., people, are those who benefit from the doctrine of provocation and who are held responsible for creating the provocation.[146] A child's act of hugging a dog,[147] stepping on a dog's tail,[148] and pulling on a dog's chain[149] have all been ruled to be acts of provocation. No case has yet held that provocation was justified by an *animal's* acts as opposed to those of a person. Again, this stems from our acknowledgment that the act of inciting can truly only come from those who can think and who can exert control upon thinking:

Amiability of disposition does not serve as a safe guarantee against violent movements. In defense or offense, the horse's heels are relied on as its most forceful weapon. They are put in motion almost involuntarily in cases of defense, when quickness of action is deemed necessary to immediate safety or relief. In the present case, should it have been possible to interpret the thoughts of the mare, it would not be surprising to learn that she really kicked at plaintiff because she believed him to be the one who applied physical force to her. The close proximity of her position to him made it possible for her offensive action to cause injury. This position was not due to her own volition but to her master's. It was he who rode her so close to plaintiff, and it was he who unnecessarily did that which provoked her to wrath, so to speak. The kicking was not the proximate cause of the injury. That cause was the act of the rider which provoked the kicking.[150]

The hard question is the one that therefore asks how an animal can display propensity, the "natural inclination or preference" to a certain type of behavior, yet not at the same time be deemed an agent capable of provoking another, "arousing them . . . to action[?]" The answer is in part that provocation carries with it an odd mixture of elements of reflex, of retaliation, of desire, and of undue influence (or at least unfair influence) and all those phenomena are intimately associated with communication in the form of human language. Provocation, in essence, seems to be a very touchstone of human consciousness and conscious communication. No machine or other inanimate object ever was sincerely provoked into action because no machine or other inanimate object exhibits the type of consciousness with which we consider sufficient to identify or converse with. To put it bluntly, animals can be "programmed," but cannot themselves "program" others and the way that language affects both thinking and behavior is the missing segment of necessary code:

[T]hinking itself is in a language [and] every language is a vast pattern-system, different from others, in which are culturally ordained the forms and categories by which the personality not only communicates, but also analyzes nature, notices or neglects types of relationship and phenomena, channels his reasoning, and builds the house of his consciousness.[151]

None of this is to deny the existence of minds in animals. It is accepted, for instance, that animals, unlike inanimate objects, can have thoughts and memories, and can be capable of remembering past incidents to connect to—and fuel—the achievement of current goals.[152] The singular phenomenon of recollecting the past, nevertheless, by itself doesn't warrant a swap out of "propensity" and a swap in of "character" as an explanation for the present action—thermostats and robotic vacuums can do as much and deserve no such benefit. Yet if animals are deemed vested with will and consequently given a right to not be harmed such as people enjoy, then the propensity rule must be jettisoned and the character evidence rule put in its place. To be consistent, the evidence rules we currently apply to animal minds versus human minds would have to be turned on their heads.

Truly, the logic of the dominos we have pushed on does not allow us the luxury of that conclusion: rights require liabilities; liabilities require exemptions; exemptions include forcibly compelled acts; provocation, a key forcibly compelled act, requires self-awareness; self-awareness requires language;

language requires a special type of brain. Evolution by natural selection has, however, fashioned that type of brain for only one species on the planet:

> When we study human language, we are approaching what some might call the "human essence," the distinctive qualities of mind that are, so far as we know, unique to man and that are inseparable from any critical phase of human existence, personal or social. Hence the fascination of this study, and, no less, its frustration. The frustration arises from the fact that despite much progress, we remain as incapable as ever before of coming to grips with the core problem of human language, which I take to be this: Having mastered a language, one is able to understand an indefinite number of expressions that are new to one's experience, that bear no simple physical resemblance and are in no simple way analogous to the expressions that constitute one's linguistic experience; and one is able . . . to produce such expressions on an appropriate occasion, despite their novelty. . . . The normal use of language is, in this sense, a creative activity. This creative aspect of normal language use is one fundamental factor that distinguishes human language from any known system of animal communication.[153]

On a purely emotional level, the lacing of rights with responsibilities seems like a mean trick to play on animals; superficially the idea of holding animals legally responsible for their own misconduct smacks of academic gamesmanship, the "poor sport" rubbing of salt into the wound of already daunting animal life burdens. On deeper reflection, however, one may come to accept the fact that our formalization of social relationships *is*, ultimately, game-playing, and that the burdens of social games are rarely, if ever, democratically balanced. Sitting at the core of every childhood pastime and adult intellectual pursuit—including the construction of morality and of law—are the ideals of rules with their hoped-for fairness, the realities of games in practice, and the concepts of what set of agreed-upon conventions might at one and the same time both *confine and liberate* certain relationships. The cynical admonition that "what the large print giveth, the small print taketh away"[154] reminds that one must beware of, and labor under, the most minute details inside the agreements and rules embracing all human activities.

The small print, the rules, the inherent unfairness, and the extrinsic need to play the games with others, all come to us through language. Language, the direct ancestor of law, is an ultimate social activity. The translation of organic processes inside our heads into "thoughts" and "ideas" requires a massively social world, with a complicated mechanical underpinning that binds members of that world together, and erects agreed-upon conventions to make sense of how expression is then used and made useful:

> It is only because we live not as individuals, but within a social community and, moreover, within a community bound together by language, that we can make

sense of our own inner thoughts and feelings. No animal possesses either language or a social network like ours. Therefore it is simply not valid to assume that they have inner experiences as we do.[155]

In turn, language leads directly and inexorably to the conception and implementation of rights. Adult humans, unlike any other animal including the great apes, "live within a web of reciprocal rights and obligations created by our capacity for rational dialogue."[156] Rights are the products of a *historically* founded social compact. *Historically*, the agreement among members of the vast majority of social groups has been that if a person does not want to be unreasonably constrained by the others, they will agree to reasonably constrain themself. *Historically*, we have cemented such agreements by talking and writing about them. If animals are to be inducted into our presently existing social compact, then their entitlement to rights—rights of freedom, rights of due care, rights of life, etc.—can arise only through their own developing history and only as a condition of two burdens: one, if they bind themselves to certain obligations, thereby to be punished or penalized if they violate the compact; and two, if sophisticated communication with them about the seriousness of the obligations can be relied upon.

A voluntary agreement to adhere to a communal standard is what incarceration, breach of contract, and termination of parental rights are all about: in governing ourselves we require ourselves to be subject to procedural and institutional strictures and we formally codify those strictures by constitution and statute. *Adhering to mutually agreed-upon written rules* is the whole point of the law game. If one cannot be a fundamental part of that agreement, one cannot play.

Currently, animals (minds, bodies, and all) are personal properties under the law, and, as with all personal properties, have owners.[157] Animal owners, in turn, are those upon whose shoulders rest the obligation to adhere to social norms emanating straight out of that ownership. As owned objects, animals are currently free of personal obligation. In essence, animals have the unfettered freedom to do whatever it is they wish to do (to the extent that their biotic and abiotic environment allows them, their genetic structure constrains them, and their interactions with others directs them); it is those who own the animals who are truly fettered by assuming the legal responsibility for the animals' actions.[158] Humans may not be the ones wearing the actual collars and muzzles, but we are the far more tightly bound captives nonetheless, our tethers being much harsher and lengthier bonds self-created through law. The prospect of social penalty yanks hard on the chain attached to our necks and levies a burden no animal has ever experienced.

As maturing children [people] begin to know what they should and should not do and are praised or censured accordingly; up to a point they become *responsible*. Yet no liberationist would wish to admit this of animals since it would allow them to be punished for *wrongdoing* (rather than for permissible training purposes) of which all are agreed they can have no conception.[159]

It will be a curious day when, perhaps, there may be "termination of animal ownership rights" proceedings that parallel the termination of parental rights proceedings, where an owner's violation of an animal's rights results in the state taking away their ownership rights. It will be a curious day when, perhaps, there may be "animal civil rights violation" suits that parallel the federal civil rights suits concerned with human rights deprivations, and when an offender's violation of an animal's privacy or personal rights would result in compensation to the animal or vindication of the animal's individual interests. If that day occurs, if animals reach maturity as rights-holders, it will only be because they have communicated to us that they know what they should and should not do and that they can self-reward or self-censure accordingly. The law could then apply to them completely, not partially, and they will have become (in the legal and moral sense) truly *responsible*.

Let's take a clear case: a 5-year-old shoots a playmate. We don't consider the 5-year-old to be blameworthy. Why not? I think it is because the intuition of blameworthiness is closely tied to the intuition of deterrability. There are certain people whose behavior can be altered by being embedded in a society that has a publicly stated limit to acceptable behavior and a commitment to punish acts that stray outside those limits. However, we tend to feel that this is not the case for a 5-year-old: the threat of criminal punishment is not factored into the brain system that causes their behavior. So if the moral goal of a system of responsibility is to deter as much harmful behavior as possible while avoiding as much suffering as possible—other than that which is justified by the first goal of deterring harmful behavior—we won't lock up the 5-year-old, because the harm done to the 5-year-old wouldn't reduce the murder rate amongst 5-year-olds generally.[160]

The reason we would allow those rights to be established and enforced would be because we had also decided to allow the animal to be punished for wrongdoing (rather than solely for permissible training purposes). All of us would have to be in agreement that the animals involved had some conception of membership in the social compact and know full well the meaning of "fault," and "blame," of "fairness" and "penalty." The trope of "blame the dog" would, instead of being a trope, be a call to action, given that human-animal legal relations would then allow the assignment of blame as a function of a reliable understanding of human-animal communication regarding the realization of blame's significance at a fundamental level. Of course, attempting to describe imposition of that blame as a realistic legal possibility reveals its unrealistic, empirical impossibility:

> [T]he human is free to select the value or goal it itself prefers. And hence what the human does is fully under the control of the individual. This is precisely, then, what is meant by saying that the human is free: its behavior is self-deter-mined, in that it itself controls which of the behavioral options it will select. [W]ith the nonhuman animal, the case is quite different. Since it does not possess an intellective power, and thus does not possess fully reflexive self-knowledge, its viewpoint is restricted to what it senses. Consequently . . . the animal is *incapable of performing a true moral act,* for the animal lacks that degree of knowledge necessary to act morally; to be able to judge right from wrong, before acting.[161]

THE SUBJECT-OBJECT RELATIONSHIP OF PEOPLE AND ANIMALS, AND ANIMAL OBJECTIFICATION

Postulating such a universe commands that animals be viewed as subjects, like us, not as objects, and correspondingly concedes that all subjects have burdens imposed upon them as a quality of being a subject. To accomplish that impossible trick, however, would require forcing an artificial transfor-mation of what both objects and subjects actually are into what they are not. Objectification seems pejorative but only for those who don't understand it and fail to grasp its intricate and involved nature.

An ordinary piece of notebook paper, an object, may be scribbled upon and then crumpled up and thrown away with no moral, political, economic, or legal concern having been triggered. The Declaration of Independence, also an object, could not be scribbled upon and then crumpled up and thrown away without overwhelming moral, political, economic, and legal concerns being activated on a global level. We mistreat the one piece of paper and venerate the second in absolute disregard of the objectification of both. As an object, our history with, social use of, and symbolic investment in, the second piece of paper has resulted in us endowing it with an immense conceptual value in a way that we have not done with the first. Similarly, a tiger is an object. In its illustrative glory as a Henri Rousseau painting, in its representative glory as a skull and pelt in a museum drawer, and in its anatomical, physiological, and behavioral glory as an actual animal in the jungle or in the zoo, we invest it with differing levels of object value as a result of our differing histories, uses, and symbolic treatment of it in each of its potential permutations as an object, writ small or writ large. Conceptually, the tiger transforms as it "moves" from the jungle den to the printed page, and it is people, not the tiger, who drive that transformation forward.

Objectification is an elegant and immensely sophisticated concept, one with the plasticity sufficient to encompass the most worthless piece of garbage, the greatest work of art, and everything in between, be it living or never having lived at all. Consider, for instance, how a cow is analogous to the "Asian forest" section of the Bronx Zoo from the previous chapter. In outward appearance, a cow seems very natural, but it is actually a complicated construction made by a large group of people taking immense effort, time, and expense to create the illusion of naturalness. Aurochs, cow ancestors, were huge, aggressive, and dangerous animals; it took thousands of years of pursuit, containment, ritual sacrifice, consumption, and careful breeding of aurochs to construct something as compact, tame, productive, and useful as a cow.[162] Just like the Asian forest, the cow's natural-looking façade hides an intricate clockwork of human exploitation and intent, the current result of which exhibits the colossal power and value of objectification.

A miscomprehension of how wide, deep, and rich the object spectrum really is, is what defines the faulty base from which exhortations about animal "rights" often arise. Carefully analyzing subject-object distinctions, and where rights develop from those distinctions, is our final task as scientists and lawyers.

NOTES

1. *Rubáiyát* of Omar Khayyám, Quatrain LXXVIII.

2. Hornaday, William Temple. *The Minds and Manners of Wild Animals: A Book of Personal Observations.* New York: C. Scribner's Sons, 1923 at p. 118.

3. See generally Lorenz, Konrad. *Man Meets Dog.* Hove, UK: Psychology Press, 2002.

4. Camerlink, Irene, Estelle Coulange, Marianne Farish, Emma M. Baxter, and Simon P. Turner. "Facial Expression as a Potential Measure of Both Intent and Emotion." *Scientific Reports* 8, no. 1 (2018): 1–9 (finding that facial expressions in pigs can communicate aggressive intent related to fight success, and that facial metrics can convey information about emotional responses involving aggression and fear).

5. See generally Lewis, Michael, and Carolyn Saarni, eds. *Lying and Deception in Everyday Life.* New York: Guilford Press, 1993.

6. Leahy, Michael PT. *Against Liberation: Putting Animals in Perspective.* London: Routledge, 2005 at pp. 132–133.

7. See generally Kerr, Norbert L., and Robert M. Bray, eds. *The Psychology of the Courtroom.* New York: Academic Press, 1982. Krauss, Daniel A. *Jury Psychology:*

Social Aspects of Trial Processes: Psychology in the Courtroom, Vol. 1. London: Routledge, 2016.

8. *Westberry v. Blackwell*, 282 Or. 129 (Or. 1978).

9. *Doe v. Barnett*, 251 N.E.2d 688 (Ind. Ct. App. 1989).

10. *Merritt v. Matchett*, 115 S.W. 1066 (Mo. Ct. App. 1909).

11. Kennedy, John S. *The New Anthropomorphism*. Cambridge, UK: Cambridge University Press, 1992 at pp. 5, 9, 22–23, 31–32, 87, 121–122.

12. See, e.g., *Cullinane v. Board of Selectmen of Maynard* 50 Mass. App. Ct. 851 (Mass. 2001).

13. *Hill v. President and Trustees of Tualatin Academy and Pacific University* 61 Or. 190 (1912); *Mitchell v. Newsom* 360 SW 2d 247 (Mo. App. 1962); *Lloyd v. Alton R. Co.* 159 SW2d 267 (Mo. 1941); *Jarvis v. Koss*, 427 A2d 364 (Vt. 1981).

14. *Rothenbusch-Rhodes v. Mason*, 2003 WL 22056565 (Ohio App. 10th Dist. 2003).

15. *Bogan v. New London Housing Authority* 366 F. Supp. 861 (D. Conn. 1973).

16. *Blaha v. Stuard* 640 NW 2d 85 (South Dakota 2002). See also *Whitmer v. Schneble* 29 Ill. App. 3d 659 (Ill. 1975) (finding no warranty by a seller that a dog's personality would not change in the future).

17. See *Graves v. Moses* 13 Minn. 335 (Minn. 1868) (regarding a horse).

18. *Johnson v. Lindley*, 41 F. Supp. 2d 1021 (D. Neb. 1999).

19. See generally Raymond, R., C. W. Bales, D. E. Bauman, D. Clemmons, R. Kleinman, and D. Lanna. "Breed Specific Legislation." *Humans and Animals*: 59.

20. See, e.g., *Cook v. Whitsell-Sherman*, 796 NE2d 271 (Ind. 2003).

21. *Newport v. Moran*, 80 Or. App. 71 (Or. App. 1986).

22. *McCullough v. Bozarth*, 232 Neb. 714 (Neb. 1989.); *Lucas v. Kriska*, 168 Ill. App. 3d 317 (Ill. App. 1 Dist. 1988); *Tipton v. Town of Tabor*, 567 N.W.2d 351 (S.D. 1997); *Burgin ex rel. Akers v. Tolle*, 500 N.E. 2d 763 (Ind. App. 1986); *Boswell v. Steele*, 158 Idaho 554 (Idaho App. 2015).

23. *Gaffney v. Kennedy*, 2003 WL 22149640 (N.Y. Slip Op. 51267(U) 9/2/03); *Cayetano v. New York City Housing Authority*, 2003 WL 21355410 (N.Y. Slip Op. 50981(U) 6/4/03).

24. *People v. Fabing*, 143 Ill 2d 48 (1991):
One reason for the domestication language in the [Illinois Dangerous Animals Act] is that the animals included in the Act are presumed to behave unpredictably even when domesticated. The snakes themselves are not entitled to due process. Thus, even though defendant's snakes may be docile, they may be found to be life-threatening due to characteristics common to other members of their species. Moreover, courts would be unable to determine whether an individual reptile possessed a threatening temperament. Human psychology is an inexact science, and we see no reason to believe that reptile psychology is capable of a greater degree of accuracy. Therefore, under the Act, the temperament of each individual reptile may not be considered when determining whether that reptile is life-threatening. Rather, we find that a determination of whether it is reasonably possible that an animal will attack humans must be made on a species-wide basis.

25. For a particularly egregious example, see *Arnold v. Lair* 621 P.2d 138 (Wash. 1980) (using "tendencies," "disposition," "demeanor," "condition," and "propensities" interchangeably).

26. *Cullinane v. Board of Selectmen of Maynard* 50 Mass. App. Ct. 851 (Mass. 2001).

27. *Hill v. President and Trustees of Tualatin Academy and Pacific University* 61 Or. 190 (Or. 1912).

28. See Posner, Richard A. *The Problems of Jurisprudence.* Harvard University Press, 1990 at p. 167: "We impute a mind to a cat in the hope that we can predict and therefore influence the cat's behavior in the same way that we try to anticipate and adjust to people's behavior by assuming they think the way we do."

29. Restatement (Second) of Torts, Section 290, comment g.

30. See *Challenger Wrecker Mfg. Inc. v. Estate of Boundy*, 560 NE2d 94 (Ind Ct App 1990) (holding that "companionship" in the instruction refers to forms of love, care, and affection in the relationship between decedent and claimant).

31. See, e.g., *Marshall v. Martinson* 518 P.2d 1312 (1974).

32. *Rich v. Cooper* 380 P.2d 613 (Or. 1963).

33. *Charmley v. Lewis* 729 P.2d 567 (Or. 1986); *Karsun v. Kelley* 482 P.2d 533 (Or. 1971).

34. *Portland Mobile Home Park v. Wojtyna* 736 P.2d 604 (Or. App. 1987).

35. *Lewellin v. Huber*, 456 NW 2d 94 (Minn. App. 1994); *Eritano v. Com.*, 690 A.2d 705 (Pa. 1997).

36. Vauclair, Jacques. *Animal Cognition: An Introduction to Modern Comparative Psychology.* Cambridge, MA: Harvard University Press, 1996 at p. 157.

37. Lewontin, Richard. *Biology as Ideology: The Doctrine of DNA.* House of Anansi, 1996 at pp. 95–96.

38. *Turudic v. Stephens*, 31 P.3d 465 (Or. App. 2001).

39. Keepers and custodians of animals "must take into account the tendencies of certain animals as a class to attack moving objects" and "exercise greater precautions" to keep such animals under control if in a public area. *Medlyn v. Armstrong*, 49 Or. App. 829 (Or. App. 1980).

40. See, e.g., W. H. Thorpe, *Learning and Instinct in Animals* (2d ed. 1966) (discussing how instincts guide the learning of worms, arthropods, fish and mammals). See generally *The Origin and Evolution of Humans and Humanness* (D. T. Rasmussen ed., 1993) (suggesting that instincts guided the learning and evolution of early hominids).

41. See *State v. Negro Will, Slave of James S. Battle*, 18 N.C. 121 (1834) ("The law demands it as a duty that we should tame our passions to suit the condition which it has assigned us.")

42. See generally S. Pinker, *The Language Instinct.* New York: William Morrow, 1995 at 268–69:
In all [human] cultures, social interactions are mediated by persuasion and argument. How a choice is framed plays a large role in determining which alternative people choose . . . [E]volving humans lived in a world in which language was woven

into the intrigues of politics, economics, technology, family, sex, and friendship that played key roles in individual reproductive success.

43. See generally Duckler, G. "Animal Wrongs: On Holding Animals to (and Excusing Them from) Legal Responsibility for Their Intentional Acts." *J. Animal L. & Ethics* 2 (2007): 91.

44. McKenna, Erin, and Andrew Light, eds. *Animal Pragmatism: Rethinking Human-Nonhuman Relationships*. Bloomington: Indiana University Press, 2004 at pp. 46, 74.

45. Niccolo Machiavelli, *The Prince* (George Bull trans.), 1999.

46. See, e.g., Robert Axelrod, *The Evolution of Cooperation* 109–23, 206–07 (1984) (developing the iterated prisoner's dilemma in which prisoners who cooperate with other prisoners gain an advantage over those who do not). *See generally* Robert L. Trivers, "The Evolution of Reciprocal Altruism," 46 *Q. Rev. of Biology* 35 (1971) (presenting a model of society in which cooperation is to the advantage of individuals and reciprocally altruistic behavior is naturally selected).

47. Safina, Carl. *Beyond Words: What Animals Think and Feel*. New York: Macmillan, 2015 at pp. 81–82.

48. Norman Malcolm, *Thoughtless Brutes*, 46 Proc. & Addresses of Am. Phil. Ass'n 5–20 (1973). "The relationship between language and thought must be . . . so close that it is really senseless to conjecture that . . . animals *may* have thoughts." Id. at pp. 17–18.

49. See generally *Wild Mammals in Captivity* (Devra G. Kleiman et al. eds., 1996).

50. For a comprehensive but dated review of some scientific studies, *See* Sara J. Shettleworth, "Constraints on Learning," in *4 Advances in the Study of Behav. 1*, 1–61 (Daniel S. Lehrman et al. eds., 1972).

51. This is not to propose equating "animal rights" with "animal protections" that aims to legislatively expand already existing rights and remedies for certain types of animal owners.

52. Dennett, Daniel C. *Freedom Evolves*. London: Penguin UK, 2004. at pp. 250–251.

53. See, e.g., Donald R. Griffin, *Animal Thinking*. Cambridge, MA: Harvard University Press, 1984.

54. The problem, when it has been acknowledged at all, is addressed as if it were merely a historical curiosity easily explained:

[In the past] it could matter whether an animal committed a deliberate or accidental harm. It could also matter whether the animal was provoked or whether it acted in self-defense against, say, the attack of other animals.

Richard A. Epstein, "Animals as Objects, or Subjects, or Rights," in *Animal Rights: Current Debates and New Directions*, 143, 146 (Cass R. Sunstein & Martha C. Nussbaum eds., 2004). The lawyer Steven Wise dismisses the topic of "legal obstacles" in the space of a single paragraph, unimpressed that animal obligations would be of much concern for the law. Steven M. Wise, "Animal Rights, One Step at a Time," in *Animal Rights: Current Debates and New Directions* 19, 25 (Cass R. Sunstein & Martha C. Nussbaum eds., 2004).

55. See generally Duckler, G. "Animal Wrongs: On Holding Animals to (and Excusing Them from) Legal Responsibility for Their Intentional Acts." *J. Animal L. & Ethics* 2 (2007): 91.

56. Searle, John R., and S. Willis. *Intentionality: An Essay in the Philosophy of Mind.* Cambridge, UK: Cambridge University Press, 1983 at p. 178.

57. See *Holloway v. United States*, 148 F2d 665 (DC Cir 1945):

There is no objective standard by which such a judgment of an admittedly abnormal offender can be measured. They must be based on the instinctive sense of justice of ordinary men. This sense of justice assumes that there is a faculty called reason which is separate and apart from instinct, emotion, and impulse, that enables an individual to distinguish between right and wrong and endows him with moral responsibility for his acts. This ordinary sense of justice still operates in terms of punishment. To punish a man who lacks the power to reason is as undignified and unworthy as punishing an inanimate object or an animal. A man who cannot reason cannot be subject to blame. Our collective conscience does not allow punishment where it cannot impose blame.

58. See Pinker, Steven. *The Language Instinct: How the Mind Creates Language.* London: Penguin UK, 2003. at pp. 334 (1995) (explaining how human language differs from other animals' means of communication):

[H]uman language has a very different design [compared to nonhuman communication]. The discrete combinatorial system called 'grammar' makes human language infinite (there is no limit to the number of complex words or sentences in a language), digital (this infinity is achieved by rearranging discrete elements in particular orders and combinations, not by varying some signal along a continuum like the mercury in a thermometer), and compositional (each of the infinite combinations has a different meaning predictable from the meanings of its parts and the rules and principles arranging them).

59. Duckler, G. "Animal Wrongs: On Holding Animals to (and Excusing Them from) Legal Responsibility for Their Intentional Acts." *J. Animal L. & Ethics* 2 (2007): 91.

60. David G. Ritchie, "Why Animals Do Not Have Rights," in *Animal Rights and Human Obligations* 181, 184 (Tom Regan & Peter Singer eds., 1976).

61. Some animal rights advocates rail at the idea of imposing obligations on animals at all, and push on the rights door to swing only one way—against humans:

In short, more attention must be given to both the needs of the animals and the culpability of the human actors. Prosecutors and judges must lift responsibility from the shoulders of the animals, and place it where it more properly belongs—with the human guardians of the offending animals. They must zealously enforce anti-cruelty laws when private citizens take the law into their own hands and kill animals suspected of harming human beings. Notions of humanity, justice, and equity require that we revisit the idea of giving animals some measure of due process before taking their lives. Perhaps it is time that we seriously consider re-extending to alleged animal offenders at least basic judicial due process protections before killing them.

From Jen Girgen, *"The Historical and Contemporary Prosecution and Punishment of Animals"* 9 *Animal L.* 97, 133 (2003). This historical review of animal punishments is heavy with anecdote and indignation, yet light on scientific support or legal analysis in assessing rights.

62. See, e.g., *Saldivar v. State*, 783 SW2d 265 (Tex App 1989).

63. See, e.g., ORS 161.085(7) (explaining that acting intentionally means that "a person acts with a conscious objective to cause the result"); *State Farm Fire and Cas. Co. v. Parker*, 1 P.3d 498 (Or. Ct. App. 2000) (finding defendant acted intentionally because he intended to shoot the victim and cause the resulting injury).

64. Most acknowledge that animals have minds, as in the curious census taken in S. L. Davis, and P. R. Cheeke, "Do Domestic Animals Have Minds and the Ability to Think?" 76 *J. Animal Science* 2072–79 (1998) (polling students, faculty, and staff at a university if they believe animals have minds).

65. *Miller v. Engle*, 172 S.W. 631 (Mo. Ct. App. 1915).

66. *Doe v. Barnett*, 251 N.E.2d 688 (Ind. Ct. App. 1969).

67. *Brown v. Minneapolis, St. P. & S.S.M. Ry.*, 180 N.W. 792 (N.D. 1920).

68. *Domenghini v. Evans*, 70 Cal. Rptr.2d 917 (Cal. Ct. App. 1998).

69. Duckler, G. "On Redefining the Boundaries of Animal Ownership: Burdens and Benefits to Evidencing Animals' Personalities," *Animal L.* 63, 69 (2004).

70. In law, dogs get the most attention of any animal. See, e.g., *Johnson v. McConnell*, 22 p. 219 (Cal. 1889) ("It is equally true that there are no other domestic animals to which the owner or his family can become more strongly attached, or the loss of which will be more keenly felt"). The majority of scientific studies on animal behavior focus on dogs. *See, e.g.,* E. B. Hale, 1969. "Domestication and the Evolution of Behavior," *in The Behavior of Domesticated Animals* 22, 22–42 (2d ed. 1969); J. P. Scott, *The Effects of Selection and Domestication Upon the Behavior of the Dog*, 15 *J. Nat'l Cancer Inst.* 739, 739–58 (1954) (explaining that dogs have existed in conditions favorable to domestication throughout history).

71. *See, e.g., Crowley v. Groonell*, 50 A. 546 (Vt. 1901) (holding owner responsible for injuries caused to another by his dog regardless of whether dog was acting in malicious or playful manner); *Mercer v. Marston*, 3 La. App. 97 (1926) (holding that a dog that is not vicious but mischievous can still cause its owner or handler to be liable for injuries to another); *Zuniga v. Storey*, 239 S.W.2d 125 (Tex. Civ. App. 1951) (reversing verdict in favor of defendant whose bull escaped and injured plaintiff's wife where defendant should have known of the bull's violent tendencies).

72. *Lewellin v. Huber*, 456 N.W.2d 94 (Minn. App. 1990) (Randall, J., dissenting) (discussing a statute covering both "playful" and "vicious" bites). Proclaiming the prohibition has hardly restricted courts over the last century from violating it, often in the same breath. See, e.g., *Johnson v. McConnell*, 22 P. 219 (Cal. 1889) (McFarland, J. dissenting) ("The rule that a man's intentions must be gathered from his conduct applies still more forcibly to dogs, and if a dog be found chasing sheep in a field of his owner's neighbor, the common judgment of mankind is that his intent is bad.")

73. Mitchell, Robert W., Nicholas S. Thompson, and H. Lyn Miles, eds. *Anthropomorphism, Anecdotes, and Animals.* Albany, NY: SUNY Press, 1997 at pp. 190–191.

74. With one exception in *Miles v. City Council of Augusta, Ga.*, 710 F2d 1542 (11th Cir 1983), the case of Blackie the talking cat:

Plaintiffs Carl and Elaine Miles, owners and promoters of "Blackie the Talking Cat," brought this suit . . . challenging the constitutionality of the Augusta, Georgia, Business License Ordinance. This Court will not hear a claim that Blackie's right to free speech has been infringed. First, although Blackie arguably possesses a very unusual ability, he cannot be considered a "person" and is therefore not protected by the Bill of Rights. Second, even if Blackie had such a right, we see no need for appellants to assert his right *jus tertii.* Blackie can clearly speak for himself.

75. Samuel D. Gosling, "From Mice to Men: What Can We Learn about Personality from Animal Research" 127 *Psychological Bulletin* 45, 48 (2001).

76. There are currently about 1.5 to 1.8 million named species, but it is estimated that the actual number of species in the world likely exceeds 10 million. *See* Mora C, Tittensor DP, Adl S, Simpson AGB, Worm B (2011) "How Many Species Are There on Earth and in the Ocean?" *PLoS Biol* 9(8).

77. Several authors think that the fact that animals feel what we feel is self-evident, i.e., it is so because it must be so to them, and thus is not a phenomenon that needs any empirical explanation. See e.g., Schaffner, J. *An Introduction to Animals and the Law*, Basingstoke, UK: Palgrave Macmillan at pp. 163:

As humans although we cannot know the full extent of a dog's pain and suffering, we do know that dogs feel pain and suffer. Thus the courts could develop a mechanism for assigning a reasonable objective value to a dog's pain and suffering.

78. Wohlleben, Peter. *The Inner Life of Animals: Love, Grief, and Compassion— Surprising Observations of a Hidden World.* Vancouver: Greystone Books, 2017 at p. 239.

79. *Lloyd v. Alton R.R. Co.*, 159 S.W.2d 267 (Mo. 1941) (internal citations omitted).

80. *Smith v. Louisiana Power & Light Co.*, 158 So. 844 (La. Ct. App. 1935).

81. Propensity evidence of humans is normally excluded. See Fed. R. Evid. 404.

82. *Eritano v. Pennsylvania*, 690 A.2d 705 (Pa. 1997).

83. See, e.g., *Ward v. Shoney's, Inc.*, 817 A2d 799 (Del 2003) ("We hold that the jury could properly find, based on its own understanding of human nature, that people sometimes cut corners, and that no expert testimony is necessary on that point").

84. Duckler, G. "Animal Wrongs: On Holding Animals to (and Excusing Them from) Legal Responsibility for Their Intentional Acts." *J. Animal L. & Ethics* 2 (2007): 91.

85. See, e.g., *Hayden v. Sieni*, 601 N.Y.S.2d 327 (N.Y. App. Div.,1993).

86. Budiansky, Stephen. *If a Lion Could Talk: Animal Intelligence and the Evolution of Consciousness.* New York: Free Press, 1998.

87. *People v. Schneider*, No. C044795, 2004 WL 2191322, at 6 (Cal. Ct. App. Sept. 30, 2004).

88. See generally B. F. Skinner. *About Behaviorism.* New York: Vintage Books, 1974.

89. See *Harrold v. Rolling J Ranch*, 23 Cal. Rptr. 2d 671 (Cal. Ct. App. 1993) ("We view sudden movements of a horse just as inherent in horseback riding as the presence of moguls on a ski slope are to skiers.")

90. Wittenberger, James F. *Animal Social Behavior.* Duxbury Press, 1981 at p. 48. *Cf.,* Ewer, Rosalie Francis. *Ethology of Mammals.* New York: Springer, 2013 at p. 7:

Because they have always stressed the importance of internal motivational factors, ethologists have preferred to use the terms *releaser* and *released* rather than stimulus and stimulated when speaking of endogenous movements. The difference is not merely terminological; it signifies a completely different picture of the central nervous organization underlying the behavior.

91. Malik, Kenan. *Man, Beast, and Zombie What Science Can and Cannot Tell Us about Human Nature*. New Brunswick, NJ: Rutgers University Press, 2002 at p. 229.

92. See Stephen Budiansky, *If a Lion Could Talk: How Animals Think.* New York: Free Press, 1998 at p. 32:

It is not as if plovers, as a predator approaches, sometimes fake a broken wing and sometimes dance the Charleston. All predators stalk, all opossums play dead, all plovers fake broken wings. No other explanation answers but these are innate, genetically programmed instincts, honed by evolution because they work.

93. Mitchell, Robert W., Nicholas S. Thompson, and H. Lyn Miles, eds. *Anthropomorphism, Anecdotes, and Animals*. Albany, NY: SUNY Press, 1997 at pp. 48–49.

94. See *Jarvis v. Koss*, 427 A.2d 364 (Vt. 1981) (finding that defendant's pig harmed plaintiff's crop and that the habits and qualities of common animals are matters of common knowledge and a proper subject of judicial notice).

95. See *Georg v. Animal Defense League*, 231 S.W.2d 807 (Tex. App. 1950) (it is common knowledge that dogs bark and howl).

96. See *Crosby v. Burge*, 1 So. 2d 504 (Miss. 1941) (it is common knowledge that any horse may lunge forward).

97. See *Bischoff v. Cheney*, 92 A. 660 (Conn. 1914) (where domestic cat exhibits neither mischievous nor vicious tendencies, liability will not attach to owner).

98. Id. at 661 (cattle, unlike cats, are a species "whose instinct is to rove").

99. *W. R. Peete & Co. v. Jackson*, 4 Higgins 678 (Tenn. Civ. App.,1913).

100. See, e.g., Crist, E. *Images of Animals. Anthropomorphism and Animal Mind.* Philadelphia: Temple University Press, 1999 at pp. 73–87.

101. See, e.g., Samuel D. Gosling, "Personality Dimensions in Spotted Hyenas (Crocuta crocuta)," 112 *J. Comp. Psychol.* 107–18 (1998) (suggesting there is some cross-species generality of personality traits such as excitability, sociability and assertiveness). For a review of the field, See Samuel D. Gosling, *"From Mice to Men:* What Can We Learn about Personality from Animal Research." 127 *Psychol. Bull.* 45–86 (2001).

102. Hayakawa, Samuel Ichiyé, and Alan R. Hayakawa. *Language in Thought and Action*. New York: Houghton Mifflin Harcourt, 1990 at p. 23.

103. See Griffin, Donald R. *Animal Minds: Beyond Cognition to Consciousness*. Chicago: University of Chicago Press, 2013; Flynn, Clifton P. *Social Creatures: A Human and Animal Studies Reader*. Brooklyn: Lantern Books, 2008.

104. Barnard, Alan. *Genesis of Symbolic Thought*. Cambridge, UK: Cambridge University Press, 2012.

105. Stangroom, Jeremy. *What Scientists Think*. London: Routledge, 2005 at pp. 33, 55–56.

106. *Samuel Ayers v. Emma Ayers*, 41 Ill. App. 226 (Ill. App. 1 Dist. 1891).

107. See, e.g., *Crooks v. White*, 290 P. 497 (Cal. App.1. Dist. 1930) (in inferring, jury may make any logical, reasonable deduction which facts permit).

108. See, e.g., *Clement v. Adams Express Company, Appellant*, 43 Pa. Super. 25 (Pa. Super. 1909).

109. *Hollingsworth v. Commercial Union Ins. Co.*, 208 Cal. App.3d 800 (Cal. App. 1989) ("The logic of words should yield to the logic of realities.")

110. Daston, Lorraine, and Gregg Mitman, eds. *Thinking with Animals: New Perspectives on Anthropomorphism*. New York: Columbia University Press, 2005.

111. Duckler, G. "Animal Wrongs: On Holding Animals to (and Excusing Them from) Legal Responsibility for Their Intentional Acts." *J. Animal L. & Ethics* 2 (2007): 91; Duckler, G. "Two Major Flaws of the Animal Rights Movement." *Animal L.* 14 (2007): 179.

112. See, e.g., Pierre Schlag, "Fish v. Zapp: The Case of the Relatively Autonomous Self," 76 *Geo. L. J.* 37 (1987).

113. Epstein, Richard A., Animals as Objects, or Subjects, of Rights (December 2002). University of Chicago Law & Economics, Olin Working Paper No. 171.

114. Hyams, Edward. *Animals in the Service of Man: 10000 years of domestication*. 1972; Serpell, James. *In the Company of Animals: A Study of Human–Animal Relationships*. Cambridge, UK: Cambridge University Press, 1996.

115. See Ryder, Richard D. *Animal Revolution: Changing Attitudes toward Speciesism*. New York: Berg, 2000.

116. See, e.g., Ingham, John Hall. *The Law of Animals: A Treatise on Property in Animals, Wild and Domestic, and the Rights and Responsibilities Arising Therefrom*. The Lawbook Exchange, Ltd., 1900.

117. See, e.g., *Allstate Ins. Co. v. Stone*, 876 P.2d 313 (Or. 1994) (actor did not intend to harm other driver when he committed suicide by driving into the path of a truck).

118. See *Allstate Ins. Co. v. Sowers*, 776 P.2d 1322 (Or. Ct. App. 1989) (officer's injury resulted from criminal conduct of the insured).

119. See *Mutual of Enumclaw v. Merrill*, 794 P.2d 818 (Or. Ct. App. 1990) ("intentional sexual abuse is the type of conduct from which an intent to cause harm must necessarily be inferred as a matter of law.")

120. Compare, e.g., *City of Boulder v. Stewardson*, 143 P. 820 (Colo. Ct. App. 1914) (declining to infer that horse had to have been frightened by a steamroller since witnesses reported that other horses were not so frightened), *with Rosenthal v. Hill Top Riding Academy*, 110 N.W.2d 854 (Minn. 1961) (holding it is common knowledge that horses are anxious to return to their stable in the evening, that many horses fear motorcycles and motor scooters, and that "as night approaches even gentle horses become restless and difficult to handle, particularly where handled by inexperienced riders.")

121. Duckler, G. "Animal Wrongs: On Holding Animals to (and Excusing Them from) Legal Responsibility for Their Intentional Acts." *J. Animal L. & Ethics* 2 (2007): 91.

122. *Click v. State*, 695 So.2d 209 (Ala. Crim. App. 1996) (witness was not testifying that appellant knew specific facts or had certain feelings). See also *Kimp v. State*,

546 N.E.2d 1193 (Ind. 1989) (police officer's opinion regarding cashier's mental state after robbery allowed); *People v. Madson*, 638 P.2d 18 (Colo. 1981) (murder victim's assertions regarding boyfriend not allowed); *Wilson v. State*, 265 S.E.2d 79 (Ga. Ct. App. 1980) (testimony by witness as to what they believed to be defendant's intent excluded); *State v. Shook*, 248 S.E.2d 425 (N.C. Ct. App. 1978) (testimony of officer relating to defendant's mental state prior to signing a statement allowed); *State v. Bennett*, 258 N.W.2d 895 (Minn. 1977) (officer may describe the meaning conveyed to him by defendant's conduct under the circumstances without opining about defendant's subjective intent).

123. See, e.g., Crist, E. *Images of Animals. Anthropomorphism and Animal Mind.* Philadelphia: Temple University Press, 1999 at p. 166.

124. See *Arnold v. Laird*, 621 P.2d 138 (Wash. 1980) ("when an issue in dispute is a dog's condition and demeanor . . . showing the dog to the jury can, in some cases, be the most probative evidence available.")

125. Jay Boyd Best, *Protopsychology*, 208 Sci. Am. 54–75 (1963) (discussing ways in which planarians behave and learn).

126. Michael P. T. Leahy, *Against Liberation* 133 (1991) (emphasis in the original).

127. Rescher, Nicholas. *Human Interests: Reflections on Philosophical Anthropology.* Vol. 6. Redwood City, CA: Stanford University Press, 1990.

128. See *People v. Schneider*, No. C044795, 2004 WL 2191322 (Cal. Ct. App. Sept. 30, 2004) (regarding jury instructions on whether defendant's dog was "mischievous").

129. Rescher, Nicholas. *Human Interests: Reflections on Philosophical Anthropology.* Vol. 6. Redwood City, CA: Stanford University Press, 1990 at pp. 6–7.

130. Malik, Kenan. *Man, Beast, and Zombie What Science Can and Cannot Tell Us about Human Nature.* New Brunswick, NJ: Rutgers University Press, 2002) at p. 366.

131. Id.

132. Ridley, Matt. *The Origins of Virtue.* London: Penguin UK, 1997 at p. 249.

133. See, e.g., Harter, Susan. "The Development of Self-Representations." (1998).

134. See, e.g., *Giles v. Russell*, 180 S.E.2d 201 (S.C. 1971) ("It is not likely that the traits of an animal will change rapidly").

135. Lumsden, Charles J., and Edward O. Wilson. *Promethean Fire: Reflections on the Origin of the Mind.* Cambridge, MA: Harvard University Press, 1983 at pp. 54–55, 105–107.

136. Denton, Derek A. The Pinnacle of Life: Consciousness and Self-Awareness in Humans and Animals. Crow's Nest, Australia: Allen & Unwin, 1993 at pp. 133–135.

137. See, e.g., *Jett v. Municipal Court*, 223 Cal. Rptr. 111 (Cal. Ct. App. 1986) ("While a child preparing for homework or cleaning a bedroom may exhibit turtle-like qualities or creep toward school in turtle pace, we decline to equate title to a tortoise to the relationship between a parent and a child. Jett owns Rocky. Parents have custody of children.")

138. *People v. Berry*, 2 Cal. Rptr. 2d 416 (Cal. Ct. App. 1991) (citations omitted).

139. Bertelsen, Preben. "Free Will, Consciousness and Self: Anthropological Perspectives on Psychology." (2005) at p. 79.

140. Duckler, G. "Animal Wrongs: On Holding Animals to (and Excusing Them from) Legal Responsibility for Their Intentional Acts." *J. Animal L. & Ethics* 2 (2007): 91.

141. *Black's Law Dictionary* 1225 (6th ed. 1990) ("The act of inciting another to do a particular deed. That which arouses, moves, calls forth, causes or occasions. Such conduct or actions on the part of one person towards another as tend to arouse rage, resentment, or fury in the latter against the former, and thereby cause him to do some illegal act against or in relation to the person offering the provocation.")

142. *Eritano v. Commonwealth*, 690 A.2d 705 (Pa. 1997).

143. *Brans v. Extrom*, 701 N.W.2d 163 (Mich. App. 2005).

144. David Favre & Peter Borchelt. *Animal Law and Dog Behavior.* Tucson, AZ: Lawyers & Judges Publishing, 1999 at p. 349.

145. Id. at 349–350.

146. *See Pisciotta v. Parisi*, 547 N.Y.S. 2d 352 (N.Y. App. Div. 1989) (Spatt, J. dissenting) (surveying older cases holding that the provoker must be a person or an individual). *But see Logan County Animal Control Warden v. Danley*, 569 N.E.2d 1226 (Ill. App. Ct. 1991) ("there is a qualitative difference between provocation by a human being and provocation by another animal.")

147. *Palloni v. Smith*, 429 N.W.2d 593 (Mich. 1988).

148. *Nelson v. Lewis*, 344 N.E.2d 268 (Ill. App. Ct. 1976).

149. *Reed v. Bowen*, 503 So. 2d 1265 (Fla. 1986).

150. *Matthews v. Gremillion*, 174 So. 703 (La. Ct. App. 1937).

151. Whorf, Benjamin Lee. *Language, Thought, and Reality: Selected Writings of Benjamin Lee Whorf.* Cambridge, MA: MIT Press, 2012.

152. See *Stroop v. Day*, 896 P.2d 439 (Mont. 1995) (holding that a dog is capable of remembering and being provoked by events from its past).

153. Noam Chomsky, *Language and Mind.* New York: Harcourt, Brace, Jovanovich, 1972 at p. 100.

154. *Murray Ohio Mfg. Co. v. Continental Ins.*, 705 F. Supp. 442 (N.D. Ill. 1989) (quoting lyrics by musician Tom Waits).

155. Malik, *supra* at 219.

156. Id. at 372.

157. See, e.g., Ohio Rev. Code Ann. § 609.020 (2003) (declaring dogs to be personal property).

158. See, e.g., *McClain v. Lewiston Interstate Fair and Racing Ass'n*, 104 P. 1015 (Idaho 1909) (emphasis added):
The dog is generally recognized as an essential part of every well-regulated family, and of a higher degree of intelligence than other domestic animals, and given privileges not generally conceded to other members of the animal family; but we are inclined to the opinion that, notwithstanding this fact, and notwithstanding the fact that the dog occupies a higher position in the social world of the animal family, and an important one in human affairs, still that the owner of such animal should not be excused from liability for injuries done by the dog when invading the rights of person or property. This position that the dog has well earned, by reason of his heroic acts and deeds of valor, might be a reason for exacting from the owner a higher duty as to

responsibility for the dog's acts; but it certainly is not a reason why the owner of such animal should not be equally responsible for the wrongs done by a dog as for wrongs done by other domestic animals, and we believe, both upon reason and authority, that when a dog invades and trespasses upon the legal rights of a person and injures person or property, and such invasion and trespass is the result of the negligence of the owner, the owner is liable for the damages done.

159. Michael P. T. Leahy, *Against Liberation.* London: Routledge, 1993 at p. 25 .

160. Stangroom, Jeremy. *What Scientists Think.* London: Routledge, 2005 at p. 33.

161. Reichmann, James B. *Evolution, Animal 'Rights' & the Environment.* Washington, DC: CUA Press, 2000 at pp. 71, 92, 101-1-2, 255, 261.

162. Ajmone-Marsan, Paolo, Jose Fernando Garcia, and Johannes A. Lenstra. "On the Origin of Cattle: How Aurochs Became Cattle and Colonized the World." *Evolutionary Anthropology: Issues, News, and Reviews* 19, no. 4 (2010): 148–157.

Chapter 8

The Case against Animal Rights

"Some Listened Perhaps but Never Talked at All"[1]

An individual comes to be a person. Personhood is that which distinguishes humans from animals. Many animals are individuals in the sense that they have distinct characters. One cat may be playful, another suspicious of human contact. One dog may be aggressive, another passive. But humans are individuals in a different sense: we are self-created beings who realize ourselves through our relations with other such beings. Humans are persons, not simply conduits for natural impulses. It is the capacity for all this that makes humans subjects and not simply objects, as animals are.[2]

Animal rights advocacy imposes hefty intellectual demands on its proponents, far beyond the cursory skills needed to proclaim an end to animal abuse, assert an allegiance to easing animal suffering, weigh in with personal anecdote, or call for increasing fines and jail terms for those accused of cruelty. Justifying how animals would be granted formal legal rights demands addressing the two pillars on which such a claim lives or dies, the precepts of law and of science.

While many authors have worked hard to make such an address and have grappled well with the mechanics of legal rules and the power of scientific knowledge,[3] core defects still abound. As lawyer paleontologists, we can approach those defects by stepping again into the past.[4]

THE PREHISTORICAL AND HISTORICAL
ESTABLISHMENT OF LAW FROM LANGUAGE

To the Roman jurist Gaius is attributed the phrase *hominum causa omne ius constitutum* ("all law was established for man's sake").[5] Today, 1,500 years later, Gaius' statement holds firm: humans alone possess legal rights, while animals—"nonhumans"—are precluded from legal rights of any type, whether of life, liberty, happiness, or otherwise. Ancient pronouncements are often eroded over time, but Gaius' proclamation has remained stable—proffering a succinct phrase that readily encapsulates a key distinction between people and animals and on a core inquiry: to whom does law belong?

The answer to that question requires an awareness of the qualitative effect of time. Prehistory can and does illuminate and inform history, and in order to appreciate Gaius' statement, an appreciation is needed of the passage of time in two respects.

The first is the passage of large-scale prehistoric time, specifically the several million years of hominid evolution preceding Gaius' statement that it took for the beatifically rich and intricate process of genetic transmission of adaptations, fueled by a constantly changing natural environment, to select for humans to be fundamentally distinct from all other animals by reaping the adaptive benefits of "social exchanges."[6] It is a process that engineered all of Gaius' ancient and immediate ancestors (and Gaius himself as well as his readers) with the astonishing ability to express what one is perceiving and evaluating in the form of "speech."[7] The not-to-be overlooked fact that Gaius wrote and spoke at all is a central factor in support of law being "established" for anyone's sake; law has become established through the evolved mechanisms of writing, reading, and speaking, i.e., human language, the core phenomenon that bases all law as a fundamental and founding principle.[8]

It is scientific studies that have primarily supported that idea, particularly in the fields of physical and cultural anthropology: from Charles Darwin to Richard Dawkins, evolutionary biology researchers interested in the inputs and outputs of human evolution have enriched our understanding that nondirectional evolutionary forces, coming to a critical point by the close of the Pleistocene, constructed humans not as anything better or worse than any other animal, but simply as something vastly different than all other animals.[9] It is from anthropological research in particular that we have come to recognize that speech and writing have played massive roles in accomplishing that change prehistorically:

> However much we tend to be obsessed by them, our cognitive capacities, epitomized by our linguistic abilities, do indeed mark us off distinctly from all of the millions of other creatures on the planet. . . . Well over three billion years after life established itself on earth, we, alone among the millions of descendants of our ancient common ancestor, somehow acquired not just a large brain—the Neanderthals had that—but a fully developed mind. This mind is a complex thing, not in the sense that an engineered machine is, with many separate parts working smoothly together in pursuit of a single goal, but in the sense that it is

a product of ancient reflexive and emotional components, overlain by a veneer of reason. The human mind is thus not an entirely rational entity, but rather one that is still conditioned by the lone evolutionary history of the brain from which it emerges.[10]

The second is the passage of (relatively smaller-scale) *historic* time, specifically the 1500 years or so of complicated social rules development that has accumulated subsequent to when Gaius made his famous statement.[11] This additional time span primarily comprises the comparatively rich and intricate sociological process of our development of informal rules, then morality emanating from those rules, and finally the common law and decisional law.[12] That process currently enables us moderns to now appreciate the social significance of the particular words that Gaius ultimately selected to utter and the mindset with which he crafted the words that were selected.

It is historical studies that have primarily developed that idea, particularly in the fields of jurisprudence and cognitive psychology. From Thucydides to Thomas Carlyle to Daniel Dennett, legal historians and linguistic psychologists have enriched our understanding that sociological forces accumulated over historic time have constructed humans—not as any more communicative or more organized than other species—but as something intricately social and expressive at several orders of magnitude above such social or expressive groups as bees, termites, seagulls, beavers, or chimps.[13] Our historical, i.e., recorded, past, has enmeshed us as a species in a communication and idea-driven sociality web that expresses itself most formally and most thoroughly through the rule and operation of law.[14] Law and writing, law and speaking, law and the difficult, painful, cumbersome, messy, time-consuming practices of transferring thoughts into words into conversations onto pages into volumes through translations across communities across generations across social boundaries through discussions among competing voices onto meetings within political processes and into a public forum—i.e., the talking about, writing out, and reading of our social agreements with each other—those phenomenal effects of expression is where our history has led us:

[T]he individuated mode of life demands for the first time that the individual must be capable of self-knowledge: capable of forming, that is, a phenomenological model of the self—a self-model or self-consciousness—in order to be able to navigate among the complex choices offered by an urbanized mode of life and to choose the 'correct' path that accords with the overall system of belief. Such discourses, representing an ongoing project for human development at both the individual and the social level, can be seen to have emerged gradually during the individuated epoch. In the first instance these discourses took the form of myths and religious systems. As time went on, the development of the written word, in particular, meant they could be formulated and disseminated far more efficiently, over much greater distances, and to a far greater number of people than hitherto. Today, as much as ever, the written text represents a medium in which one may give material and lasting expression to one's thoughts, feelings, reflections and so on, creating an object 'outside' oneself that offers a basis for more sustained reflections. Unlike mere passing thoughts, the thought captured in writing remains before us. At the private level we know this from the act of writing a diary: by literally seeing the thoughts one has recorded, one endeavors to arrive at a greater understanding of oneself.[15]

The yawning void of any possible "history" for animals is critical. Certainly their bodies leave an enormous library of traces of their physical existence: the entire science of paleontology alone richly details the internment, fossilization, disinterment, exhumation, and reconstruction of physical forms of animal (and all organic) life in all of its bewildering manifestations. But their past mental lives, if any such existed, are an absolute cipher. Because they are inarticulate, because they do not memorialize or transcribe, because they can't leave documents or records of any type that track observations about their place in their own past and possible future, then there can be no proper history of them, and thus there can be no possible mechanism by which they can have developed an awareness of anything greater than their own individual and transitory experiences:

> [With humans] spoken texts continue to be more central than written ones in political as well as popular culture. However, the historian of animals has no such argument available to her: a dog can bark, and that bark can be recorded, documented, but it cannot be understood. The only documents available to the historian in any field are documents written, or spoken, by humans. Another problem for the history of animals emerges in the ways in which we organize the past in our histories. This is a problem which exacerbates one that is recognized in other fields of history. In 1977, Joan Kelly famously asked the question "Did Women Have a Renaissance?" She answered it by arguing that the term being used to epitomize a historical period actually represented what happened to only a tiny minority of literate men; that it immediately evacuated from the interest of the historian those who were not involved in the intellectual debates—women, the poor, the illiterate. Likewise, in histories of the non-European, a similar question of periodization emerges. . . . Animals, as far as we know (and this is the only perspective available to us) have no sense of periodization. So, given the question "did dogs have a Renaissance?" the answer is clearly no; dogs did not partake of the intellectual debates which define the period, nor did they have the concept of historical periodization so central to our understanding of the past.[16]

Multiple lessons abound then from both human history and human prehistory, and a suite of scientific studies can more than adequately explain why we should not treat animals like humans, or apply legal rules to them as if they were no different than humans. It may well be true that we can always do better to continue to tweak and restructure some of the more antiquated rules that we have used in the past about protecting animals from harm, that we can always legislate and litigate further to accommodate and to reflect more enlightened schema by which we value or convey animals as properties, especially in the roles they play as domestic counterparts or educational tools.[17] Nevertheless, with no history attending them and with no means of expression by which to connect physical events that occur to them with psychological events that occur as a result, then the most valuable and legitimate interactions we can have with animals are those founded at heart on clear scientific principles of their objectification, interactions and understandings that employ scientific reasoning and that take into account lessons from biology, anatomy, anthropology, and paleontology as to just what animals are to us as intricate and animate objects forming part and parcel of our adaptive environment.[18]

DIFFICULTIES ANIMAL RIGHTS PROPOSALS ENCOUNTER AS TO BOTH SCIENCE AND LAW

Those passages of time reveal Gaius' remark as an insight to be appreciated rather than as an insufficiency to be remedied. If we appreciate the gritty mechanics of how organisms evolve and operate, we can acknowledge that humans and animals have separated out of a mutual past and traced distinctly independent trajectories into the present. While in general a bid to erect animal entitlements is thus inconsistent with prehistory and history, with scientific knowledge both ancient and modern, a proposal for animal rights is more particularly beset by two distinct basic problems.

The first is a failure to be scientific in the standard and valuable sense of "systematically analyzing the true manner in which the natural world works" and then "applying rules about the occurrence of natural phenomena in explaining certain events and mechanisms."[19] Certainly, for engaging in a topic that demands a clear understanding of a large and complicated component of the natural world, the animal rights movement has not always adhered to the rigors of the scientific method or to the constraints of scientific analysis about what animals are in general. Anthropomorphism is often substituted in place of taxonomy, such that the parameters within which animals are addressed are inaccurate given what we actually know about animals from scientific studies.[20]

When a dog defecates on the oriental rug and greets us at the door cringing, we without hesitating say he is feeling guilty over what he has done. When a horse nuzzles us, we say he likes (or even loves) us. If we are particularly competitive, we say our dog or our horse loves to win blue ribbons at shows. If we are particularly given to New Age mystification, we can suggest the following explanations for why a mother lion ate her dead cub after it was killed by a male from another pride: "Maybe she felt closer to her dead offspring when it was part of her body once again. Maybe she hates waste, or cleans up all messes her cubs make, as part of her love. Maybe this is a lion funeral rite." Or maybe she was hungry. Anthropomorphism, the tendency to view an animal's actions in terms of our own conscious intentions, thoughts, and motives, is viewed by many as an act of generosity toward the species we aim it at, and humility on our part. The ultimate compliment: You're almost human! But a more honest evaluation may be that anthropomorphism betrays an utter lack of imagination on our part-not to mention a slavish obedience to an instinct that may well have been pounded into our genes over the course of millions of years of evolution.[21]

Disinterest in using taxonomic classifications of *Animalia* leads to a skewed focus on mammals alone (and a small percentage of mammals at that). Disinterest in attending to the basic anatomical and physiological composition of animals leads to a skewed focus on the real relations between animal function and form and on how organismal organization tracks phyletic organization. The result is an employment of careless designations of animals, as "relatives," "bloodlines," "cousins," "sharing a common heritage," "family members," and "kin"[22]—ironically, a few terms of which, in a different historical context, derive from misconceptions about ancestor-descendant links used by overt racists to justify acts of racial and gender segregation and discrimination.[23]

The consequences of such disregard are stark. The sciences of anatomy, taxonomy, organismal evolution, and cladistics are fluid and rich fields of inquiry, and—regulated by the intellectual rigor of actual field and laboratory research and peer-reviewed publication—reflect whatever the current state of knowledge is about complex phylogenies, about genetic and developmental links, and about the specific exchange and passage of physical and physiological traits between and among interbreeding animal individuals over time.[24] Where rhetoric about animals becomes detached from laboratory, fieldwork, and museum research and studies, the apertures through which our mixture is sieved become so large as to make filtration meaningless—no valuable filtrate is obtained since everything pours right through, subjective and objective experiences alike.

The lack of adherence to science has two polar aspects. One aspect comprises a refusal to address all of *Animalia*, to be principled in accounting for *every animal*—an unwillingness, in other words, to lump the earthworm in with the elephant in talk about how all animals deserve rights. The other aspect comprises a counterpart failure to account for the fundamental distinction between humans and all other animals—a different unwillingness, this one to remove from the group the one species, Homo sapiens, that is evolutionarily different.

A DECISION PROCEDURE FOR APPLYING RIGHTS ACROSS ANIMALIA

In the first aspect, some animal rights advocates will almost arbitrarily pick and choose among animal taxa to separate, subjectively, those they feel deserving of rights, from those that are too unfamiliar, too unattractive, or just too poorly held in esteem to merit the application. Peter Singer, for instance, identified those most worthy as "nonhuman animals that appear to be rational and self-conscious beings, conceiving themselves as distinct beings with a past and future."[25] A core challenge would be to identify how any such entities exist at all, given the nonexistence of tests for self-consciousness, but to the extent that such could exist the end result is still that the winners of this unusual lottery turn out to be mid-to-large-size mammals, either the larger primates or the more familiar of the cetaceans.[26]

It is often said that we are members of a "global community" which includes, in addition to ourselves, all other living creatures from chimpanzees to blue-green algae, and it is said that we have duties to the other members of this community just as each of us has duties to other members of the human community. However, "community"—in the only sense in which it can possibly have any moral significance—requires at least the potential for shared beliefs and values. The universe of living creatures simply does not amount to a community in any morally relevant sense. The "global community" usually turns out to be a metaphor for the fact that all life is part of a complex ecological web. We are dependent on many other species; and almost every other species (perhaps absolutely every other species) is dependent on us in the sense that we could destroy it if we tried. What follows from these facts? Nothing of interest. Our power to affect other species may be a necessary condition of our having duties regarding them; but the mere fact of our having this power does not tell us what duties we have, if any, in the use of it. Similarly, our dependence on other species means that if we do too much damage to other living things we are likely to end up hurting ourselves as well; but any argument from this premise will make our duties regarding nature instrumental, which is just what the argument from global community was meant to avoid.[27]

Other animal rights advocates don't engage the term "animal" so much as they adjust the term "person" in contrast, shoehorning the more aesthetically appealing members of the apes and marine mammals at focus into a conveniently accommodating "personhood" term, manipulated rhetorically so as to nearly eviscerate the word's root "person" of any real semantic meaning.[28] For them, possessors of rationality and self-consciousness (or at least of their sporadic appearance) are rewarded with legal rights because humans are rational and self-conscious—the pedestrian part of the idea being that anything pretty much like us should also get rights pretty much like ours.

This is neither law nor science in any sense, but an appeal to anthropomorphic sentiments, and substituting that unhappy prejudice in place of real applications of anatomy, taxonomy, or biology to animal actions and relationships is impoverishing.[29] The overall result is that earthworms are snubbed and apes are celebrated. Yet, other than the subjective appeal that complicated central nervous systems and their emergent sensory epiphenomenon seem to have to some, an answer is still needed as to what is either the logical or scientific reason that all those poor earthworms—dumb, nearly senseless, and irrational though they may be, yet animals as they most certainly are—remain left out in the legal cold?

The "earthworm omission problem" necessarily forms part of the landscape on which the animal rights argument rests, and the exclusion of animals with simple nervous systems from rights-type arguments has the effect of eroding the terrain precariously downward into absurdity as one approaches refusals to address all members of the animal kingdom, to account for every animal.[30] Only the smallest semantic shift may cause the argument to career in a dangerous direction, such as with pleas for universal inclusion:

> In order to make a case for "animal rights," some philosophers, lawyers, ethologists, and others are eager to demonstrate that other non-human species have some degree of humanlike self-awareness. Such an approach in the final analysis is human-centric and "species-bound" since it assumes that only humanlike (or supra-human) beings are worthy of being accorded rights. Surely all living creatures of creation, by virtue of their existence and being an integral part of the interdependent whole which constitutes the biosphere, have the basic right to exist, live, reproduce and fully actualize their natural potentials (within the natural constraints of ecological harmony rather than under the constraining forces of human dominion).[31]

One, the cautionary tales of *LeBlanc* and *Shanklin* should hopefully raise a high alert here as to where forays into that territory lead. Two, if rights are to be accorded to "all living creatures of creation, by virtue of their existence and being . . . part of the biosphere" then the scientific word "animal" is instantly drained of its academic and linguistic meaning, and merely becomes a convenient, but content-empty, term on which to drape the implementation of a moral, not a legal or scientific, policy. Three, as moral positions go, that position presents what must surely be the most irrational and unworkable moral policy ever conceived. "All living creatures," its religious phraseology aside, delineates a massive group to which a billion squared members belong,[32] with barely a single valuable distinction to divulge between this blue whale over here or that dust mite over there—and it presents a practical application problem that would make the determination of war crime reparations seem like county fair pie-judging in comparison. At its core, proposing the ill-fitting insertions of the square pegs of animal behaviors into the round holes of human forms is an ill-advised activity pointing valuable routes of inquiry in the entirely wrong direction:

> As the linguist Noam Chomsky said recently in exasperation over experiments attempting to teach humanlike language to apes, "If you want to find out about an organism you study what its good at. If you want to study humans you study language. If you want to study pigeons you study their homing instinct. Every biologist knows this." Sara Shettleworth, a psychologist at the University of Toronto, contrasts the "anthropocentric program" of cognitive research with an "ecological program." She notes that anthropocentric questions such as, "Can any nonhuman species count?" lead to search for *demonstrations*, not *understanding*. It leads us to ignore the most "cognitively rich" behaviors of animals in favor of ones chosen purely because they resemble *our* abilities. And it leads us to totally neglect "consideration of what cognitive processes animals might be expected to have evolved for dealing with their natural environments." Certain birds, for example, such as Clark's nutcrackers, are very good at remembering where they have cached food. If we really want to understand animal cognition, and to place that in its true ecological and evolutionary context, Shettleworth says, study how nutcrackers accomplish this-not whether they can count the way humans do.[33]

A DECISION PROCEDURE FOR DISTINGUISHING RIGHTS BETWEEN PEOPLE AND OTHERS

Additionally, animal rights advocacy is hard-pressed to acknowledge that distinctions affecting what "rights" are exist between humans and all other animals, distinctions that ground the significance of a legal right as something that can apply only to humans. While animals can certainly accomplish extraordinary tasks without recourse to the conscious thought that arises from language, the manner of thought that produces language appears only in us.[34]

Many advocates abhor the concession that language forms a critical dividing line between rights-holders and non-rights-holders. They do not like it that rights are embodied in some form of linguistic expression. They do not like it that to have a right means to be responsible for one's actions. They do not like it that an entity incapable of accepting responsibility, as with a child, can be accorded only protections, not rights.[35] They do not like it that the difference between a right and a protection is significant in that the former requires an entity to make its own decisions, while the latter requires holders to make decisions for another. That dislike compels animal rights advocates to try to substantiate independent decision-making among animals—but accomplishing such a task turns out to be an obstacle of immense proportions.

Many animal rights advocates especially do not like it that humans make the decisions on which law is founded because we can distinguish between right and wrong in a moral sense, and that we can do that solely because language enables us to do so.[36] The base ability to "communicate"—an activity that even unremarkable non-rights holders such as car alarms and toaster ovens regularly engage in—is far, far below the rich and complex activity of true human language.[37] To get past this conceptual speed bump, rights advocates also maneuver the terms "language" and "communication" about but ultimately cannot surmount the extensive observational-based scientific evidence about the massive evolutionary difference between the two terms.[38]

It remains nonetheless and undeniably true that the requisite manner of thought required for language to be assigned to animals as an integral characteristic is simply absent in animals. That absence, in turn, draws a critical dividing line that cannot logically or empirically be denied:

> All non-human animals are constrained by the tools that nature has bequeathed them through natural selection. They are incapable of striving towards truth; they simply absorb information and behave in ways useful for their survival. Both their knowledge of the world, and their behavior towards it, has been largely preselected by evolution. Language, in other words, helps turn humans into conscious agents: individuals with distinct personalities and abilities who only 'realise' themselves through their interactions with each other, and with the social and natural world. Humans are individual personalities, but they are equally social beings. Animals are neither truly individual, nor truly social. They are not truly individual because, while they may have distinct personalities, they lack the capacity to take individual responsibility. They are not truly social because while they may live within groups, those groups cannot take collective decisions (whether conscious or unconscious) to transform themselves.[39]

Symbolic thought—as a biologically oriented process that has evolved and expanded in us alone—takes us out of our past as simply another genus of midsize Neolithic primate, and has pushed us into a new life as uniquely

social, rationalizing organisms.[40] We have moved from wilderness to metrop-
olis in a breathlessly short span of geologic time, and it is the evolution of
language itself, not simply the development of intricate modes of communicating in and out of language, that has enabled us to make that journey.[41]

PRINCIPLED AND UNPRINCIPLED
EVALUATIONS OF ANIMAL BEHAVIORS

In assessing where "language" truly fits within *Animalia*, discipline in making objective observations about the conduct of animals in nature and in
captivity should really rank far above a pandering to the personal account
or compassion-filled story. Compare the following two passages, the first a
snippet of impersonal scientific restraint, the second—an imaginary conver-
sational exchange projected by the author onto his dog—a classic of intensely
personal speculation:

> It is not always easy to decide what counts as communication in animals. As
> one researcher notes, "Students of animal behavior have often noted the extreme
> difficulty of restricting the notion of communication to anything less than every
> potential interaction between an organism and its environment." So that, at the
> very least, sticklebacks mating, cats spitting, and rabbits thumping their back
> legs must be taken into consideration—and it isn't at all clear where to stop. . . .
> There is no way yet in which we can be sure about making the right decision
> when it comes to interpreting such phenomenon.[42]

> I love dogs; it has always been clear to me that they lead extremely intense emo-
> tional lives. "No, Misha, no walk just now." What? The ears would cock. Can
> I have heard right? "Sorry, Misha, but no." Unmistakable. The ears flop. Misha
> would throw himself onto the floor. There was no mistaking the pure disappoint-
> ment he was feeling. Just as unmistakable was his intense joy when I would say,
> "Okay, get your leash, we're going for a walk," and the sheer pleasure Misha felt
> on his walks, his delight at racing ahead, chasing leaves, doubling back, tearing
> off into the forest and returning behind and ahead of me.[43]

The first account simply posits a healthy caution about research goals on,
and legitimate knowledge of, the communicative content of an animal's
conduct. The second passage invites engagement in a wish-fulfillment fantasy yet infers that the description somehow has empirical value. In their
conjunction, the two passages carve out a forceful reminder that behavioral
and ecological interactions between and among animals can be massively
sophisticated affairs; disentangling their myriad influences has occupied both
fiction authors and field scientists for the better part of three centuries with

no end in sight.[44] In their contrast, the two passages reflect the unhappy fact that solid explanations for most animal behaviors simply stump the observer. Consternation, nevertheless, is no justification for preferring conjecture over conservatism.[45]

When they do address research, advocates are adept at raising moral concerns about the treatment of certain animals—by scientists dealing with chimpanzees in captivity, for instance, or through impacts on biodiversity by industrial processes, at modern farming technologies creating inroads in "natural" environments, or at the subjugation or reintroduction of captive wildlife by field biologists.[46] Yet they proceed no further than the moral concerns; they often decline to take the hard step of "doing science" themselves, or to look further than nature essays and public opinion polls on the larger epistemological significance of how animals and people are eventually affected by various forms of treatment.[47]

Ultimately, the idea that granting rights affords a remedy for poor treatment demands an appreciation of what right-holding really entails. When the suffrage movement led to a recognition that women were abysmally treated in the political process by being denied the right to vote, the "granting" of voting rights to them was attended by obligations tagging along with the benefit: obligations to register, abide by regulations, accept contest outcomes, and pay the price of marshalling power or violating voting rules no differently than all other voters.[48] As with appreciating what the behavior of "voting" signifies, comprehension and communication are absolutely mandatory to a participant valuing both the attendant entitlements and the attendant duties.[49] Granting rights to animals doesn't afford a remedy for their poor treatment since they have no concept of either associated benefits or burdens and have no option to be participatory in valuing the status of right-holding.

The fundamental legal rights that we have granted to ourselves are considered such "not simply because they implicate deeply personal and private considerations, but because they have been identified as 'deeply rooted in this Nation's history and tradition and implicit in the concept of ordered liberty, such that neither liberty nor justice would exist if they were sacrificed.'" [50] Fundamental legal rights are, therefore, at one and the same time both historically derived intellectual concepts as well as prehistorically derived cognitive artifacts.[51]

> In dealing with our hunting evolution, we have documented at length what these needs are: needs for space to move about in; for a share of the communal kill; for participation in the predatory activity of the whole group; for a chance to rise in status through merit; for an opportunity to take risks; for the means to make deals and alliances; for exploration and novelty when young; for a sense of security derived from close association with the mother; for education geared

to the realities of the life cycle; for accurate knowledge of the environment; for a chance to be brave and prove oneself; for a place at the triumph feast; for an acknowledgement of individual worth; for children and the caring for them and the protection and security that accompany this; for recreation and free use of the imagination; for support in times of stress; and above all the intense need to contribute with dignity to the community of which one is part. These and more are the basic behavioral needs of the creature. They should not be things it has to claim and justify, any more than it has to claim and justify its right to breathe, or the chicken has to justify its right to peck, the hawk to swoop. We do not ask whether the cock has a right to crow; we accept that crowing is what the cock does. To prevent it from crowing is to take away something that is intrinsic to being a cock. The same is true, for example, of the so-called "right to work" in human societies, or the "right to vote." It is heartless to claim that these are abstract symbolic things that must be justified on the basis of divine intent or rational political theory; they are statements about what it is to be a human being: that a human being is the kind of animal that, of its very nature, contributes its labor to the group and participates in the conduct of the group's affairs. The "right" to a minimum wage, for example, or to adequate and inexpensive medical care, or to an education, or to a free and creative use of the intellect, is simply a "right" to behave in a way that is intrinsic to being human; it needs no more justification than the crowing of the cock.[52]

Even ignoring rights of personal privacy and personal autonomy (areas that seem like they should be fundamental but aren't), a basic right to liberty that we have preserved for ourselves is only denominated a "right" as a result of actions we have taken all throughout our past in slowly establishing a value to liberty that was not initially apparent to us, but that only became apparent over time and on account of discrete historical events. Lacking that history, lacking that tradition, lacking that dawning realization and development of perceived value based on significant social incidents of importance to large groups of people, animals cannot have developed legal rights in the way we have.[53]

[A] person who torments a cat to death the way a cat might torment a mouse deserves our moral condemnation—not because cats have rights, but because people have responsibilities. Likewise, we insist it is wrong for people to burn books, deface a masterpiece, or desecrate a church—not because these things have rights, but because people have responsibilities. Rights are a serious business. They are the linchpin of a free society. Without them, people would not be able to go about their business free from arbitrary interference by government. Rights offer a people freedom to convince others of different points of view without having to resort to violence and the resulting breakdown of civilization. The animal rights movement would allow people no more rights than rats or cockroaches. The real agenda of this movement is not to give rights to animals, but to take rights from people—to dictate our food, clothing, recreation, and whether we will discover new medications or die. Animal rights pose an extraordinary threat to our health, freedom, and even our lives.[54]

A call to "respect the rights of individual animals in the same way as we respect the rights of humans" has nevertheless rung through the voices of animal rights advocates ever since Singer put those words down nearly 50 years ago.[55] Singer and adherents to his philosophy have consistently discounted the law's acknowledgment that rights concern matters that are basic to our conception of justice and that define the community sense of fair play.[56] It seems to matter little to animal rights advocates that animals do not have a concept of "justice" or of "fair play" at all, much less a communal one. The requisite "collective conscience" is—troubling enough—missing.[57] In omitting the need to first show a sense of justice, fair play, or social conscience, the corollary that to have a right means also to be responsible for one's actions is sorely discounted.

DISTINCTIONS PRODUCED BY LANGUAGE SEPARATE PEOPLE FROM ANIMALS

Yet it is for that very reason that an entity incapable of accepting responsibility, as with a child for instance, can be accorded "protections," but never rights. A right requires the entity to make its own conscientious decisions, while common law and statutory *protections* require rights-holders to make conscientious decisions for others. Once again, the effect of language is unquestionably key: rights-holders make conscientious decisions because they can distinguish between right and wrong in a moral sense, and they can do that because language allows formulation of how individual conduct affects groups with whom the individual interacts. The generic ability to simply "communicate" to the contrary, does not rise to the requisite level. That difference—between language specifically and communication generally—is immense:

> It has in fact been established that animals are able to communicate with one another and that much of their behavior depends on signals sometimes consisting of movements, sometimes of sounds, and sometimes of smells, and it is often difficult to know what aspect of an animal's total behavior constitutes a signal and what part of it is just coincidental. In the case of horses, however, there are already several well-known signs and signals. A snort signifies a warning of danger to the whole herd. A whinny stands for pleasure. Ears back mean "look out," and if the tail is lashed as well it means that a kick will probably follow. As well as these, there are probably innumerable other signs recognized

by horses but unknown to us. One single snort may mean something quite different from a double one. A foot lifted in one way may mean something quite different from a foot lifted in another. It needs a great deal of careful observation to find out the true basis of different animal languages, but that the time and energy spent on this is often well rewarded has been shown in several instances recently. Von Frisch's discovery of the language of the honey bee and Lorenz's discovery of duck language are among the most interesting examples and have helped greatly in our understanding of animal behavior. . . . The signals identified by these observers, however, and those mentioned above in the case of horses, are all of a more or less automatic character. That is to say that they are made by the giver spontaneously in response to particular situations and evoke spontaneous, unlearned (and even uncontrollable) responses from those that receive them. They are similar to laughter and tears in us. They do not have to be learned and their appreciation does not depend on past experience.[58]

Animals use a universe of communication modes and forms, many in a fashion that clearly seek influence over the behaviors of others in their environment. None, however, seek influence over the internal processes, thoughts, knowledge, or intentions of others. We have evolved to be able to grasp that members of our species have minds that work analogously, and that the thoughts, knowledge, and intentions of others can be altered by words combined with actions.[59]

Many animal rights advocates also mistakenly believe that rights are disconnected from duties—but only for animals other than people. Somehow, people are required to fulfill duties to respect the rights of animals to life, to freedom, from human-induced pain, and from confinement, but animals are apparently not required at all to have similar duties reciprocally imposed. That proposed inequity misconstrues the methodology of "rights." If rights are to be accorded to "all living creatures of creation, by virtue of their existence and being . . . part of the biosphere" then not just animals, but "rights" as well become illusory objects. Rights become as amorphous and ethereal as "creatures," objects apparently determined to exist by the sheer force of the beholder's will to want them to exist, ghostly forms roving in shapeless herds free of definitional chains.

Animal rights advocates' beliefs about the necessity of granting rights tend to spring from two core axioms: That freedom confers greater happiness and less suffering on animals than does encroachment, and that animal "happiness" outweighs any interests that people might have in curtailing that happiness. The idea that animal happiness is a function of "freedom," a distinctly human-oriented concept, is itself a nonsequitur. "Animals would be happier if they were freer" is logically equivalent to "Animals would be better artists if they had opposable thumbs." Opposable thumbs being a hallmark of human anatomy, and artistic appreciation being a hallmark of human culture, the only animals then that have opposable thumbs and an appreciation for art happen—not by chance, but by definition—to be humans. The same goes with concepts such as freedom; the only animals that could appreciate what "freedom" actually is, are those that "happen" to have the ability to conceive of the concept of freedom in the first place.

> Rights and duties, then, are corollaries of freedom, and all those who are the subjects of rights are persons, for a person is "whatever subsists in an intellectual or rational nature" [citation omitted]. It is because the nonhuman animal does not have an intellective orrational nature that it is not a person and cannot, therefore, be considered the subject of rights. To apply the term "person" to the nonhuman animal, as Singer and others do, on the basis of its being conscious, is to play word games, since it undermines the true, authentic meaning of personhood and of consciousness. If a living thing is a person simply because it possesses sensory consciousness, then there is little point in referring either to animals or to humans as "persons" in the first place, since "person" would add absolutely nothing not already contained in the term "animal."[60]

Romanticizing wildlife as well as life in the wild is as damaging as is definitional wordplay. It is an inescapable fact that animals in the wild are not free at all but are the "prisoners of space and time" lamented by Hancock.[61] Evolution by natural selection has permeated "the wild" with, and shaped it by, abusive, cruel, and unblinkingly predatory and destructive activities. More often than not the construction of a cage will alleviate, not exacerbate, that harshness. Even when an artificial enclosure such as a home, a zoo, a laboratory, or a kennel, simply replaces those impacts with ones with different names, whatever the enclosure, it is certain that the act of opening its door and allowing the animal "to go free" does not send the animal into any more free or favorable environment in any respect worth describing. As we have seen in the chapter on zoos, captivity has its inescapable origins, its undeniable benefits, and its likely trajectory to contend with.

A few in the animal rights movement would yet rather bowdlerize evolution by natural selection or nature (often unrealistically defined as animal life outside of human influences) through what the science writer Matt Ridley has called "condescending sentimentalism" by "desperately play[ing] up the slimmest of clues to animal virtue . . . and clutch[ing] at straws suggesting that humankind somehow caused aberrant cruelty."[62] They discount the reduction of natural horrors that captivity, farming, and ranching has effected on animals, preferring to trumpet the benefits that freedom has brought to humans and then apply the unsupported syllogism that those benefits are readily translatable to animals. In doing so, they mistake where our freedom comes from and what life is like for an animal who is "truly free," and in doing so they risk exposing animals to higher levels of pain and suffering than currently experienced in captivity, on farms, on ranches, and in our homes.[63]

All animals are at one and the same time both liberated and constrained by the traits bestowed on them by evolution by natural selection, as well as by the biotic and abiotic environments of which they necessarily form an integral part. Where such observations are counterproductive to attaining certain political goals, animal rights advocates will substitute illusory traits and illusory environments instead. Here is a passage illustrative of this approach:

> Those of us at the heart of the animal law movement envision a world in which the lives and interests of all sentient beings are respected within the legal system, where companion animals have good, loving homes for a lifetime, where wild animals can live out their natural lives according to their instincts in an environment that supports their needs—a world in which animals are not exploited, terrorized, tortured or controlled to serve frivolous or greedy human purposes. This vision guides in working toward a far more just and truly humane society.[64]

A workable definition of "sentience" notwithstanding, one would have to be unfamiliar with the last 150 years of accumulated scientific study of how evolution by natural selection works in the natural world to sincerely make such a plea. Not only is "a world in which animals are not exploited, terrorized, tortured or controlled to serve frivolous or greedy human purposes" an unobtainable, inherently biologically impossible world, but the world of nature to which the author fervently hopes to somehow return animals to already *is itself* a world in which animals are "exploited, terrorized, tortured or controlled"—but there it is to serve the frivolous or greedy purposes of all the other animals, not just predators and competitors but an animal's own conspecifics and descendants as well.

A serious ethical dilemma is created by the double standard that advocates apply to prohibitions against animal mistreatment under the rubric that "allows" animals to be cruel to each other but prohibits humans from being cruel to animals. If animals are rights-holders, then animal cruelty laws should apply to them—yet when animal rights advocates are confronted with the possibility of truly adjudicating competing rights among all rights-holders as a intrinsically defined group, they falter: they know in their hearts that the lion is not planning on laying down with the lamb any time soon, yet neither can they imagine having to hold the lion legally accountable for what lions naturally do to lambs (and to other lions), acts invariably involving intentional violations of every animal cruelty law imaginable and then some. That choices must be made reveals the unity of rights and responsibilities and in the scenario where the lion attacks the human infant and one must choose whom is to be protected, a denial of that unity creates an irrational impasse.[65]

[P]roponents of animal rights want to influence what people do rather than judge or alter the behavior of other animals. They want people to stop eating animals, to stop experimenting with animals, to stop using animal skins for clothing. They do not claim that humans have a duty to train carnivores to stop eating other animals in order to protect herbivores from their "natural" predators. We demand consistency in our moral reasoning and it is appropriate to challenge individuals if they embrace distinct and incompatible ethical perspectives, one creating duties toward animals and another creating duties to our fellow human beings. Whatever basic principles we embrace must be applied to both the human and nonhuman domains . . . [R]ather than occupying the moral "high ground," animal rights advocacy may reflect a lack of moral insight and a failure in public moral discourse.[66]

INSERTING MORALITY INTO THE RIGHTS EQUATION

So the demand goes thus: a dog is to have a right and a human is to respect it, but the dog is itself to have no obligation back to anyone, either to humans or to other dogs (or to other animals). Yet any "non-reciprocity of rights" would unfairly exempt the new rights-holder from having to even respect the new right simply among themselves as a defined rights-holding group.[67] Where, within an intellectually principled dialogue on how rights work, may it be justified that a human biting a dog is a clear rights violation while a dog biting a human or a dog biting another dog is neither sanctioned nor addressed at all?

If the answer is simply because "dogs are different than people," than good conscience demands that valuable observation not be eroded with semantics and skewered by exception. If the answer is that a dog is to have a right because it is moral for humans to recognize it, but the dog need not itself be bound by any morality in exercising the right, then that "non-reciprocity of moral obligations" is fundamentally inconsistent with how morality works— it drains meaning entirely from morality to impose a moral code on all yet to enforce violations about it against only some. Only humans act morally; no other animal in the world has ever concerned itself with "moral" conduct. Examining human behavior through a moral lens is an important and con- scientious task for society to engage in; examining animal behavior through a moral lens almost instantaneously becomes Bernard's epistemological "recipe for disaster."

Not only could one not envision an individual dog, cat, horse, or bird making a morality-based decision, one could not envision such behavior across any taxon either. The prokaryotes[68] that compose all of *Animalia* have engaged in the most outrageously "immoral" acts that have ever been exhibited on the planet: throughout earth history, prokaryotes have created immense global crises of starvation, pollution, and extinction that make recent human activities puny and laughable in comparison. Prokaryotes destroy and have destroyed other organisms by the great multitude, transfer and have transferred mountains of genetic material freely from individual to individual, alter and have altered every gene complex conceivable in order to create chimeras at a level that the most ill-advised bioengineers could only dream about, and hijack and weaponize, and have fundamentally hijacked and weaponized, nearly every usable resource of the biotic and abiotic world in doing so.[69] If morality transcends humans, then a lot of non humans have a lot of explaining to do as they receive their rights assignments. If morality is limited to humans, then assigning rights to others accepts and rewards immorality as a valuable commodity if not divorcing rights from morality altogether. Both paths present the horrible prospect of existentially devaluing people, animals, rights, and moral conduct all in the same breath.

THE ANIMAL RIGHTS LAWSUIT AND ITS INHERENT PROBLEMS

A social movement implies at least three basic assumptions: that political power fuels its goals, that its goals serve a social good, and that its adherents use the political power to become beneficiaries of the power (or alternatively that the movement's adherents work to help a group of beneficiaries who cannot use the political power themselves).[70] Certainly, the animal rights movement uses political power to fuel its goals, which charitably serve a social good.[71] It is a movement sporadically blemished by an overly earnest use of melodrama[72] and a susceptibility to shifting market forces.[73] A few courts have noted some merit to what the movement hopes to accomplish,[74] but in the majority the movement's intellectual rigor has not withstood any serious scrutiny, specifically via "animal rights suits."

As lawsuits go, animal rights suits are problematic. They must initially surmount procedural obstacles such as the concept of standing; they tend to encounter substantive problems such as the scarcity of precedential case law; and they all ultimately face social and political barriers such as the psychological reluctance of judges and juries to take them seriously. A currently pending example in the Oregon Court of Appeals, *Justice v. Vercher*[75] illustrates several of these flaws.

In *Justice*, the Animal Legal Defense Fund (ALDF) named a horse as a plaintiff and under his (melodramatically human-constructed) name filed a state court lawsuit against the horse's former owner as the defendant. The action sought $100,000.00 in damages, the claim for relief was described as "negligence per se," and the allegations were that the defendant had abused him and thereby caused a horse rescue to incur expenses in repairing his injuries. The horse's material problems were solved readily by the rescue, but his (ALDF's) lawsuit ran into legal problems immediately upon filing.

First, the *Justice* case showed that animal rights suits are problematic in that animals just don't have *capacity to sue*, that is, the right to even come into a courtroom brandishing a gripe in the first place. Animals aren't entities with a recognized legal ability to bring, or appear in, a civil or criminal action. A dog, cat, horse, etc. is neither a *natural* person, nor an *artificial* person, nor a *quasi-artificial* person, and there is no city, county, state or federal statute, nor trial or appellate opinion, anywhere that defines "person" to include any animal at all. The absence of capacity is nearly overwhelming by itself to the unviability of an animal rights suit.

Second, *Justice* showed that animal rights suits are problematic in that animals also don't have *standing to sue*, the right to pursue relief as what is called "a real party in interest." Standing is conferred by either a provision in a constitution or a section in a statute, and no constitution or statute in any jurisdiction anywhere grants any animal the right to relief in a civil court, so the absence of an express statutory right giving standing also stops animal rights suits dead in their tracks.

Third, *Justice* showed animal rights suits as problematic in that animals don't even have an *implied right to sue*. The right can't be indirectly derived from thoughts posed in, between, or behind the words or lines of any constitutional or statutory text. To imply a private right of action, a constitution or statute's terms or its legislative history must clearly indicate that the legislature intended there should be liability for violation of a certain provision, yet somehow didn't take the pains to set it out in a specific writing. None, including even animal cruelty statutes in the various state criminal codes, do so or refer in any manner to a private right of action or the imposition of civil liability at all.

Even recent oddities in the civil law in this area—such as the puzzling appellate opinion in the Oregon case of *State v. Hess*, adopting the reasoning from the Oregon Supreme Court case of *State v. Nix* characterizing animals as "victims" for certain purposes—don't help, since "victim" and "litigant" are categorically separate concepts. A "person against whom a crime has been committed" and a "person engaged in a legal proceeding" are unrelated entities to each other legally; the happenstance of being the subject of a crime just doesn't correlate with the entitlement to a civil remedy, so "sympathy card" cases positing animals as victims does nothing to advance their proposed status as empowered litigants.

Fourth, *Justice* showed that animal rights suits are problematic in that animals just don't have any *natural right* to sue either, fundamentally because there is just no phenomenon at all called "natural rights" in the first place.

Those abstractions inhabit the fantasies of philosophers exclusively since true rights are the fruit of the law and of the law alone. There are "no rights without law—no rights contrary to law—no rights anterior to the law"[76]— there simply are no rights *other* than legal rights, no natural rights, no rights higher or above those which people have already created *through* law. The assertion of "nonlegal" rights is absurd in law and logic: a right is, and only is, "a legally enforceable claim by one against others accompanied by corresponding obligations to others,"[77] codified through the democratic process. The absence of any illusory natural right also fatally terminates the pursuit of an animal rights suit.

Fifth, *Justice* showed that animal rights suits are problematic in that they open a gate to a boundaryless field whose legally defined edges cannot be discerned even with the sharpest of scopes. The proposal that horses might have a right to sue people for damages for harming them brooks no natural stopping point to that right as applied. Under the same reasoning, horses must also thus be able to sue people for racing them for money; for selling them at auctions; for fencing them in pastures and stockyards; for separating them from their mothers; for riding them improperly upon the highway; for drugging them without their owner's consent; for branding them; for quarantining them; for slaughtering them; and for even using them as horses *at all in any form*. Horse rights suits would wrap a prohibitory blanket around putting them in shows, fairs, competitions, performances, or parades; engaging them in dressage, hunter and jumper shows, grand prix jumping, three-day events, combined training, rodeos, driving, pulling, cutting, polo, steeplechasing, endurance trail riding, or western games and hunting; in training them, grooming them, breeding and teaching them, boarding them, riding them, inspecting them, or evaluating them, all activities a) currently permitted and regulated under most state statutes[78] and b) performed by hundreds of thousands of people on a daily basis.

There being nothing jurisprudentially unique about equids, of course, then once those statutory obstacles for horses are thrust aside by implementation of the right, the analysis must necessarily continue forward with parallel concerns regarding dogs, cats, rabbits, chickens, fish, and insects, ad infinitum.[79]

Sixth, *Justice* showed that animal rights suits aren't even supported by basic principles of jurisprudence. The rapid dismissal of such suits as soon as they are filed[80] is consistent with protecting the most cherished of those principles, an axiom all law is founded upon: that the participants in our legal system make conscious choices and consciously intend the consequences of their actions. That core assumption allows us to justify holding people responsible for their behavior—its why in criminal law we treat confessions as reliable unless they were compelled, its why in tort law we hold people to a standard of care based on how a reasonable person would have behaved, its why in contract law we enforce agreements according to the objective meaning of the words used. The assumption of a participant's rationality is the cornerstone supporting every mortar and brick of civil and criminal law we have constructed.

A foundation of rationality is absolutely essential to furthering the goals of a legal system in which rights arise from the ideal of respecting individual liberties. The only way in which a dog, cat, or horse's right to sue could even work would be to assume the dog, cat, or horse's rationality no differently than everyone else's rationality—that is, accept that the dog, cat or horse has free will, autonomous choice, and transparent self-knowledge, the same suite of assumptions imposed on every other rights-holder.[81]

The "non-reciprocity" concerns we raised before then raise their ugly head; were we to grant rights to an entity but then excuse it from any responsibility to adhere to the standards of conduct to which everyone adheres, the rationality foundation would collapse in a sorry heap. Basic reason demands that we don't allow rights-holders to be absolved of personal responsibility, we don't let antisocial conduct go unsanctioned and unpunished, and we don't release liberties to float free, untethered from the constraints of the social compact. Doing so would erode the very concept of individual liberty, since rights unsecured by obligations reject the value that rights have to anyone in the first place. The absence of any rational basis in jurisprudence at all also terminates the pursuit of an animal rights suit.

The common law is dynamic—ever-growing, ever-changing, and fluid enough to embrace novel ideas as they arise, including accounting for changes in political, economic, and social structures, policies, and agendas. Animal rights advocates should sincerely be commended for their ideas and aspirations and law does, and should, match social change, including the social changes that they propose. Using methodology as the vehicle, however, that is, using procedural rules and legislation to circumvent the doctrines of standing and capacity, however, would not be the end of any analysis of animal rights but merely the beginning. Carving out the details of a horse's right to sue would be critical for us to truly grasp the scope of three things: what the new right actually entails, what specifically are its burdens, and who actually obtain its benefits.

As to the first mandate, limning the *scope* of a horse's right to sue, we would need to discern its procedural reach. Is the right only the right to sue in a state trial court, or does it also embrace the right to file a small claims action, to appeal to a review court, or to participate in an arbitration? Does a horse's right to sue include allowing horses to also join class actions, present anti-SLAPP motions, and petition for federal bankruptcy protection? If not, why not? What is the decisive factor that would enable a civil right to sue for damages, but preclude a civil right to petition for other types of relief?

As to the second mandate, pinpointing which *burdens* accompany the right, we would need to discern the responsibilities attaching to the right's expression. The horse would need to be subject to oath, as with any other litigant, discovery would need to be available against the horse, counterclaims and liens would need to be available against the horse, and costs and fees would need to be available to be imposed against the horse, just as with any other litigant. Those basic obligations that all litigants shoulder would need to be practically enforceable against the horse under the evidence code and the civil procedure code in order for the right to sue to satisfy basic tenets of due process.

As to the third mandate, cementing who specifically *holds* the right, we would need to discern if its benefits extend anywhere beyond a particularly named plaintiff. Is the right to sue just for an individual horse, or is it also for some group to which horses belong as members? If the latter, is it for all horses regardless of age in which they get the right from the moment they are born, or only adult horses, or only stallions, or only horses who have been hurt? Is it only for the single species *Equus equus* or is it for all equid species including donkeys? If not, why not? What exactly is the defining criterion that distinguishes any in-group from any out-group? If horses, why not donkeys, or all herbivores, or all quadrupeds, or all mammals, or all vertebrates? If the right is for all animals regardless of taxon, from corals to caracals, then we will need to clearly identify that boundary and stay responsibly within its borders.

If the defining criterion for plaintiff status is even broader than membership in the phylum *Vertebrata*, and is a thing that animal rights advocates parade about called "sentience," then the critical question becomes *why?* Why sentience? Assuming you could responsibly define that term, one with no scientific definition at present, we would need to substantiate the link; how a horse's status of possessing sentience then creates a right to sue. If the claim is that sentient things experience pain, that claim simply begs the same question: what endows the sensation of *pain* with legal significance such that rights then flow from feeling *that* sensation?[82]

In fact, what endows the experience of *any* bodily sensation as legally momentous? The fortuity of people experiencing sensations, of pain or pleasure, is certainly not what has turned us into rights-holders. The phenomenon of horses having similar experiences does not turn them into rights-holders either. It is clear to most normal observers that horses are conscious, that they perceive the world through sensation, and that they can and do react to those sensations in complex ways. What is legally momentous however is not their reactions to those experiences—it is their lack of reflective self-awareness that would enable them to *comprehend* those experiences as their own, ones for which they could therefore then agree with us that social responsibility attaches. That is what people do and that is why people have rights:

> When I put a bowl of WONDERCHUNKS in front of my car, nothing happens; when I put a bowl of WONDERCHUNKS in front of my dog, a frightful scene ensues. As everyone accepts, my dog but not my car reacts, perhaps, it must be said, impulsively, perhaps in the vice of his drives and instincts; but he reacts. And the very fact that he reacts so emphatically at the appearance of his meals suffices, I think, to dispel any doubts about whether he is conscious. To continue to doubt that he is conscious when he reacts to WONDERCHUNKS in the way is possible, I think, only if one is very, very securely in the grip of a theory; and I do not think I am. My dog lacks desires, beliefs, and language in my view, but he is conscious' and because he is conscious, he can suffer unpleasant sensations. But though he is conscious, he lacks a concept of self, to which his subjective experiences are ascribed; and, as I have made plain, I agree with Hacker that he could not have such a concept, unless he were blessed with language.[83]

Without that corresponding acceptance of individual responsibility for one's conduct as an integral part of the social compact, a right, including the right to sue, can't be earned by a horse, much less gratuitously bestowed on a horse, because it can't be comprehended, appreciated, or enforced against a horse. Simply having sensation and experiences alone, even painful ones, doesn't suffice at all. In the history of jurisprudence, the status of having the ability to experience sensations has never been identified as the basis from which rights arise. There is no legal document, constitution or otherwise, which posits a psychological state of mind or a condition of the body as the underpinning for rights.

TESTING ANIMAL MINDS FOR MENTAL
EXPERIENCES AND LEGAL SIGNIFICANCES

There is also no scientific basis for all this. Our epistemological, ontological, and methodological tools direct us to the idea that a rigorous scientific analysis of a phenomenon requires that the event being determined be "intersubjectively testable," that is, have the capacity to be accurately communicated between different investigators and to be reproducible under varying circumstances in order to be confirmed as valid.[84] One way of obtaining that manner of assurance is to require that the event be ultimately describable in the language of physical things. While scientists frequently struggle with what benchmarks are sufficient to do so in different circumstances and contexts, the focus on empirical measures is paramount:

It is rather difficult to describe accurately what can be included as physical things or intersubjectively testable events. Informally, what is important is that the event described can be witnessed by more than one person and that the description of the event can be understood by most other people. It is interesting to note that sensations and pains do not meet this criterion; they cannot be witnessed by more than one person. But reports of sensations and pains are acceptable. In other words, the event that is acceptable as scientifically observable is someone's saying that he or she has pain, not the pain itself. . . . The criterion of intersubjective testability is an important one, and one that is generally thought to be necessary. It means that what you see in a dream is not a scientifically observable event, because no one else can see your dream. If you have an itch or a pain, that is not admissible directly as a scientifically observable event because no one else can feel your itch. Psychologists can accept as a scientifically observable event your report of a dream, a pain, or a wild sensation; but it is accepted as a report, not as the actual event. They can gather some supporting evidence from other sources, such as neural activity, rapid eye movements, or other physical indices. We, however, have no way of directly verifying a sensation such as a pain, nor do we have any expectation of being able to do so in the future. . . . The second criterion for an event to be admissible to science is the requirement of a high degree of agreement among different people on the description of the event. This criterion of *reliability* is related to but somewhat different from the criterion of intersubjective testability. Intersubjective testability requires the event to be open to public view and not entirely personal. Reliability requires the event to be described in such a way that different individuals can agree on the description. It is this description of events, not the events themselves, that scientists enter as a datum, although to simplify communication many scientists refer to the event rather than its symbolic representation as the datum. Most events can be described so that different individuals will agree on the description. For example, one might simply say that an event occurred. Since everyone would agree that an event occurred, that description is highly reliable, but it is not very informative. Reliability has associated with it a criterion of *precision*. The more accurately and specifically an event can be reliably described, the more acceptable the description is to scientists.[85]

An animal's psychological sensations and internal mental experiences— whether of pain or pleasure or cognitive awareness or of something else entirely—are simply not testable events. They cannot be contemporaneously narrated or subsequently reported, cannot be measured or weighed, cannot be described in any manner by the one directly experiencing them, nor can they be reliably revealed through an exposure of some physical state the animal is in at the moment the sensation or experience occurs. With no reliability to fall back on, with no precision to constrain, and with no predictability to propose, the inner workings of a horse's mind are unreachable and incomprehensible to people—and thus are useless to presume as a basis for anything, much less for the assertion of rights.

To the extent that the animal rights movement entangles moral judgments with political agendas, and expends energies advancing political causes by appealing to moral outrage, a disciplined application of the rule of law is not really impacted by those types of actions, regardless of the level of their stridency.[86] To the extent that authors and writers in the movement use or abuse specific legal terminology to express their opinions, again, there is no actual effect on the operation of law in our courts or legislatures in spite of how vehement the writers themselves are. It is only when animal rights advocates take on the litigation or legislation role itself and propose to a jurist, fact finder, or legislative body that it formally memorialize the proposition that an animal should be granted a "right," it is then when the integrity of many interlocking legal concepts—of property, of tort, of contract, and of constitutional command—are jeopardized.

Immensely lengthy evolutionary processes, in slowly but inexorably crafting the organisms self-described as "people," have resulted in a remarkable adaptation: an ability to construct and comprehend abstractions called "laws," intellectual concepts produced by language and forged in the fire of intricate social entanglements. The adaptive power of abstractions has—in a remarkably short time geologically through human-oriented historical processes— uniquely benefited the holders of those processes to inhabit and exploit every imaginable niche on the planet, and have separated them from animals by a conceptually immense gulf:

> How do you determine whether nonlinguistic creatures understand and respect others' rights, and assume responsibility for what they do? The respect part is potentially the easiest, as we can see whether individuals follow certain kinds of principles: tolerating another's property, harming and helping others in specific, societally defined contexts. But it is not clear how one tests for comprehension. Nor is it clear how one determines whether they understand the concept of responsibility. That animals take care of others who require such care is one thing. It is something else altogether to feel the weight of obligation, cognizant of the consequences of breaking a commitment to help. The reason I dwell upon this distinction here is because for many scholars writing about our moral sense, and especially our sense of justice, the cooperative actions of animals are *merely* coordinated social behaviors. What they lack is the explicit recognition of why there are rules for cooperation and why there must be a group-level acknowledgment and adherence to such rules. In discussing his guiding principle of justice as fairness, Rawls makes this point explicitly: "Social cooperation is distinct from merely socially coordinated activity—for example, activity coordinated by orders issued by an absolute central authority. Rather, social cooperation is

guided by publicly recognized rules and procedures which those cooperating accept as appropriate to regulate their conduct.[87]

Individuation, and the concept of individual responsibility, finds both its origin and its highest expression only in social *groupings* of humans, not in individuals in isolation from their social groups. One of the most important facts about the genesis and power of our ordinary strong sense of personal freedom is how it seems to have always been there from the start—we never get the internal feeling of *developing* responsibility via stages, only of already possessing it when we call on it. Spinoza attributed that oddity to our ignorance, specifically, "the ignorance of the causes of our desires."[88] That sterile view might be valid were we isolated agents with no connections to any other, but that is not the case: humans by evolution and by definition are links in a complex social network of other humans, and as participating members of social groups are very much *not* "ignorant of the causes of our desires." We are sharply cognizant of those causes and not only expend considerable energy, time, money, thought, and effort into monitoring, assessing, and regulating those causes, but find that we and they evolve in tandem across time based on their expression.

> We want incompatible things, and want them badly. We are fairly aggressive, yet we want company and depend on long-term enterprises. We love those around us and need their love, yet we want independence and need to wander. We are restlessly curious and meddling, yet long for permanence. Unlike many primates, we do have a tendency to pair-formation, but it is an incomplete one, and gives us lot of trouble. We cannot live without a culture, but it never quite satisfies us. All this is the commonplace of literature. It is also, to a degree, the problem of the other intelligent species too. In each, a group of counteracting needs and tendencies holds life in a rough but tolerable equilibrium. In each there are endemic conflicts. Yet an individual depends for his satisfaction on the repertory of tastes native to his species; he cannot jump off his feet. What is special about people is their power of understanding what is going on, and using that understanding to regulate it. Imagination and conceptual thought intensify all the conflicts by multiplying the options, by letting us form all manner of incompatible schemes and allowing us to know what we are missing, and also by greatly increasing our powers of self-deception. As against that, they can give us self-knowledge, which is our strongest card in the attempt to sort conflicts out.[89]

Hume appreciated what he called "the natural motives" of sexual appetite, affection for children, limited benevolence, resentment and interest, all shared sources for developing the rationale of responsibility. This is in large part because freedom and responsibility are not just consequences arising out of individual human histories, those developed from one person's cradle to their grave—they are consequences arising out of our entire species' history and prehistory as well, those weighty effects developed from even before the Paleolithic cradle of humanity to even beyond the Neolithic tomb.

NOTES

1. *Rubáiyát* of Omar Khayyám, Quatrain LXXXIII.
2. Malik, K. *Man, Beast and Zombie.* New Brunswick, NJ: Rutgers University Press, 2002 at p. 390.
3. For some strong and principled writing on the animal rights position, *See* Armstrong, Susan J., and Richard G. Botzler, eds. *The Animal Ethics Reader.* Taylor & Francis, 2016; Rowlands, Mark. *Animals Like Us.* Verso, 2002; Flynn, Clifton P. *Social Creatures: A Human and Animal Studies Reader.* Lantern Books, 2008; Mack, Arien. *Humans and Other Animals,* Ohio State University Press, 1999; Dawkins, Marian Stamp. *Through Our Eyes Only?: The Search for Animal Consciousness, Oxford University Press,* 1993.
4. Sections of this chapter are extensions of ideas first articulated in Duckler, G. "Two Major Flaws of the Animal Rights Movement." *Animal L.* 14 (2007): 179.
5. Edward Poste, *Gai Institutiones or Institutes of Roman Law by Gaius.* Oxford, UK: Clarendon Press, 1904.
6. See, e.g., Leda Cosmides and John Tooby, "Cognitive Adaptations for Social Exchange" in Barkow, J. Cosmides, L. and J. Tooby (eds.) *The Adapted Mind: Evolutionary Psychology and the Generation of Culture.* Oxford, UK: Oxford University Press 1992.
7. See, e.g., Andrew, R. J. "Evolution of Intelligence and Vocal Mimicking," *Science,* August 24, 1962; MacDonald, C. "The Evolution of Man's Capacity for Language," in *Evolution After Darwin,* Vol. 2, Chicago; University of Chicago Press, 1960; Hockett, C. F. and R. Ascher "The Human Revolution" *Current Anthropology,* June 1964.
8. Duckler, G. *"Animal Wrongs: On Holding Animals To (And Excusing Them From) Legal Responsibility for Their Intentional Acts,"* 2 *University of Pennsylvania Journal of Animal Law and Ethics* 91–121 (2007).
9. See, e.g., Daniel Dennett, *Kinds of Minds.* Basic Books, 1996, 147. There is no step more uplifting, more explosive, more momentous, in the history of mind design than the invention of language. When Homo sapiens became the beneficiary of this invention, the species stepped into a slingshot that that has launched it far beyond all other earthly species in the power to look ahead and reflect.
10. Ian Tattersall, *Becoming Human: Evolution and Human Uniqueness.* New York: Harcourt Brace and Co., 1998, 233–234.
11. See Alexander Marshack, *The Roots of Civilization.* New York: McGraw-Hill, 1972.
12. Oliver Wendell Holmes, *The Common Law.* New York: Little, Brown and Co., 1963.

13. See Elaine Morgan, *The Descent of the Child: Human Evolution from a New Perspective.* New York: Oxford University Press, 1992, 247. Once the child has learned the meaning of the words "why" and "because," he has become a fully paid-up member of the human race.

14. See generally Herbert Lionel Adolphus Hart, *The Concept of Law.* Oxford, UK: Clarendon Press, 1961.

15. Bertelsen, Preben. "Free Will, Consciousness and Self: Anthropological Perspectives on Psychology." New York: Berghahn Books, 2005 at pp. 79–80.

16. Rothfels, Nigel, ed. *Representing Animals.* Bloomington: Indiana University Press, 2002 at pp. 5–6.

17. See, e.g., Serpell, J., R. Coppinger and A. H. Fine, "The Welfare of Assistance and Training Animals" at 524–529 in *The Animal Ethics Reader,* Armstrong, S. J. and R. G. Botzler, eds. London: Routledge Press, 2003.

18. See, e.g., Trivers, R. L. "The Evolution of Reciprocal Altruism" *Quarterly Review of Biology*, March 1971.

19. See, e.g., Ronald Giere, *Understanding Scientific Reasoning.* New York: Harcourt Brace, 1991; Carl G. Hempel, *Aspects of Scientific Explanation.* New York: Free Press, 1965.

20. Bernard E. Rollin, "Scientific Ideology, Anthropomorphism, Anecdote, and Ethics" at pp. 67–74 in *The Animal Ethics Reader, supra.*

21. Budiansky, Stephen. *If a Lion Could Talk: Animal Intelligence and the Evolution of Consciousness.* New York: Free Press, 1998 at pp. xv–xvii.

22. See, e.g., Jeffrey M. Masson, *The Emperor's Embrace: Reflections on Animal Families and Fatherhood.* New York: Pocket Books, 1999; Alison Hills, *Do Animals Have Rights?* London: Icon Books, 2005.

23. Jonathan Marks, *What It Means to Be 98% Chimpanzee: Apes, People, and Their Genes.* Berkeley: University of California Press 2002, 61–69.

24. See, e.g., Alfred Sherwood Romer, *Vertebrate Paleontology.* Chicago: Chicago University Press, 1966.

25. Peter Singer, *Practical Ethics.* Cambridge, UK: Cambridge University Press, 1979.

26. Bekoff, M. "Deep Ethology, Animal Rights, and the Great Ape/Animal Project: Resisting Speciesism and Expanding the Community of Equals" at pp. 119–124 in *The Animal Ethics Reader, supra* [primates]; Midgley, M. "Is a Dolphin a Person?" at pp. 166–174 in *The Animal Ethics Reader, supra* [cetaceans]. It would be inaccurate to reframe the movement to constitute a "mammal rights" movement since 85% of the mammalian taxa are left out of consideration.

27. Norton, Bryan G. "Conservation and Preservation: A Conceptual Rehabilitation." *Environmental Ethics* 8.3 (1986): 195–220 at pp. 181, 197, 198–199.

28. For a critique of this point, see Michael P. T. Leahy, *Against Liberation* Oxfordshire: Routledge Press, 1991, 24–26.

29. Richard Morris and Michael Fox (eds.) *On the Fifth Day: Animal Rights and Human Ethics.* Washington, DC: Humane Society of the United States, 1976, 137–204.

30. In Washington state, King County Code Section 11.04.020C defines "a'nimal" as "any living creature except Homo sapiens, insects and worms," brazenly dealing

with the "earthworm omission problem" by just taking worms out of the "animal" equation altogether.

31. Michael W. Fox, *Species Identity and Self-Awareness* in *Species Identity and Attachment* (M. Aaron Roy, ed.). Garland STPM Press, 1980 at pp. 347–353.

32. See Claus Nielsen, *Animal Evolution: Interrelationships of the Living Phyla.* Oxford, UK: Oxford University Press, 1995.

33. Budiansky, Stephen. *If a Lion Could Talk: Animal Intelligence and the Evolution of Consciousness.* New York: Free Press, 1998.

34. Mary Midgley, "Is a Dolphin a Person?" at pp. 166–174 in *The Animal Ethics Reader, supra.*

35. Tom Regan, "The Case for Animal Rights" at pp. 17–24 in *The Animal Ethics Reader, supra.*

36. *See* Frey, R. G. *Rights, Interests, Desires and Beliefs* at pp. 50–53 in *The Animal Ethics Reader, supra.*

37. *See* Stephen Anderson, *Doctor Dolittle's Delusion.* New Haven, CT: Yale University Press, 2004; *See also* Michael Bright, *Animal Language.* Ithaca, NY: Cornell University Press, 1984.

38. *See generally* Steven Pinker, *The Language Instinct.* New York: Harper Collins, 1995 at pp. 368–69.

39. Malik, K. *Man, Beast and Zombie.* New Brunswick, NJ: Rutgers University Press, 2002 at pp. 349–50.

40. Janet Astington, *The Child's Discovery of the Mind.* Cambridge, MA: Harvard University Press, 1993.

41. While it is true that we became hominids at around the six-million-year mark when an ancestor characterized by an upright posture diverged from the proto-chimpanzees and proto-gorillas, we only became human around 100,000 to 150,000 years ago when our ancestors evolved the species-specific distinctive patterns of anatomical structure, manual dexterity, and cognitive behavior we exhibit today.

42. Jean Aitchison, *The Articulate Mammal: An Introduction to Psycholinguistics* New York: Routledge, 1976, 35 .

43. Jeffrey M. Masson, *When Elephants Weep: The Emotional Lives of Animals.* New York: Dell Publishing, 1995, xvi–xvii.

44. See Sara J. Shettleworth, "Constraints on Learning," in D. S. Lehrman, R. A. Hinde, & E. Shaw, *Advances in the Study of Behavior: IV.* Academic Press, 1–61..

45. Following Wittgenstein, we could call it a form of "aspect blindness," that is, not an organic defect but an inability to work through a table of possibilities to discern how one animal might materially differ from another within a taxonomic array. The reference is to the missed connection between one "seeing an aspect" of something and one "experiencing the meaning" of that same thing. *See* Wittgenstein, Ludwig. "Philosophical Investigations. Blackwells." (1953).

46. *See* Michael Fox "To Farm without Harm and Choosing A Humane Diet: The Bioethics of Humane Sustainable Agriculture" in Robert Garner (ed.) *Animal Rights: The Changing Debate.* New York: New York University Press, 1996, 92–103.

47. For an example involving two writers both examining insect "intelligence," contrast an animal rights advocate's two-word conclusion that honeybees must be

given legal rights since they are "sentient," citing as his sole authority a "personal communication" with a psychologist (Steven Wise, *Drawing the Line*. New York: Perseus Books, 2002, 81: "Do their tiny brains produce sentience? Apparently so"), with an evolutionary biologist's explanation of how the rigors of the scientific method might generate real answers about certain insect interactions using, as his example, coevolutionary behaviors of wasps and figs (Richard Dawkins *Climbing Mount Improbable*. New York: W. W. Norton and Co., 1996, 308:

Much of the deciphering of the wasp-pollination story would simply have involved slicing figs open and looking inside. But "looking" gives too laid-back an impression. It wasn't a passive gawping but a carefully planned recording session yielding numbers to be fed into calculations. Don't just pluck figs and slice them. Systematically sample figs from a large number of trees, from particular heights, and at particular seasons of the year. Don't just stare at the wasps wriggling inside: identify them, photograph them, accurately draw them, count them and measure them. Classify them by species, sex, age and location in the fig. Send specimens to museums for identification by detailed comparison with internationally recognized standards. But don't make measurements and counts indiscriminately just for the sake of it. Make them in the service of testing stated hypotheses. And when you look to see if your counts and measurements fit the expectations of your hypothesis, be aware, in calculated detail, how likely it is that your results could have been obtained by chance and mean nothing.

48. See, e.g., Harvey, Anna L. "The Political Consequences of Suffrage Exclusion: Organizations, Institutions, and the Electoral Mobilization of Women." *Social Science History* 20, no. 1 (1996): 97–132.

49. It is not coincidence that political discourse is rife with communication-dependent assertions, from Herschel's "What starts out as a sound, ends in a deed" to Martin Luther King Jr.'s "Our lives begin to end the day we become silent about the things that matter."

50. *Williams v. Attorney General of Alabama*, 378 F.3d 1232 (11th Cir. 2004).

51. See, e.g., James B. Reichmann *Evolution, Animal 'Rights,' and the Environment.* Washington, DC: Catholic University of America Press, 2000, 256–63.

52. Tiger, Lionel, and Robin Fox. *The Imperial Animal.* Laurel: Dell at pp. 136, 238.

53. See, e.g., *Kihlstadius v. Nodaway Veterinary Clinic*, 697 F. Supp. 1087 (W.D. Mo. 1988) (holding that dogs do not have civil rights).

54. Marquardt, Kathleen, Herbert M. Levine, and Mark LaRochelle. *Animalscam: The Beastly Abuse of Human Rights.* Washington, DC: Regnery Publishing, 1993 at p. 6.

55. Peter Singer, *Animal Liberation: A New Ethics for Our Treatment of Animals.* New York: New York Review/Random House, 1975.

56. *State v. Amini*, 175 Or. App. 370 (Or. App. 2001).

57. *Cf. Smith v. State*, 6 S.W.3d 512 (Tenn. Crim. App. 1999); *King v. South Jersey Nat. Bank*, 66 N.J. 161 (N.J. 1974).

58. Williams, Moyra. *Horse Psychology.* New York: A. S. Barnes, 1969 at pp. 43–44.

59. Stephen Budiansky, *If a Lion Could Talk: How Animals Think.* London: Weidenfeld and Nicolson, 1998, 161.

60. James B. Reichmann *Evolution, Animal 'Rights,' and the Environment,* Washington, DC: Catholic University of America Press, 2000, 261.

61. See David Hancocks, *A Different Nature: The Paradoxical World of Zoos and Their Uncertain Future.* Berkeley: University of California Press, 2001.

62. Matt Ridley, *The Origins of Virtue.* Penguin Books, 1996, 215.

63. See, e.g., John R. Campbell and John F. Lasley, *The Science of Animals that Serve Humanity.* New York: McGraw-Hill, 1998.

64. Joyce Tischler, "Toward Legal Rights for Other Animals" at pp. 691–693 in *Animal Law,* 3rd ed. Waisman, S. et. al. eds. Durham, NC: Carolina Academic Press, 2006.

65. See Daniel A. Moros, "Taking Duties Seriously: Medical Experimentation, Animal Rights, and Moral Incoherence" in *Birth to Death: Science and Bioethics.* David C. Thomasma and Thomasina Kushner, eds. New York: Cambridge University Press, 1996 at pp. 313–324.

66. Kushner, Thomasine Kimbrough, and David C. Thomasma, eds. *Birth to Death: Science and Bioethics.* New York: Cambridge University Press, 1996 at pp. 314–315.

67. See generally Frans de Waal *Good Natured: The Origins of Right and Wrong in Humans and Other Animals.* Cambridge, MA: Harvard University Press, 1996.

68. Prokaryotes are the most primitive and ubiquitous of organisms, single-celled entities with no nuclear membrane and classically exemplified by *E. coli*, the common bacteria of the gut. They were the dominant form of life on the planet for billions of years. Eukaryotes, entities with more complicated cell structure, arrived late in the game, and include all the multicellular organisms one finds on the planet today, from slime molds to philosophers.

69. Lynn Margulis and Dorion Sagan, *Microcosmos: Four Billion Years of Microbial Evolution.* Berkeley: University of California Press, 1997, 29–31..

70. See generally Della Porta, Donatella, and Mario Diani. *Social Movements: An Introduction.* New York: John Wiley & Sons, 2020.

71. Wesley V. Jamison, *Every Sparrow That Falls: Understanding Animal Rights Activism as Functional Religion* at 556–62 in *The Animal Ethics Reader, supra.*

72. In 2006, for instance, animal rights advocates lauded a) a pet fashion show in California proclaiming that "Animal Law is In Fashion" and awarding prizes to dogs in human costume, b) a court ruling in Philadelphia directing a farm to stop referring to its chickens as "happy and well-treated" but to call them "contented and well-treated" instead, and c) proposed legislation in Connecticut to remove the definition of an invasive monk parrot species as "invasive." For more, *See* James Jasper "The American Animal Rights Movement" in Robert Garner (ed.) *Animal Rights: The Changing Debate.* New York: NYUy Press,1996 at pp. 129–142.

73. See, e.g., *American Soc. for Prevention of Cruelty to Animals v. Board of Trustees of State University of New York,* 165 A.D.2d 561 (N.Y.A.D. 2 Dept. 1991) ("[T]he humane treatment of animals may well constitute public business.")

74. *People for Ethical Treatment of Animals v. Bobby Berosini,* Ltd., 111 Nev. 431 (Nev. 1995) ("Although we recognize a degree of merit in the animal rights

movement, we feel working within the needs and sentiments of the community yield far greater participation and progress.").

75. *Justice v. Vercher*, 2018 WL 11189952 (Circuit Court of Oregon, Washington County 2020).

76. Doyle, Oran. "Legal Positivism, Natural Law and the Constitution." *Dublin ULJ* 31 (2009): 206 (quoting the English philosopher Jeremy Bentham (1832)).

77. Third, Restatement. "Property (Wills and Other Donative Transfers)." *Washington, DC: The American Law Institute* (2010).

78. See, e.g., ORS 30.687.

79. See Carere, Claudio, and Jennifer Mather, eds. *The Welfare of Invertebrate Animals*. Vol. 18. Springer, 2019:

Welfare is a broad concern for any animal that we house, control or utilize—and we utilize invertebrates a lot. What is pain in crustaceans, and how might we prevent it? How do we ensure that octopuses are not bored? What do bees need to thrive, pollinate our plants and give us honey? Since invertebrates have distinct personalities and some social animals have group personalities, how do we consider this? We have previously relegated invertebrates to the category 'things' and did not worry about their treatment. New research suggests that some invertebrates such as cephalopods and crustaceans can have pain and suffering, might also have consciousness and awareness.

See Barron, Andrew B., and Colin Klein. "What Insects Can Tell Us about the Origins of Consciousness." *Proceedings of the National Academy of Sciences* 113.18 (2016): 4900–4908:

How, why, and when consciousness evolved remain hotly debated topics. Addressing these issues requires considering the distribution of consciousness across the animal phylogenetic tree. Here we propose that at least one invertebrate clade, the insects, has a capacity for the most basic aspect of consciousness: subjective experience.

80. *Hawaiian Crow ('Alala) v. Lujan*, 906 F Supp 549 (D. Haw. 1991) (bird has no standing to sue); *Citizens to End Animal Suffering & Exploitation, Inc. v. New England Aquarium*, 836 F Supp 45 (D. Mass. 1993) (dolphin has no standing to sue); *Cetacean Cmty. v. Bush*, 386 F3d 1169 (9th Cir. 2004) (whale, porpoise, or dolphin has no standing to sue); *Tilikum ex rel. People for the Ethical Treatment of Animals, Inc. v. Sea World Parks & Entm't, Inc.*, 842 F Supp 2d 1259 (SD Cal. 2012) (killer whale has no standing to sue); *People ex rel. Nonhuman Rights Project, Inc. v. Lavery*, 124 AD3d 148 (N.Y. 2014) (chimpanzee has no standing to sue); *Naruto v. Slater*, 888 F3d 418 (9th Cir. 2018) (macaque monkey has no standing to sue).

81. See Petrinovich, L. *Darwinian Dominion: Animal Welfare and Human Interests*. Cambridge, MA: MIT Press, 1999.

82. The deficiencies of "sentience" are not just empirical but moral as well:

It is ironic, to say the least, that this result of the application of a sentiency criterion, in large measure in order to combat discrimination (against the "higher" animals), is itself, as Rodman has noted, blatantly discriminatory in character. For, to put the matter rather pompously, it condemns the whole of non-sentient creation, including the "lower'"animals, at best to a much inferior moral status or, as we shall see, at worst to a status completely outside morality. In essence, non-sentient creation is "simply there" for sentient creation to do with as it sees fit. Animal rightists and animal liberationists in general have often objected to the Christian view of man as having dominion over the rest of creation; but the only revolution they effect by means of an appeal to a mental state of view of value is to give man and the "higher" animals dominion over the rest of creation. The criterion of sentiency, then, does not eliminate discrimination; on the contrary, it broadens the category of those who can practice it, or, in the case of the "higher" animals, who can have it practiced on their behalf.

Hauser, Marc. *Moral Minds: How Nature Designed Our Universal Sense of Right and Wrong*. New York: Ecco/HarperCollins Publishers, 2006 at p. 44.

83. Frey, Raymond Gillespie. *Interests and Rights: The Case against Animals*. Oxford, UK: Clarendon Press, 1980 at pp. 108–109.

84. Popper, Karl R. *Objective Knowledge*. Vol. 360. Oxford, UK: Oxford University Press, 1972.

85. McCain, Garvin, and Erwin M. Segal. *The Game of Science*. Boston: Thomson Brooks/Cole, 1988 at pp. 48–49.

86. Keith, Lierre. *The Vegetarian Myth: Food, Justice and Sustainability*. Oakland: PM Press, 2009 at p. 75:

The [animal rights] movement is liberal individualism applied to animals. It is a reflection of human needs and desires, not the needs and desires of animals themselves.

87. Hauser, Marc. *Moral Minds: How Nature Designed Our Universal Sense of Right and Wrong*. New York: Ecco/HarperCollins Publishers, 2006 at pp. 21, 343, 414–415.

88. See LeBuffe, Michael. "Spinoza's Psychological Theory." (2001).

89. Midgley, Mary. *Beast and Man: The Roots of Human Nature*. Brighton, 1979. at pp. 282–283.

Conclusion

"Past Regrets and Future Fears"[1]

We must not deceive ourselves: morals do not forbid making experiments on one's neighbour or one's self; in everyday life, men do nothing but experiment on one another.[2]

The methodological tool of inquiry from chapter 1 suggests the idea that conflicts between opposing legal theories, much like conflicts between opposing scientific theories, may be resolved if opponents can agree on a test as to which theory has better support and on the particular tools by which to run such a test. In law, that test arrives in the form of a trial shackled by the rule of law, and in science it arrives in the form of an experiment shackled by the rule of verifiability, and in both, the contestants must ultimately agree to abide by principled use of the tools and accept that a certain outcome will be decisive. We have also noted that the disciplines' paths diverge where principles of stare decisis and precedent can dictate a very sturdy "decisiveness" for the former (mostly via documents in the form of judgments and appellate opinions), whereas "decisiveness" for the latter is malleable and dynamic and can fluctuate drastically with the results of further experiment, perception, and inquiry. In either case, whichever theory in particular lawyers and scientists end up adopting nevertheless depends upon which strengths in argument each participant is persuaded by and which weaknesses they are willing to overlook. Being only human, we accept that objective pleas to logic, tempered by subjective pleas to individual opinion, are yoked together in every determination reached.

For that reason, neither lawyers nor scientists are ultimately obligated to favor or reject specific proposals since additional routes to a solution can always be generated by new facts, new techniques, and new proposals. Publicly, subsequent explanations and rising contradictions in the outside world may revise the apparent rightness or wrongness of what seemed like a solid conclusion. Privately, subsequent obstinacy and rising concessions within the personal convictions of the respective investigators may subtly disarm the apparent significance of any study or verdict.

> The mind is a complex thing, not in the sense that an engineered machine is, with many separate parts working smoothly together in pursuit of a single goal, but in the sense that it is a product of ancient reflexive and emotional components, overlain by a veneer of reason. . . . Because the fossil and archaeological records show us that the final step in becoming human was more than a simple extrapolation of earlier trends, it is hardly for a paleontologist to attempt an explanation of the complexities of modern human behavior, at least beyond pointing out the interaction of the old and the new that goes on inside our symbol-manipulating brains and that underpins our vaunted consciousness. Exegesis of the way we are lies in the domains of psychologists, neurobiologist, philosophers, novelists, playwrights, and others. How we ought to conduct our lives (and how we are encouraged to live them) is the province of ethicists, philosophers, and, God help us, lawmakers.[3]

There is, nevertheless, a backstop to all that. Even additional hypotheses and novel legal rulings need to be plausible and supported by some manner of reliable evidence. People can't avoid the difficulty inherent in making choices in all walks of life, but they can do their best to avoid the inanity of basing choices on implausible scenarios, illogical lines of thought, or the absence of any evidentiary support whatsoever. Unhelpful detritus—in particular, purely political or religious agendas—should not, but currently do, infect every determination as to what animals are, how animals are treated, and what laws and rules should apply to them.

The objectification of animals and their necessary role as valuable objects inside of complex human communal arrangements have numerous strengths in argument, and the authority I've provided may guide the reader to be persuaded that those strengths outweigh their weaknesses. Even accepting their problems, science and law both have ways to make animal-related legal problems tractable in the disciplines' joint search for understanding. Order and unity in the chaotic world of experience can be identified, especially regarding human-animal interactions, and the disputes and queries persistently bubbling up from the froth of that world can be reasonably handled in several ways.

One, both disciplines can look to, and rely on, the past for guidance. The evolution of all animals well preceded human social relations, relations that themselves well preceded the development of written laws. The capacities of prehistoric humans for reciprocity, retaliation, aggression, dispute resolution, and empathy form the raw materials of social regularity and moral systems, and it is these basic building blocks from which legal behaviors became constructed.[4] The cement between those blocks concerned animals—their evasion, their acquisition, and their exploitation. Because assemblages in death can inform assemblages in life, then a close and detailed taphonomic examination of the myriad links bridging prehistorical groups and events with historical groups and events can inform us about the large gaps we currently notice between how we treat animals and how we treat ourselves.

Two, both disciplines can attend to constructing and supporting clear definitions. Our words of choice direct our inquiries of choice: in forming a hypothesis, the ontological component, the definition of "A" crucially affects the path taken in supporting beliefs about A, the epistemological component, and the mechanisms sufficient to test beliefs about A, the methodological component. Good definitions create good directions toward knowledge. Archaic perceptions of animals cause law to waver on the brink of constructing workable categories. While scientific classifications of animals have their problems, they allow substantial room to maneuver in defining animals and people and can establish the right parameters to frame burdens and benefits on both groups.

Three, both disciplines can recognize that the disparate natures and evolutionary trajectories of different animal species, including our own, materially affect the varying need for the control by one over another—information usable to reliably distinguish cats from cars in a manner that doesn't require equating cats with people or equating either with cars. We can lead ourselves to then responsibly answer questions as philosophically large as should cats have owners at all, as well as questions as legislatively small as how many owners of a certain cat there can legally be. Enfolding in how manufactured properties arose in the first place, we can use criterion of care to explain why a cat's owners may be different each day, criterion of custody to explain why there may be a single owner of a cat throughout the animal's life, and criterion of control to explain why no one may qualify to own the cat at all (particularly with a certain difficult cat of whom the author is well aware and who shall remain unnamed).

Four, both disciplines can use filters, filtrate, and particulate models to usefully distinguish cats from crickets as well. *Animalia* is internally and externally complicated and those complications should not be overly simplified or overly exaggerated—or outright ignored. There is a reason that "pets," "livestock," and "game animals" are extensively regulated by people while amoebae, earthworms, and millions of other less "useful" species live their lives untouched by any law. Principled distinctions are discernible from sensible classification schemes, and avoiding anthropomorphic biases and tendencies is a worthy goal for lawyers and scientists in their consciences and in their practices.

Five, both disciplines can stay grounded in the practical realities of animals as objects. Though animals can't have rights in the way that only people can, their value isn't thereby diminished. As subjects to the objects around them, people locate animals as one set of immensely valuable inhabitants in a thorny nest in which innumerable other equally problematic objects reside as well. We worship animals and we consume them; we create beautiful works of art about them, and we unblinkingly exploit them for the practical utility of their various component parts. Most of the same could be said for precious gems, mountains, and herbaceous biomass. With animals there are serious distinctions of course, and most distill down to retraining some sort of control over their complicated writhings, part of our never-ending scouting out of boundaries of creative power we would like to, but often cannot, wield over all manner of enthralling things in our environment.

> Belongings is an interesting word, referring to membership and therefore to parts of a whole. If that whole is Me, then perhaps the acquisition of mostly man-made objects can contribute in some way to my identity—a way that may compensate for some earlier means lost when people became sedentary and their world mostly man-made landscapes. Or, if objects fail to fully suffice, we want more and more, as we crave more of a pain-killing drug. In short, what is it about the domesticated civilized world that alters the concept of self so that it is enhanced by property?[5]

As belongings, in the practical sense of physical possessions and the emotional sense of desired acquisitions, there is nothing wrong with celebrating animals' appropriate place in the messiness of the natural world. That role necessarily embraces a historical development of rights for ourselves as part of a social compact and necessarily prohibits animals from joining in the compact or from either benefiting or being burdened by such an imposition.

Lawyers and scientists have always asked how people can be so like animals but at the very same time so not like them, have always asked how people can be related to animals biologically and anatomically in the most intimate ways and yet so different from them socially and intellectually, have always asked which animals deserve respect or destruction, which animals must be protected, which animals must we be protected from, and which animals do we just not care a whit about at all. A clear view of answers responsive to those puzzles—in the form of judgments and appellate opinions or in the form of scientific experiment and development of the published literature—is imperative. Above all, on account of such a view, we can at least acknowledge that we are different from them at a foundational and transcendent level based on how our minds have evolved and now work:

> Self-understanding makes self-governance possible. Interpreting selves can create meaningful societies. That is, a species capable of understanding the rules that govern its behavior can direct its social organization to the accomplishment

of goals defined by the members of that species as meaningful. . . . The more modern people become, the more their affairs are governed by something other than both biology and culture. That something else is mind. Unlike our biological destiny, it enables us to have a say in the rules that govern how we reproduce ourselves. Unlike our cultural destiny, it confronts the way we usually have done things with an imagined capacity to do things in other ways. We cannot, nor should we ever, rule out the biological and cultural sciences as ways of understanding some of what we do.[6]

Lawyers and scientists, being lifetime members of the human social community, treat animals with the same odd mixture of empirical knowledge, economic reality, and moral concern that others utilize in reaching decisions about object value. Valuation, however, shouldn't be dissociated from evaluation. If one is completely ignorant of values altogether then one is incapable of making a rational decision about valuable things, whether for or against their preservation, conveyance, or regulation. Answering the question of what exactly a dog is useful for should invoke thoughts about what a star or an ant is useful for—and why rights of possession and ownership are critical concepts holding human communities together in their construction of what it means for something to be *invaluable*.[7]

Valuing animals requires the employment of accurate comparisons and the formation of applicable criteria; it requires the use of reliable models and the implementation of sound economic principles. As an evaluator, the lawyer-scientist therefore needs to be a good economist in addition to knowing about animal bodies, behaviors, taxonomies, development, and evolution. A bank of zoological and economic knowledge must be drawn from for conceptual wealth to generate. Inserting animals into the "manufactured product" slot of an object's economic trajectory from attainment to divestment—the contribution, investment, enjoyment, and return factors from chapter 5—reveals animal value as unfolding from that knowledge, from animal objectification. The contribution is the animal's *Pierson v. Post* capture, the investment is the work put into its captivity and nurture toward replication, its enjoyment is in its utility, and its return emanates from its conveyance to others. Grasping that model leads to real insight; the weak proclamation simply that "I value animal welfare," in comparison, is a poor substitute given what roles animals truly play as fixtures in our homes, as captives, as ritualistic emblems in our communities, and as goods in our markets.

Finally, we need to continually affirm the momentousness of language as a dividing line between us and them. The adaptation of language that has evolved in us at one and the same time informs and deforms conversations we have with ourselves about ourselves as subjects and animals as objects:

Language . . . is the indispensable mechanism of human life—of life such as ours that is molded, guided, enriched, and made possible by the accumulation of the *past* experience of members of our own species. Dogs and cats and chimpanzees do not, so far as we can tell, increase their wisdom, their information, or their control over their environment from one generation to the next. But human beings do. . . . To be able to read and write, therefore, is to learn to profit by and take part in the greatest of human achievements—that which makes all other achievements possible—namely, the pooling of our experiences in great cooperative stores of knowledge, available (except where special privilege, censorship, or suppression stand in the way) to all. What we call society is a vast network of mutual agreements. We agree to refrain from murdering our fellow citizens, and they in turn agree to refrain from murdering us; we agree to drive on the right-hand side of the road, and others agree to do the same; we agree to deliver specified goods, and others agree to pay us for them; we agree to observe the rules of an organization, and the organization agrees to let us enjoy its privileges. This complicated network of agreements, into which almost every detail of our lives is woven and upon which most of our expectations in life are based, consists essentially of *statements about future events which we are supposed, with our own efforts, to bring about* . . . [I]n order that we shall continue to exist as human beings, we *must* impose patterns of behavior on each other . . . [D]irective utterances with collective sanction, which try to impose patterns of behavior upon the individual in the interests of the whole group, are among the most interesting of linguistic events. Not only are they usually accompanied by ritual; they are usually the central purpose of ritual. There is probably no kind of utterance that we take more seriously, that affects our lives more deeply, that we quarrel about more bitterly. Constitutions of nations and of organizations, legal contracts, and oaths of office are utterances of this kind; in marriage vows, confirmation exercises, induction ceremonies, and initiations, they are the essential constituent. Those terrifying verbal jungles called laws are simply such directives, accumulated, codified, and systematized through the centuries.[8]

The illustration on the front of this book visualizes some of its major themes. On the left, six modern paleontologists diligently remove rocks from the entrance to a cave. On the right, seven hominids in the cave just as diligently set more rocks in place. The two groups clearly are working at cross-purposes, with those on the left ostensibly seeking to make the past yield its secrets and those on the right ostensibly seeking to obstruct that very goal. Upon first viewing the picture, the frustration of purpose is palpable and progress on both sides seems effectively stymied. In that sense, it is a pictorial translation of a short poem about immobility.

Resonant with that frustration, the paleontologist may see themselves in the illustration portrayed literally, at a field excavation striving hard to unearth the mysteries of hominid prehistory. Similarly, the psychologist may see themselves in the illustration portrayed broadly, at a difficult counseling session, perhaps, striving to uncover a patient's repressions while the patient struggles bitterly to keep them interred. The lawyer may see themselves figuratively in the illustration as well, digging industriously with their evidence code shovels and procedural rule picks in a cavernous courtroom in efforts to discover the occurrence of a previous event the opposition is doing their best with objections and exclusionary motions to cover from view.

I have looked at that picture thousands of times, and in it I see something slightly different than interpretive representations of the various difficulties that stasis inserts into people's professions and vocations. Faintly, among its lines and shading, I can glimpse an illustration of the art of inquiry itself.

In abstract terms, the ontological inquiry is reflected in the picture's use of two contrasting spaces: the modest open space on the left and the larger closed cave on the right, what we know and what we don't. The epistemological inquiry is reflected in all those asymmetrical and hard-to-balance rocks: their placement in or away from the gap, how we are alternatively aware or kept unaware of what has actually occurred in the world. Finally, the methodological inquiry is reflected in the respective deliberate motion of the people's hands: the living tools with which rocks get placed and removed, how the competing tasks in the drama are actually being completed in light of the goals that have been set. It is, in that sense, an austere image of what knowing and not knowing looks like.

Lawyers are keenly aware that a good metaphor can be a form of poetry, and for me the metaphor of knowledge that this picture offers rather poetically highlights the significance of the active passage of time. Time flows from the right to the left in that, as modern cave dwellers, the actions we take in our present create consequences that impact the future, specifically, what our descendants might come to learn. Time flows from the left to the right in that, as modern paleontologists, the forays we can make into learning of the world can materially affect what we decipher of our own past. The caption to the picture translates into "The prehistorian must sometimes encounter incomprehensible difficulties." The past only offers up incomprehensible difficulties to the investigator, however, if we have made no efforts in the present at all or have made efforts to deliberately make knowledge incomprehensible. Lawyers and scientists as investigators stand on both sides of the picture traveling back and forth in time affecting facts in both directions; with some effort truths can be blocked and with some effort truths can be revealed, and all the efforts are our own.

I will close suggesting that the richness of the illustration offers one further metaphorical insight, one directly connected to the discussions in this book. Language, an evolutionary adaptation with a heft and substance weightier than the heaviest of boulders, can be manipulated by people for any number of competing purposes, including to increase knowledge or to suppress it. As they roll forward and roll back the stones of their respective arguments about what animals are and what rights are, the lawyer-scientist and the animal rights advocate each focus intensely on that gap between the daylight and the darkness, a gap that could be opened and illuminated in awareness, or covered and buried in ignorance, as the case may be.

Law, science, and poetry are each independent but interrelated manifestations of human ingenuity and human culture, and each reflect the current culture in which they operate and the past culture from which they have arisen and evolved. Depending on how they are employed, each may at times enhance and at times obstruct valuable insights into the human condition. At the end of the day, it is the mindset of the actors—lawyer, naturalist, or poet—that curves the track in one or the other direction.

The epic project of applying tools to the raw material of lives to develop insight, to develop understanding, is a project that cannot take even the smallest step without the use of language, from the most basic rhyme to the most intricate judicial opinion. Mindsets are the organic products of that language use. The author J. B. White remarked that lawyers act as poets "to bring to bear the materials of the past upon a present question, remaking those materials as they do so, with the idea of creating a new set of relations in the present and the future."[9] To White, law is a moment in time, specifically, *the* moment when the lawyer must speak and in speaking make something new out of their language. The animal as a legal object is one of those new things, a remarkable insight derived from aggregates of mindsets employing concepts developed in law and science, a moment sparked by evolutionary forces, a moment exhorted across generations, and a moment entrenched in the lyric, meter, and rhythm of human discourse in all its forms, the scientific study, the field report, the data table, the civil complaint, the jury verdict, the judicial opinion, the philosopher's quatrain, and the poet's ode.

> By firm immutable immortal laws
> Impress'd on Nature by the Great First Cause,
> Say, Muse! How rose from elemental strife
> Organic forms, and kindled into life;
> How love and Sympathy with potent charm
> Warm the cold heart, the lifted hand disarm;
> Allure with pleasures, and alarm with pains,
> And bind Society in golden chains.[10]

NOTES

1. *Rubáiyát* of Omar Khayyám, Quatrain XXI.

2. Bernard, Claude. *An Introduction to the Study of Experimental Medicine.* Translated into English by Copley Green, with an introduction by Lawrence J. Henderson and a Foreword by I. Bernard Cohen. New York: Dover Publications, 1865.

3. Tattersall, Ian. *Becoming Human: Evolution and Human Uniqueness.* New York: Houghton Mifflin Harcourt, 1999.

4. Gruter, Margaret, and Monika Gruter Morhenn. "Building Blocks of Legal Behaviour." (2000).

5. Shephard, P., *The Only World We've Got.* San Francisco: Sierra Club Books, 1996.

6. Wolfe, Alan. *The Human Difference: Animals, Computers, and the Necessity of Social Science.* Berkeley: University of California Press, 1993.

7. Midgley, Mary. *Animals and Why They Matter.* Athens, GA: University of Georgia, 2007.

8. Hayakawa, S. J. "Language in Thought and Action." New York: Harcourt, 1949.

9. White, James Boyd. *Heracles' Bow: Essays on the Rhetoric and Poetics of the Law.* Madison: University of Wisconsin Press, 1985.

10. Darwin, Erasmus. *The Temple of Nature, or The Origin of Society.* Baltimore: Bonsal & Niles, 1804.

Bibliography

Akhtar, S., and V. Volkan. *Cultural Zoo: Animals in the Human Mind and Its Sublimations*. Madison, CT: International Universities Press, 2005.

Baker, Steve. *Picturing the Beast: Animals, Identity, and Representation*. Urbana: University of Illinois, 2001.

Bergler, R. *Man and Dog: The Psychology of a Relationship*. New York: Howell Book House, 1988.

Bernard, Claude. *An Introduction to the Study of Experimental Medicine*. Vol. 400. Courier Corporation, 1957.

Budiansky, S. *The Covenant of the Wild*. New Haven, CT: Yale University Press, 1992.

Bulliet, R. W. *Hunters, Herders, and Hamburgers: The Past and Future of Human-Animal Relationships.* New York: Columbia University Press, 2005.

Bustad, L. K. "Man and Beast Interface: An Overview of Our Relationships" in *Man and Beast Revisited.* M. H. Robinson and Lionel Tiger (ed.) Washington, D.C.: Smithsonian Institution Press, 1991.

Clutton-Brock, J. *Domesticated Animals from Early Times*. Austin: University of Texas Press, 1981.

Clutton-Brock, J. "Origins of the Dog: Domestication and Early History" at pp. 8–20 in *The Domestic Dog*. Serpell, J. (ed.). Cambridge, UK: Cambridge University Press, 1995.

Coppinger, Raymond, and Lorna Coppinger. *Dogs: A New Understanding of Canine Origin, Behavior, and Evolution*. Chicago: University of Chicago, 2002.

Coren, Stanley. *The Intelligence of Dogs: A Guide to the Thoughts, Emotions, and Inner Lives or Our Canine Companions*. New York: Free Press, 2006.

Crist, Eileen. *Images of Animals: Anthropomorphism and Animal Mind*. Philadelphia: Temple University Press, 2000.

Daston, Lorraine, and Gregg Mitman. *Thinking with Animals: New Perspectives on Anthropomorphism*. New York: Columbia University Press, 2005.

Deacon, Terrence William. *The Symbolic Species: The Co-Evolution of Language and the Brain*. New York: W. W. Norton, 1997.

Decker, A., and G. Goff. *Valuing Wildlife: Economic and Social Perspectives*. Boulder: Westview, 1987.

Faigman, David L. *Legal Alchemy: The Use and Misuse of Science in the Law*. New York: Macmillan, 2000.

Fox, Harold Munro. *The Personality of Animals*. Melbourne: Penguin, 1952.

Fox, Michael W. *Behaviour of Wolves, Dogs, and Related Canids*. New York: Harper & Row, 1972.

Franklin, A. *Animals in Modern Cultures: A Sociology of Human–Animal Relations in Modernity*. London: SAGE Publications, 1999.

Haraway, Donna Jeanne. *When Species Meet*. Minneapolis: University of Minnesota, 2008.

Hare, B. et al. "The Domestication of Social Cognition in Dogs." *Science* 298: 1634–36 (2002).

Hauser, Marc D. *Moral Minds: The Nature of Right and Wrong*. New York: Harper Perennial, 2007.

Hearne, Vicki. *Adam's Task: Calling Animals by Name*. New York: Knopf, 1986.

Hoage, R. J. *Perceptions of Animals in American Culture*. Washington, D.C.: Smithsonian Institution, 1989.

Holmes, Oliver Wendell. *The Common Law*. Cambridge, MA: Belknap of Harvard UP, 2009.

Hyams, E. *Animals in the Service of Man*. Philadelphia: J. B. Lippincott Company, 1972.

Janovy, John. *On Becoming a Biologist*. New York: Harper & Row, 1985.

Katcher, A. H., and A. Beck, "Animal Companions: More Companion Than Animal" in *Man and Beast Revisited*. Washington, D.C.; Smithsonian Institution Press (eds. M. H. Robinson and Lionel Tiger), 1991.

Kay, William J. *Euthanasia of the Companion Animal*. Philadelphia: Charles, 1988.

Kellert, S. "Urban American Perception of Animals and the Natural Environment," *Urban Ecology* 8: 209–28 (1984).

Kennedy, J. S. *The New Anthropomorphism*. Cambridge, UK: Cambridge University Press, 1992.

Leahy, M. *Against Liberation: Putting Animals in Perspective*. London: Routledge, 1991.

Lorenz, K. *Man Meets Dog*. New York: Kodansha International, 1953.

Machan, Tibor R. *Putting Humans First: Why We Are Nature's Favorite*. Lanham, MD: Rowman & Littlefield, 2004.

Malik, Kenan. *Man, Beast and Zombie: What Science Can and Cannot Tell Us about Human Nature*. London: Weidenfeld & Nicolson, 2000.

Manning, A. *Animals and Human Society: Changing Perspectives*. London: Routledge, 1994.

Mason, I. (ed.) *The Evolution of Domesticated Animals*. London: Longman Press, 1984.

Midgley, Mary. *Animals and Why They Matter*. Athens: University of Georgia, 2007.

Midgley, Mary. *Beast and Man: The Roots of Human Nature*. Ithaca, NY: Cornell University Press, 1978.

Mitchell, Robert W., Nicholas S. Thompson, and H. Lyn. Miles. *Anthropomorphism, Anecdotes, and Animals*. Albany: SUNY Press, 1997.

Petrinovich, L. *Darwinian Dominion: Animal Welfare and Human Interests*. Cambridge: MIT Press, 1999.

Renteln, Alison Dundes., and Alan Dundes. *Folk Law: Essays in The Theory and Practice of Lex Non Scripta, Vol. I and II*. Madison: University of Wisconsin, 1994.

Robinson, Michael H., and Lionel Tiger. *Man & Beast Revisited*. Washington: Smithsonian Institution, 1991.

Room, Adrian. *The Naming of Animals: An Appellative Reference to Domestic, Work, and Show Animals, Real and Fictional*. Jefferson, NC: McFarland, 1993.

Rothfels, Nigel. *Representing Animals*. Bloomington: Indiana University Press, 2002.

Rowan, A. (ed.) *Animals and People Sharing the World*. Hanover: University Press of New England, 1988.

Rowlands, Mark. *Animals like Us*. London: Verso, 2002.

Ryder, Richard D. *Animal Revolution: Changing Attitudes toward Speciesism*. Oxford, UK: Berg, 2000.

Schaffner, Joan. *An Introduction to Animals and the Law*. Houndmills, UK: Palgrave Macmillan, 2011.

Schwartz, Marion. *A History of Dogs in the Early Americas*. New Haven, CT: Yale University Press, 1997.

Serpell, J. *In The Company of Animals*. Oxford, UK: Basil Blackwell., 1986.

Shephard, P., *The Only World We've Got*. San Francisco: Sierra Club Books, 1996.

Snyder, L. M., and E. A. Moore, *Dogs and People in Social, Working, Economic, and Symbolic Interactions*. London: Oxbow Books, 2006.

Srivastava, P. *Economic Zoology: The Role of Animal Life in Human Welfare, Agriculture, and Industry*. New Delhi: Discovery House, 2003.

Tattersall, I. *Becoming Human: Evolution and Human Uniqueness*. New York: Harcourt Brace and Co., 1998.

Waldau, P., and K. Patton (eds). *A Communion of Subjects: Animals in Religion, Science and Ethics*. New York: Columbia University Press, 2006.

Willis, Roy G. *Man and Beast*. London: Hart-Davis MacGibbon, 1974.

Yates, B. C., and J. Koler-Matznick, *The Evidentiary Dog: A Review of Anthrozoological Cases and Archeological Studies*. New York: Free Press, 2002.

Zajonc, R. B. "Attraction, Affiliation and Attachment" in *Man and Beast: Comparative Social Behavior*. J. F. Eisenberg and W. S. Dillon, eds. Washington, D.C.; Smithsonian Institution Press, 1971.

Zeuner, F. *History of Domesticated Animals*. New York: Harper & Row, 1964.

Index

"actions, attitudes, and understandings" as test, 76

ADA, *See* Americans with Disabilities Act

adaptations: evolutionary, 57; generally, 19, 43, 226; physical, 23; in zoo animals, 140

agreements: about animals, 159; generally, xxi, 5, 37, 173, 177, 185, 186, 203, 222, 240 with animals, 159

ALDF, *See* Animal Legal Defense Fund

Americans with Disabilities Act, 106

"animal crimes," 46–47, 55

animal cruelty, 61–62, 217

animal law, ix, xiv, xvi, 14

Animal Legal Defense Fund, 219, 220

animal rights advocates, xvii, xix, 132, 193n61, 201, 207, 208, 212, 215, 217, 226, 232n72

animal rights lawsuits, 219–223

Animalia, 34, 36, 80, 206–207, 211, 218, 237

animals: appearance of guilt in, 47; as "actors," 126–27; affirmative acts, engaging in, 51; as "belongings," 80; behavior of, 36, 60, 68n99, 71, 80, 105, 127, 149, 159, 167–68, 170, 175–76, 195n90, 208, 211; as biological resources, 89; as

"blameworthy," 50; bodies, 42, 204, 239; capture, restraint, and confinement of, 70; cars, compared with, 78; children, compared with, 57, 78, 81–82, 133, 138, 178, 180–81, 198n137; "classes" of, 147n21; cloning of, 147n31; in collections, 123; commission of crimes by, 50, 53, 60, 66n61; commoditization of, 19; communication in, 215; confinement of, 120, 122; consciousness in, 87n25; control of, 25, 79, 178; as "criminals," 48, 56, 62; in courtrooms, 164; deaths of, 40; definitions of, 31, 32, 36, 71, 124; in displays, 123, 142, 147n29; domestication of, 19, 190n24; "domestic," 36; as economic resources, 89; experiences, 225; expression by, 52, 189n4, 195n77; generally, xiii, xv, xvii, xviii, xx, xxi, 12, 13, 16, 238; as goods, 90; guardians for, 79–80, 147n26; habits of, 154, 156; history, lack of, 204; husbandry of, 16; identification of, 91; instincts of, 195n92, 196n98; intelligence, 230n47; intent determined in, 150, 161, 177; intent, forming, 18, 72; killing of, 18, 41,

About the Author

Geordie Duckler received his PhD in Biology from UCLA in 1997. His dissertation addressed the paleopathological diagnosis of diseases in late Pleistocene and Holocene mammals in North American assemblages, examining fossil evidence for increased physiological stress using paleopathological indicators such as skull and tooth abnormalities. As a vertebrate paleontologist focusing on the decline of Ice Age megafauna, his publications in Journal of Vertebrate Paleontology, Zoo Biology, and Animal Conservation contributed to assessments of prehistoric animal health and the evolution of biological stresses in endangered Florida pumas, and established the first use of Harris lines in paleontological research as a general health indicator for large mammals. His original research on cranial formations and masticatory musculature of felids raised in captivity contributed to comprehensive assessments of the relative health of predators in zoos.

Additionally, Dr. Duckler has also been a trial attorney since 1987 heading a specialty practice devoted exclusively to the litigation of animal cases, having handled over 3,000 such cases in 30 states in state and federal civil and criminal trial courts and appellate courts on issues ranging from exotic animal ownership disputes and veterinary malpractice to animal death cases and prosecutions of animal cruelty. He has instructed lawyers on every animal law issue imaginable, including for the Oregon and California State Bars and via numerous law review articles and lectures, and has been profiled in numerous regional and national newspapers, magazines, television shows, and radio programs about animal law issues and cases, including *The National Law Journal*, *Court TV Radio*, *Geraldo*, *Newsweek*, *The New Yorker*, *Playboy*, *Bark*, National Public Radio, the BBC, and in two National Geographic documentaries.

www.ingramcontent.com/pod-product-compliance
Lightning Source LLC
Chambersburg PA
CBHW050634280326
41932CB00015B/2638